silver surfers'

COLOUR GUIDE TO

word. processing

wendy hobson

withdr...

foulsham

LONDON • NEW YORK • TORONTO • SYDNEY

foulsham

The Publishing House, Bennetts Close, Cippenham, Slough, Berkshire, SL1 5AP, England

Foulsham books can be found in all good bookshops or direct from www.foulsham.com

ISBN-13: 978-0-572-03234-0
ISBN-10: 0-572-03234-X

Copyright © 2006 W. Foulsham & Co. Ltd

Cover photograph © Alamy Images

A CIP record for this book is available from the British Library.

Printed in China through Colorcraft Ltd, HK

Contents

Introduction

This book is designed specifically for those who want a practical, targeted, step-by-step approach to getting to grips with word processing on the computer – whatever their age. You may already have tried out some skills on a computer and want to know more, you may never have touched a computer or a keyboard before. Whatever your skill level, there's something for you in this book.

If you watch youngsters using new technology – whether it's using a mobile phone, working in a word-processing program or surfing the net – they look so comfortable with the set-up and simply have the confidence to try anything and learn as they go along. For those who have grown up with fountain pens, manual typewriters and carbon paper, it doesn't always come quite so naturally. But that does not mean you cannot master those same skills – you can!

What's in this book?

In this book, you'll find all the basic skills you need to use word-processing programs with confidence because it will help you to learn gradually, to remember what you have learned, and to move ahead at your own pace.

- All the information is broken into manageable chunks.

- I'll give you the information you need when you need it and not try to cram in too much all at once.

- When you need to know the right terminology to make things simpler to understand, I'll explain the words clearly.

- I won't assume knowledge you don't necessarily have.

- I'll target practical tasks because by finding a use for your skills you will master them more quickly and remember them more easily.

- You can take everything at your own pace, and go over things as often as you like.

- I won't expect you to remember everything you've learnt on one task, but will repeat the basic instructions for you.

- Everything is clearly laid out so you can find things easily.

- There are step-by-step projects to help give you the confidence that you can achieve some really professional-looking documents on your PC.

- There are screen shots all the way through, plus pictures to show you what buttons to press and what to expect.

It will help you to work through the book systematically, as skills you learn early on will apply to many different tasks throughout the book, and I've tried to structure the tuition so you learn the easiest things first, and those things you are most likely to use. You will also find that some terms come up so often that they will soon become second nature. Even if you don't know where your 'Main menu' is now, you soon will! However, I have also tried to make each section self-sufficient so, for example, if you are eager to put some colour into your document, you can jump straight to the instructions you need and apply them to your work.

You won't find that this book covers absolutely everything about word processing. If you've seen how thick and intimidating the books that claim to be comprehensive can be, you'll know why! In fact, even some that claim to include everything, actually leave out some of the more complex options because computer programs are just so sophisticated. You will find, however, that it includes all the basics you need to make you proficient in word processing – and plenty more besides! – focusing on getting the jobs you want done quickly and simply, and giving you the confidence to work forward and try things out for yourself.

There will be plenty more you can discover when you have finished working through this book, but if you have mastered these skills, you will have the knowledge, ability and above all confidence to try out options for yourself or move on to more advanced training.

Don't worry

> Throughout the book, you'll find these 'Don't worry' boxes. They reassure you about things or explain extra bits and pieces you are likely to come across, shortcuts or different ways of doing things, but are not essential to understand at that stage. Just ignore them unless something is bothering you, or until you are comfortable with what you are doing and want to go back over them. Remember: you can go at your own pace!

What do you need to get started?

To work on the projects in this book, you need a personal computer – or PC – running a Windows operating system. If you've bought it in the last ten years, that's what you'll have. 'Windows' simply means that when you use the computer, the programs you are working on open up in a rectangular box – spot the connection! – on the screen.

The various parts of the computer are: the monitor; the processor; the keyboard; the mouse and the printer.

Don't worry **about laptops**

> A laptop is a portable computer that opens up like a book to reveal a screen, keyboard, processor and mouse all in one. Although much smaller, they can be just as powerful and you can do word-processing tasks just as easily on a laptop as on an ordinary PC.

ImagExtra
(www.andyjonesdesign.co.uk/imagextra)

The monitor

Looking just like a TV screen, this is not actually where the processing is done but is the screen on which everything is displayed. If you have a new computer, you are likely to have a flat screen. These are more stylish and take up much less space than a standard monitor but both styles do exactly the same job.

The processor

This is the actual working part of the computer, housed in a metal or plastic box. It either sits flat on the desk – hence the name 'desktop computer' – or upright beneath the desk – hence the common name 'tower'.

iStockphoto

Don't worry **about iMacs**

If you have an iMac, the monitor and processor are all in one. You will also only have one button on your mouse. There are some differences when using word-processing programs, but you can still use these instructions and you will soon get used to the slight modifications you will need to employ when following the instructions.

The keyboard

Just like a typewriter, you type letters and numbers on the keyboard and they appear on the screen. You can also use certain keystrokes to move around your document or make changes to it.

www.burningwell.org

The mouse

The mouse has two buttons and a scrolling wheel and is usually connected to the computer by a cable – although you can now buy a mouse without a cable. Moving the mouse on your desk controls the movement of a cursor – a bar or arrow – on the screen, so you can point your cursor at a particular point on the screen or use it to 'press' various buttons on screen to perform specific tasks.

The printer

There is a huge variety of printers you can buy, varying in quality from basic to high quality. You will be able to do all the projects in this book with a basic colour inkjet printer, which is what comes with most computer packages. If you find you want to produce higher-quality prints, you can ask the advice of your local computer supplier on what would best suit your needs.

Colour printers use four colours – magenta, cyan (blue), yellow and black – combined to make any colour you want, and the ink is supplied in cartridges. If you are choosing a new printer, check the price of the cartridges, especially if you plan to do a lot of printing. The cheapest printers have one cartridge that contains all four colours. The problem with these is that you will almost always use more black than anything else, so you'll have to replace the cartridge as soon as the black runs out, even if other colours remain. You might therefore want to think about choosing a printer that has one black and one colour cartridge, or separate cartridges for each colour.

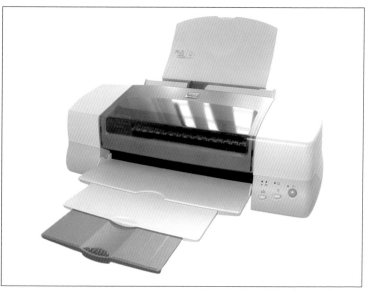

ImagExtra (www.andyjonesdesign.co.uk/imagextra)

The scanner and three-in-one printer

Many computer packages now come with a scanner so you can scan images on to your computer. A scanner is similar to a photocopier but instead of reproducing an image on paper, it appears on your computer screen so you can then print it out, manipulate it, e-mail it or just view it on screen.

Many printers are now three-in-one printer-copier-scanners, which offers an economical way to add extra capacity to your computer set-up.

Don't worry **about laser printers**

Faster, quieter and much more expensive, laser printers are really more suitable for business use or for printing large quantities. Some print in black and white only.

Setting up your computer

When you set up your computer, make sure you position it comfortably on a standard-height desk with a stable chair with an adjustable backrest. Your feet should be flat on the floor, your elbows at right angles, and your eye line level with the screen. Try to be in good light, but not have any reflected light on the screen. Position everything you need so you don't have to stretch, and don't sit for too long at the computer without getting up for a break.

A few words you'll find useful

When you are reading a computer book, you don't want a lot of jargon, but it is helpful to understand a few words that make things easier. If you were talking about putting together some flat-pack furniture, you'd need to know what 'screwdriver', 'hammer', 'nails' and 'bad instructions' meant before you started; this is just the same.

Apple: Apple, AppleMac, Mac or iMac are all names for a type of computer that works in a slightly different way from a PC. There are some minor differences in how you use word-processing programs on a Mac but you can still use this book.

Cursor: A bar or arrow on the screen that shows you where you are working.

Desktop: When you switch on your computer, what appears on the screen is called your desktop.

Hardware: This just means the parts of the computer itself.

PC: Personal computer.

Printer cartridge: Replacement ink for your printer in a small sealed unit.

Program: A piece of software designed to do a specific job, such as word processing.

Software: Any program in the computer that makes it work.

Word processing

On your computer, you will need a word-processing program. There are many of these, most performing similar tasks, but the industry standard is Microsoft Word, and this book is based on that program. When you start using a word-processing program, you can start on simple projects like typing and printing a letter, just like the most basic typewriter. However, you will soon realise that they are much more powerful than that because you can alter your text as much as you like, move whole sections from one place to another, change the style of the text and the colours, add pictures – and that's just the beginning!

But we are not going to try to run before we can walk, so don't worry. In this book, you'll get a thorough grounding in the basics to set you well on the way to discovering the options for yourself. The best way to learn is to open up your word-processing program, read once through the instructions for the task you are going to try out in this session to give yourself a general idea of what you are trying to achieve, then go through step by step, carrying out each instruction as you read it. This will really give you a feel for the programming and help you to remember how to do it next time.

Don't worry **about how it works**

One thing it may help to keep in mind is that you don't need to know how or why anything works on the computer as long as it does what you want it to. When you switch on the television and surf through the channels to find what you want to watch, you don't spare a thought for wavelengths, transmitters or signal strength. Why should you when you've found *Inspector Morse* and he's coming through loud and clear? Using a computer is just the same. Learn which buttons to press and what happens when you do – that's it! Although, it's not quite 'it' because, unlike the TV remote, you have help options always at hand: pictures on the buttons, labels on everything telling you what it does, a **Help** option, and an **Undo** button so you can cancel anything you've done!

Chapter 1

What's Word Processing All About?

Word processing just means playing around with words, but with a computer you can do that in a big way! You don't need any special skills – although obviously if you can type, it makes it faster – because modern computers and programs are designed to be so easy to use. Fundamentally, they work just like a typewriter, so you type your words on the keyboard and they appear on the screen instead of on the paper in a typewriter.

Once you have done that, you can make the words larger, put them in CAPITAL LETTERS, *italic* or **bold**, print them in different colours, include symbols – ✝ ✡ ✳ – or even pictures.

You can move them around the page,

• put them in bullet points,

1. number them,

copy them, paste them, change the order of sections, or wrap them in a box.

You can then save them, open them up again, add more, change some, and keep on doing that until you are happy to save and print your work. In fact, word-processing programs are so powerful that they open up a whole new world of possibilities.

Don't worry **about making mistakes**

The great thing about working on a computer is you can make as many mistakes as you like and it really doesn't matter. Probably the worst thing you can do is work on a document then forget to save it, so you have to do it all again! But that is quite hard to do, so relax and feel free to experiment.

Microsoft Word

Microsoft Word is the industry standard word-processing program and you can buy and load this on to your PC. It comes as part of a package called Microsoft Office. A slightly less sophisticated version of Word is called Microsoft Works and this is usually loaded on to all PCs when you buy them. It does not have all the more complex features of Word but it works in a similar way and all the instructions in this book will look familiar and be equally easy to follow.

Depending on which version of which program you use, and which operating system your computer uses (whether the screen says XP, or ME or something else when you switch it on), you'll find some differences in what you see in this book and what you see on the screen. However, even if they are not identical, they will all look fairly similar and easy to recognise. For example, all programs have what's called a toolbar at the top of the screen. Yours may look like this:

like this:

like this:

or slightly different from all three. But they will use common options and images, the instructions in this book will still be easy to follow and it won't make any difference to the results.

If you are using a completely different program, such as Notebook, the display may not be quite the same, but it will have many similar features and there will be common tasks and common symbols used so you can still learn to use it following the instructions in this book.

Finding your way around a keyboard

Before you even switch on, it's worth taking a look at your keyboard and familiarising yourself with it. Don't try to learn where everything is – it's much easier to do that when you start using the keys – but just get an idea of where the main keys are positioned.

Basic keyboards are called QWERTY, after the order of the letters on the top row. Interestingly enough, the letters were originally arranged in this order not to make it easier to type but to make it more difficult! They wanted to slow typists down as the original manual typewriters could only cope at a slow speed!

www.burningwell.org

Don't worry **about the very top row**

The row of keys labelled F1 and so on can be set up to perform special jobs, or be used as shortcuts. Just ignore them for now. In the list of shortcuts at the end of the book, you will find some of them useful. If you have a very new keyboard, you may also have more controls at the top that relate to music and DVD programs; you don't need them for word processing. You may also have a couple of Windows flags and a pop-up menu key; again, you don't need to worry about them.

- The letters are arranged in this fairly random order in the centre of the main part of the keyboard.

- The numbers are along the top row.

- The space bar is the long bar at the bottom.

- Punctuation marks are on the right.

- On the right, the **Enter** key takes you on to a new line.

- The **Backspace** at the top right deletes the previous keystroke.

- The **Tab** key is at the top left. This allows you to move across the page in even spaces.

- One key up from the bottom left and right, the **Shift** key is pressed to get capital letters, or the symbols printed above the numbers and punctuation marks. If you press the **Caps lock** key on the left, all your letters appear in capitals until you press it again to switch it off.

- At the bottom left and right of the keyboard are the **Control** (Ctrl), **Options** and **Alt** keys. These are not important until later on!

- To the right of the main keys is a block of five or six keys (depending on your keyboard) labelled: **Delete, Home, End, Page up, Page down** and possibly also **Insert. Home** takes you to the beginning of a line; **End** to the end of a line; the others are self-explanatory.

- On some keyboards, this group has nine keys and includes the **Print screen, Scroll lock** and **Pause** keys that are usually on the top row. Don't worry about them – you don't need them.

- Also to the right of the main keys, are four arrows for moving your cursor up, down, right and left in your document.

Don't worry **about overtyping**

When you type in the middle of a document, you add the text, moving any existing text down the page. On some computers, when you press the **Insert** key, you change this so that you type over any existing text. Just press it again to switch back to normal.

- On the right-hand side is a separate number keypad. You don't have to use it, but it can be quicker when you are typing lots of figures or especially if you are working in a spreadsheet.

 Don't worry **about numbers not working**

> If you find when you key numbers into your number keypad that they do not appear on the screen, press **Num lock**.

Teach yourself to type

Although you don't need to touch type, it does make things much easier if you can. Typing tutor programs are not expensive – in fact, you may even have one loaded on to your computer when you buy it. They go through step by step, teaching you how to type properly. It takes a bit of practice but it's well worth it.

Words you need to know

Before you actually get started, you need to know just a few more computer terms. It doesn't really matter what you call things if you know what you are doing, but it will make it much easier to follow instructions and to learn your way around if you take a moment to make sure you know these few useful terms.

Menu: A list! The Main menu always appears across the top of your screen when you are in Word.

Drop-down menu: If you click on an item on a menu, another list of items appears for you to choose from. If you are already at the bottom of the screen, it will pop up instead of drop down. If you are at the side, it will pop out!

Toolbar: A strip at the bottom of the screen or the top of the window containing a series of buttons that you click on with your mouse to turn specific functions on or off.

Button: The buttons on each toolbar work just like an on/off button on a TV or any electrical appliance: you press it to switch on, then press it again to switch off.

Icon: Each button has a little picture on it to tell you what the button does if you press it.

Document: Each letter or item you work on is known as a document.

Switch on and learn to tame the mouse

Switch on your computer and when it has 'booted up' – that just means it has stopped whirring and is ready to go – you will be looking at your desktop. You may have set it up with a beautiful beach scene or a snap of your grandchildren, or it may be something more basic.

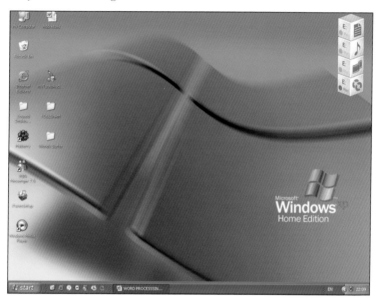

Don't worry about a different screen

The screen shots in this book will help to show you what you are likely to see on your screen while you are working through the book. No two computers are identical, so you may find some things are slightly different. For example, you will not have exactly the same icons on your desktop as in the image above. However, in all essential elements, it's the same.

How to tame a mouse

You will need to use a mouse for many jobs, so first, take a minute to get used to it.

- **Pointing:** Hold the mouse in your hand and move it around on the desk; it will soon feel comfortable in your hand. Watch what happens on the screen: the mouse will move a cursor – remember: the bar on the screen – around the desktop. This is called pointing and takes you to where you want to be on the screen, in your document or on the toolbars.

- **Clicking:** Press and let go the left-hand button; this is called clicking and tells the computer where you want to be in your document, or presses a toolbar button.

- **Double-clicking:** Press and release the left-hand button quickly twice; this is called double-clicking and is another way of switching things on.

- **Scrolling:** 'Stroke' the scrolling wheel in the centre; when you are in a document this will move you up and down the page.

Don't worry **about right-clicking**

You won't need the right-hand button on your mouse just yet. I'll explain some of its functions as we come to them. You can use it for more options than we'll get through in this book, so do experiment as soon as you want to, as it offers some neat shortcuts.

Opening the program

The next thing you need to do is to open the word-processing program. If you have a Microsoft Word icon on your desktop, simply double-click on the icon to open the program. If not, look along the bottom of the screen at the toolbar with the **Start** menu in bottom left-hand corner.

• Click on **Start** and a menu will pop up.

- Move your mouse so your cursor is on **All programs** (or **Programs** if you have an older computer). Click on this and another menu will pop out listing all the programs on your computer.

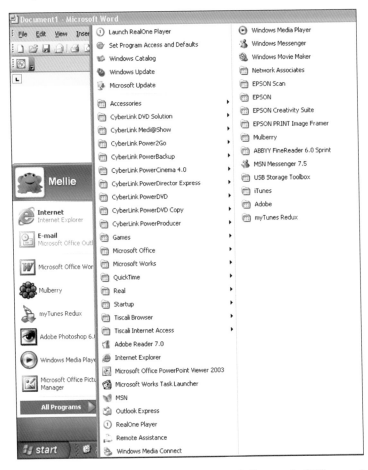

- Move your mouse so your cursor is on **Microsoft Office** and click once so a further menu pops out. Click on **Microsoft Word** to open the program.

If you have another word-processing program, follow the same route and click on the program name to open it up.

Once you have opened your program, the name of the program, or the document you are in, will appear on the blue bar at the bottom of the screen. If you have more than one document open, you can simply click on the name to bring it to the front.

Opening up on a Mac

- If you have an Apple computer and are working in OSX, click on the Word icon on the toolbar (called the 'dock') at the bottom of the screen. If you can't see the toolbar, drag your mouse to the bottom right-hand corner of the screen and it should pop up.

- If you have an earlier system, click on the Apple icon in the top left-hand corner, click on **Programs**, then on **Microsoft Word**.

If you would prefer the dock to remain on your screen – rather than bobbing up and down – you can adjust the settings.

- Go to the blue apple in the top left-hand corner.

- Choose **Dock**, then **Dock preferences**.

- Untick **Automatically hide and show the dock**.

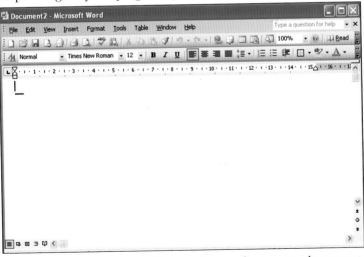

What to expect

Depending on your program, you'll see something like this:

which is the program toolbar and your first open document. This is what we are going to work with.

If you only see this:

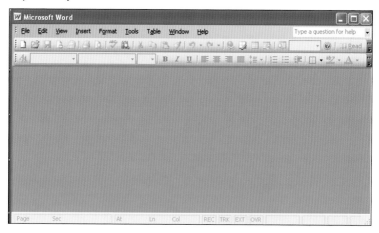

move your mouse so your cursor is pointing to the **New blank document** button on the left, which looks like a piece of paper with the corner folded down, and click once. Your first document will open.

If you have a document with a Getting started screen on the right-hand side of your document, click on the cross at the top right-hand corner of that section of the screen and it will disappear.

A word about templates and wizards

Most programs offer you ready-made templates for documents, or mini programs-within-the-program, called wizards, that guide you through specific jobs. These can be really helpful and make many jobs easier, but they don't teach you how to do things for yourself, so we are not going to use them in this book. In any event, they are so user-friendly, you only need your onscreen instructions.

If you do want to use templates in Word, click on **File**, then **New** and a list will open on the right-hand side of your screen. Under the Templates heading, click on **On my computer** and a window will open up.

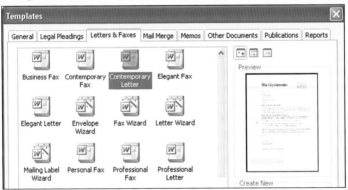

Click on any of the tabs along the top to see a selection of templates. Click once on a template to see a preview of what your document will look like if you use it. Double-click on the template icon to open it up, then simply follow the instructions to type in your text and it will be styled according to the template.

If you double-click on an item labelled 'wizard', you will be led through a complete step-by-step route through the job, such as writing a letter or making a card or a calendar, so all you need to do is read the screen, make your choices from the options available, then press the **Next** button to take you to the next screen until you click on **Finish**.

Using the whole screen

There is a blue bar across the top of the document saying 'Document 1 – Microsoft Word'. Look at the right-hand side and you'll see three small buttons. We are interested in the middle one, the **Restore/Maximise** button. If it looks like this:

your Word document is using the whole screen – that's the best option to use to show the whole area of your document. Click on it once and it will change to look like this:

and your window will be smaller, and you will probably be able to see some of your desktop behind it. Use your mouse to position your cursor on the blue bar across the top of the document window, where it says Document 1. Click and hold your mouse button, then move the mouse and you will drag the window across the screen. You can use this to move your document so it is easy to see.

Click on the **Restore/Maximise** button to maximise the window.

Don't worry **about the size of the window**

If you have reduced the size of your window so you can see the edges, you can change the size and shape of the window. Move your mouse so your cursor is over the side of the window and it will turn to ↔. Click and hold down the left-hand mouse button and you can move the mouse to adjust the width of the window. Move your mouse so your cursor is over the corner and it will turn to ↘. Click and hold down the mouse button to change the size. You can use this option if you want to display two documents on the screen at the same time.

Your reminder box

- There are many different word-processing programs, but they all share similar basic functions.

- You don't need to worry about making mistakes, as they are so easy to correct.

- Familiarise yourself with the keyboard.

- Use the mouse to point, click, scroll and double-click.

- To open a program, click on **Start**, **All programs**, **Microsoft Office**, **Microsoft Word**, or double-click the icon on the desktop.

- To fill the whole screen with your Word document, use the **Restore/Maximise** button.

Chapter 2

Your First Document

Now you can begin your word processing with confidence! If you get no further than this chapter, you'll still be able to do all the basics – it's that simple.

You should have switched on your computer and opened up your word-processing program, so you will see a large white window, filling the screen, with various bars along the top.

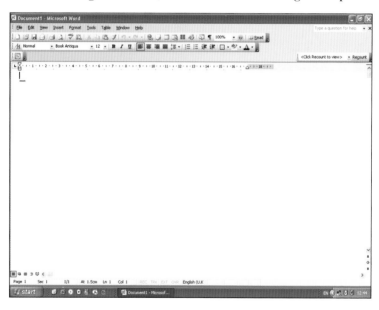

Take a look at the screen but don't be put off if you think there's a lot to see. You can take your own time to learn each item as and when you need it. Don't think you need to work out what everything means; you don't. In fact, many people who profess to be experts don't know everything! The buttons will not be the slightest bit offended if you ignore them completely. By the time you finish this book, you will be familiar with most of them but, as I have said, there is so much scope in Word that we cannot cover everything in this book. As and when you are ready, just play around!

The Main menu

The three bars at the top of the screen are: the Main menu, the Standard toolbar and the Formatting toolbar. These are your routes into the program functions. I will show you what each menu item or button is for as you need to use it. For now, just notice which bar is which so you recognise them when you need them later.

The words **File, Edit, View** and so on are the Main menu. At the risk of putting you off entirely, it works a bit like those ghastly menu options on automatic phone lines – but much easier to use! Each word is an entry point to a whole list of other options.

File	Edit	View	Insert	Format	Tools	Table	Window	Help

Practise using your mouse to take a look. As you move your mouse up to the toolbars, it will change to a left-pointing arrow, and as you move it over each item the word will change colour.

- Click on **Tools**, for example, and the drop-down menu will appear to show you the most common choices from that menu.

- Slide your mouse down so your cursor is pointing to **Word count** and it will be highlighted.

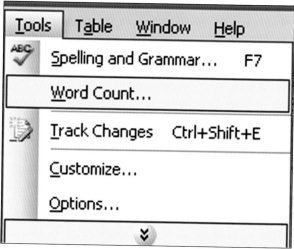

- Click on **Word count** and a window will open up telling you all about your document – which is not much because you haven't done anything yet, but it's a nice, simple window to show you.

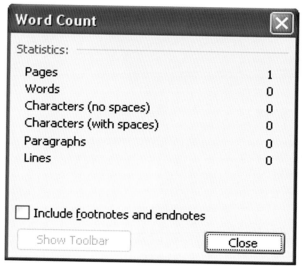

- Click on **Close** to go back to your document.

Don't worry **if your item is not listed**

Click again on **Tools** to open the drop-down menu and you will see a double arrow at the bottom of the list. That means that Word is only showing you the most common options under that menu instead of all of them. Slide your cursor down over the double arrow and click – or just wait for a moment – and the menu will expand to include all the options. If ever you cannot see the choice you are looking for on a menu, that's where you'll find it.

Sometimes you'll see an arrow next to an item on the drop-down menu, which simply means you have more options on another list. On **Tools**, you see **Language** has an arrow on the right, meaning there are more options. If you hold your cursor on **Language**, another menu will pop out. Simply click on each chosen option in turn to lead you through the menus. If you get confused, or whenever you want to go back to your document, just move your cursor back over your document and click.

Don't worry **if menu items are greyed out**

You may also find when you look at a menu that some items are grey instead of black. That means you have to do something else before you activate them. For example, click on **Edit** and you will see that **Copy** and **Paste** are greyed out; this is because you have to choose the section of text you want to copy before you can copy it, and obviously you have to copy something before you can paste it somewhere else.

The Standard toolbar

Under the Main menu, the Standard toolbar has buttons for all the main jobs you'll want to do, such as opening a document, saving it in a file, printing a document and undoing something you didn't mean to do. You simply click on the button you want.

Again, as you move your cursor over the toolbar, it will change to an arrow pointing left and the buttons will change colour. If you hold your cursor over a button for a second, a little box will appear telling you the function of that particular button. I'll introduce you to each option as you need them. Some of the icons are instantly recognisable, such as the **Print** icon. Many others you'll learn; even more you can ignore until you get to an advanced book.

Don't worry **about missing toolbar icons**

If you find your toolbar does not seem to have one of the buttons I mention, don't worry. At the right-hand end of the toolbar is a Toolbar options arrow – a tiny, downward-pointing arrow. Click on it and a selection of extra icons will appear. Click on the one you want and it will appear on your toolbar.

The Formatting toolbar

This works in exactly the same way as the Standard toolbar but performs jobs that relate to how your document looks: putting text in bold or italics, changing the text size, and so on. We'll begin to use this toolbar in chapter 5.

Don't worry **if you can't see the toolbars**

In the unlikely event that you only see the Main menu and only one or neither of the toolbars, click on **View**, then on **Toolbars**. You'll see a tick next to the toolbars that are appearing on the screen. Click next to **Standard** or **Formatting** if it is not ticked and the toolbar will appear.

Keying in the text

Now let's get back to your document: the white window like a sheet of paper with the Main menu, the Standard toolbar and the Formatting toolbar above it.

The cursor should be flashing at the top of the document to tell you it's ready to go. Start typing. You can type anything you like, but I'm going to use the letter opposite as an example, so you might like to do the same. Here are a few tips that cover all the basic skills.

Don't worry **about predictive text**

While you are typing, you may see a little box appear above the word you are typing. That's the computer guessing you are going to type a common word, such as December. If that's what you want, stop keying and press **Enter**. If it's not what you want, just ignore it and keep typing.

- **To type in the text:** Simply use the keyboard at your own pace.

- **To type capital letters:** Press and hold the **Shift** key, then press the letter.

- **To delete text:** Press the **Delete** key to delete the letter immediately after the cursor. Press the **Backspace** key to delete the letter immediately before the cursor.

- **To start a new line:** You don't need to do anything at the end of a line as the computer will automatically move on to the next line. However, if you want to start a new line at a specific point in your text, simply press **Enter**. Each new line will start on the left-hand side.

- **To add a line space:** Press **Enter** twice.

- **To type numbers:** Use the top row or the number keypad.

- **To move around the document:** Use the arrows on the keyboard or move your mouse so the cursor is where to want to be, then click.

28 December 2007

45 The Street
Mytown
Mycounty WP10 5XP

Dear David

It was lovely to see you over Christmas and thank you so much for coming all the way from University in Durham to spend some time with us and bring us such lovely gifts. We know you have a busy schedule and exams looming in the new year so it's appreciated all the more.

Your course sounds really exciting and you must have been thrilled to get a 2:1 in your first essay! Well done! We know you have worked very hard to get this far and we are very proud of your achievements. We are delighted you have settled in well and made so many good friends. Granddad was particularly interested in the rugby club so perhaps we could get to see you play some time before the end of the season.

We have been getting to grips with our new computer and are in the process of trying to get the hang of word processing, so you can expect to be receiving some pretty fancy letters during the next term! We've decided to try to learn this first, then treat ourselves and go on the internet at Easter, so by summer it'll be e-mails too! Watch this space!

With all our love

Grandma and Granddad

Don't worry **about wiggly red lines**

The computer will automatically correct common spelling mistakes as you type. It will also put a wiggly red line underneath anything it doesn't recognise as a word in the dictionary. This is just to draw your attention to it so you can go back and correct it if you wish; nothing will happen if you just ignore it. I'll show you how this works on page 153 so you can use this Spellcheck option (it's actually called a 'Spellchecker' but I can't bear the word!).

Making it easy to see

Word usually shows you your document actual size. If you would like to make the text larger on the screen so it is easier to see, you can easily do so.

- On the Standard toolbar, you'll see a box showing 100% and a small arrow.

- Click on the arrow and a menu will drop down. Move the cursor to highlight the size you want, then click again.

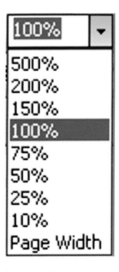

If you click on 500% by accident, just go back and try again at another percentage!

Where's my letter gone?

If you do go to 500%, then back to 100%, you may find you can't see all the document on the screen any more. Look on page 55 and you'll see how to move the scroll bar along the bottom to restore your page.

Printing your first document

Now you want to see how clever you are and print out your letter. Make sure you have paper in the printer.

• On the Standard toolbar, press **Print**.

• The computer will send the information to the printer and automatically print one copy of the document.

We will learn about how to print more copies, or sections of the document later on (see page 63).

Don't worry **about things going wrong**

If you accidentally hit a key or click on a toolbar and something unexpected happens, don't worry. If menus are open, click anywhere in the document and you'll go back to your work. If that doesn't work, press the **Escape** key on the top left-hand corner of your keyboard.

Saving your first document

With a word-processing program, you can keep a copy of every document you create on the computer; you don't have to keep a copy on paper. I always give a document a name and save it before I do anything else, just in case of power cuts, other unforeseen circumstances or just making a mistake!

A copy on the computer is called a 'soft copy'; a printed copy is called a 'hard copy'. Keep a soft copy of this document to practise on, even if you don't want to keep it for anything else.

If you look at the blue band at the top of your document, you will see it says 'Document 1'. Each time you open the program, it will start with this, then if you open more documents, they will be numbered in sequence. That's no use when you want to store and keep things to find later, so you need to give your document a name so you can find it when you want it again.

- On the Main menu, click on **File**, then **Save as**.

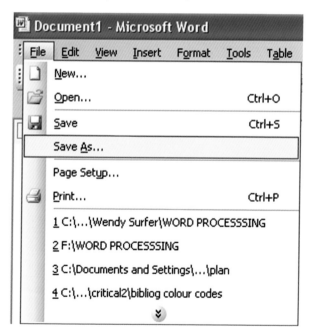

- In the window that opens up your cursor will automatically be in the File name box. Type a suitable name for your document. You can call it anything you like, but I'm going to choose 'My first document'. You could call it 'David thank you letter', 'Letter to David', or anything else you like.

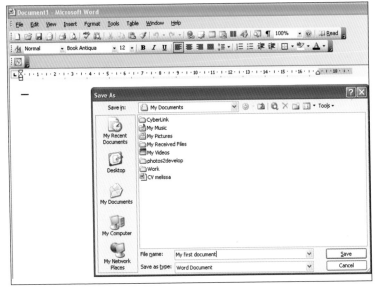

- You will see that the computer will automatically save the file in **My documents**, so that's where you'll find it when you want it again.

- Click **Save** and you will return to your document, but you'll see its name is now at the top, instead of 'Document 1'.

Later on, I'll show you how to organise your work into folders to make it easier to keep tidy (see page 66).

Don't worry **about moving the toolbars**

If you want to move a toolbar position, move the cursor until it is over the line of dots on the left-hand end and it turns to a cross with arrows on each end. Click and hold down the mouse button then drag to move the toolbar where you want it.

Don't worry **about centimetres**

At the top of your screen, you'll see a ruler calibrated in centimetres. If you prefer to uses inches, click on **Tools** on the Main menu, then on **Options** and a window will open up. Click on the **General** tab, then look towards the bottom and you'll see an arrow next to the Centimeters box. Click on it and change it to Inches, then press **OK**. Your program will then display everything in inches.

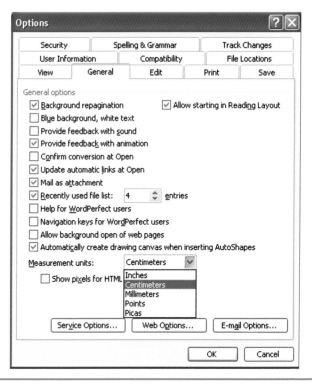

Finding the exit

It must be time for a cup of tea! You can just leave everything to sit and wait until you come back, but when you want to exit, this is what you do.

At the top right-hand corner of the window, you'll see two buttons – possibly one red and one black – with a cross on each one.

You can exit your document and leave your word-processing program open so you can open a new document or work on something else.

• Click on the lower black cross to exit your document.

• If you have already saved it, the document will disappear – but don't worry because it is in **My documents**.

• If you have not saved it, Word will ask you if you want to save it. Click **Yes**, then follow the instructions on page 45 on saving your document.

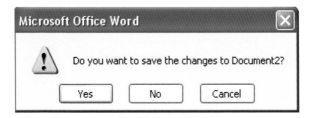

- If you have changed anything since you saved it, Word will ask you if you want to save your changes. Click **Yes** and Word will update the copy in **My documents**.

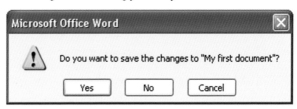

You can also exit both the document and the word-processing program at the same time.

- Click on the top red cross to exit the whole program.

- The same applies to saving your document as if you had simply exited the document: you will be asked if you want to save it or save changes.

If you are using a Mac

Mac toolbars are almost identical. The main difference is that your exit box will be at the top left-hand corner. Click the red circle on the corner of the document to exit. To close **Microsoft Word**, click on the name on the top menu, then drag down and click on **Quit**.

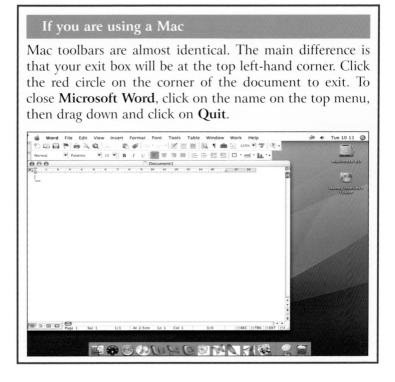

Using help

As I mentioned before, there are plenty of ways the computer is set up to help you and one of these is the onscreen help. It used to be the case that help options were guaranteed to confuse you completely by answering every question except the one you needed the answer to. The problem is that the programs are very complex, and the help screens are written by people who know the program inside out, so they don't tend to focus on a simple answer to a simple question. However, they have improved a great deal, so do try them out. If you find they only addle your brain, don't worry, just ignore them – it's *them* not you!

- At the top right-hand corner of your Word document screen is a help box.

- When you have a query, simply type your question in the white box, using the most relevant words, then press **Enter**.

- A window will open offering you a list of search results. Click on the one that you think will help to solve your problem and an explanation will be shown to you.

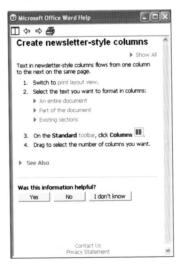

- Click on the **X** in the top right-hand corner, as usual, to close the windows.

Your reminder box

- Click on Main menu items to reveal the drop-down menus.

- To activate a button on the Standard or Formatting toolbars, simply click on it.

- Type your text into your document using the keyboard.

- Use the arrow keys or point and click with the mouse to move around the document.

- To display your document larger or smaller, use the % box on the Main menu.

- Click the **Print** button on the Standard toolbar to print your document.

- To name and save your document, use **File, Save As** from the Main menu.

- To exit your document, use the lower cross in the top right-hand corner.

- To exit Word, use the top cross in the top right-hand corner.

- Type a query in the Help box in the top right-hand corner of the Word screen, press **Search** and select from the options offered to you.

Chapter 3

Developing Your Skills

You can practise the skills you learnt in chapter 2 for as long as you like until you feel really comfortable with what you are doing. Once you start to find you are doing things automatically, without having to think about them, you'll probably want to learn more. It's a lot like learning to drive; at first you have to think consciously about everything but after a while, you do most things automatically – like steering and changing gear – without even thinking about it.

There's a lot of information in this chapter, so don't feel you have to work on it all at once; do it a section at a time at your own pace.

Opening your documents

We are going to work on My first document again and there are two simple ways to find it.

- If you have a **My documents** icon on your desktop, double-click on it and the window will open up. If not, click on **Start**, then on **My documents**.

- Double-click on **My first document** and you will open Word and the document at the same time.

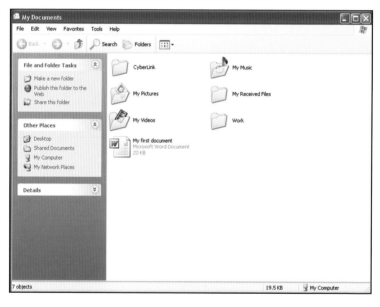

If you prefer, you can open Word first then open the document. Obviously if you are already in Word, you would also use this route to open any document. If you have a Microsoft Word icon on your desktop, double-click on it. If not, click on **Start, All programs, Microsoft Office**, then **Microsoft Word**. (From now on, I'll assume you don't need to reminded how to do that.)

- On the Main menu, click on **File**, then on **Open** and a window will open up.

- In the small window at the top, you'll see **My documents**.

- In the large window, you'll see some folders and 'My first document'.

- Either double-click on the document or single click on the document to highlight it, then click **Open**.

Don't worry **about recent documents**

From the Main menu, click on **File** and you'll see at the bottom of the drop-down menu a list of the documents you have worked on most recently. If the document you want is in that list, simply move your cursor down to highlight it, then click to open it up.

Adding another paragraph

Now you have your letter open on your screen. If you decided before that you would not print and send your letter until you had added a bit more, that's easy to do.

- Move your cursor to after 'Watch this space!' and click.

- Press **Enter** twice to start a new paragraph, then type in another paragraph. Your sign-off will simply be pushed down the page.

Don't worry **about alternative routes**

You will find that there are often a number of different ways to do the same job on a computer: using the menus, using shortcut keys, using the toolbar icons, and using special icons surrounding your document. In this book, I have concentrated on trying to help you feel comfortable with using the program, so I have not always included all the different options as that can be confusing at first. You only need to know one way so if you are happy with the first way you learn, stick with it. As and when you want to experiment to try out another option, go for it.

Scrolling around

You have already learnt that to move around your document, you can use the mouse and the arrow keys, but there are some other ways, too.

- Use the **Page up** and **Page down** keys; these do exactly what it says on the keys!

- Use the scroll bars.

- Use the scrolling wheel on your mouse.

The scroll bars

The main scroll bar is on the right-hand side of your document.

The little box on the scroll bar shows you where you are, in percentage terms, in your document. If you are half way down the document, the box will be half way down the scroll bar, regardless of whether it is a one-page document or a 50-page one.

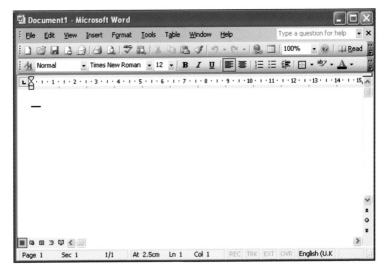

Click on the scroll bar and drag it up and down to move up and down the document.

If it is a long document, a little box will appear, telling you which page of the document is appearing on the screen.

There is also a scroll bar along the bottom of the window. It works in exactly the same way but moves you left and right across the document.

The scrolling wheel

Stroke the scrolling wheel on the mouse and you will move up and down the page.

Highlighting text

You are now going to learn to use your mouse to highlight text. This is a skill you will use a lot in the following chapters because once you have highlighted a section text, whatever instruction you give will affect that whole piece of text.

You can highlight individual letters, words, lines or paragraphs.

• Move the cursor to the left of a word or group of words, click and hold down the mouse button while you move the mouse to the right, highlighting the words as you go, then release the mouse button. The words will stay highlighted.

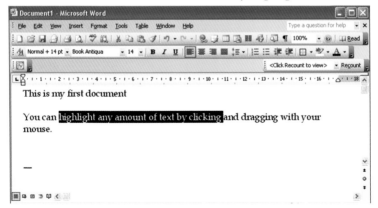

- This is called clicking and dragging.

- If you then click somewhere else in the document, you cancel the highlight.

- You can highlight a whole line of text at once. Move your cursor to the left-hand margin and it will turn into an arrow pointing to the right.

- Click once and the whole line will be highlighted.

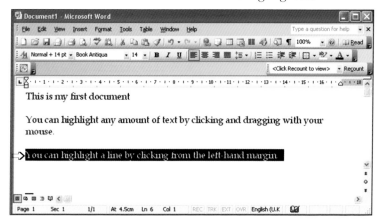

- If you keep holding down your mouse button and drag down the page, you will highlight a line at a time.

Click once back on your document to cancel the highlight and try something else. Move your cursor to the left-hand margin so it changes to a right-pointing arrow, as before. This time, click quickly three times and you can highlight all the text in your document in one go.

Don't worry **about the scrolling wheel**

If you want to highlight a long piece of text, you can click and hold on the left mouse button with your index finger, then scroll with the scrolling wheel with your middle finger. It just takes a bit of practice!

Replacing highlighted text

You can use this facility to replace a piece of text in your document. Let's say you want to change 'in the new year' in your letter to 'in February'.

- Click and drag to highlight 'in the new year'.

- Now type in 'in February' and these words will replace the highlighted text.

Deleting highlighted text

If you decide you want to delete a block of text, you can do it in one go instead of by repeatedly pressing **Delete** or **Backspace**.

- Click and drag to highlight the text you want to delete.

- Press the **Delete** button.

Undoing the last action

If you have highlighted and deleted a paragraph, then changed your mind, you can undo the last action.

- On the Standard toolbar, click on the **Undo** button.

- To the right of the **Undo** button is a small arrow. If you click on this arrow, you will see a list of the last things you did to your letter.

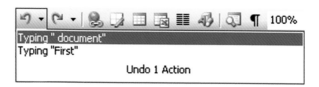

- If you drag down that list, highlighting the actions, you can undo several things at once.

The arrow next to it is the **Redo** button so you can change your mind back if you want to.

How to move text

You can move single letters, a word, sentence or whole chunk of text from one place to another in your document. This is called dragging and dropping.

- Click and drag to highlight the text you want to move.

- Hold the cursor over the highlighted text and it will change to an arrow pointing to the left.

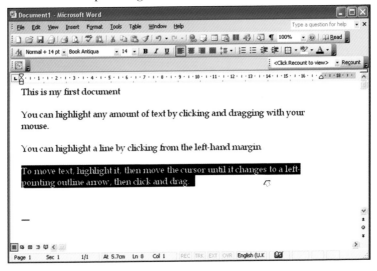

- Click again and hold.

- As you drag the text to where you want to move it, you'll see a shadow image of the text you are moving. When you have positioned it where you want it, then release the mouse button.

- If you drop it in the wrong place, just pick it up and move it again.

How to copy and paste text

You can copy and paste text in a similar way if you want to repeat a word or a section of text.

• Click and drag to highlight the text you want to copy.

• On the Standard toolbar, press **Copy**.

• Move your cursor to where you want to place the copy of your text and click once.

• Press **Paste** and the text will be pasted again into your document.

Copy and paste

You can also copy and paste using the Main menu: **Edit**, **Copy** or **Edit**, **Paste**.

You may not use this much in a short letter, but once you go into longer documents, it can be useful. You can also copy and paste between two documents. Let's say that having written to your grandson David, you write a letter to a friend and you want to include the same paragraph about how well you are getting on with the computer.

- Click and drag to highlight the paragraph you want to copy.

- On the Standard toolbar, press **Copy**.

- On the Standard toolbar, press **New blank document** to open another document.

- Now your cursor is in the new document, press **Paste** and the paragraph will copy into the new document.

- You can add to this document, change it, do whatever you like to it. You'll then need to save it with a different name, just as you did the first one (see page 44).

Adding text to a document

Don't forget that you can add text to a document in any order you like – you don't have to start at the beginning and work through to the end. You can type the last bit first, then move your cursor to the top and write the first paragraph. You can then add more in the middle, changing and adding for as long as you like, moving it around and changing sentences, words or whatever.

Take some time to practise with your first document. It never has to go anywhere except your computer and you can throw it away whenever you want to, so you can try out anything you like as often as you like.

Different ways of viewing your document

There are two main ways of looking at your document on the screen. It doesn't make any difference to the text itself, just how you look at it. Word usually displays the document in **Normal view**. If you look at the bottom left-hand corner of the screen, you will see the first box is switched on.

If you click on the third box, **Print layout view**, it will show you how the text actually looks on the page so instead of a dotted line across the page to show you where you move from one page to another, you will see the margin at the top and bottom of each page and a thick bar where the pages separate.

Print preview

You can also look at exactly how your document will look when it is printed.

• On the Standard toolbar, click on **Print preview**.

• You will see your document as it will be printed.

- Click on the **Multiple pages** button and choose how many pages you want to see on the screen at once.

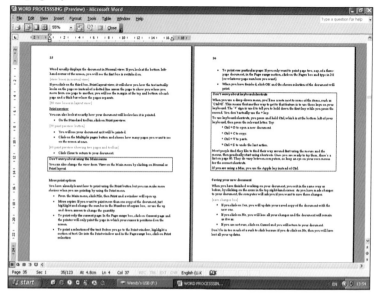

- Click **Close** to return to your document.

As well as the buttons at the bottom of the screen, you can also change how you view your document from **View** on the Main menu by clicking on **Normal** or **Print layout**.

More print options

You have already learnt how to print using the **Print** button but you can make more choices when you are printing by using the **Print** menu.

- From the Main menu, click **File**, then **Print** and a window will open up.

- **To print more copies:** If you want to print more than one copy of the document, just highlight and change the number in the **Number of copies** box, or use the up and down arrows to change the quantity.

- **To print only the current page:** In the **Page range** box, click on **Current page** and the printer will only print the page in which your cursor is positioned on the screen.

- **To print a selection of the text:** Before you go to the Print window, highlight a section of text. Go into the Print window and in the **Page range** box, click on **Print selection**.

- **To print one particular page:** If you only want to print page two, say, of a three-page document, in the **Page range** section, click on the **Pages** box and type in 2–2 (or whatever page numbers you want).

- When you have finished, click **OK** and the chosen selection of the document will print.

Don't worry **about paper not loaded**

If a window pops up telling you the paper is not loaded correctly, this is most likely just the printer's way of telling you to fill up with paper. Simply put some more paper in your printer, then click **OK** or **Continue**. If the paper has misaligned, straighten it and click **OK**.

Saving your new document

When you have finished working on your document, you exit in the same way as before, by clicking on the cross in the top right-hand corner. As you have made changes to your document, the computer will ask you if you want to save them.

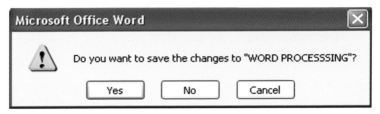

- If you click on **Yes**, you will update your saved copy of the document with the new one.

- If you click on **No**, you will lose all your changes and the document will remain as it was.

- If you are not sure, click **Cancel** to return to your document.

Don't be in too much of a rush to click because if you do click on **No**, then you will have lost all your updates.

Don't worry about keyboard shortcuts

When you use a drop-down menu, you'll see a note next to some of the items, such as **Ctrl+Z**. This means that another way to get to that feature is to use those keys on your keyboard. The '+' sign is used to tell you to hold down the first key while you press the second. You don't actually use the + key.

To use most keyboard shortcuts, you press and hold **Ctrl**, which is at the bottom left of your keyboard, then press the relevant letter.

Most people discover they like to find their way around first using the mouse and the menus, then gradually start using shortcuts. Once you are ready to try them, there's a list on pages 218–19. They do vary between computers, so keep an eye on your own menus for the correct shortcuts.

If you are using a Mac, you use the **Apple** key instead of **Ctrl**.

Your reminder box

- To open a document, double-click on **My documents** on the desktop, then double-click on the document name.

- You can also open a document by clicking on **Start**, **All programs**, **Microsoft Office**, then **Microsoft Word** to open Word, then clicking on **File** and **Open** from the Main menu and double-clicking on the document name.

- Simply type additional material into the document as you wish.

- Move round a document using the **Page up** and **Page down** buttons, the scroll bar and the scroll button on the mouse.

- To highlight text, click and drag across the text you want so you can replace or delete it.

- Use the **Undo** button if you change your mind and want to undo the last action.

- To move text, highlight it, move the mouse over the text until it changes to an arrow, click and drag it to its new position, then release the button.

- Highlight text, then use the **Copy** and **Paste** keys to copy and paste text.

- To change the way you view your document, click on **Normal view** or **Print layout view** on the toolbar at the bottom of the document.

- Use **File**, then **Print** from the Main menu to select more printing options.

- When you exit a saved document, remember to choose **Yes** to save any changes you have made.

Chapter 4
Getting Organised

It is very important to get into the habit of organising your work on the computer so that you can find your documents again when you need them. Just like keeping a desk or bureau tidy, it simply makes life much easier.

Remember to start as you mean to go on. A habit is much harder to break than a principle, so if you get into good computer habits, they'll become second nature, whereas if you start by leaving your documents all over the place, you'll always be intending to do something to tidy them up but probably never get round to it.

My documents

First, let's take a look at the virtual filing cabinet where you will store all your documents. On your computer is a folder called **My documents**, which is where you saved 'My first document'. You may have an icon on your desktop, or you may find it by clicking on **Start**, then on **My documents**. This is your virtual filing cabinet.

If you only had one document – or even ten – you would be able to find it easily by clicking on **Start**, then on **My documents** (or clicking on the icon on the desktop), then double-clicking on the document name to open it up.

However, by the time you have been working on your computer for a few weeks, you are not going to have just a few documents, you are likely to have quite a lot, so simply to drop all your documents individually into that virtual filing cabinet would be about as efficient as just dropping all your papers jumbled up in a filing cabinet! Not a good move! Instead you can create individual folders to keep all the relevant documents together – just like a manila folder in a filing cabinet – and you can create as many folders as you need. If you want to, you can also put one folder inside another – and another one inside that! So, for example, in **My documents**, you and your partner might each have a folder, then within those folders, individual folders for each of your interests.

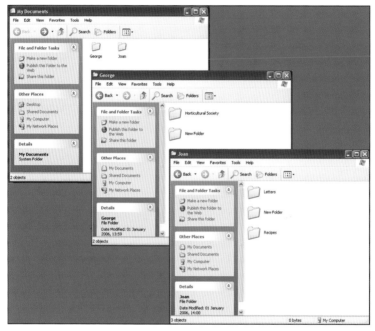

There is no limit to the number of folders you can create.

If you have not already done so, click on **Start**, then on **My documents** to open it up. At the top of the window – as you might expect – are the Main menu and the Standard buttons bar.

They work in just the same way as the toolbars we have been using in documents, and you'll learn the individual buttons as you need to use them.

Creating and naming folders

Take a few moments to think about how you might like to organise your documents, so that you can make a few folders on your computer. Here's an example to show you how it might work.

- You already have your **My documents** window open.

- From the Main menu, click on **File**, then **New**, then **Folder** and a folder icon will appear in the window with a highlighted box next to it saying 'New folder'.

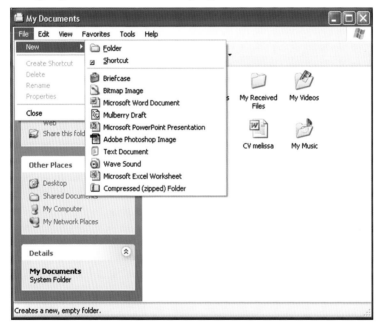

- Type in the name you want to give to the folder, then press **Enter** and the folder will appear in the window in alphabetical order.

- Let's say, you and your partner are going to use the computer, so make one new folder for each of you.

- Double-click on your folder to open it up.

• Within that folder, you can create some more folders in exactly the same way. Name them: Letters, Dance club, Horticultural society, Art class ... whatever you think you might need.

• When you have done that, press **Back** on the Standard buttons bar to take you back to the main folder. There's also a **Forward** button to take you the other way.

• Then you can double-click on the other folder and make some more folders within that.

Don't worry about the panes on the left

The panes on the left-hand side will change if you are viewing folders or text or pictures, depending on what you can do with them.

Viewing your documents

Now you have something to look at, you can try out the different ways of viewing your document folders. It doesn't matter which you use; you can simply select whichever you prefer and change your mind as often as you like. Try them out and see which suits you best.

With **My documents** window open, click on **View** buttons on the Standard buttons bar or click on **View** on the Main menu. The second section of the drop-down menu will give you a variety of options.

• **Thumbnails** is especially useful for photographs as it shows a small image of the document. If you are looking at a folder, it will simply show an image of a folder; if you are looking at a document, it will show an icon like a sheet of paper.

- **Tiles** displays each folder as a fairly large image of a folder, and each document as a piece of paper.

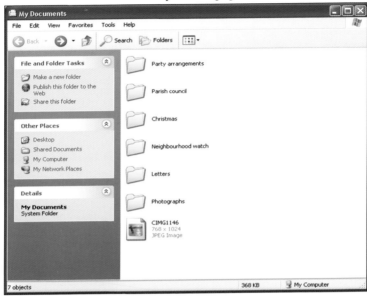

- **Icons** displays similar but smaller images.

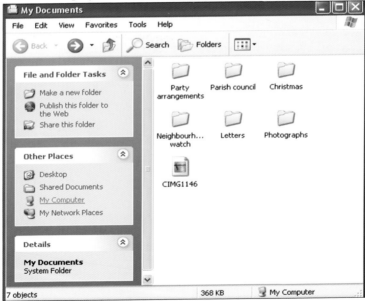

- **List** simply gives you an alphabetical list of folder and file names.

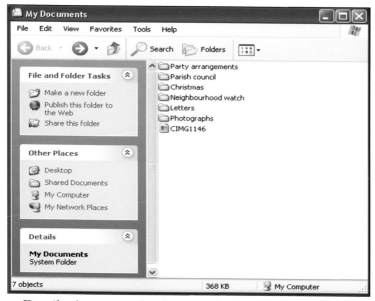

- **Details** shows you the date you last modified the folder or document, how big it is and what type of file it is.

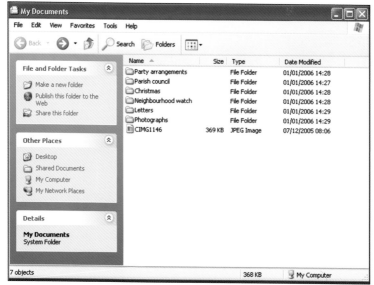

Naming and saving documents

Now, each time you save a document, remember to choose a suitable name: something short and neat that describes what the document contains and that you will remember when you want to go back to it.

Think back to the sequence you used to name your first document (see page 44). You use basically the same sequence, but now you have a choice of folders in which to store your document, so you need to learn how to 'navigate' to put the document in the right place. The first two steps are the same.

- On the Main menu, click on **File**, then **Save as**.

- In the window that opens up, type your chosen document name in the **File name** box.

- The top bar will show you that you are in **My documents** and you will see your list of folders underneath.

- Double-click on the folder in which you want to store your document (or single click, then click on **Open**). If you want to save your document in one of your sub-folders, keep clicking until you open the one you want.

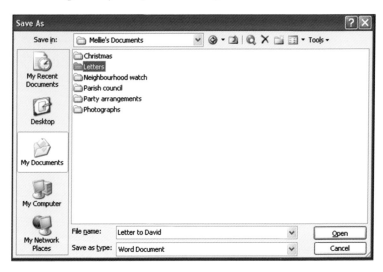

- Click **OK** and your document will be safely stored where you want it.

> **Save as**
>
> A quick way to reach the Save as window is to press the **F12** key at the top of your keyboard.

Save a document before you format it

You don't have to wait until a document is finished until you save it. If you want to take a break, or if you have just done quite a lot of keying and don't want to lose your work, just save the document as described above. You can continue to work on it, close it and open it again and change it as often as you like. Remember, when you exit a saved document, you need to choose **Yes** when asked if you want to save your changes (see page 64).

If you are going to format a document – using different fonts, colours and so on, as we will in the next chapter – it is a good idea to save the text document first before you start on the formatting. That way if anything does go wrong, or you don't like what you have done, it's easy to go back to your original text and start again.

Don't worry **about Close and Cancel**

Sometimes, you will see a **Close** button to exit from a window and sometimes you'll see **Cancel**. Don't worry about the reason for now; they do the same job of taking you out of that window.

Saving as you work

For extra peace of mind, when you are working on a saved document, you can save your changes as you go. Let's say you are writing a long letter and have saved it one day, then you are working on it again. You've done another long paragraph and want to break for a cup of tea. Simply press the **Save** button on the Standard toolbar and your file copy will be updated.

Don't worry **about autosave**

While you are working on a document, Word will automatically save it every so often. Occasionally your computer may crash, which usually means it freezes and refuses to do anything. Press the **Reset** button on your computer processor to restart. When you reopen Word, it will bring up the recovered document so you don't lose all your work. You can adjust how often your computer saves your work.

- From the Main menu, click on **Tools**, then **Options** and a window will open up.

- Click on the **Save** tab.

- Next to **Save AutoRecover info** is a box indicating how often your work is saved, which is usually at 10-minute intervals.

Browsing to find a document

Once you have quite a few documents, you'll need to find your way around the filing system so you can find what you are looking for. This is called 'browsing'.

The simplest way is to click on **Start**, then on **My documents**, then keep double-clicking on folders until you reach the document you want. Double-clicking on the document name or icon will open it up.

You also have some buttons on your Standard buttons bar to help you when you are in the **My documents** window.

- Click on the **Back** button to go to the window you have just left.

- Click on the **Forward** button to go to the next level of folders.

- Click on the **Up** button also goes to the next level of folders, so from **Recipes** to **Joan**, in the example on page 67.

Practise meandering around the folders you have created until you feel comfortable browsing to find your documents and folders.

Don't worry **about losing documents**

Although it's always better to know where everything is so you can find it easily, if you do forget where you put something on the computer, you can do an automatic search to find it again. Go to **Start**, then **Search**, then follow the instructions in the search window to identify the type of file you are looking for. Key the name of the document – or an appropriate keyword – into the box and click on **Search**.

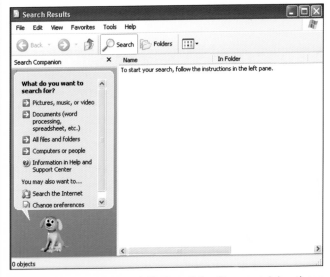

The computer will find and display all the files containing those keywords. Simply double-click on the one you want to open it.

Moving documents and folders

As the number of folders and documents grows, you are bound to want to make some changes to where you have filed things, just as you might move a letter from one file to another. It's just as easy as moving that piece of paper!

- Open your **My documents** folder by clicking on **Start**, then **My documents**.

- If you have made some folders, you will see the folder names or icons.

- Click on the name of the document you want to move and it will highlight. Hold down the mouse button and drag the document on top of one of the folders so it is also highlighted. Release the mouse button and the document will be placed inside the folder. Remember, this is called dragging and dropping.

- You can drag and drop a document from one place to another, or a folder from one place to another.

How to change a document or folder name

If you decide you want to change the name of a document or folder, you can do so as often as you like.

• Open the window in which you can see the document name.

• Hold the cursor over the name and right-click the mouse. A drop-down menu will appear.

• Click on **Rename** and the folder or document name will be highlighted.

• Simply key in the new name and press **Enter**.

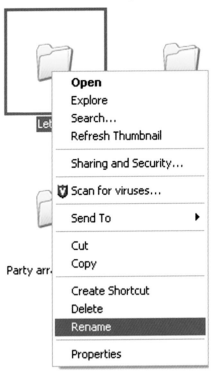

If you look again at the menu that dropped down when you right-clicked, you will see that you can also use this right-click option to delete or copy folders or documents. Simply right-click on the document name, then click on the option you want.

Creating a shortcut

If you use a folder or document frequently, you can put a shortcut to it on your desktop so you only have to double-click on the shortcut icon to open it up instead of going through the menus. Right-click on the folder or document, as before, then click on **Create shortcut** and a copy will appear in the window. Drag and drop it on to the desktop.

Copying and backing up

Modern computers are very reliable, but if they do go wrong, you stand to lose all your documents. It is a good habit to get into to back-up your work regularly, using a floppy disk, USB or memory stick, or CD. You can also copy information quickly and easily to send it to someone else.

Floppy disks

It's the magnetic disk inside the hard plastic case that is floppy! Each disk can hold about 1.44 MB, which is not much in computer terms but is plenty for quite a few text documents. The advantage of a floppy disk is that you can copy documents on to it, over-save them with a new version of the document, add more and throw old ones away as often as you like.

A floppy disk simply slots into a designated slot on your computer known as the A drive. Some PCs no longer support floppy disks as other storage methods have taken over.

ImagExtra (www.andyjonesdesign.co.uk/imagextra)

USB stick

USB sticks are tiny, efficient, very convenient and not expensive. They vary in capacity from 64 MB to 2 GB, so they can hold a huge amount of information. You can also use them as many times as you like, in the same way as a floppy. There are USB1 and USB2 media sticks. A USB2 stick can be used in either a USB1 or USB2 connection.

A USB stick is inserted into the USB slot on your computer known as the E (or sometimes F) drive.

Pixmania.co.uk

CD

A compact disk can store up to 700 MB of data. All modern PCs have a CD-writer so you can copy information on to a CD. Once you have copied on to a CD, it is permanent and you can't change it.

Your computer will have a small tray that emerges from the computer housing when you press a button. Put the CD in the tray and press the button to close it. This is called the D drive.

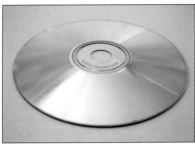

ImagExtra (www.andyjonesdesign.co.uk/imagextra)

Don't worry **about DVDs**

A DVD looks the same as a CD but can hold a full-length film – you won't be worrying about that just yet! You can almost certainly play a DVD on your computer, but to create a DVD you need a DVD writer.

How to copy to a floppy disk

If you want to copy information to a floppy disk, it is quick and easy. You can copy individual documents or whole folders, as long as they don't contain too much information (on the quart into a pint pot principle).

• Insert a floppy into the disk drive.

• Open **My documents** and navigate to the window in which the document or folder name appears.

• Click on the document to highlight it.

• Click on **Edit**, then **Copy to** and a window will open up.

• Double-click on **My computer**, then on 3½ floppy (A:), then click **Copy**.

• Press the button to eject the floppy from the computer. Label it with the name of the file.

If you are saving an updated document

If this is the case, you will be asked if you want to replace the old document with the new one. Simply press **Yes**.

How to copy to a USB stick

You use exactly the same method to copy to a USB stick as to a floppy, although you navigate to the **Removable disk (E:)**. Some computers may recognise the USB stick as **Removable disk (F:)**. You can also over-save a document in the same way as on a floppy disk.

How to look at what's on your floppy or USB

Double-click on the **My computer** icon on your desktop or from the **Start** menu, then double-click on **3½ floppy (A:)** or **Removable disk (E:)**. A window will open up showing you which documents or folders are saved on that disk.

You can also use this route to copy documents. When you have opened the (A:), (D:) or (E:) drive – whichever one you want to copy your document to – click on the **Maximise/Restore** button to reduce the size of the window. Now open the window in which the document name appears on your computer so that window is next to the first one. Then drag and drop the folder or document you want to copy from the main window to the second window.

How to copy to a CD

Copying to a CD usually uses a separate program but it is completely automatic and easy to follow. The instructions may vary slightly between computers.

- Put a blank CD into your CD drive.

- Open the window in which your document name appears.

- From **My computer**, open the **CD-RW** or **DVD-RW** drive (D:).

- Drag and drop the files on to the CD window.

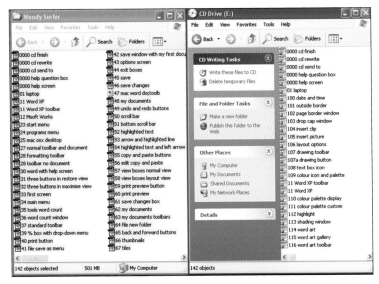

- Click on **Write these files to CD**.

• A CD wizard will open and prompt you to name the CD.

• It will then copy the files and eject the disk when it is ready.

Remember to write the name of the files on the CD on the disk in indelible pen or on the CD case.

Earlier Windows systems

If you have an older computer, burning to a CD may work differently.

- Put a blank CD into your CD drive and a window will open up.

- When asked to choose, select **Data**.

- In the top left-hand window, you will see all the items on your computer. Navigate to the ones you want to copy, click and drag the folders you want to the bottom right-hand window.

- Once all the folders you want to copy are listed, click on **Burn CD** or **Create CD** and the information will be burned on to the disk.

- Once it is finished, you will be prompted to name the CD, then click on **Exit**.

Throwing things away

Although your computer can store huge amounts of information with no problem, it is easier to find things if you keep it tidy. Here's how to have a clear-out of documents you no longer need.

- Open your **My documents** by clicking on **Start**, then **My documents**, as usual.

- Click on a document or folder and drag it to the **Recycle bin** icon on your desktop until the icon darkens, then let go – just like putting something in the waste bin. The icon will change so you know there's rubbish in the bin.

- If you miss – my aim was never that good to begin with! – you will copy your document to the desktop. It doesn't matter. Just pick the copy up off the desktop and put it in the bin, then throw away the original.

- The documents will stay in your waste bin until you empty it in the dustbin – once you have done that, it's gone for good. To empty the bin, hold the cursor over the bin, right-click on your mouse, select **Empty recycle bin**, then let go. The computer will flash up a window asking if you are sure; select **Yes** and press **Enter**.

On a Mac, press **Ctrl** and click on the bin, then select **Empty recycle bin**.

Your reminder box

- Start with good habits and they will be easy to maintain.

- Create folders from the Main menu using **File, New, Folder** and name them as you create them.

- View **My documents** by thumbnail, tile, icon, name or details.

- Name your documents sensibly and use **File, Save as** from the Main menu to save them to **My documents**, navigating to the folder you want.

- Use the **Back, Forward** and **Up** buttons to browse through your folders.

- Use **Start, Search** if you can't find a document.

- Drag and drop documents or folders to move them from one place to another.

- Right-click on a document and choose **Rename** to rename it.

- You can copy information on to a floppy disk or a USB memory stick using the **Copy to** option.

- You can copy to a CD by dragging and dropping on to the CD window.

- You can view what's on your floppy, USB or CD via **My computer** and the appropriate drive.

- To throw away a document, drag and drop it into the recycle bin, then right-click and select **Empty recycle bin**.

Chapter 5

Making It Look Good

So far, you have mainly used the default settings on your program, the most commonly used styles and ways of doing things. Now you are confident enough to begin to experiment a bit more with the look of your document.

Don't worry **about making mistakes**

I can't stress too often that you can play around as much as you like and you always have the choice to save what you've done, save another copy that is slightly different, or ignore your changes and go back to your original.

Choosing the font

The font is the typeface you use for your document. You can choose from a wide range programmed on to the computer. Different computers have a different selection of fonts. The default is usually Times New Roman.

You can:

- put the whole document in the same font;
- **choose** a different font for every individual word – or for every letter;
- put headings in a different style;
- select classic fonts, *fancy fonts*, **silly fonts** and *handwriting fonts*;
- decide you like sans serif fonts (simple fonts with no little hooks on the ends of the letters);

- prefer serif fonts (with little hooks on the ends of the letters);

- or anything in between.

If you have an open document and want to select the font for your document, you can set the font before you start and everything you type will appear in that font.

- Open Microsoft Word and click the **New blank document** button to open an empty document.

- From the Formatting toolbar, click on the arrow next to the box containing the font name, which will almost certainly be 'Times New Roman', and a menu will drop down.

- You will see a list of the choices you have, displayed in the actual typefaces so you can see what they look like.

- Scroll down the list using the scroll bar at the side of the window, the scroll button on your mouse, or the up and down arrows on the keyboard, then click on the typeface you want.

- Everything you type in the document will be in that font.

Using the menu to look at fonts

If you have an older program, the list may not display in the actual font styles so you may want to use the menu route to look at fonts; you can also use this route in any program if you prefer. Click on **Format** on the Main menu, then on **Fonts** and the fonts window will open up. The font you click on in the top panel will display in the bottom panel.

If you have a formatting window – such as the font window – open on top of your document, it may cover up some of the document you want to see. Simply move your cursor on to the blue bar at the top or the thin bar at the sides, click and hold, then drag to where you want it.

If you have already typed your document, you can then change the fonts in just the same way; you just need to highlight the words, letters or line you want to change.

- Highlight the word or words you want to change.

- Click on the font drop-down arrow.

- Scroll down and click on the font you want.

- The highlighted words will change to the selected font.

Don't worry **if you want more fonts**

You can buy more fonts for your computer, or download hundreds free from the internet. If you want something unusual for a poster, for example, try searching for 'free fonts' on Google and you'll have far too much choice!

Setting the type size

The size of type you use is measured in points, abbreviated to 'pt'. 12pt is a normal text size. As with the font style, you can change the whole document to the same size, put every word – or every letter – in a different size, or anything in between.

You can choose any size for your text, from tiny – if you are printing a card, for example and wanted to put an acknowledgement at the bottom – to a normal text size for letters or documents, to huge words for posters. You use just the same process as changing the font.

• Highlight the text you want to change.

• From the Formatting toolbar, click on the arrow next to the point size – which defaults to '12'.

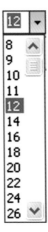

• Drag down the list and click on the size you want.

• The highlighted text will change size.

> ### Quick-change text size
>
> Another way to do it is to highlight the text you want to change, highlight the size in the box on the format toolbar, key in the size you want, then press **Enter**.

Changing text to bold, italic or underline

The principles you have now learnt apply to all formatting of text: choose any amount of text and highlight it, click on the relevant button to change the format – and that's it. If you change your mind, click the button again to switch it off.

You can put text into bold, italic or underline using the buttons on the Formatting toolbar.

- Highlight the text you want to change.

- On the Formatting toolbar, click on **Bold**, **Italic** or **Underline**, depending on which style you want.

- You can also click on any combination of the buttons for ***bold italic***, *underline*, and so on.

Quick-change formatting

You can use keyboard shortcuts for formatting text. Take a look at the list on page 218 if you want to start trying them.

Changing to upper or lower case

If you decide you would like to change the text from lower case to upper case – capital letters – you don't have to re-key it.

- Highlight the text you want to change.

- From the Main menu, select **Format**, then **Change case**.

- You can then choose the style you want from the window, then press **OK**.

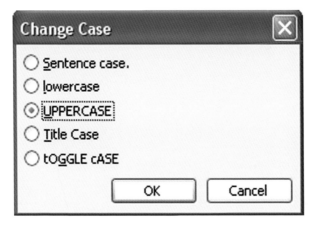

Quick-change to capitals

Highlighting text and pressing **Shift F3** will change the case of the text.

Changing the line spacing

Text will normally appear in single-line spacing, but if you want the lines to appear more widely spaced, you can change it however you like.

- Highlight the text you want to change.

- On the Main menu, click on **Format**, then **Paragraph** and a window will open up.

- Click on the arrow beneath **Line spacing**. The most usual choices are: single, 1.5 or double spacing.

- If you want just slightly more widely spaced lines, choose **Exactly**, then key into the next box a number that is two more than your font size; so if you are in 12pt type, key in 14. For very widely spaced lines, increase the second number.

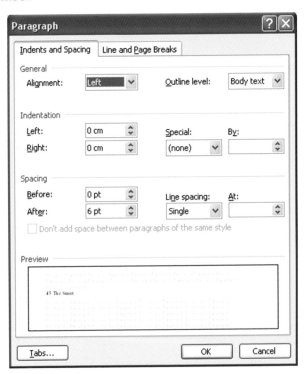

Don't worry **if you want to exit from a menu**

If you have opened a drop-down menu and it is the wrong one, or you have changed your mind, simply slide your mouse back over the document and click to return to the document. If you have opened a format window by mistake, click on **Cancel**, or the **Exit** button in the top right-hand corner.

Using other font features

Another way to format the font is to use the toolbar to access the font window – as you may have done already if you tried the alternative route to choosing the font, above. This allows you to change the font, plus it gives you lots of other options.

• Highlight the text you want to change.

• From the Main menu, choose **Format**, then **Font** and a window will open up.

- You can use this method to choose your font face, size and style, using the top boxes.

- If you tick the box next to one of the featured styles in **Effects**, the program will change the font to that style: strikethrough, superscript and so on.

- If you want small caps, key in lower case (not capital letters), highlight, then tick the box.

We'll look at using colour, which you can also change from this menu, in chapter 8.

Don't worry **about too much choice**

Once you start using these kinds of windows, there are lots of options for you, both things explained in this book and other possibilities that are beyond the scope of a beginners' guide. Home in on what you need, learn things a step at a time as you need to know them and just ignore the rest until you are ready to try them out.

Your reminder box

- To choose the font, highlight the text, then click on the arrow next to the font name box on the Formatting toolbar.

- To set the type size, highlight the text, then click on the arrow next to the font size box on the Formatting toolbar.

- To put type into bold, highlight it, then press **Bold** on the Formatting toolbar.

- To put type into italic, highlight it, then press **Italic** on the Formatting toolbar.

- To underline type, highlight it, then press **Underline** on the Formatting toolbar.

- Line spacing can be adjusted from the Main menu by clicking on **Format, Paragraph** and adjusting from the drop-down menu.

- Other font features can be changed from the Main menu by clicking on **Format, Font** to open the font formatting window.

Chapter 6
Getting Fancy

You should now be feeling really confident with your word-processing skills and you are probably jumping ahead and trying things out for yourself – good for you! Here are some more skills you can use to perfect your documents.

Adjusting the margins

The margins on a document are usually set to about 2.5 cm (1 in) top and bottom and 3.17 cm (1¼ in) left and right, although the default may vary. You can set your margins to whatever you want, and change them for each document.

- From the Main menu, choose **File**, then **Page setup**.

- Select the **Margins** tab.

- Key in the margin sizes you want in the four boxes – Top, Bottom, Left and Right – or use the up and down arrows.

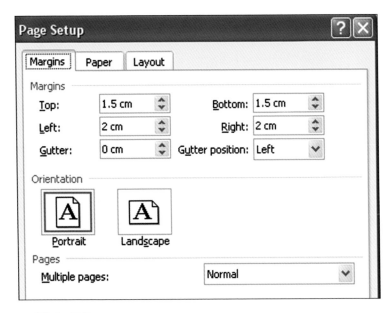

- Click **OK**.

- If you want all your documents to open with this size of margin, instead of clicking **OK**, click **Default**.

- You will be asked to confirm that this is what you want. Click **Yes**.

You can override the default margins for any document.

Changing the paper orientation

If you want to turn your document on its side so the long edge is along the top, you can easily do so. This is called 'landscape' format rather than 'portrait'.

- From the Main menu, select **File**, then **Page setup** as you did above.

- Select the **Margins** tab.

- Under **Orientation**, click on **Landscape**, then click **OK**.

Setting the alignment

You can position text so that each line starts on the left-hand side of the page,

so that each line starts
on the right-hand side of the page,

so that each line is centred between the margins,

or so that each line is spaced evenly across the line with a straight edge on each side, like the main text in this book; this is known as justified text. You are already familiar with the process now.

- Highlight the text you want to change.

- On the Formatting menu, click on the style you want: **Align left**, **Centre**, **Align right** or **Justify**.

- The highlighted text will be repositioned.

Creating indents

If you want to indent the first line of a paragraph, press the **Tab** key at the beginning of the line.

You can also indent a whole section of text.

• Highlight the text you want to change.

• On the Formatting toolbar, click on **Increase indent**.

• The text will automatically indent. You can press the key again to indent further.

• If you don't like it, press **Decrease indent**.

You can also tell the computer to indent the first line of a paragraph automatically whenever you press the return key.

• Highlight the text you want to change.

• From the Main menu, choose **Format**, then **Paragraph**.

• From the **Special** drop-down menu, choose **First line**.

• The first line of any paragraphs will automatically be indented without you having to press the **Tab** key.

Changing the tabs

If you press the **Tab** key, you move on 1.27 cm (½ in), so you can use it to put words neatly into columns. If you are typing a list with several columns, you can set your tabs to an appropriate position so your text is neatly aligned.

• You can key in the text first, pressing **Tab** once between each entry, then highlight the text you want to change; or you can format the tabs first, then the new tab stops will be valid from the position of the cursor.

• From the Main menu, choose **Format**, then **Tabs** and a window will open up.

• Click **Clear all**.

- In **Tab stop position**, key in the position you want your first tab, then click **Set**. Use the ruler at the top of the document to work out where you want them to be.

- Key in the remaining tab positions, pressing **Set** each time, then click **OK**.

- Your tab stops will be indicated by a little marker on the ruler at the top of your document.

Jill and Bob	67 Littleton Way	01458 452369
Pete and Marjorie	88 The Street	01569 456874
Jim and Mary	75 Hampton Road	01592 165986
George and Joan	96 The Ridge	01266 129636

Tab alignment

Normally, tabs will automatically align on the left of the new column. If you want the text to align right or to centre, click in the appropriate box when you set your tab, before you press **Set**. If you click on **Decimal**, columns will align on a decimal point. If you click on **Bar**, it will put a vertical bar in the tab position.

If you would like leader dots between your tabs, you have the option in the same window to include that as well.

Don't worry **about shortcut tabs**

If you simply want to add an additional tab, you can do so quickly by clicking on the ruler at the top of the document so the little marker appears. If you want to control the tab alignment as well, keep clicking on the key to the left of the ruler until it changes to the type of tab you want, then click on the position on the ruler to set your new tab.

Setting up columns

If you want your text to appear in two or more columns, you can do it automatically. You can set the whole document in columns or just one or more sections of it.

- Move your cursor to the left-hand margin and triple-click to highlight the whole document, or highlight the text section you want to change.

- Click on **Columns** on the Standard toolbar, then on one, two, three or four columns.

- The text will automatically be laid out in columns. It will only display in columns on your screen if you are in Print layout view (see page 61).

You can add a column break at any point, so your text continues from the beginning of the next column. Follow the instructions on page 148.

Don't worry **about more column options**

Once you get more confident, you can adjust the width of columns or the spaces between them to customise your document. On the Main menu, click on **Format**, then on **Columns** to see the various options.

Using bullet points

You can make a list appear with bullet points without having to key them in. Each time you press **Enter**, the list will create another bullet point.

• Highlight the text you want to put into bullet points.

• On the Formatting toolbar, click on **Bullets**.

• The highlighted text will change to a bulleted list.

Using numbered points

You can also number a list automatically. If you add another point to the list – in any position – it will automatically renumber.

• Highlight the text you want to number.

• On the Formatting toolbar, click on **Numbering**.

• The highlighted text will change to a numbered list.

Fancy bullets and numbers

If you want to change the style of bullets or numbers, from the Main menu, choose **Format**, then **Bullets and numbering** and a drop-down menu will appear. Click on the **Bulleted** or **Numbered** tab, click on the window that shows the style you want, then click **OK**.

Adding symbols

You can add symbols to your document, such as accented letters, fractions, Greek letters and so on.

- From the Main menu, click on **Insert**, then on **Symbols** and a window will open up.

- Use the scroll bar at the side to look through the options.

- Single-click on a symbol to enlarge it.

- Double-click on the symbol you want to select, or single-click then click on **Insert**.

- Click on **Cancel** to exit the window.

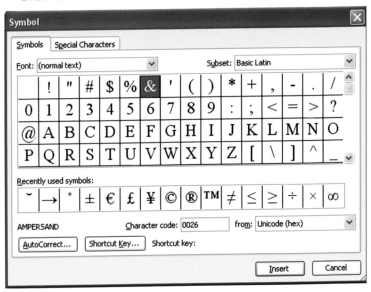

Adding the date and time

If you want to include the date in a document, or the time, you don't have to key it in.

- From the Main menu, click on **Insert**, then **Date and time**.

- You will be offered a list of ways to display the information.

- Click on the option you prefer.

- If you click the **Update automatically** box, the program will automatically give you that day's date whenever you open the document.

- Click **OK**.

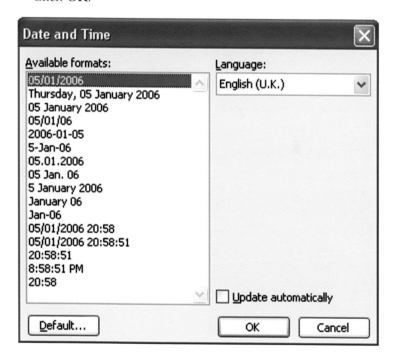

Your reminder box

- To adjust the margins, from the Main menu, choose **File**, then **Page setup**.

- To change the alignment, click on the relevant **Align** button on the Formatting toolbar.

- Indent paragraphs using a tab, or from the Main menu, choose **Format**, then **Paragraph** and **First line** from the **Special** box.

- Change tab settings from the Main menu by clicking on **Format**, then **Tabs** and keying in the tab stops you want.

- From the Standard toolbar, choose **Columns** to set highlighted text in your chosen number of columns.

- Use **Bullets** on the Formatting toolbar to add bullets to a list.

- Use **Numbering** on the Formatting toolbar to number a list automatically.

- To add symbols, from the Main menu, use **Insert**, **Symbol**, click on the one you want and click on **Insert**.

- Click on **Insert**, then **Date and time** from the Main menu to add the date and time to a document.

Chapter 7

Adding Boxes and Pictures

By now you are ready to get into some sophisticated graphics, and word-processing programs can offer you some great options. If you are creating birthday cards, newsletters or invitations, you can really make things look professional.

Adding borders

You can add a border to a page or to a short – or long – section of text within a document. There are plenty of complicated border options, but I am going to concentrate on the simplest ones. Once you have mastered these, you will be perfectly able to experiment with others yourself.

To put a box around a paragraph

The simplest way is to use the highlight skill you have already learnt and the toolbar button.

- Highlight the section of text to which you want to add a border.

- Click on the **Outside border** button on the Formatting toolbar.

- If you don't like what you've done, simply click the button again.

- If you click on the arrow next to the button you'll activate a drop-down menu showing you a series of other options.

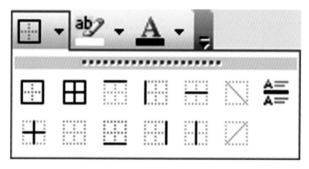

- You can put a rule on any side of the text.

- The border will affect whatever you have highlighted, so you can even put a box round a single word if you like.

To add a fancy border

- Highlight the text you want to surround with a border.

- From the Main menu, select **Format**, then **Borders and shading** and a window will open up.

- Select the **Borders** tab and click on **Box**.

- From the **Setting** options, choose the style of border you prefer.

- From the **Style** options, click on the border pattern you like.

- Select the width of the line for your border from the **Width** options.

- In the **Preview** window, you will see the effects you are about to apply to your highlighted text. You will see that by clicking on the boxes around the preview pane, you can add or remove parts of the border.

- When you are happy, click **OK**.

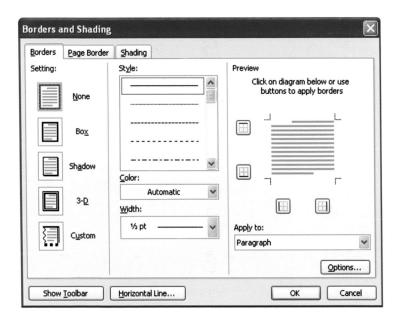

Once you have selected different border options from the drop-down menu, you will apply those options – instead of the simple default box – if you use the **Outside border** key on your Formatting toolbar.

Don't worry **about colour**

You can also choose the colour of your border. If you are ready to have a go, make a selection of which colour you want before you apply your box. Alternatively, you can wait until we deal with colour on page 124.

To add a border to a page

You have even more options, including picture borders, if you want to put a border round each page.

- From the Main menu, select **Format**, then **Borders and shading** and a window will open up.

- Select the **Page border** tab.

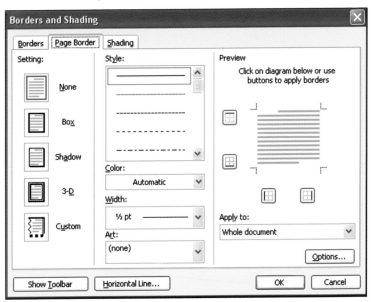

- Make your selections in exactly the same way as you did for your box border.

- In the **Preview** window, you will see the effects you are about to apply to your whole document. There is another drop-down menu allowing you to apply the border to only a section of your document. You will see that by clicking on the boxes around the preview pane, you can add or remove parts of the border.

- When you are happy, click **OK**.

Other border options

There are other things you can do with borders – either a box border or a whole-page border – so when you have mastered the basics, you can experiment with some alternatives.

- If you click on **Shadow** instead of **Box**, the box style will display a shadow on the right and bottom borders. Make all the other selections as before.

- If you choose **3D**, you will get a three-dimensional box style combined with all your other options.

- Click on **Custom**, then click on your chosen style. You can then click on one border in the preview pane to select that style. Click again on a different style and click on a second border in the preview pane, and so on to mix and match border styles for each side of your box.

- If you click on the **Options** button, you can add a larger space between the text and the surrounding border. The default setting is a 1pt space top and bottom and a 4pt space on either side. If you increase those numbers, you'll increase the space between the text and the border.

- If you click on the **Options** button in the page border window, you can adjust the space between the border and the edge of the page.

Don't worry **about shading**

You can also add shading within your box, but since this is more interesting in colour, we'll deal with that on page 129.

Adding drop caps

If you are writing a novel – or perhaps a short story for a grandchild – you may want to add a drop cap at the beginning of the story or chapter. You will need to be in Print layout view (see page 61) to see your drop cap displayed.

- Position your cursor at the beginning of the paragraph.

- From the Main menu, choose **Format**, then **Drop cap** and a window will open.

- You can choose a traditional option, or a drop cap in the margin. You can adjust how large the letter is by changing the number of drop lines; the standard setting is three.

- When you have chosen, click **OK**.

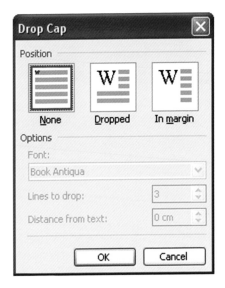

Don't worry about what it will look like

Experiment with options. If you don't like what you have done, simply press the **Undo** button, or go back to the Drop cap window and click on **None**.

How to add clip art

Now you are going to add some illustrations to your document. The easiest way to do this is to use the ready-made clip art collection on your computer. You will need to be in Print layout view to display your pictures properly (see page 61).

- From the Main menu, select **Insert**, then **Picture**, then **Clip art**.

- In the window that opens up on the right, key in a search word and press **Go** and you'll be offered a selection of images.

- Scroll down and click on any image that you want to insert in your document.

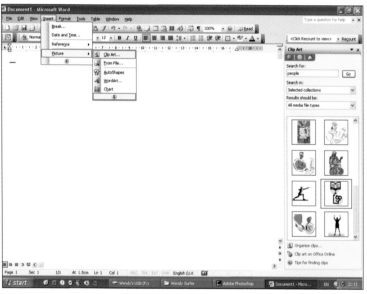

- Click on the **X** in the top right-hand corner to exit from the screen.

If you decide you don't like the picture after all, simply click on the clip art to activate it so a border appears around it, then press **Delete**.

Changing the size of the clip art

It is quite likely that the artwork you insert will be larger than you want it.

- Click on the art so a border appears with boxes on each corner and on each side.

- Click and drag from the corners to reduce or enlarge the image.

- Click and drag from one side to make it wider, thinner, taller or shorter – but remember that this will change the proportions of the image.

Don't worry **about online collections**

In your clip art window, you will also have the option to search online collections of clip art – if you are connected to the internet – and download them to your computer.

How to add pictures

You add photographs or any illustrations to your documents in the same way, also in Print layout view.

- From the Main menu, select **Insert**, then **Picture**, then **From file**.

- The computer will automatically take you to a file called My pictures.

- If the picture you want is in that file, click on it to highlight it, then press **Insert**.

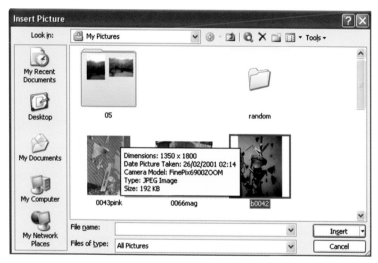

- If not, use the **Back** button, or the **Up one level** button to navigate to where you have stored the photo you want.

- When you have found it, click on the name to highlight it, then press **Insert** and it will appear in your document.

If you want to change the size, you do it in exactly the same way as you did with the clip art. It's also the same if you want to delete a picture: click on the picture to activate it, then press **Delete**.

Don't worry **about format picture options**

Another way to change the size is to click on **Format**, then **Picture** from the Main menu and select the **Size** tab. You can then type in the measurements you want for your picture, or the percentage of the original size you want it to appear.

Scanning your own images

If you have a scanner, you will be able to scan in your own images and save them on your computer. You can then insert them in your documents in exactly the same way, navigating to where you have saved them in **My documents** or **My pictures**.

Wrapping text around a picture

When you insert a picture in your document, the text will appear either above or below it. You may want the picture on one side, with the text flowing round it. This is called text wrapping.

- When you have inserted your picture or clip art, click on it to activate it. The border will appear round the outside and a picture toolbar will open up.

- Click on the **Text wrapping** button and choose how you want the text to wrap around the picture. You can choose to position the illustration in line with, square to, tight to, behind or in front of the text, top and bottom, through, behind, and so on.

Experimenting with the options is the easiest way to see how they will look, and if you have tried out the options for yourself, you are more likely to remember the procedures.

If your computer does not offer you a Picture toolbar, simply activate the picture by clicking on it, then click on **Format**, then **Picture** from the Main menu. Click on the **Layout** tab and make your selections in the same way.

Creating text boxes

In the same way as you can insert a picture into a document, you can insert a text box into a document. You can format the text in the box to be different from your main text and keep the text separate. You can adjust the box size however you want, and adjust the text wrapping to arrange your main text around the box. Display your document in Print layout view.

- Click on the **Drawing** icon on the Standard toolbar.

- An additional toolbar will appear on your screen. It may be at the bottom of your screen.

- Click on the **Text box** icon and your cursor will change to a cross.

- Imagine this is the top left-hand corner of your text box and, holding down the mouse button, drag it diagonally to create a box on the screen.

- As with the picture, click in the text box to activate it. You can change its size and shape in the same way as you did a picture by clicking and dragging on the control boxes on the corner or the sides.

- Click inside the box and type in your text.

- Highlight the text inside the box to format it in the same way as you would ordinary text.

- From the Main menu, click on **Format**, then **Text box**, then the **Layout** tab to decide how you want your main text to wrap around the box, as you did with clip art and pictures.

- To delete a text box, click on it, then press **Delete** but don't forget that you'll delete the whole thing, including the text.

Don't worry **about the drawing toolbar**

Drawing toolbar repeats some of the buttons that appear on the Formatting toolbar, plus there are more options that will be dealt with in the next chapter. Even then there's more scope for experimentation, drawing shapes, lines and 3D images.

Your reminder box

- To add a border, highlight the text and use the **Outside border** button on the Formatting toolbar, or from the Main menu, choose **Format, Borders and shading**, then the **Borders** or **Page border** options.

- Insert a drop cap using **Format**, then **Drop cap** from the Main menu.

- Insert clip art via **Insert, Picture, Clip art** from the Main menu.

- To insert a picture, select **Insert** from the Main menu, then **Picture**, then **From file**.

- Click on a picture or clip art to activate it so you can change its size or position.

- Use the box on the corner of a picture or clip art to re-size it.

- From the Main menu, use **Format, Picture, Layout** to alter how the text wraps round the image.

- To create a text box, click on **Drawing**, then **Text box** and click and drag to create your box and work within it.

Chapter 8

Making It Colourful

So far, we have worked only in black and white, but now it's time to bring in some colour. The principles you have learnt for formatting in other ways apply here just the same: highlight the text you want to change; click on the relevant icon or use the drop-down menu to make your choice; click **OK**.

Choosing the font colour

You can choose to display your text in any colour you like, either from a palette of common choices or from a complete colour wheel to give you infinite choice. You change the colour from the Formatting toolbar using the Font colour icon.

- Highlight the text you want to change.

- Click on the arrow next to the **Font colour** icon on the Formatting toolbar to display the drop-down menu.

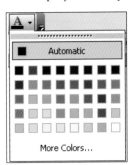

- If you see a colour you want on the palette, click on it.

- If you can't see a colour you like, click on **More colours** and a new window will open up.

- On the **Standard** tab, click on any coloured hexagon. The screen will display the existing colour in the bottom box on the right, and the new colour above it.

- When you are happy with your choice, click **OK**.

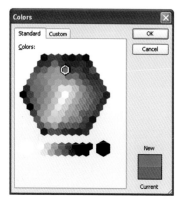

- If you choose the **Custom** tab, you have even more choices. Click anywhere in the rainbow window to select a colour. Again, the new colour will appear in a box above the old.

- When you are happy with your choice, click **OK**.

You will see that the coloured line on the **Font colour** icon has changed to your chosen colour. If you now want to change a block of text to that colour, simply highlight the text, then click on the button. If you want a different colour, choose from the drop-down menus as before.

Don't worry **if the text is not highlighted**

If you don't highlight text, but simply click on a new colour, when you continue to type, the program will start to type in the chosen font colour. To go back to black, click on the **Font colour** arrow, then on **Automatic**.

Coloured highlights

We have become used to using the word 'highlight' to indicate how to select blocks of text. You can also do this on your documents, in just the same way as you would colour over a block of text on paper with a coloured highlighter pen to emphasise it.

- Highlight the text you want to change.

- Click on the arrow next to the **Highlight** button on the Formatting toolbar.

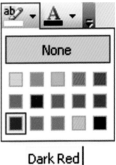

- Click on the colour you want and your chosen text will have a block of the highlight colour behind it.

As before, the coloured bar on the **Highlight** button will change to your chosen colour, so highlight text and click on it if you want to use the colour again. To delete the highlight, highlight the text, click on the arrow, then click on **None**.

Choosing a background colour

If you want a block of colour to appear behind your text, you can choose any colour you like. You can then alter the font colour on top to create different effects.

For example, to get an effect like this, you can choose a pink shading with white text.

- Highlight the text you want to put a coloured panel behind.

- From the Main menu, select **Format**, then **Borders and shading**.

- Click on the **Shading** tab.

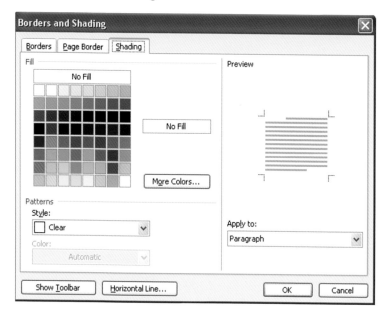

- As before, you can click on any colour you want, then click on **OK**.

- Or you can click on **More colors** to give you both Standard and Custom options, as with the font colours on page 125.

If you continue to type while you are within the shaded area, it will grow to fit the text. If you want to move to your normal background, simply move the mouse outside the colour and click on the white 'paper'.

You can, of course, add a background colour within a text box by using exactly the same process.

Inserting coloured borders and boxes

You have already mastered putting boxes around your text, but they can be done in colour as well. The process is the same as adding a fancy border as you did on page 112; you just need to select your colour before you choose your border style.

- Highlight the text you want to surround with a border.

- From the Main menu, select **Format**, then **Borders and shading** and a window will open up.

- Select the **Borders** tab and click on **Box**.

- As before, choose from the **Setting** style and **Width** options.

- This time, select a colour as well from the **Colour** menu.

- Your border will now appear in the Preview window in the colour you have selected.

- When you are happy, click **OK**.

Adding fancy shading

You have already added coloured backgrounds to your text, both with and without borders. You can use the same menu options to add shading within your border, introducing coloured dots and patterns behind your text.

• Highlight the area where you want to add a shaded panel.

• From the Formatting toolbar, click on **Format**, then **Borders and shading** and a window will open up.

• Select the **Shading** tab.

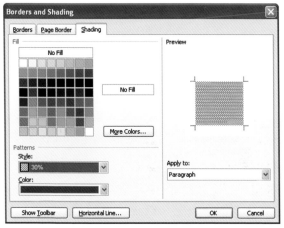

• Instead of clicking on the colour you want, go down to the **Style** options and, from the top window, click on the arrow and choose a percentage from the drop-down menu.

• Then on the second window, labelled **Color**, click on the colour you want from the drop-down menu.

• If you then go back to the **Style** menu, you can see how the patterns display in that colour, and change them if you wish.

• When you are happy, click on **OK**.

Use the shading options in combination with borders in exactly the same way as above to fill your box with any colour or pattern of shading.

WordArt

WordArt offers you a simple way to get seriously creative with display headings. You don't have to use colour for WordArt, but it does look much more interesting, so I thought this topic fitted comfortably in this creative chapter.

To find out what you can do with WordArt, just look at the appropriate window.

- Click on the **Drawing** icon on the Standard toolbar to display the Drawing toolbar.

- Click on the **WordArt** icon to open up the window.

- Click on the style of text you like from the options available.

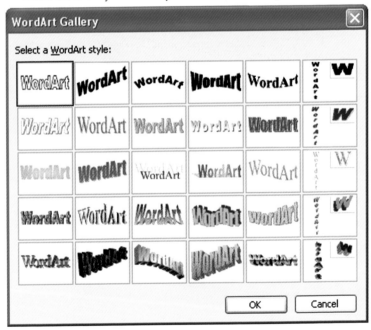

- Click **OK** and another window will open up.

- Type the text you want to display in the main window. If you want to change the font or size of your WordArt, you can make choices from the drop-down menus.

- When you have made your choices, click **OK** and the text will appear in your document in the chosen display style.

If your WordArt text is not where you want it, move your cursor over the text and the cursor will turn into a cross. Simply click and drag to move it where you want.

Don't worry **about the extra toolbar**

When you click on the WordArt text, another small toolbar will appear. You can click on the various buttons to change: the text; the style; the colour; the type of line; the size; the text wrapping; the shape; the letter height; and the alignment. If you click on the rotate tool, then move your cursor over one of the green circles that appears, you can even rotate the text clockwise! You can spend hours experimenting!

Your reminder box

- Change the font colour from the Formatting menu by clicking on **Font colour**.

- To highlight text, use the **Highlight** button on the Formatting toolbar.

- Add a background colour by clicking on **Format, Borders and shading** from the Main menu, choosing the **Shading** tab and clicking on the colour you want.

- Use the same route to choose a background pattern, but select the **Style** percentage and colour.

- From the Standard toolbar, click on the **Drawing** icon, then choose **WordArt** from the Drawing toolbar to create and format WordArt in your document.

Chapter 9

Using Tables

You have already learnt how to set up your tabs in order to align columns of text. Using tables gives you another useful way of displaying information. You can include as many columns and rows as you like, and each box in the table is called a cell. Tables are ideal for timetables, lists of addresses, or anything that requires separate cells of information.

The easiest way to play around with the table options and find out the possibilities is to key in a short list – like the one on page 105 – and play around with the program so you can see the effect of the various instructions.

How to set up a table

The first thing to do is to decide how many columns of text you want in your table. If you also know how many rows you want, you can specify that as well, but it is not necessary to do so now as the table will just keep growing as you add to it.

- Position your cursor where you want the table in your document.

- From the Main menu, click on **Table**, then **Insert**, then **Table** and a window will open up.

- Choose the number of columns and the number of rows you want. If you are not sure how many rows, just start with three for now.

- Click **OK** and a table will appear in your document.

- To key text into the table, simply click in a box and start typing. The box will grow as you add text.

- Use the **Tab** key to move from box to box, or simply click in the box you want with your mouse.

Working in a table

You can highlight cells and format the text within each one in a different way if you want, or simply leave them all the same. For example, you may want to have the column headings in bold. Simply highlight the row – or a cell or any number of cells – and click on the **Bold** icon.

You can manipulate text in a table in exactly the same way as you do normally, typing in, deleting, moving, correcting and formatting. The only major difference is that if you highlight a section of text, you can move it to another cell and add it to any text already in that cell. However, if you highlight the whole cell and move it, it will replace the original cell.

In this cell, the text is highlighted.	In this cell, the whole cell is highlighted.

You can also use copy and paste in the same way as in normal text (see page 59).

One additional option in a table is that you can copy one complete cell, then highlight a number of cells and click on **Paste** and the copied text will be repeated in each highlighted cell.

How to convert text to a table

If you have already keyed in your text, then decide it would be easier to work in a table, that's easy to do.

- Highlight the text you want to include in the table.

- From the Main menu, click on **Table**, then **Convert**, then **Text to table** and a window will open up.

- Depending on what is in the text, the computer will make its best guess about how many columns and rows you want.

- Before you adjust the number of columns, look at the bottom of the window to the **Separate at** options. If you have used tabs to separate your columns, click on the Tab option and the number of columns should alter to the correct number. Adjust the separator and the column number until you get what you want, then press **OK**.

On the other hand, you may have set up text in a table, then decided you want it as basic columns. Simply highlight the table, then from **Table** on the Main menu, click on **Convert**, then **Table to text**. You may then want to adjust your tab stop positions to make sure the list is neatly aligned (see page 104).

Adding and deleting rows and columns

If you want to add more rows to your table, click on the last box, then press the **Tab** key and another row will appear. You can do this as often as you like, adding more rows as you key in.

Alternatively, you may want to add rows in the middle of the table.

- Hold the cursor in the margin to the left of the row and the cursor will change to ⏴.

- Click once and the whole row will be highlighted.

- From the Main menu, select **Table**, then **Insert**, then click on **Rows above** or **Rows below**, and you will add rows to your table.

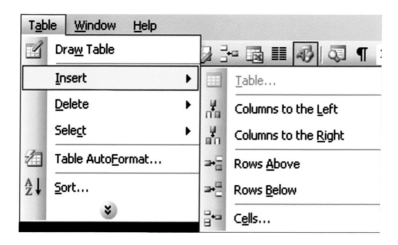

If you want to add an additional column, you use the same procedure.

- Hold your cursor above a column until it changes to ↓.

- Click on your mouse to highlight the whole column.

- From the Main menu, choose **Table**, then **Insert**, then click on **Columns to the left** or **Columns to the right**.

Deleting columns or rows

To delete a column or row, highlight it – as you did above – then press the **Cut** key on the Standard toolbar.

You can also select **Table** from the Main menu, then **Delete** the **Table**, **Columns**, **Rows** or **Cells**.

Moving rows and columns

Once you have created a table, you can easily move a complete row to somewhere else in the table.

- Hold the cursor in the margin to the left of the row and the cursor will change to ↰

- Click once and the whole row will be highlighted.

- Move the cursor over the highlighted row until the cursor changes to a left-pointing arrow.

- Click and drag the row to where you want it.

You can do a similar operation to move a column.

- Hold your cursor above a column until it changes to ↓ .

- Click on your mouse to highlight the whole column.

- Move the cursor over the highlighted column until the cursor changes to a left-pointing arrow.

- Click and drag the column to where you want it.

Don't worry **about fancy rules**

Normally if you work in a table, the computer will supply a plain rule round all the cells, or boxes, in the table. However, you can work from the Main menu with **Format, Borders and shading, Borders** to use any style you like for any of the rules within the table. You could have a thicker rule round the outside and a dotted rule in the centre, for example, or any combination either across the whole table or in individual cells. Just use the same process as you did when adding rules to ordinary text (see page 111).

Adjusting the column width

If you don't want your columns to be all the same size, you can change them to any combination of options.

- Move your cursor over one of the upright lines between the columns and it will change to ← | →.

- Click and drag to change the column width.

Don't worry **about colours**

You can also use colours in tables in the same way as you do in ordinary text documents, selecting the colours for the fonts, the rules or the background from the Formatting toolbar. Simply follow the instructions on pages 124–129 for using colour in text.

Sorting text into order

Another useful option on the Table menu is **Sort**. You can use it both in tables and in general text to sort the rows, or lines of text, in a particular order. For example, you might want to key in a list of names, then sort them alphabetically.

• Highlight the text list or the whole table. You can do this by clicking in the first cell and dragging to highlight the table, or from the Main menu, click on **Table, Select**, then **Table**.

• Again from **Table** on the Main menu, select **Sort** and a window will open up.

• If you are sorting text, the first window will say 'Paragraphs', the second one 'Text', and there will be a mark next to 'Ascending'. If you leave these default settings and click **OK**, the list will sort into alphabetical order.

• Choose 'Descending' to sort in reverse alphabetical order.

• If you are sorting a table, it will give you the option of sorting by Column 1 or Column 2, and so on.

• If you have named the columns and indicated the headings in bold or another font, the computer will recognise these as headings and list the column names.

- Click on the arrow and highlight the column you want to control the sort. For example, if you have headings called 'First name' and 'Surname', you would probably want to sort by surname. You can then click on the next column, if you want a secondary sort. If the computer has recognised them as headings, it will not include them in the sort; if you don't put the headings into bold, it will sort them with the rest of the list.

- Finally, click **OK**, as usual.

For example, in this table, I have keyed in some friends' names in any order. If I highlight the table and select **Sort**, then sort by Surname, First names, then Children, I can put the list into the most logical order. The computer will put the surnames in alphabetical order. Then, because there are three Smiths, it will put Mary and Stan, then the two sets of Joan and George, then Owen and Glenda. Finally, it will put Joan and George and Anita before Joan and George and Paul. Remember, if you do not differentiate the column headings, the computer will treat them as part of the list.

Surname	First names	Children
Smith	Owen and Glenda	Bernadette and Elizabeth
Jones	Roger and Christine	James, Callum and Sophie
Smith	Joan and George	Paul
Barber	Mike and Viv	Sally, Peter and Jack
Smith	Joan and George	Anita
Houseman	Phil and Linda	Sarah and Leigh
Smith	Mary and Stan	Daniel

Surname	First names	Children
Barber	Mike and Viv	Sally, Peter and Jack
Houseman	Phil and Linda	Sarah and Leigh
Jones	Roger and Christine	James, Callum and Sophie
Smith	Joan and George	Anita
Smith	Joan and George	Paul
Smith	Mary and Stan	Daniel
Smith	Owen and Glenda	Bernadette and Elizabeth

Using Autofit

If you want to avoid having your table take up too much space, you can change how it is set up. When you create a table, it automatically divides into equal columns spread across the width of your text. If you choose **Autofit**, you can make each column as wide as the longest text within it.

• Highlight the table.

• From the Main menu, select **Autofit**, then **Autofit to contents**. The computer will create columns just wide enough for each set of names.

• If you then add text to a cell, it will grow with the text.

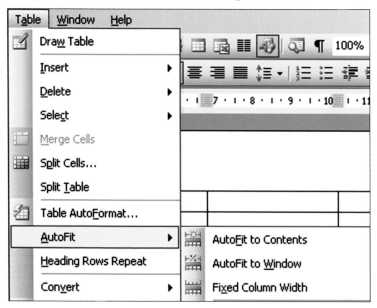

Other options under **Autofit** allow you to **Distribute the columns evenly** or **Distribute the rows evenly**. You may want to use either of these if you have adjusted the column widths or added columns, then want to make them all the same dimensions.

Using Autoformat to create different styles

Another option on the **Table** menu gives you the opportunity to display your table in fancy ways, instead of just in boxes.

• Highlight the table.

• From the Main menu, select **Table**, then **Table autoformat** and a window will open up.

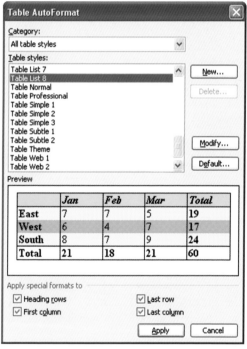

• In the left-hand **Table styles** window, highlight one of the options and the style of that table will appear in the **Preview** window. You can select from about 40 different options.

• By ticking or unticking the boxes at the bottom – Heading rows, First column, Last row, Last column – you can also make amendments to each individual style.

• When you have found a style you like, click **OK** and your chosen style will be applied to your table.

Merging and splitting cells

If you have created a table and you decide you would like to merge two cells together, you can easily do so.

- Highlight the cells you want to combine.

- From the Main menu, select **Table**, then **Merge cells**.

- The two cells will be amalgamated into one.

If you want to split cells into two or more separate cells, you have to decide how you want them to be divided.

- Highlight the cell you want to split.

- From the Main menu, select **Table**, then **Split cells** and a window will open up.

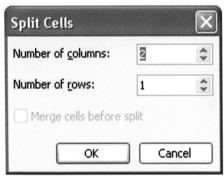

- Type in or use the increase and decrease arrows to decide whether you want to split the cell into two or more columns or two or more rows.

- Click **OK**.

You can use this option to make complex tables – or a pattern for your next patchwork quilt!

Barber	Mike and Viv Sally, Peter and Jack				
Houseman	Phil and Linda		Sarah and Leigh		
Jones	Roger and Christine		James, Callum and Sophie		

Your reminder box

- To work on a table, use **Table** from the Main menu for all options.

- **Insert table** will insert a table in your document with your chosen number of columns and rows.

- Choose **Convert**, then **Text to table** or **Table to text** to perform either task.

- To add rows to a table, select **Insert**, then click on **Rows above** or **Rows below**.

- To add columns to a table, select **Insert**, then click on **Columns to the left** or **Columns to the right**.

- Adjust the column width by moving the cursor over the column edge until it changes, then clicking and dragging.

- Highlight text to be sorted, then select **Sort**, choose the order into which you want your text to be reorganised, then click **OK**.

- Use **Autofit** to space rows or columns evenly, or make the columns fit the length of the text.

- Use **Autoformat** to apply a new display style to your table.

- Use **Merge cells** or **Split cells** to amalgamate or split cells in a table.

Chapter 10

Advanced Skills for Bigger Documents

As I mentioned at the beginning, Word has many sophisticated options, some of which you may have discovered if you have already found your confidence and started experimenting. This section covers those you are most likely to use. In some cases, Word offers you further options that are beyond the scope of this introductory guide. If you don't need to know, just ignore them. If you are intrigued, go for it! Move on to a more advanced book or experiment with the program for yourself and you'll soon work out all kinds of other possibilities.

Numbering the pages

If you are working on a long document, you can automatically number the pages.

- From the Main menu, click on **Insert**, and choose **Page Numbers** and a window will open up.

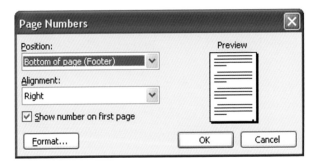

- Use the top drop-down menu to choose the position of your page numbers at the top or the bottom of the page.

- From the second menu, decide if you want them positioned on the left, right, centred, or on the inside and outside of each page.

- If you do not want the number 1 to appear on the first page of your document, untick the box.

- The preview will illustrate your choices. Once you are happy, click **OK**.

Don't worry **about formats**

If you click on the **Format** button, you have even more options. You can start your numbering somewhere other than 1 – if you are working on a two-part document, for example – or use 'A, B, C' or other options for sequencing your pages.

To remove page numbers

- From the Main menu, go to **View**, then **Header and footer**.

- If your page number is at the top, highlight and delete it.

- If it is at the bottom, press **Switch between header and footer**, then highlight and delete, then press **Close**.

Adding page breaks

You can start a new page anywhere you like in your document.

• From the Main menu, go to **Insert**, then **Break** and a window will open up.

• Choose **Page break** and click **OK**.

If you are in Normal view, the program will automatically switch to Print layout view (see page 61). You can stay in that option, or click back to Normal view, in which case, you will see a dotted line marked 'page break' in the appropriate position.

You can also choose to insert a column break in the same way, so if you are working in columns of text, you can automatically indicate where you would like your next column to start.

Go to

Whether or not you have added page numbers, you can go directly to a particular page in your document.

- From the Main menu, choose **Edit, Go to**.

- Insert the page number you want to find, then press **Next** and you will be taken directly to that page.

- Press **Close** to return to your document.

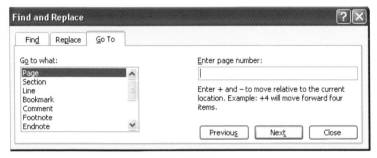

Shortcut to Go to

Ctrl + G is a useful keyboard shortcut for this option.

Find and replace

You can search a document for a specific word or phrase you want to find, or you can search for it and replace it with another. Whether you are finding or replacing, you can key in just a few letters, one word or a whole sentence.

- From the Main menu, choose **Edit**, then **Find** and a window will open up.

- Type in the word or words you want to find and press **Find next**.

- Word will scroll through the document and highlight the next occurrence of your selected word or words.

- If that's what you want, press **Cancel** to return to your document and make the change you want. If not, continue searching.

> ### Shortcut to Find
> The keyboard shortcut for find is **Ctrl + F**.

If you know you have spelled a name incorrectly throughout a document, or you want to replace any group of words, you can simply find and replace them.

- From the Main menu, choose **Edit**, then **Replace**.

- Type in the word or words you want to find, then whatever you want to replace them with.

- If you are sure you want to replace them all, press **Replace all**.

- If you want to go through one at a time, press **Find next**, then **Replace** individually as the program scrolls through and highlights each occurrence of the words.

- Press **Cancel** to return to your document.

Don't worry **about more options**

On either screen, press **More** for more options. The most common choice is to search for something in the same case, for which you tick the **Match case** box. Using this option, you can search only for 'The Street' and not for 'the street', for example. Using the other buttons, you can search for a word in bold or another format and replace it with italic, for example, or a whole host of other combinations.

Adding headers and footers

If you are preparing a long document, you may want the title to appear at the top or bottom of each page. You can do this in combination with page numbers, or just use headers and footers.

- Go to the start of your document.

- From the Main menu, select **View**, then **Header and footer** and the display of your document will change so the main text is greyed out, and a text box at the top of your page is activated. A new toolbar will also open up.

- Click in the box and type in the heading you would like to appear. You only need to do this once and the program will repeat the same heading throughout.

- If you want to format the header text – you may want it centred and in a slightly smaller font size from your main text, for example – do it in the same way as you would any text by highlighting and making your changes from the Formatting menu.

- If you want to add a footer, click on the **Switch between header and footer** button and it will take you to a similar active box at the bottom of the page.

- Add your text, as before, then click on **Close**.

Don't worry **about the new toolbar**

On the header and footer toolbar, you also have more options: to add or format the page numbers, to insert the date and time, or to move around the headers and footers.

Using Spellcheck

While you are working in Word, the computer checks everything you type against a dictionary. It automatically corrects common spelling and typing errors, so if you type 'seperate', it would automatically correct it to 'separate', for example.

The Spellcheck automatically underlines with a wiggly red line any words it believes are wrongly spelled. This is useful if your spelling is not too good, of course, but can also pick up typing errors if you are not a perfect typist. It will also notice notice if you repeat a word when you are typing.

Common proper names – John, Ann, London, New York, Calcutta – will be recognised by Spellcheck, but anything more unusual will defeat it – Mr Arbuthnot, Cippenham, eBay.

Don't worry **about Spellcheck**

The red lines are for your use only – their only function is to draw things to your attention. You don't have to do anything about them if you don't want to, or you can switch them off (see page 157).

Set the right language

First, make sure your Spellcheck is set to the correct dictionary. Look along the bottom of your document window and you should see 'English (U.K.)' or 'English (U.S.)' in a little box. If you are not sure, simply type 'color' and 'colour' into a document. If you want UK English, 'color' should be underlined. If you want US English, 'colour' should be underlined.

If you don't have what you want, it is easy to change.

- From the Main menu, click on **Tools**, then **Language**, then **Set Language**.

- Click on the language you want.

- Click **OK**.

You'll see that you can also set to a whole range of other languages if this is appropriate, although the relevant dictionaries will only be loaded on more sophisticated versions of the program.

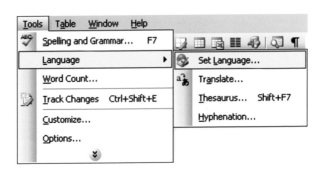

A word of warning

English spelling being what it is, you can't expect Spellcheck to do everything for you. For example, it won't notice if you have missed out a word, missed out a letter to make another word (bought and brought, for example), used a word in the wrong context, or misused apostrophes or other punctuation.

Deer Sire,

Eye agree with yew. It is grate two bee able too cheque spelling. This letter has bean chequered buy won, sew eye no awl the word's inn it must bee spelt write.

Running your document through Spellcheck

If Spellcheck underlines a word, you can simply correct it as you go by using the backspace and delete keys. Alternatively, you can run the whole document through Spellcheck when you have finished.

- Click at the top of the document.

- From the Main menu, click on **Tools**, then **Spelling and grammar** and a window will open up.

- You will see a section of your document in the top window with the first doubted word in red. Simply click on the button that reflects what you want to do, then Spellcheck will move on to the next word.

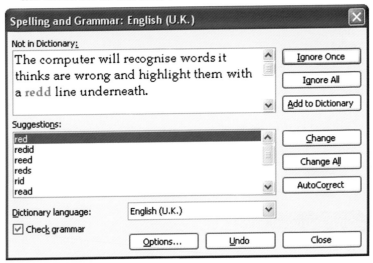

The buttons on the right give you the option to:

- **Ignore once:** Ignore the word if you know it is right – and remember Spellcheck is not always right.

- **Ignore all:** This option allows every instance of that word – so if you mention Mr Arbuthnot more than once, you only have to click once.

- **Add to dictionary:** Clicking on this adds the word to your dictionary so it will recognise it if you use it again.

- **Change:** In the bottom window, you will see a list of one or more words that the computer thinks are what you should have typed; click on the right one. If you don't see the one you want, click in the top window and make the change. Finally, click on **Change**.

- **Change all:** If you click on this, the computer will change every instance of this word in your document, so if you have typed 'Mr Arbuthnot' all the way through, then find out it should be 'Mr Arbuthnott', you can use this option.

- **Autocorrect:** If you click this button, Spellcheck will add this word to the list of things it corrects automatically.

If you change your mind when you have corrected something, press **Undo**.

When you have finished, a window will pop up to tell you the Spellcheck is complete. If you want to stop at any time before then, click on **Close**.

Don't worry **about options**

On that same menu, clicking **Options** will give you more choices in how you set up your Spellcheck but don't bother with them unless you want to. If you don't want the computer to check that item, untick the box.

Switching off Spellcheck

If it really annoys you, you can switch off Spellcheck. You can switch it on again any time you wish.

- From the Main menu, choose **Tools**, then **Options**.

- Choose the **Spelling and grammar** tab.

- Untick the box next to **Check spelling as you type**.

- Click **OK**.

> ### Shortcut to Spellcheck
> To go straight to Spellcheck, press **F7**.

Checking grammar

Word can also check your grammar as you type. It works in exactly the same way as Spellcheck but underlines in wavy green lines and leaves you to 'correct' what you have done in the document. I say 'correct' because, personally, I find this an intrusion into my writing style and I don't usually agree with it! Remember it's only a machine!

It is easy to switch the grammar check on or off in the same way as spelling.

- From the Main menu, choose **Tools**, then **Options**.

- Choose the **Spelling and grammar** tab as you did above.

- Tick or untick the **Check grammar as you type** box and the **Check grammar with spelling** boxes.

You should also tick or untick the box at the bottom left-hand corner of the **Tools, Spelling and grammar** window.

Don't worry **about the thesaurus**

If you are finding it difficult to find a different word to use for something, Word has an in-built thesaurus. Highlight the word you want to look up. From the Main menu, choose **Tools**, then **Language**, then **Thesaurus**. You will be offered a series of alternatives. Click on the one you want, then press **Replace** to replace the word in your document.

Using Autocorrect and Autotext

Both these options can help to make your life easier when you are keying in documents.

- From the Main menu, click on **Tools**, then **Autocorrect options** and a window will open up.

- Select the **Autocorrect** tab.

- By ticking the boxes, you set up the computer to correct your typing as you go. It can correct two capital letters, add capitals after a full stop, capitalise the names of days and make a correction if you leave the **Caps lock** on by mistake.

- It will also automatically correct the selection of common typing errors listed in the bottom window. If you know you often make specific keying errors, you can add your own by keying the incorrect version in the **Replace** window and the correct version in the **With** window, then press **Add**.

- To delete entries, click on them, then click **Delete**.

- To finish, click **OK**.

Using Autotext

Autotext is a similar section of the Word program that allows you to type in words, phrases, or even sentences that you use regularly. When you start to type, as soon as the computer recognises the phrase, it will show you the words in a yellow box. If that is what you want to type, press **Enter** instead of having to type the whole phrase. If not, just carry on typing.

- From the Main menu, click on **Tools**, then **Autocorrect options** and a window will open up.

- Select the **Autotext** tab.

- In the bottom window, you will see a list of Autotext words and phrases. Click on any and press **Delete** to remove them from the list.

- To add to the list, type in what you want in the top window, then click on **Add**.

- To finish, click **OK**.

Word count

If you want to find out how many words are in your document – for an evening-class essay, for example – you don't have to count a single word!

- Highlight the whole document by positioning your mouse in the left-hand margin and clicking quickly three times. Alternatively, you can highlight any smaller portion of text.

- On the Main menu, click on **Tools**, then **Word count** and a window will open up.

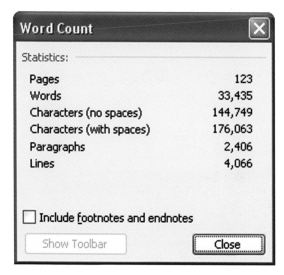

- The window will list not just the number of words, but also the number of pages, characters (counting or not counting spaces between words), paragraphs and lines.

- To exit, click **Close**.

Your reminder box

- To number pages, from the Main menu, click on **Insert**, then **Page numbers**.

- Add page breaks or column breaks from the Main menu via **Insert**, then **Break**.

- From the Main menu, choose **Edit**, then **Go to**, or use keyboard shortcut **Ctrl + G**, then key in the number of the page you want to go to and press **Enter**.

- From the Main menu, click on **Edit** then **Find**, or **Edit** then **Replace** to search through your document for specific words.

- Add headers and footers to your document using **View**, then **Header and footer**, then typing in once the copy you want to appear throughout the document.

- Set the correct language for your document by choosing **Tools** from the Main menu, then **Language** and **Select language** and selecting English (U.K.) or English (U.S.).

- From the Main menu, click on **Tools**, then **Spelling and grammar** to run a document through Spellcheck.

- To switch Spellcheck or grammar checking on or off, tick or untick the box on the **Tools, Options, Spelling and grammar** tab.

- From the Main menu, choose **Tools**, then **Autocorrect** for both **Autocorrect** and **Autotext**, selecting the relevant tab from the main window.

- To count the number of words in a document, or part of a document, highlight the text, then click on **Tools, Word count**.

Chapter 11

Mail Merges

A mail merge is the computer term for a method of creating personalised letters – at worst, those personalised mailshot letters you get if you haven't signed up to the no-junk-mail systems!

It is best to tackle a mail merge – if you want to – once you have become reasonably confident in your word-processing skills. It is extraordinarily easy, but you do need to do things in the correct sequence, so it helps if you are familiar with following instructions and don't worry if you do something 'wrong'. If in doubt, just exit the documents without saving them and start again. Once you have mastered it, you'll wonder what the fuss was about.

What would you use a mail merge for if you are not in an office scenario? There's plenty of useful applications: you never need to write out your Christmas-card labels again; you can easily personalise your round-robin letters or club newsletter; change-of-address notices or party invitations can all be done with a real professional finish.

How does mail merge work?

A mail merge takes one set of information, usually a list of some kind, and – surprise, surprise! – merges it in a specific way of your choice with another set of information, usually a letter or similar document. Let's outline how it works before we go on to the step-by-step instructions.

Source information

Your first set of information is known as your data source and you must establish this before you start. The simplest way is by setting up a table, as we did in chapter 9 (see page 133). Each column in the table stores a type of information known as a Field, so in our table on page 140, the fields are defined as: surname, first names, children. The computer shows you this is a field by displaying it like this: <<Surname>>. You can have as many fields as you like. Each box, or cell, in the table stores a separate piece of information within the field defined by that column.

Don't worry **about Microsoft Excel**

You can also use a Microsoft Excel database as a data source for a Word mail merge in exactly the same way as a Word table.

Main document

Your main document is obviously the base into which you flow the data you have stored. It's much easier to see how it works with an example, so let's use the table information we already have to demonstrate.

To create your main document, you simply type the words you want, but instead of typing in each name, you use mail merge to insert a field.

To: <<First names>> <<Surname>>

I would be very pleased if <<First names>> would bring <<Children>> to join me for drinks on Saturday 12 December at 6pm. I do hope you can come.

Wendy

Notice that you need to include spaces between the fields if you want a space to appear, so there has to be a space between <<First names>> and <<Surname>>. If you want to go to a new line – in the lines of an address, for example – you press the return key as usual so the fields appear on separate lines. If you want a page break between each letter, add one at the end of the document.

The merged document

Once you merge your two sets of information, the computer takes the data you have asked for and places it in the main document to create individual notes like these ones.

To: Mike and Viv Barber

I would be very pleased if Mike and Viv would bring Sally, Peter and Jack to join me for drinks on Saturday 12 December at 6pm. I do hope you can come.

Wendy

To: Phil and Linda Houseman

I would be very pleased if Phil and Linda would bring Sarah and Leigh to join me for drinks on Saturday 12 December at 6pm. I do hope you can come.

Wendy

To: Roger and Christine Jones

I would be very pleased if Roger and Christine would bring James, Callum and Sophie to join me for drinks on Saturday 12 December at 6pm. I do hope you can come.

Wendy

To: Joan and George Smith

I would be very pleased if Joan and George would bring Anita to join me for drinks on Saturday 12 December at 6pm. I do hope you can come.

Wendy

If any of the fields are empty, the computer will ignore them. In an address, for example, it doesn't matter if one address has fewer lines. However, in this example, you would need to check and amend the details of anyone without children.

Don't worry **about defining your fields**

When you do a mail merge, you are quite likely to find you need to make the odd change once you've set up your document. For example, you would usually sort a list of names in a table by surname, so that would be your first column. When you input your fields in the main document, surname will be first on the list, so if you list that first, you'll send your letters to 'Smith Carolyn and Peter'. Similarly, if you forget to put a space between your fields, you'll get 'SmithCarolyn and Peter'. Don't worry! If you have merged the document, throw it away, change the order of the fields in the main document (by highlighting and moving the text), then re-run the merge.

Step-by-step mail merge

Follow these instructions and you can't go far wrong. This will show you how to create a letter; you can adapt it to create whatever you want. If you do get confused, it's usually easiest just to exit and start again.

- Create and save a table of names and addresses as outlined on pages 133–134. This is my example document.

Surname	First	Children	Address 1	Address 2	Town	County	Postcode
Houseman	Peter and Mary	Scott and Ian	86 Whiteknights Road		Bristol	Avon	BS8 7HJ
Jones	Miranda and Bob	Sarah and Charlotte	7 Church Road	The Maltings	Leeds	South Yorkshire	LS6 5TH
Smith	John and Mary	Simon	The Cottage	34 The Street	Dunsfold	Gloucester-shire	GL6 7UJ
Whitehouse	Sarah and Jim	Callum, Jackie and Sam	10 The View		Eastbourne	Sussex	EH7 8HY

- Press **New blank document** to open a new document.

- From the Main menu, click on **Tools**, **Letters and mailings**, **Mail merge** and a window will open up on the right-hand side.

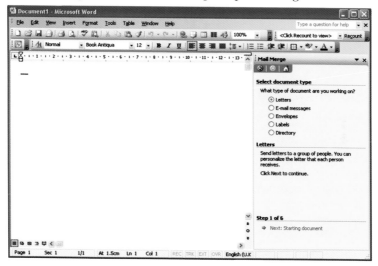

- Select **Letters** as your document type and click **Next**.

- Select **Use the current document** as your starting document, then click **Next**.

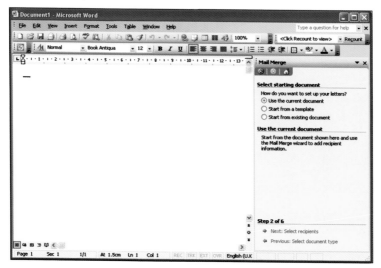

- To select the recipients, click on **Use an existing list**, then click **Browse** and navigate to your address document.

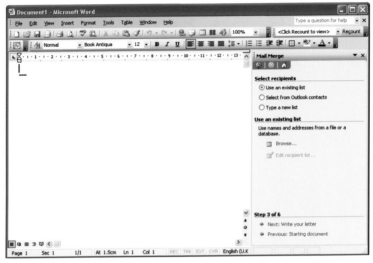

- Click on it, then click **Open** and the document will open up in a special screen.

- You can simply click **OK**, then click on **Next** to move to the next screen, or you can sort your recipients according to the instructions if you wish, then click **OK**, then **Next**.

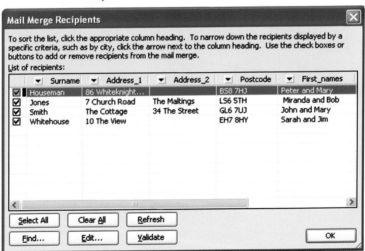

- Start to write your letter.

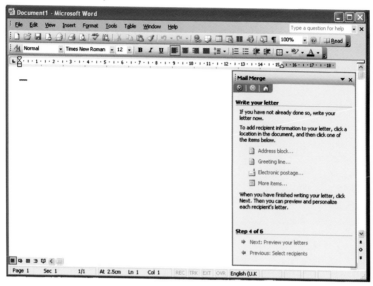

- Where you want to include a field, click on **More items** to open the **Insert merge field** window. Click on the item you want to include from the list, then click **Insert** and **Cancel**. Press the space bar or the return key to position the next piece of information correctly, then go back to **More items** to insert your next field until you have completed your letter. You can include your own address details at the top, or if you are printing on headed paper, remember to allow enough space at the top so the letter prints out in the correct position.

- You can choose the style of address you want for the greeting line by clicking on **Greeting line** and making a selection.

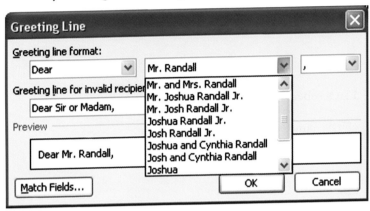

- You can choose how to display the address by clicking on **Address block** and making a selection.

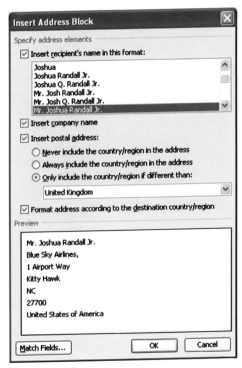

• Your document will look like this.

---

37 Mortimer Street
Monkton
Somerset
BA15 9JH

15 October 2007

«First_names» «Surname»
«Address_1»
«Address_2»
«Address_2»
«Town»
«County»
«Postcode»

Dear «First_names»

This is just to let you know that we will be holding the next meeting of the camera club at my house on Friday 23 October at 6.30 pm. Do feel free to bring «Children» with you if you think the topic might be of interest – we could do with some new members!

With kind regards

Wendy

- Click on **Preview** make sure you are happy with the individual letters. If not, go back and make any changes.

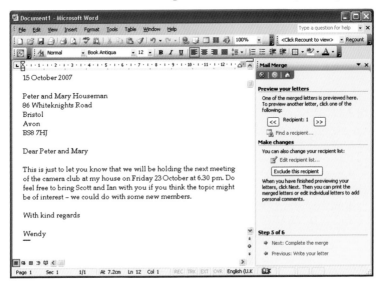

- When you are happy, press **Complete the merge**. On the next screen, press **Print** and each person will have an individual letter. Alternatively, you have the option to **Edit individual letters** if, for example, you want to add a specific note to one letter.

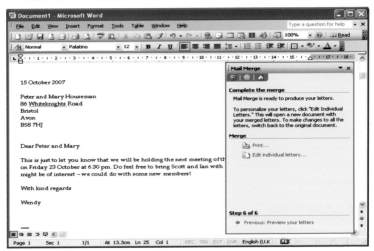

- Each of your letters will be personalised.

---

37 Mortimer Street
Monkton
Somerset
BA15 9JH

15 October 2007

John and Mary Smith
The Cottage
34 The Street
Dunsfold
Gloucestershire
GL6 7UJ

Dear John and Mary

This is just to let you know that we will be holding the next meeting of the camera club at my house on Friday 23 October at 6.30 pm. Do feel free to bring Simon with you if you think the topic might be of interest – we could do with some new members!

With kind regards

Wendy

You can save your file in the usual way if you want to, or exit.

Earlier Windows or Mac programs

If you are not using Windows XP, the mail merge process is slightly different, so follow these instructions instead.

- Press **New blank document** to open a new document.

- From the Main menu, click on **Tools**, then **Mail merge** and a window will open up.

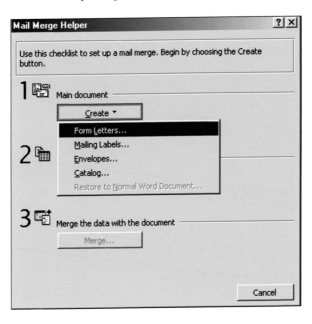

- At number one, select **Create**, then **Form letters**, then click on **Active window**.

- At number two, select **Get data**, then **Open data source**, and a window will open up showing **My documents**. Navigate to your address list, if necessary, click on it to highlight it, then click on **Open**.

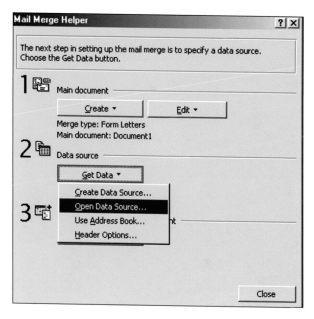

- You will be told you need to set up your main document. Click on **Edit main document** and the computer will return you to your empty document but you will see an extra icon **Insert merge field** on your Formatting toolbar.

- Start to type your document. Where you want to include a different name or detail, click on **Insert merge field** and choose the item you want to include from the drop-down menu.

- When you have finished your letter, open the mail merge window again from **Tools, Mail merge**. At number three, click on **Merge**, then **Merge** again in the next window.

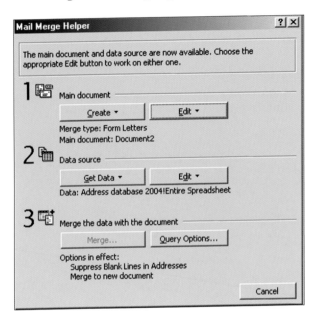

- Click on **Print** to print out your letters.
- You can save your document in the usual way if you wish.

Printing mailing labels

You can use exactly the same principles to print out a set of labels from your database, with just a couple of changes.

- As your document type, choose **Labels** instead of **Letters**, then click **Next**.

- Click on **Label options** to select the type of labels you have, clicking on **Avery A4 and A5 sizes**, then clicking on the code number printed on the labels.

- Finally, click **OK**.

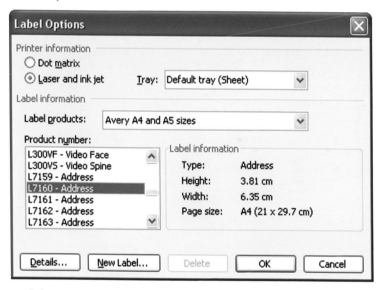

- Select your recipients and set up your document in the same way as you did for the letter. Click **Update all labels**, then preview and print as before.

Printing individual labels and envelopes

Although not strictly part of the mail merge options, it seems a logical place here to show you how to print individual labels, or a sheet of the same label. I print out sheets of university address labels to forward mail to my children during term time.

- If you are in a letter or document that contains the name and address you want to appear on the label, highlight it.

- From the Main menu, click on **Tools, Letters and mailings**, then **Envelopes and labels**, then click on the **Labels** tab on the window that opens up. The small window will contain the highlighted text. If you have not highlighted the text you want, simply key it into the window.

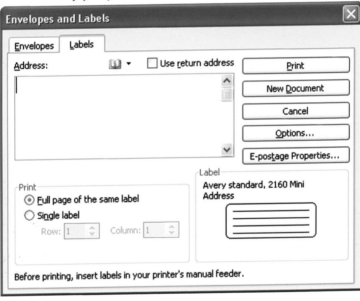

- If you want to print a full page of the same label, simply press **Print**.

- If you only want one copy, click on **Single label** and choose which label on the sheet you want to print. If you have a full sheet of labels, print at row 1, column 1, but once you have used that label and peeled it off, you can print on row 1, column 2, and so on.

Don't worry **about Options**

This allows you to choose your label size by code number, as described on page 177.

Printing envelopes

To print an envelope, follow exactly the same instructions as for labels, but select the **Envelopes** tab. The little picture will show you which way to feed the envelope into the printer.

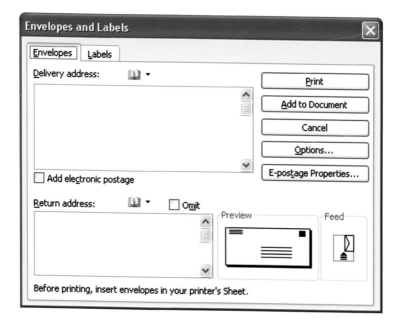

Your reminder box

- A mail merge is a way of creating personalised letters or other communications by inserting one set of data into specific positions in a letter or document.

- From the Main menu, choose **Tools**, then **Mail merge** and follow the step-by-step instructions to create Form letters or Mailing labels.

- To print a single label, a sheet of labels or an envelope, click on **Tools**, then **Envelopes and labels** from the Main menu.

Chapter 12

Improving Accessibility

The displays on computers are set up for the 'average' user – whoever that might be. If that's not you – perhaps you find the text too small to see easily or the keys repeat too quickly when you are typing – you can adjust the options on the computer to make it easier for you to use. These are functions of the computer, not the word-processing program, so they will vary depending on your operating system.

The accessibility wizard

The easiest way to activate the right settings for you is to go through the accessibility wizard.

- From **Start**, click on **All programs**, then **Accessories**, then **Accessibility**, then **Accessibility wizard** and a welcome window will open up. Read the instructions on each page, make your choices, then click on **Next**.

- On the first screen you will be asked to select a font size.

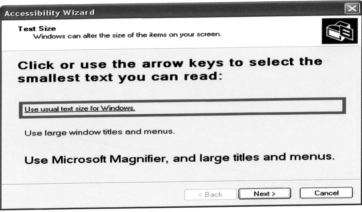

- In the next screen, you can change the display settings.

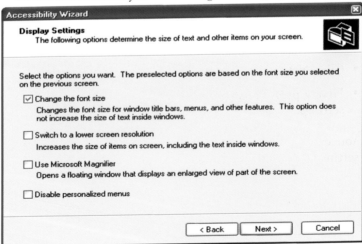

- You then specify your individual needs by clicking on various boxes to indicate if you have difficulty with vision, hearing or using the keyboard.

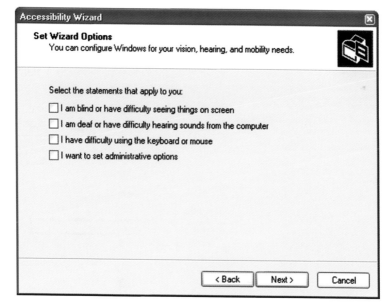

- Follow through the remaining windows, which will vary depending on the boxes you ticked, until you have completed the wizard. For example, you can change the icon size, alter the size of the cursor, change the mouse to left-handed operation and change the keypad if you find that easier to use than the mouse.

- Click **Next** when you have completed each window.

- Finally, press **Finish** and the computer will store your chosen settings.

You can go through the wizard at any time to change the settings if you are not happy with them.

Using the control panels

If you prefer, you can adjust various options using the control panels instead of using the wizard. In each case, click on **Start**, then on **Control panels** to open the window. On the left, click on **Switch to classic view**, then double-click on the relevant icons explained on the following pages.

Accessibility options

The accessibility options can all be adjusted individually. Go through those panels you think might interest you and try them out one at a time.

- Double-click on **Accessibility options** in the Control panels window and a window will open up with five tabs: **Keyboard, Sound, Display, Mouse** and **General**.

- Under each tab, you will have various options to tick or untick, then click on **Apply**, then **OK**.

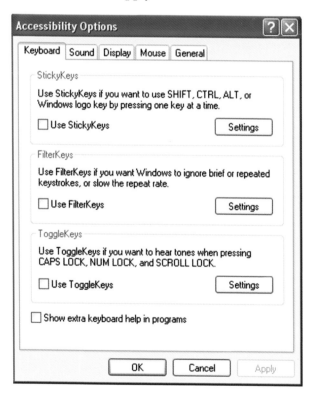

Slowing down the keyboard

If you hold down a key, it will continue to repeat. This may be useful if you want to put a row of kisses at the end of an e-mail to a grandchild, but it's really annoying if keys keep repeating when you don't want them to.

- Double-click on **Keyboard** in the Control panels window and a window will open up.

- Under the **Speed** tab, you can adjust the **Repeat delay, Repeat rate** and **Cursor blink rate**, then click **OK**.

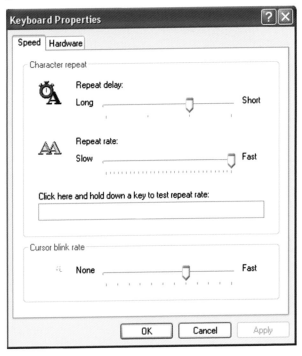

You can do this as often as you like until you have adjusted the keyboard to your liking.

Customising the mouse

There are similar options for making the mouse easier to use.

- Double-click on **Mouse** in the Control panel window and a window will open up.

- Under the **Buttons** tab, use **Button configuration** to switch to a left-handed mouse.

- Change the **Double-click speed** to make it faster or slower.

- Switch on **Click-lock** if you find it difficult to hold down the mouse button when you are clicking and dragging.

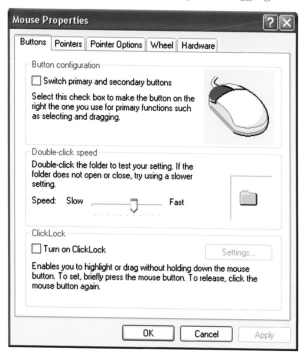

Don't worry **about pointers**

There are some more sophisticated options under the **Pointers** and **Pointer options** tabs if you want to change the cursor options on the screen.

Enlarging your display

If you want to customise the display options, it is best to try one thing at a time as otherwise it can be difficult to remember what you have done if you want to go back and change it.

- Double-click on **Display** in the Control panels window and a window will open up. Choose the **Appearance** tab.

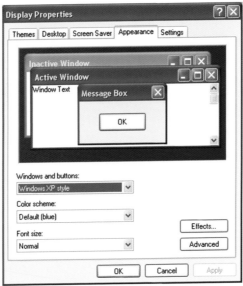

- Under **Item**, use the drop-down menu to select one item, then adjust the size and font sizes using the drop-down menus. The preview window will demonstrate the changes.

- Under **Active title bar**, you can change the width of the blue bar at the top of a document.

- Under **Caption buttons**, you can change the size of the buttons in the top right-hand corner of the window.

- Under **Icon**, you can change the size of icons in main windows, such as in the Control panels window.

- Under **Menu**, you can change the width of the Main menu bar and the font size.

- When you are happy, click on **Apply**, then **OK**.

Don't worry **about the Desktop tab**

But you'll notice that you can choose from a range of different desktops, or you can navigate via the **Browse** button to any image you have on your computer and use it as your desktop picture.

The magnifier

The magnifier helps people who are visually impaired by showing a small section of the screen around the cursor position enlarged at the top of the screen.

- From **Start**, click on **All programs**, then **Accessories**, then **Accessibility**, then **Magnifier**.

- Choose the settings you want from the window options, then click back into your document and begin working.

- To switch off the magnifier, click on **Exit**.

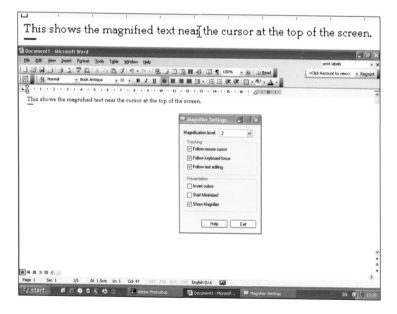

The onscreen keyboard

If you find it difficult to use the keyboard, the computer can display an onscreen keyboard, which you can activate using your mouse.

- From **Start**, click on **All programs**, then **Accessories**, then **Accessibility**, then **Onscreen keyboard**.

- You'll see an introductory window with some details of the program. Click **OK** for the keyboard to appear.

The narrator

Most computers offer the option of using the narrator to speak characters or commands.

- From **Start**, click on **All programs**, then **Accessories**, then **Accessibility**, then **Narrator**.

- Read the introductory window and click **OK**, then tick the boxes in the window to activate them.

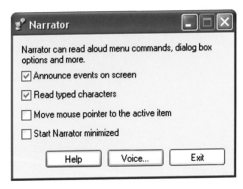

Your reminder box

- Click on **Start, All programs, Accessibility, Accessibility wizard** to activate the wizard to customise the computer display to your needs.

- From **Start, Settings, Control panels**, you can adjust the computer display to make it easier to use via the **Keyboard, Mouse** and **Display** icons.

- To turn on the magnifier or the narrator, click on **Start, All programs, Accessories, Accessibility**, then choose **Magnifier** or **Narrator**.

Chapter 13

Step-by-step Projects

This chapter offers you some step-by-step projects to help you practise your skills. You don't have to wait until you have read through the whole book before you try them, although the instructions will be more familiar if you have made a start with your word-processing skills as the full instructions are given in the main chapters in the book. These projects will help you combine various techniques, give you lots of experience – and hopefully a lot of fun, too!

Follow the instructions one stage at a time, personalising your document as you go and using any additional skills you have acquired. For each step of the project, you will be referred to the full instructions if you need to refresh any sequences.

Each of the projects can be adapted to a range of uses. For example use the:

- Headed notepaper project to design notelets or cards.

- Letter project to write any kind of document from an invoice to a novel.

- List of things to do project for a meeting agenda or any kind of listed information.

- Invitation project for any handouts or notices.

- Table of addresses project for any information that is most easily stored in units.

- Christmas-card labels project to create labels from a database for any kind of circulation from telling people about a meeting to inviting them to an event.

- Jar labels project to create labels for gifts, work boxes, screw jars, or business cards by using ready-made card sheets instead of labels.

- Family history project for organising and storing information.

- Poster project for pictures, handouts or notices.

- Newsletter project for any display information.

All the projects start with Word, or your word-processing program, open on your computer.

I generally recommend that if you are going to produce a number of any document – an invitation, for example – you print one copy and check it on paper before you commit to producing a quantity.

How to create headed notepaper

Step 1	Press **New blank document** to open a new document.	Page 30
Step 2	Key in your name on the top line. Key in your address either on the next line, or on separate lines, depending on how you would like it to appear.	Page 40
Step 3	Add your telephone number, mobile phone number and e-mail address if you want to include them.	Page 40
Step 4	Check that all the details are correct and make any corrections.	Page 40
Step 5	Go to **File**, **Page setup**, **Margins** and adjust the margins so the copy appears the right distance from the top and sides of the page.	Page 100
Step 6	Highlight the sections of text and choose the font you would like to use from the Formatting toolbar. You may want to use more than one font.	Pages 90–92
Step 7	Highlight the text and choose the font size you would like to use from the Formatting toolbar. You may want to use more than one size.	Page 93
Step 8	Decide whether you want the text ranged left, right or centred, highlight it and position it by clicking on the relevant icons on the Formatting toolbar.	Page 102
Step 9	Highlight the text and choose the font colour you would like to use from the Formatting toolbar. You may want to use more than one colour.	Pages 124–125
Step 10	Press **Print** to print a copy of the page and check all the details on paper.	Page 43
Step 11	Click on **File**, then **Save as** to name and save your document to an appropriate folder in **My documents** so you can use it again.	Pages 44–45
Step 12	Select **File**, then **Print** to print the number of copies you want.	Page 63

SARAH AND PETE MONTAGUE

15 High Street
Worplesden
Lancashire
LR6 8PZ
01753 256952
sarahpete4@btinternet.com

How to display a letter

Step 1	Press **New blank document** to open a new document or open up your headed paper.	Pages 30 or 51
Step 2	If you have not done so, create your letterhead by following the first step-by-step project.	Page 194
Step 3	Position your cursor after the letterhead. Decide on the font you would like to use for the copy in the letter and select it from the Formatting toolbar.	Pages 90–92
Step 4	Select the font size you want from the Formatting toolbar.	Page 93
Step 5	From the Main menu, choose **Insert**, then **Date and time** and insert the date in your letter in the format you prefer. Highlight it and range it left or right.	Pages 109 and 102
Step 6	Type in the address of the recipient and range it left.	Pages 40 and 102
Step 7	Type in your text. Highlight the text, then range it left or justify the text from the Formatting toolbar.	Page 102
Step 8	Adjust your margins by clicking on **File**, **Page setup**.	Page 100
Step 9	When you have finished, click on **Print preview** to see how your document looks on the page.	Page 61
Step 10	Click on **Close** to return to your document and make any changes you want.	Page 40
Step 11	Click on **File**, then **Save as** to name and save your document to an appropriate folder in **My documents**.	Pages 44–45
Step 12	Select **File**, then **Print** to print the number of copies you want.	Page 43

SARAH AND PETE MONTAGUE

15 High Street
Worplesden
Lancashire
LR6 8PZ
01753 256952
sarahpete4@btinternet.com

03 February 2008

Guy and Mary Martin
The Lodge
Long Lane
Greenfields Park
Bristol
BS7 6HY

Dear Guy and Mary

It was lovely to see you at the weekend and thank you so much for your hospitality. We had left it far too long to come and visit you and we must not leave such a long gap next time.

We particularly enjoyed the delicious home cooking and catching up on what you have been doing, and how your family are growing and succeeding in their various schools and jobs. We would hardly have recognised the children after all this time! Fortunately, Pete managed to resist the temptation to say 'Haven't you grown!'.

I have put a note in my diary for a couple of months' time to make sure we book a return visit.

Thanks again and we look forward to seeing you soon.

With kind regards

Sarah and Pete

How to keep a record of things to do

Step 1	Press **New blank document** to open a new document.	Page 30
Step 2	Key in the headings under which you want to include information: the house, the garden, places to visit, holidays, and so on.	Page 40
Step 3	Add lists of the things you want to do under each one of relevant items.	Page 40
Step 4	Highlight each item, then click and drag it to the order it should be in importance in the list.	Page 58
Step 5	Highlight the text and choose the font style you would like to use from the Formatting toolbar.	Pages 90–92
Step 6	Use a different style for the headings, or change them to bold from the icons on the Formatting toolbar.	Pages 90 and 94
Step 7	Highlight each heading and use the drop-down arrow on the **Borders** icon to add a rule underneath each one.	Pages 111–112
Step 8	Highlight sections of the text, then add colour from the Formatting toolbar if you wish.	Pages 124–125
Step 9	Highlight each list and click on **Numbering** in the Formatting toolbar to number the lists in priority.	Page 107
Step 10	Scroll through your list to make sure there is nothing you have left out. Add any new jobs you think of.	Pages 54 and 60
Step 11	Click on **File**, then **Save as** to name and save your document to an appropriate folder in **My documents**.	Pages 44–45
Step 12	Select **File**, then **Print** to print the list if you want a hard copy.	Page 43

Things to do

The house

1. Clean the windows – inside and out!
2. Replace the outside tap
3. Buy paint for the front door
4. Paint the front door
5. Tidy the garage

The garden

1. Spread the compost
2. Buy a new compost bin and reorganise
3. Cut back the pyracantha
4. Trim the hedge

Places to visit

1. Windsor Castle – check opening times
2. Savill Gardens – find out best times to visit
3. Bekonscott Model Village (when the grandchildren visit)

Holidays

1. Cornwall – look up weather for May
2. Sicily – send off for brochure
3. Rome – research tourist sites online

How to create an invitation

Step 1	Press **New blank document** to open a new document.	Page 30
Step 2	Type in the text you want to include, pressing **Enter** to indicate where you want to start new lines.	Page 40
Step 3	Highlight the text and choose the font style you would like to use from the Formatting toolbar. You may want to use more than one style.	Pages 90–92
Step 4	Highlight the text and choose the type sizes you want from the Formatting toolbar. You may want to use more than one size.	Page 93
Step 5	Highlight the text and choose the colours you want from the Formatting toolbar. You may want to use more than one colour.	Pages 124–125
Step 6	Highlight the text, then centre it, or align it right or left from the Formatting toolbar.	Page 102
Step 7	Highlight the text, then from the Main menu, click on **Format, Borders and shading** to add a fancy border around the edge.	Pages 111–115
Step 8	If it is a short invitation, such as our example, you may want to copy and paste more than one copy on a page, so you can then cut them out. Make sure you allow enough space between each one.	Page 59
Step 9	If your invitation fills a full page, check your margins on **File, Page setup** so the invitation is well positioned on the page.	Page 100
Step 10	Press **Print** to print a copy of the page and check all the details on paper.	Page 43
Step 11	Click on **File**, then **Save as** to name and save your document to an appropriate folder in **My documents**.	Pages 44–45
Step 12	Select **File**, then **Print** to print the number of copies you want.	Page 63

To ....

Come and help me celebrate my 60th birthday

on Saturday 15 May
at 8 pm
at 106 The Drive, Buckhurst Hill

Mary Jones

Please call 01256 459625 or e-mail mary.jones@aol.com
to let me know you can come

How to create a table of your addresses

Step 1	Press **New blank document** to open a new document.	Page 30
Step 2	From the Main menu, select **Table**, then **Insert table**.	Page 133
Step 3	Choose 7 or more columns depending on how much information you want to include: surname, first names, address 1, address 2, town, county, postcode. Choose 4 rows to start.	Page 134
Step 4	Key in the column headings in the first row. If you use this table for a mail-merge project, these column headings will be called 'fields'.	Page 134
Step 5	Highlight the row of column headings and click on **Bold** on the Formatting toolbar.	Page 134
Step 6	Key in your names and addresses in the appropriate cells.	Pages 134–135
Step 7	When you reach the final cell on the table, press **Tab** to create a new row.	Page 134
Step 8	If you want to add additional rows or columns, use **Table, Insert**.	Page 136
Step 9	If you want to change the column widths, position your cursor over the border, then click and drag to change the columns.	Page 138
Step 10	Highlight the text, then use **Table, Sort** to sort the names into alphabetical order.	Page 139
Step 11	Click on **File**, then **Save as** to name and save your document to an appropriate folder in **My documents**.	Pages 44–45
Step 12	Click on **File, Print** if you want to print out a hard copy.	Page 63

Surname	First	Address 1	Address 2	Town	County	Postcode
Houseman	Peter and Mary	86 Whiteknights Road		Bristol	Avon	BS8 7HJ
Jones	Miranda and Bob	7 Church Road	The Maltings	Leeds	South Yorkshire	LS6 5TH
Smith	John and Mary	The Cottage	34 The Street	Dunsfold	Gloucestershire	GL6 7UJ
Whitehouse	Sarah and Jim	10 The View		Eastbourne	Sussex	EH7 8HY

How to print your Christmas-card or party-invitation labels

Step 1	First you need to create a table of the names and addresses on your list, so complete the previous project.	Page 202
Step 2	Press **New blank document** to open a new document.	Page 30
Step 3	From the Main menu, click on **Tools**, **Letters and mailings**, **Mail merge** to activate the mail merge wizard. Select **Labels** for your document type and move on to the next screen.	Page 167
Step 4	Click on **Label** options then click on the label code on the screen that matches the one printed on your labels. Click **OK**.	Page 177
Step 5	Select **Use the current document** as your starting document and move on to the next screen.	Page 167
Step 6	To select recipients, click **Browse** to navigate to your address list, click on it to highlight it, then click on **Open**.	Page 168
Step 7	Sort your recipients if you wish, according to the instructions; this is not essential so if you are not sure whether or not they need sorting, just ignore it.	Page 168
Step 8	To set up your main document, position your cursor at the top, click on **More items**, click on the first field you want to include, then press **Insert**. Continue to do this until all the fields appear as you want them on the label. Click **Close**.	Page 169
Step 9	Click **Update all labels**.	Page 177
Step 10	Click on **Preview** to check your labels.	Page 172
Step 11	Put enough label sheets into your printer. When are happy, press **Complete the merge** and **Print**.	Page 172

| Step 12 | Click on **File**, then **Save as** to name and save your document to an appropriate folder in **My documents** if you want to use it again. You do not need to do this, however. It is probably best to keep your address list up to date, then do the mail merge when you need it. | Pages 44–45 |

John and Mary Smith
The Cottage
34 The Street
Dunsfold
Gloucestershire
GL6 7UJ

Peter and Mary Houseman
86 Whiteknights Road
Bristol
Avon
BS8 7HJ

Miranda and Bob Jones
7 Church Road
The Maltings
Leeds
South Yorkshire
LS6 5TH

Sarah and Jim Whitehouse
10 The View
Eastbourne
Sussex
EH7 8HY

How to print a set of jar labels

Step 1	Press **New blank document** to open a new document. Key in the text you would like to appear on the label.	Page 30
Step 2	Highlight the text and choose the font style you want to use from the Formatting toolbar.	Pages 90–92
Step 3	Highlight the text and choose the font size you want to use from the Formatting toolbar, keeping in mind that it should fit on a label.	Page 93
Step 4	Highlight the text and choose the font colour you want to use from the Formatting toolbar.	Pages 124–125
Step 5	Insert a piece of clip art by clicking on **Insert, Picture, From Clip art**.	Page 117
Step 6	Change the size of the clip art or picture by clicking on it to activate it, then moving the cursor to one corner and clicking and dragging on the arrow cursor.	Page 118
Step 7	Adjust how the text wraps round the picture by clicking on it, then clicking on **Format, Picture** from the Main menu, then selecting the **Layout** tab and clicking on your choice.	Pages 120–121
Step 8	Highlight your text, then from the Main menu click on **Tools, Envelopes and labels** and select the **Labels** tab. Your text will appear in the window; the clip art will not show.	Page 178
Step 9	Click on **Options**. From the top menu in the window that opens, choose **Avery A4 and A5 labels**. From the list of label options, click on the code number that appears on your labels. Click **OK**.	Page 177
Step 10	Click on the circle next to **Full page of the same label**. You can simply press **Print**, but to see how your label will appear before you print it, click on **New document**.	Page 178
Step 11	Click on **File**, then **Save as** to name and save your document to an appropriate folder in **My documents** if you want to use it again.	Pages 44–45

Step 12	Put enough label sheets into your printer. Click **File**, then **Print**.	Page 63

Home-made
Apple Jelly
August 2008

How to record data on your family history

Step 1	Press **New blank document** to open a new document.	Page 30
Step 2	From the Main menu, click on **File, Page setup** and click on the **Paper size** tab. Select **Landscape** format.	Page 101
Step 3	From the Main menu, select **Table**, then **Insert table**.	Page 133
Step 4	Choose 10 or more columns, depending on how much information you want to include: surname, maiden name, first names, date of birth, place of birth, parents, school, date and place of marriage, occupation, date of death. Choose 4 rows to start.	Page 134
Step 5	Key in the heading names in the first row. Highlight the headings and make them bold by clicking on the **Bold** icon on the **Formatting** toolbar.	Page 134
Step 6	Highlight the table, then choose to centre or left-align the text from the Formatting toolbar.	Page 102
Step 7	Key in your own name and details, then begin to key in your immediate family.	Page 134
Step 8	When you reach the final cell on the table, press **Tab** to create a new row.	Page 134
Step 9	If you want to reorder the columns, highlight a column and click and drag it to where you want it.	Page 137
Step 10	Use **Table, Sort** to sort the names into alphabetical order or chronological order.	Pages 139–140
Step 11	Click on **File**, then **Save as** to name and save your document to an appropriate folder in **My documents**.	Pages 44–45
Step 12	Click on **File, Print** if you want to print out a hard copy.	Page page 63

My family

Surname	Maiden name	First names	Date of birth	Place of birth	Parents	Schools	Date and place of marriage	Occupation	Date of death
Green	Pargiter	Susan Amy	8 July 1947	Islington, London	Samuel and Mary Pargiter	High Mount, Islington	31 June 1970	Environmental Health Officer	
Green		Thomas Graham	24 March 1947	Doncaster, South Yorkshire	William and Elizabeth Green	Main Road, Doncaster	31 June 1970	Teacher	
Green		Sarah Anne	27 January 1980	Reading, Berkshire	Susan and Thomas Green	Highdown, Caversham			
Green		Paul Michael	19 April 1981	Reading Berkshire	Susan and Thomas Green	Highdown Caversham			

How to create a poster

Step 1	Press **New blank document** to open a new document.	Page 30
Step 2	Type in the text you want to include, using the **Enter** key to indicate where you want to start new lines.	Page 40
Step 3	Highlight the text to centre it, or align it right or left from the Formatting toolbar	Page 102
Step 4	Highlight the text and choose the font style or styles you would like to use from the Formatting toolbar.	Pages 90–92
Step 5	In the same way, choose the type sizes from the Formatting toolbar.	Page 93
Step 6	Click on the **Drawing** icon on the Formatting toolbar, then use **WordArt** to display the main heading.	Pages 130–131
Step 7	Highlight the text and choose the colours from the Formatting toolbar.	Pages 124–125
Step 8	If you want to add a background colour, click on **Format, Borders and shading** from the Main menu and select the **Shading** tab, then make your choices. Add borders from the **Borders** tab.	Page 127
Step 9	Add pictures by clicking where you want them to appear, then from the Main menu choosing **Insert, Picture, From file**. Alter the text wrapping and the picture size if you need to by clicking on the picture to activate it, then choosing **Format** from the Main menu, clicking on **Picture**, then the **Layout** tab and making your choice.	Pages 119–120
Step 10	Press **Print** to print a copy of the page and check all the details on paper.	Page 43
Step 11	Click on **File**, then **Save as** to name and save your document to an appropriate folder in **My documents**.	Pages 44–45
Step 12	Select **File**, then **Print** to print the number of copies you want	Page 63

Bring all the family to the 50th Annual

Horticultural Society Show

Best fruit, flower and vegetable competitions
Craft displays and prizes
Bouncy castle and games for the children
Tombola, lucky dip and many stalls

The Showground, Mountfield, Battle
Saturday 25 June
from 2–6pm
Entry £2.50 adults, £1 children and concessions

For full details on categories for competition entries,
call the Show Secretary, Ruth Morrell, on 01288 785625

How to create a family newsletter

Step 1	Press **New blank document** to open a new document. Type in the text you want to include.	Pages 30 and 40
Step 2	Highlight the text and choose the number of columns from the Formatting toolbar.	Page 106
Step 3	Highlight the text and choose the font style or styles you want from the Formatting toolbar.	Pages 90–92
Step 4	Highlight the text and choose the type sizes you want from the Formatting toolbar.	Page 93
Step 5	Highlight the text and choose the colours you want from the Formatting toolbar.	Pages 124–125
Step 6	Highlight the text and centre it, or align it right or left.	Page 102
Step 7	If you want to add any borders, highlight the relevant text, then click on **Format, Borders and shading** from the Main menu and make your choices.	Page 111–115
Step 8	If you want to add a separate text box, click on the **Drawing** icon on the Standard toolbar, then on **Text box** on the Drawing toolbar that opens up. Click and drag to create your text box. Key in the text and format it in the same way as you did the main text.	Pages 121–122
Step 9	Add pictures by clicking where you want them to appear, then from the Main menu choosing **Insert, Picture, From file**. Change the picture size by clicking on the picture, then clicking and dragging the cursor arrow from one corner.	Pages 118–119
Step 10	Alter the text wrapping round the picture by clicking on the picture, then selecting **Format, Picture** from the Main menu, clicking on the **Layout** tab and making your choice.	Page 120
Step 11	Click on **File**, then **Save as** to name and save your document to an appropriate folder in **My documents**.	Pages 44–45
Step 12	Press **Print** to print a copy of the page and check all the details on paper. Select **File**, then **Print** to print the number of copies you want.	Page 63

The Green's Christmas message

Hello everyone! We hope you have had a happy and eventful year and enjoy reading a bit about what the family have been up to this year.

Holidays

Our short trip to Ireland is really best forgotten as the weather wasn't kind and the travelling arrangements were appalling! However, we did spend several delightful weeks in Cornwall and loved visiting the Gardens at Heligon and all the fabulous sites of interest.

The blind club

We've been helping out at the club for a couple of years now and this year took all the members down to Pett to enjoy the sea air and fresh fish and chips. We all had a lovely time.

Diamond wedding

We celebrated our diamond wedding this July and spent a wonderful day with almost all the family (Melissa and Danny couldn't make it) on a lovely day in the garden. Everyone brought something for the picnic so we didn't even have to do any work! It was super.

Rounding up the grandchildren!

As you know, we are hugely proud of our grandchildren and can't resist bragging about how well they are doing.

Leyla is starting rehearsals for the *Starlight Express* tour as Arlene Philips' Assistant Choreographer.

Esther and Danny are going to be married in Las Vegas in April.

Chris graduated from Exeter University with a BSc (Hons) and has gone back to do a Masters.

Melissa got 4 As in her A levels and is now reading English at Bristol University.

Madeleine has taken her GCSE options and will be taking her English exam in the summer a year early.

Isobel continues to excel at sport and has been playing in the England hockey squad.

Happy New Year

Let's hope next year is a good one for all of you.

Lots of love Joan and George

Word-processing Terms You Might Come Across

You only need to know word-processing terms if it helps you to do what you want to do, so this is provided as a helpful reminder should you need to look up any words you can't remember, or if you come across words you would like to understand.

Bold A thicker typeface used for headings or emphasis, such as the headwords in this glossary.
Boot up Start up your computer.
Border Plain or fancy edge round text or the page in your document.
Browse Look around the computer to find what you want.
Bullets Also known as bullet points, a list displayed with a dot at the beginning of each line.
Button A virtual button on your computer screen that you 'press' by clicking on it with your mouse to activate it.

Centred Text that is evenly positioned between the margins and jagged on both sides.
Click Press the mouse button.
Click and drag Click and hold down the left-hand mouse button and drag across text to highlight it.
Control key The bottom left-hand key on the keyboard, used to activate many shortcuts.
Copy Highlight and copy a section of text. You can then paste it somewhere else in the same document or in another document.

Crash When a computer either freezes or starts behaving badly. You can usually restart the computer to sort out the problem.

Cursor The marker on the screen that indicates your position in a document. It is controlled by the mouse or the keys.

Default The setting a computer uses if you have not made your own modifications.

Desktop The main computer screen.

Document Each item you create in your word-processing program is called a document.

Double-click Quickly click twice on the left-hand mouse button.

Drag and drop Pick up and move highlighted text from one place to another.

Drop-down menu A list that drops down if you click on a Main menu item. Depending on where the Main menu is positioned on the screen, a sub-menu may also pop up or pop out.

Field A specific type of information contained in one column of a table.

File A document saved on a computer.

Find Automatically search for a word or words.

Folder Just like a manila folder, you save collections of documents in a folder.

Folio Page number.

Font The style of the letters displayed in your document; it means the same as typeface.

Footer Text that appears at the bottom of every page.

Go to An option to go directly to a specific page in your document.

Hard copy A printed copy of your document.

Hardware All the bits of the computer you can see.

Header Text that appears at the top of every page.

Highlight Isolate a block of text by clicking and dragging with your mouse; sometimes called Select.

Icon A picture or graphic that indicates what a button will do or what kind of document or file you are looking at.

Indent Positioning type a little way in from the left-hand margin.

Input Put in!

Italic Type that is *slanted to the right*.

Justified Type that is evenly spaced with a straight margin on both sides.

Keyboard shortcuts Quick ways of performing a task using keys instead of the menus on the screen.

Keys The buttons you press on your keyboard.

Landscape When a page has the long side along the top.

Mail merge A way of creating a series of personalised letters using information stored in a table.

Main menu The list across the top of your document screen.

Memory or media stick *See* USB stick.

Menu A list of options.

Monitor The screen on which you view your documents.

Mouse The hand-held device you use to move the cursor round your document and activate buttons on the screen.

Navigate Move around the computer files to find what you want.

Operating system The software system that controls how the computer works.

Paste Once you have copied a piece of text you can paste it in another place in the same document or in another document.

PC Personal computer.

Pop-up menu A list that pops up if you click on a Main menu item.

Portrait When a page has the short side along the top.

Preview A window that shows you what your document will look like.

Print Print a copy of your document on paper.

Program A set of instructions for a computer that enable it to perform specific jobs, such as a word-processing program.

Ranged left Type that aligns to the left-hand margin with a jagged right-hand margin.
Ranged right Type that aligns to the right-hand margin with a jagged left-hand margin.
Replace Replace one chosen word with another.
Right-click Click on the right button on the mouse.

Sans serif A plain font without any little ticks on the ends of letters (like the text in the Don't worry boxes).
Save File your work so the computer stores it for use when you want it.
Scroll bar A bar down the right-hand side of your document that shows you where you are in the document. You can click and drag the scroll bar to move from one place to another. There is also a horizontal scroll bar along the bottom of the screen.
Serif The little tick on the ends of letters (like the main text in this book).
Software The programs inside the computer.
Spellcheck A part of the program that can automatically check the spelling and grammar in your document.

Table Information presented in a series of cells, or individual boxes.
Toolbar A collection of buttons that perform specific tasks.
Typeface The style of the letters displayed in your document; it means the same as font.

USB stick A small device that slots into the computer on which you can copy data to transport it or back up your files. It is also called a memory or media stick.

Keyboard Shortcuts

This is a selection of the main shortcuts you can use on your keyboard rather than going through the Main menu or the buttons on the toolbars. The + simply means that you need to hold down the first key while you press the key you need; you don't need to key in +. The **Ctrl (Control)** key is on the bottom left-hand corner of your keypad.

Remember, you still need to highlight the relevant text first if you are using formatting options.

Action required	Keystrokes
Align left	Ctrl+L
Align right	Ctrl+R
Bold	Ctrl+B
Centre text	Ctrl+E
Change case	Shift+F3
Copy	Ctrl+C
Decrease font size by 1pt	Ctrl+Shift+< or Ctrl+[
Delete	Ctrl+X
Deletes the word to right of the cursor	Ctrl+Delete
Deletes the word to left of the cursor	Ctrl+Backspace
Find	Ctrl+F
Go to	Ctrl+G or F5

Action required	Keystrokes
Highlight the whole document	Ctrl+A
Increase font size by 1pt	Ctrl+Shift+ or Ctrl+]
Indent paragraph	Ctrl+M
Insert the date	Alt+Shift+D
Insert the time	Alt+Shift+T
Italic	Ctrl+I
Move cursor one word to the left	Ctrl+ →
Move cursor one word to the right	Ctrl+ ←
Move cursor to the beginning of paragraph	Ctrl+ ↑
Move cursor to the end of paragraph	Ctrl+ ↓
Move cursor to beginning of document	Ctrl+ Home
Move cursor to end of document	Ctrl+ End
Open the help menu	F1
Open a document	Ctrl+O
Open print window	Ctrl+P
Open thesaurus	Shift+F7
Paste	Ctrl+V
Print	Ctrl+P
Replace	Ctrl+H or Ctrl+Shift+H
Save	Shift+F12
Save as	F12
Sets 1.5-spaced lines	Ctrl+5
Sets double-spaced lines	Ctrl+2
Sets single-spaced lines	Ctrl+1
Spellcheck	F7
Underline	Ctrl+U
Undo last action	Ctrl+Z

Index

Communicating Science

Professional, Popular, Literary

In recent years governments and scientific establishments have been encouraging the development of professional and popular science communication. This book critically examines the origin of this drive to improve communication, and discusses why simply improving scientists' communication skills and understanding of their audiences may not be enough.

Written in an engaging style, and avoiding specialist jargon, this book provides an insight into science's place in society by looking at science communication in three contexts: the professional patterns of communication among scientists, popular communication to the public and science in literature and drama. This three-part framework shows how historical and cultural factors operate in today's complex communication landscape, and should be actively considered when designing and evaluating science communication.

Ideal for students and practitioners in science, engineering and medicine, this book provides a better understanding of the culture, sociology and mechanics of professional and popular communication.

NICHOLAS RUSSELL is Emeritus Reader in Science Communication in the Department of Humanities at Imperial College London.

Communicating Science

Professional, Popular, Literary

NICHOLAS RUSSELL

Imperial College
London

CAMBRIDGE
UNIVERSITY PRESS

CAMBRIDGE UNIVERSITY PRESS
Cambridge, New York, Melbourne, Madrid, Cape Town, Singapore,
São Paulo, Delhi, Dubai, Tokyo

Cambridge University Press
The Edinburgh Building, Cambridge CB2 8RU, UK

Published in the United States of America by
Cambridge University Press, New York

www.cambridge.org
Information on this title: www.cambridge.org/9780521131728

First published 2010

Printed in the United Kingdom at the University Press, Cambridge

A catalogue record for this publication is available from the British Library

Library of Congress Cataloguing in Publication data
Russell, Nicholas J.
    Communicating science : professional, popular, literary / Nicholas Russell.
        p. cm.
    Includes bibliographical references and index.
    ISBN 978-0-521-11383-0 (hardback)
    1. Communication in science. 2. Science–Social aspects. I. Title.
    Q223.R87 2009
    501'.4–dc22   2009027849

ISBN 978-0-521-11383-0 Hardback
ISBN 978-0-521-13172-8 Paperback

Contents

Part V   Science in literature

Introduction
What this book is about and why you might want to read it

This is a book about the benefits and problems of communicating science, not a book about how to actually communicate. There are many useful things to say about practising science communication: writing, speaking, presenting, being interviewed, building websites, making podcasts and so on, and they are all well said in a variety of other places. This book has a different purpose.

Rather than assuming that the main problem in communicating science is that many scientists are not good at it (because they have no training or are not interested) it suggests that there are other questions to ask. Some of these are obvious; why communicate science in the first place, what science should be communicated, to whom should it be addressed and whose interests are served? Such questions are central to the analysis of any communication process and the answers (in science as elsewhere) are complicated.

It is not only the factual communication of science that is important. Fiction and other entertainment media create and reflect social attitudes towards science and scientists, so it is valuable to look at how science is presented in novels, short stories, feature films, plays, comics, graphic novels, computer games, social networking sites and so on. The range of such cultural artefacts is large and in this book there will only be space to cover fiction and drama.

The material here was originally developed for post-graduate Science Communication students at Imperial College London preparing to enter communication careers in journalism, broadcasting, work in museums and galleries or in public relations. While this book has useful things to say to such specialist students, its main aim is to show that analysis of science communication is relevant to all students interested in the relations between science and wider culture. In particular, it is aimed at science graduates and post-graduates who are told they have a duty to improve their professional communication and to undertake science popularization.

Professional communication is covered in Part I. For graduate and post-graduate students their primary communication task is learning the conventions of professional writing, which might be less stressful if they knew something about the history, strengths and weaknesses of these conventions. It is a serious omission that communication is seldom cited as an essential element in the 'scientific method' because research articles are claims to new knowledge and the primary output of those working at the leading edge of science, while the body of scientific knowledge is set out in monographs and textbooks. The machinery for publishing science is also a mechanism of quality control (distinguishing between good and less good science and scientists) and a means of patrolling the borders of the discipline (determining who can be called a scientist and who cannot).

Popular communication of science is discussed in Parts II and III. Since the middle of the nineteenth century, science has become a closed and financially demanding profession. Scientists need specialized education, expensive spaces (laboratories) and expensive devices (instruments), and professional science communication is now intended only for other professionals. The community has had to develop a separate communication strand to popularize its work to non-scientists. This popular communication is necessary to justify science to those who fund it (governments, industry, charities and the public).

The strength of this popularizing impulse has varied but entered a particularly strong phase in the United Kingdom at the end of the twentieth century with movements for Public Understanding of Science (PUS) and Public Engagement with Science and Technology (PEST), and there has been a parallel Scientific

Literacy movement in the United States. What has characterized all these movements is the duty of scientists to explain what they do and present it in the best light. But a properly informed public must be able to critique science as well as support it. Popular science communication therefore has twin duties, to inform and educate the public about science on the one hand, but also to probe and criticize it on the other. All science is not necessarily a public good which just needs to be disseminated to invite approval.

Science in fiction and drama are examined in Parts IV and V. Scholars have revealed a great deal about the relationships between science and society from the study of real science in actual contexts, but the cultural significance of science in fiction has been relatively neglected. Part IV shows that, at certain key points in the history of science, a number of canonical plays provided insight into how science was evolving. Part V describes several further dramas, which show that long-standing ethical problems with science have persisted across the centuries and also demonstrates that readers can learn much about science and its culture from fiction.

While the chapters of the book are arranged to make sense in sequence, they can all be read on their own. Each chapter explores an element of science communication from the perspective of an author who has studied biology, taught applied biology and liberal studies in technical education, been a student of the history of science and technology, worked as a freelance science journalist and contributed to science communication teaching at Birkbeck College London and Imperial College London. These experiences determine the attitudes taken towards the three strands in this collection; another author would tell different stories with different emphases.

The book draws on a variety of sources, some of them venerable because they first set out the central issues. The book is not a comprehensive review of the academic literature; that would have demanded several monographs. Each chapter begins with a short scenario, a story (sometimes fact, sometimes fiction) that introduces or rehearses some of the chapter themes. I hope these stimulate readers to peruse the drier material in the bodies of the chapters (though I hope this material is itself clear and easy to read).

Before the book starts there is a short Prologue setting out historical connections between the now dissimilar practices of professional science communication, factual journalism and fiction writing. There is no need to read this first, or indeed at all. Like all the other chapters it is designed to be as free-standing as possible. However, since there are connections running through the chapters, the more that are read, the greater may be the benefit gained from each one.

Everything here has benefited from discussions with, and what I have learned from, colleagues at both Birkbeck College London and Imperial College London, together with cohorts of enthusiastic students at both institutions who have been a pleasure to teach. The students have been too many to mention but I am much indebted to my colleagues who have included Wendy Barnaby, Giskin Day, John Durant, Shani Gbaja, Joan Leach, Felicity Mellor, Gareth Mitchell, the late John Newell, Rachel Souhami, Robert Sternberg, Jon Turney, Stephen Webster and Peter Wrobell. While they (and others) have all contributed to whatever may be virtuous here, they are entirely innocent of blame for tedium, error or other malfeasance.

I am also grateful to Lyn who has been tolerant for many years of energy that a teaching life demands, and to the science editors of various newspapers and magazines in the late 1980s and early 1990s (especially Tom Wilkie, then of *The Independent*) who accepted the contributions submitted in an intensive period of learning how to communicate science by doing it. My thanks as well to Andrew Hunt, who proved a stimulating colleague at the Nuffield Foundation in the early 1990s, and to Anthony Tomei, then Assistant Director of the Foundation, who gave me the opportunity to move from teaching into educational development, a change of career that contributed much to how I set about teaching science communication.

Prologue
Three orphans share a common paternity: professional science communication, popular journalism and literary fiction are not as separate as they seem

NATURE SPEAKS

The weekly magazine, *Nature,* is a strange beast. It began in the mid nineteenth century popularizing science but has subsequently evolved into a leading technical journal for the scientific profession. Its original popular remit remains in a section where specialists explain the significance of their latest work for a wide readership. But the bulk of the magazine consists of 'letters' to *Nature* where scientists announce progress in exciting or fashionable fields. These letters make few concessions to the ordinary reader. In form, language and content they are written by professional scientists for professional scientists.

Nature also carries news and editorial opinion on matters of importance to the profession. The three editorials in the 27 March 2008 issue happened to deal explicitly with the three themes of this book; the professional, the popular and the literary communication of science. Their joint appearance in *Nature* suggests that the scientific community is aware of the importance of all three genres.

The editorial on professional communication concerned a paper on adult stem cells modified by genetic manipulation to behave as if they were embryo cells. The work is exciting because such cells can be used in research and disease treatment. The editorial worried about errors in a hastily prepared paper which the lead author admitted and plausibly explained. Cutting corners in the laboratory and in preparing documentation is a result of intense competition. In this case there were honest errors, but mistakes are hard to distinguish from dishonesty and the profession is concerned that error could shade into fraud, which is a serious professional problem. Detecting and rooting out fraud are hard; the best mechanism is rigorous policing of the channels of professional communication.

This editorial demonstrates the central role of professional communication, not only in making scientific claims, but to the quality control of science.

The second editorial dealt with popular communication and public scrutiny of science. The American Pew Research Centre's *State of the News Media 2008* reported a drop in media science coverage since 2001, partly caused by increased attention to political news following the 9/11 attack squeezing out minority concerns like science. Reduced coverage of science does not allow the media to carry out their democratic watchdog role; to check on government and business investment and responses to science, correct misrepresentations of science by non-scientific pressure groups, and expose over-enthusiastic manipulation of the media and other unethical behaviours by scientists themselves. Science should be tested for its public benefit, a principle to which *Nature* (and by implication the scientific community) subscribes. The social contract for public funding between scientists and society has to be justified by the benefits that science brings.

This editorial suggests that a healthy democracy needs a free press in which the coverage of science is as important as the coverage of politics or business.

The lead editorial was about literature; a paean of praise to the science fiction writer Arthur C. Clarke who had died aged 91. Clarke was a techno-visionary who fantasized about distant times and places when mankind could roam through the solar system

and beyond. *Nature* admired Clarke's transcendent vision of the
future in a universe understood through science and explored
by technology. The editorial is suffused with science as a force
for progress and good, emblematic of the mind set of many in
the scientific community. Science fiction and fantasy are the
main literary genres where such 'scientism' is displayed and the
science fiction which Clarke and others wrote stimulated many
young people to take up science. Conversely, there has been an
opposing trend in literary fiction of pessimism about science and
its consequences.

This editorial makes it clear that the treatment of science
and scientists in fiction is a key factor in the culture of science, in
the making of scientists and in the forming of attitudes towards
science by other professionals and by the public.

WHAT DO THESE THREE COMMUNICATION GENRES HAVE IN COMMON?

Today, the professional, the popular and the literary
communication of science are different genres with different
practices, but the foundations of all these practices were first
articulated by one man, the seventeenth-century statesman and
philosopher, Sir Francis Bacon. Bacon called for a grand renewal of
knowledge, not based on the interpretation of ancient authoritative
texts, but on direct observation of the natural and human worlds.
This emphasis on accurate observation and reporting of events
underlay the early practice of natural philosophy (science),
reportage journalism and literary fiction.

Popular magazines and papers gained a foothold in England
only in the eighteenth century, the first daily paper, the *Daily
Courant*, appearing in 1702. Many writers for these periodicals
were shadowy informers employed by the two main political
factions, the Whigs and the Tories. The periodicals produced
propaganda, 'spinning' news of current events to further particular
political ends. But the most prolific and unscrupulous informers

founded a new profession, journalism. The most famous early exponent was Daniel Defoe, who was also a major contributor to the invention of a second genre, the socially realistic novel.

Although Defoe's novels and journalism were written in the early eighteenth century, the historian Ilse Vickers argues that his mind set was determined by his education in the previous century. His parents were Dissenters who sent him to Dr Morton's Dissenting Academy at Newington Green in the 1670s. Morton was a keen student of the ideology of Francis Bacon, and Vickers contends that Defoe embraced this Baconian philosophy, which informed both his factual journalism and his fiction.

After leaving the Academy, Defoe became a Presbyterian Minister but soon left the church to become a merchant and ultimately polemicist and spy, in which capacities he did not follow Bacon's ideal of gathering objective information. Although he was still writing polemic at the time, in November 1703 he (and all other inhabitants of southern England) witnessed the most violent storm in British history, which he reported in a piece of early reportage as *The Storm* in 1704. Defoe then continued to act as a political spy and propagandist for the Tory cause, only in 1715 beginning to write *Robinson Crusoe* and following this up with several other novels and fact-based works of proto-reportage including the famous *Journal of the Plague Year*.

The Storm marked a new departure upon which Defoe drew for all his later books. He aimed at a comprehensive factual account of events. The interpretation of these events then drew its authority from this accurate reporting. This was a fresh rhetorical strategy in journalism; starting with objective reports as opposed to the earlier tradition of news as polemic written on behalf of one or other party interested in the events. The new natural philosophers of the seventeenth century used the same technique; the reports of facts about nature were so thorough and accurate that they lent authority to the interpretations which followed. In both cases the emphasis on starting from a baseline of objective fact comes from Bacon.

Besides advocating careful observation of events, Bacon proposed two other principles; the systematic recording of data using language as plain and transparent as possible, and that natural philosophy should improve technology for human benefit. On the first principle, Defoe consciously evolved a plain style of writing and framed his fiction according to Bacon's advice on compiling 'histories'. Clarity in the communication of natural philosophy (and science) apparently has not survived into the twenty-first century but remains a central professional virtue in journalism. On Bacon's second additional principle, the scientific community has been successful in using his argument that pure science should be supported because new scientific knowledge underlies new technology.

Common elements in the practices of natural philosophy and journalism can be extended to the literary novel. Serious fiction reflects fundamental human values, otherwise only addressed by factual disciplines like philosophy, science and religion. Lamarque and Olsen, for instance, argue that great literature (like great philosophy or religion) develops these values, leading rather than simply reflecting culture. Other strands in the origin of the literary novel in the eighteenth century were factual history, on the one hand, and fantasy, fable and allegory ('romance'), on the other. Mayer argues that early novelists aligned themselves firmly with history and claimed to be as much concerned with factual truth as were non-fiction writers. In the seventeenth century historians started to compose accounts based on documents and interviews; history began to mean accounts of 'matters of fact' operating according to the same Baconian agenda that inspired early science and journalism. While serious fiction was not legitimate history, a clear boundary developed to separate it from fantasy. It claimed to be based on 'matters of fact'; fiction accurately imitated social and personal reality.

The literary novel therefore shared with natural philosophy (science) and reportage journalism a central concern with giving an objective account of the world. While this process is fraught with problems, representing and explaining reality remain key aspirations for both scientists and good journalists. In literature, as in other high art forms, the early realistic project was first abandoned and then actively attacked. Nevertheless, fiction still deals in forms of factual and social truth, and the literary novel remains a natural communication sibling to both professional science communication and journalism.

GEORGE GISSING AND THE CONNECTIONS BETWEEN SCIENCE, JOURNALISM AND LITERATURE AT THE END OF THE NINETEENTH CENTURY

The worlds of science, of journalism and of literary fiction appear together in two late nineteenth-century novels written back to back by George Gissing; *New Grub Street* (1891) and *Born in Exile* (1893). In these autobiographical books, fictional versions of the intelligent but over-sensitive and depressive Gissing appear as the struggling lower middle-class novelist Edwin Reardon (*New Grub Street*) and the struggling lower middle-class chemist and journalist Godwin Peak (*Born in Exile*).

After the Education Act of 1870 all children could attend primary school and learn to read and write. A decade later this fed into increased publishing opportunities to satisfy these new readers. The genteel publishing world of the mid nineteenth century, dominated by three-volume literary novels and scholarly cultural periodicals designed for middle-class readers, was expanded with daily newspapers, middle and low-brow magazines and short novels breaking the stranglehold of the 'three decker' of literary fiction. As cultural and news journalism both became more populist, there were opportunities for a new cadre of practitioners not necessarily 'properly' educated in the classics nor bound by gentlemanly snobbery as to what activities should concern reporters and commentators. But the new commercialization deeply divided the educated literary community, leading to a split between journalists and novelists.

In *New Grub Street* the scholarly Reardon does not have
an aptitude for the new commercial magazine world. He marries
above his class and is pressured by his wife when she realizes that
his literary reputation is not high and his income not adequate
for a respectable life. His antithesis is Jasper Milvain, who is
determined to make his living in popular journalism, where
success comes from ruthless networking and a facility to write
about anything from the most trivial to the most elevated. He and
his type are displacing the older literary tradition of scholarly
writers and editors to which Reardon hopelessly clings.

New ideas from science and continental philosophy diffused
among the educated in the late Victorian period and Reardon's
wife, separated from her struggling husband, reads about Herbert
Spencer and Charles Darwin and the application of their ideas to
society. All this also interests the populist coming man, Milvain,
with whom she discusses these matters and which eventually
leads to their marriage after Reardon's death. Her engagement
with issues around science and philosophy is symbolic of the
central cultural role played by science in late nineteenth-century
society. Science had become professional and scientists addressed
only each other in their books and journals. But many of them
were also active in promulgating their ideas to a wider public and
practised popular as well as professional science writing. Gissing's
other *alter ego* in *Born in Exile*, Godwin Peak falls into this
category.

If Reardon was a failed novelist, then Godwin Peak is a failed
scientist. He is a lower middle-class northern boy who wins a
scholarship to a thinly disguised Owens College, Manchester. Here
he and his similarly underprivileged friend John Earwaker take a lot
of second prizes, the first prizes going to their upper middle-class
colleagues Bruno Chilvers, an extravagant and orthodox Christian
destined for the church, and Buckland Warricombe, a star geology
student and confirmed atheist, stereotypically combining new
science with scepticism about established social conventions. Peak

and Earwaker share these rationalist attitudes and atheism with Buckland.

Throughout his studies Peak leaned towards science, stimulated by holiday work in the Moxey chemical works and childhood friendship with a retired railwayman with a passion for geology and strongly anti-religious views. Peak winds up working at a London chemical firm as an analyst, bored and resentful because he would like to devote himself to the pure science of geology. He saves money to give himself a year off to do some proper geological field work, goaded by Moxey's languid nephew Christian who also works for the same chemical firm but has the money to set up a small domestic laboratory for his own pleasure.

John Earwaker is also in London, working as a journalist and encourages Peak's freelance writing efforts on the impact of new scientific ideas. Peak controversially publishes an article, 'The new sophistry', in the radical *Critical*, in which he (anonymously) attacks philosophers and theologians trying to find compromise between the atheist implications of Darwin's ideas and a role for God and religion. Peak argues that no such compromise is possible and comes down firmly on the side of scientific atheism.

Peak is travelling to Cornwall on holiday when in Devon he re-encounters his old friend Buckland Warricombe and his sister Sidwell. He is invited into the local circle at the Warricombe estate and is smitten with Sidwell and envious of her clergyman father's life as a gentleman geologist with the resources to undertake pure research. Peak therefore lights on a path of extreme hypocrisy, he will pretend to orthodox religious belief, support old Warricombe in his pursuit of a compromise between Darwinism and Christianity, and even train for the church, all in order to win Sidwell's hand.

This hypocrisy is eventually exposed when Buckland establishes that Peak was the author of the 'new sophistry' article and Peak has to confess his devious strategy to Sidwell. Ironically, she has been moving to a more agnostic position herself and their views meet in mutual distaste for democracy among what they

regard as the semi-educated working class. In the end Peak loses
Sidwell and returns to being an analyst and freelance science
writer. Christian Moxey's plain but intelligent sister Marcella (who
always took a shine to Peak which he never reciprocated) is killed
in an accident and leaves Peak a small legacy. He determines to use
it to allow him the old-fashioned gentlemanly privileges of travel
and thought, but falls ill and dies of malaria in a Vienna hotel
room.

Gissing's novels demonstrate that reasonably close
relationships existed between the three genres of science
communication, journalism and literary fiction just over a century
ago. Professional and popular science communication had diverged,
but it was still conventional for working scientists to write in both
genres; no specialist trade of science journalism had yet emerged.
Cultural journalism and serious literature are still penned today by
the same hands, but the majority of cultural journalists and literary
novelists tend now to be specialists in their separate activities.

The practice of science has seldom been a subject for literary
fiction. Gissing was probably the one nineteenth-century English
novelist, apart from H.G. Wells, who made science and scientists
major fictional subjects and uniquely combined them with an
examination of the lives of literary authors and cultural journalists.
Gissing's two novels provide us with insightful accounts of
the practices of these three trades when they were still closely
connected.

BIBLIOGRAPHY

Anon (2008). Editorials. *Nature*, 27 March, **452**, 387–8.

Black, J. (1993). Politicisation and the press in Hanoverian England. In Myers, R.
and Harris, M. (eds.). *Serials and Their Readers 1620–1914*. Winchester: St Paul's
Bibliographies.

Cyranoski, D. (2008). Five things to know before jumping on the iPS bandwagon. *Nature*,
27 March, **452**, 406–8.

Hamblyn, R. (2003). Introduction, *The Storm, Daniel Defoe* (first published 1704). London:
Allen Lane.

Gissing, G. (1978). *Born in Exile* (first published 1893). Brighton, Sussex: Harvester Press.

Gissing, G. (1997), (ed. D.J. Taylor). *New Grub Street* (first published 1891). London: J.M. Dent (Everyman).

Lamarque, P. and Olsen, S.H. (1996). Literature and value. In *Truth, Fiction and Literature.* Oxford: Clarendon Press, Chapter 17, pp. 440–56.

Mayer, R. (1997). *History and the Early English Novel.* Cambridge: Cambridge University Press.

Probyn, C.T. (1987). *English Fiction of the Eighteenth Century 1700–1789.* London: Longman.

Rivers, I. (ed.), (1982). *Books and Their Readers in Eighteenth-century England,* Leicester: Leicester University Press.

Rogers, P. (1972). *Grub Street. Studies in a Subculture.* London: Methuen.

Vickers, I. (1996). *Defoe and the New Sciences.* Cambridge: Cambridge University Press.

Part I Professional science communication

1 Spreading the word: problems with publishing professional science

One afternoon in January 1693 the sign outside the coffee house at the Blackfriars end of the Strand groaned in the wind howling off the Thames. At half past two the bookseller John Dunton reached the coffee house, quickly moving inside to the fire, candles and scattering of occupants. He paused once the door had closed and spotted Benjamin Steele in a corner. Beside him sat Richard Holden chewing the end of a quill. Dunton greeted them as he sat down, opening his satchel from which a heap of pamphlets and books fell onto the table, each marked with slips of paper. He fished out some blank sheets from the satchel's nether reaches and put them in front of his henchmen.

"Ben, you had best start with this German report. You should be able to run up a draft, then we'll get Harrington to make sure we have it authentic. Richard, the introduction in this botanical tome looks interesting though the Latin is awful. Show me when you've a draft. I can probably make a sensible judgement. Meanwhile I will make a start on this French piece which claims to be a lost essay by Monsieur Descartes. About that, we shall see."

All three set to work drafting English translations of the three pieces of foreign natural philosophy; one cosmological, one botanical, one mathematical. Steele and Holden's threadbare clothes quickly became aromatic and Dunton made extensive use of a strongly scented handkerchief. That was one problem of working with Cripplegate hacks. Another was their greed for payment. They existed on the trifles earned for commissioned work or from selling the odd article to the new commercial magazines.

After an hour's graft, the trio's concentration was broken by the arrival of Harrington D'Arcy, younger brother to Earl Crompton. Although he was a Fellow of the Royal Society, a genuine natural philosopher, D'Arcy joined Dunton and his hacks in putting together the periodical of the learned (but entirely fictitious) Athenian Society. This was the *Athenian Mercury*, a fake that sold better than the genuine *Philosophical Transactions of the Royal Society*. D'Arcy disliked many officers of the Society and wanted the mythical Athenian Society and its *Mercury* to flourish instead. "Any correspondence?" asked D'Arcy. "Of course", said Dunton pulling a bunch of letters from the satchel, "several; you'll enjoy them. You'll be able to contradict Boyle for the chemical enquiry". D'Arcy grinned; he was no fan of the late Robert Boyle.

Another hour's work and most of the next issue of the *Athenian Mercury* was ready. Dunton had made several translations beforehand, Holden had prepared three philosophical letters in the styles of different Royal Society luminaries, and with what they had just translated and D'Arcy's detailed natural philosophical replies to genuine public enquiries, the *Mercury* was virtually put to bed. The fictional Athenian Society turned out excellent philosophical discourse with a ready readership. The *Mercury* was more regular than the halting *Philosophical Transactions* of the real Royal Society.

PROFESSIONAL SCIENCE COMMUNICATION BEGINS WELL, EVEN IF AUTHENTICITY IS DIFFICULT

John Dunton, the Athenian Society and the *Athenian Mercury* are real, Steele and Holden are invented hacks and D'Arcy an invented natural philosopher (at least two actual members of the Royal Society helped Dunton with his fake publication). The hall of mirrors goes on because, while the Athenian Society was a virtual copy of the real Royal Society, the *Athenian Mercury* was itself imitated by a second-order fake, the *Lacedomonian Mercury*. These two publications poured ordure over each other in print until the *Athenian Mercury* came unstuck when the Tory hack and playwright, Elkanah Settle, sent in a false reader's letter citing a number of learned sources which Dunton took to be genuine and replied in supportive vein. That gave Settle the ammunition to expose the Whig Athenian Society and *Mercury* as lies, which he did in a coruscating satire, the *New Athenian Comedy*. The learned fakes were exposed and disappeared, but their existence demonstrates the ease with which trust in printed material could be undermined by unscrupulous mimics in the uncontrolled print market at the time.

Publishing scientific work for professional natural philosophers (and later scientists) has continued to be difficult; what to present, how to present it and how to ensure that it is published. The Royal Society published the first issue of its proto-learned journal, the *Philosophical Transactions*, in May 1665 edited by Henry Oldenburg, its first Secretary. The journal had a job of persuasion to do as many contemporaries regarded natural philosophy as strange. Adrian Johns has shown that the production of the *Transactions* was anything but smooth, and uncovered the scenario story of the virtual societies and the fake publications. The Royal Society had to establish a reputation for trustworthiness, otherwise natural philosophy would never be accepted. Its decision to allow Oldenburg to launch the *Transactions* was odd. The respectable way to present natural philosophy at the time was in Latin monograph books. Oldenburg was proposing to publish an ephemeral record of 'work in progress' in vernacular language, using the freshly evolved periodical form, a close relative of the tract and the pamphlet, already well established as the home of political cant and pornography. To use a modern analogy, it was as if (say) a society representing new British human rights lawyers decided to publicize their professional activities by publishing an illustrated comic.

So why did Oldenburg suggest such a periodical and why did the Society approve? Johns gives three main reasons. Printers did most of their work on small contracts and preferred limited runs of repeating units (small but regular periodical issues were more attractive than one-off monograph books), books required a much larger capital outlay to set and print (which printers often wanted authors and potential buyers to help finance), and there was gentlemanly distaste for the demonstration of ambition, implied by putting one's name to a large publication. It was much easier for the Royal Society's virtuosi to publish small authored papers because they did not then appear over-pushy.

Oldenburg made a good start with the *Philosophical Transactions*, but things soon began to go wrong. The plague forced the Society out of London in 1666 and the Great Fire of London in the same year nearly ruined the London printers, because they used vaults of old St Paul's Cathedral as storage and most editions went up in smoke along with the edifice itself. Costs, regularity of printing, distribution and sales all went haywire in the later 1660s and 1670s and issues of the *Philosophical Transactions* were pirated, sometimes by the Society's own printers. People were deceived by these imposter versions, which contained different arrangements of items, and were mistranslated on the Continent, severely undermining the Society's reputation overseas.

But the Society's ultimate success with the *Philosophical Transactions* encouraged imitators like Dunton. The success of both real and false natural philosophy reveals its popularity in the late seventeenth century, a popularity consolidated in the eighteenth. Natural philosophy periodicals circulated freely in the London coffee-houses, with their promiscuous mix of the educated and the ignorant, noble and humble, rich and poor, professional and gentry. Natural philosophy also appeared in the political and social periodicals and booksellers made tidy sums selling volumes on selected aspects of natural philosophy. Royal Society Fellows were the original authors of much of this material, but the market was too big for the virtuosi to satisfy alone, it created space for hacks and literary figures to write popular natural philosophy. This evidence of enthusiasm runs counter to the ridicule and satire that some literati heaped on the new natural philosophy in drama and verse (see Part IV).

Newton and his work dominated the trade in popular natural philosophy in the early eighteenth century. Between 1680 and 1750 expositions of his ideas came off the presses in huge numbers, while Newton's own writings enjoyed steady sales. From the mideighteenth century, interest in Newton declined, while natural history increased. The pioneer natural history writer was the French savant, Count Buffon, a leading naturalist with a writing style that bewitched his readers. In England, followers of Buffon were often laymen like Oliver Goldsmith, the accomplished stylist in poetry, drama and fiction who also wrote a best-selling *History of the Earth, and Animated Nature*. Its significance can be judged from the fact that publishers were prepared to pay £840 for it, comparing well with the sums offered to leading literary fiction writers of the time, such as the £210 offered to Smollett for *Humphrey Clinker* or the £600 to Fielding for *Tom Jones*. By the last quarter of the eighteenth century, natural history books out-sold most other types of serious literature.

Natural philosophy influenced most of the literary figures of the age; even those deeply opposed to it like Swift and Pope. Newtonian mechanical metaphors abounded in early eighteenth-century poetry, while the libraries of the great Whig aristocrats were stuffed with natural philosophy books. By the end of the eighteenth century, the rationale for the foundation of the Royal Society had been met, a public respectful of, and eager to learn about, natural philosophy and the practical applications that supposedly arose from it.

PROFESSIONAL AND POPULAR COMMUNICATION DIVERGE

During the nineteenth century, popular passion for natural philosophy was undermined by its increasing professionalism, symbolized by the adoption of a new term to describe the activity, 'science'. Many scientists found it easier to communicate only with their peers and there was less need to deal with a wider public, leading to the danger that the public might turn against science. The problem was acute by the mid nineteenth century and several new popular science journals (including *Nature*) were founded to carry on the task of convincing the public that science was an important pursuit. *Nature* has been a long-term success, although most other popular nineteenth-century science journals disappeared. Among professional scientists, writing for popular outlets became the specialized activity of a subgroup with the talent and inclination to undertake it (or the necessity; even by the late nineteenth century there were too few posts in science for those who wanted to make a living from it).

Moves to keep science in the public eye were generally successful in the nineteenth century with ordinary periodicals carrying news about science. Coverage was dominated by biology, the biggest topic being evolution; together with anthropology, archaeology and philosophy. Oceanography, vivisection and spiritualism were also well represented. The voyage of the *Challenger*, examining the science of deep oceans in a circumnavigation of the world, caught the public imagination, much as space travel did 100 years later.

THE EVOLUTION OF THE SCIENTIFIC JOURNAL

While science may have proved popular, the business of professional communication encountered problems. The modern professional pattern of specialized academic journals containing stereotypically structured research articles only matured in the twentieth century. The evolution of this modern publishing institution from the few pioneering proto-journals of the Royal Society and other early learned societies proved long and tortuous.

Despite the ultimate triumph of the short article, throughout much of their history, natural philosophers and scientists made claims for new knowledge by writing monograph books. These had only limited audiences and this problem bedevilled professional science publication. Early printers and publishers required authors to obtain sponsorship (especially for expensive illustration), or get up a list of subscribers who would pay for the volume in advance, before the printer would set the book. For a subscription list, authors had to collect subscriptions themselves and pay from their own pockets for subscribers who failed to contribute promised money.

Publishing learned scientific journals proved no easier. Scientific and medical journals started as newsletters disseminating matters of interest to the community they served and were not devoted to publishing fresh research. From the late eighteenth century, more specialized journals began to appear, reflecting the fragmentation of science. Many such journals were produced by learned societies, whose lectures and meetings provided a steady stream of material to publish. Even so, journals were often financed and administered by an individual on a freelance basis, a sure recipe for instability. Science journals eventually changed from trade magazines to primary reporting of new research because of increasing pressure of claims for new knowledge from an increasing number of working scientists.

Learned societies were often inefficient at converting meetings into published reports, 5-year delays were not uncommon in the nineteenth century. This stimulated commercial publishers to start journals, which guaranteed faster publication. By late Victorian times, these commercial journals were the majority, although the failure rate of all titles remained high. The lack of big enough commercial markets for scientific research continued to dog learned journal publication into the twentieth century. No ideal system for publishing scientific journals which satisfies all parties has yet been devised.

THE EVOLUTION OF THE SCIENTIFIC PAPER

Since the *Philosophical Transactions of the Royal Society* has been published continuously since the seventeenth century, it has been subject to historical analysis, notably by Atkinson. In the seventeenth and eighteenth centuries most reports to the journal were letters. The authors presented themselves at the centre of action, referred to themselves in the first person, and freely described their thoughts, feelings and actions. The texts resembled the spoken discourse of everyday life. From the early eighteenth century, a majority of articles began to report original work.

Between 1775 and 1825, texts in the *Philosophical Transactions* underwent a major change. The essay format overtook the letter; authors took a decreasing place in their reports, while the experiments and observations became the core and were described in much greater detail and with more precision. The later stereotyped framework of the science article began to emerge and became the norm later in the nineteenth century. This period also saw a swing to the passive voice, the 'nominal' voice of long strings of noun phrases (a prose style from which the author/scientist is curiously absent), and a rising level of abstraction. By 1900 the passive voice was almost universal.

By the mid nineteenth century, jargon was creeping into *Philosophical Transactions* reports together with tables and mathematical and chemical formulae. By the 1870s, improvements in printing technology allowed more illustrations and some papers were organized round sequences of pictures. Things then remained fairly static until the last quarter of the twentieth century when, in some papers, experimental results and their interpretation began to lose their dominant position and became more focused on extended discussion of theory.

Gross, Harmon and Reidy have made a more comprehensive analysis of texts from an international range of learned scientific journals from the seventeenth century to the present day. They show that, while the emphasis on facts remains dominant, modern scientists are well aware that facts do not speak for themselves. The narrative around the raw data is increasingly cast in the form of an argument; new work derives from the existing canon through extensive citation. We are no longer invited to trust scientists as virtuous members of the gentrified elite, but to accept them as trained professionals, working at appropriate institutions and publishing in journals whose quality is guaranteed by professional peer review.

The modern scientific paper is a rigidly stereotyped document. There are sections following each other labelled (with minor variations): Introduction, Methods, Results, Discussion and/or Conclusion, References, together with a relatively free-standing Abstract. This standard arrangement implies that science proceeds by induction, gathering data (uncontaminated by pre-conceptions about what these might mean) from which hypotheses or theories (interpretations) are teased out. Presentation of data has been at the core of natural philosophical writing since the seventeenth century from Francis Bacon's principle that knowledge of nature can only be obtained from data about nature, 'The Book of Nature'. But scientific knowledge is an interpretation of that data and it is that interpretation which the author wants readers to accept. Making experimental data (hard, verifiable stuff at least in principle) the central point, together with a quasi-logical framework of interpretation from that data (an inductive progress which moves from specific, concrete events to inclusive generalizations), are designed to persuade readers of the validity of new knowledge claims.

Bacon and Oldenburg both advocated that natural philosophers write as plainly as possible. Language was not to be used as a device to trigger emotion; appeal should be made only to reason and commonsense. Language was to be literal, figurative tropes like metaphors, similes or personifications were not to be used. Modern scientific writing makes every effort to conform to these precepts but the presentational techniques of natural philosophers in the seventeenth and eighteenth centuries showed considerable variations in style. In the late seventeenth century Robert Boyle carried out experiments using an elaborate piece of apparatus (the air pump) producing highly artificial conditions (a vacuum). Shapin and Schaffer argue that Boyle wrote to convince readers of the truth of his observations by describing what had been done in such detail that the reader could imagine that he/she had been there him/herself. His goal in writing was to achieve 'virtual witnessing'. But there are other interpretations of Boyle's reports. Montgomery, for instance, sees an unfocused mind rambling round the issues without good editorial discipline, rather than a deliberate attempt to convince readers that they were there in the room with Boyle and his associates.

Alan Gross argues that Newton learned between youth and maturity to devise a presentation style that would better persuade others of the truth of his ideas. He compares the short article on light and colour that Newton wrote in 1672 with the massive monograph on the same theme, *Optiks*, published in 1704. In the 1672 article Newton announced that white light was made up of the seven colours in combination. He claimed that colours were primary and white derivative, and not the other way round as previous theory had suggested. The core of the later *Optiks* consists of the same insight, but presented in a different way. The 1672 paper was brash and assertive but could be easily challenged. It stressed the importance of a single, crucial experiment, which Newton felt should have been completely persuasive. But it wasn't, several virtuosi attacked his conclusions. Thirty years later in the 1704 book, experiment was piled on experiment and Newton set out a programme that dominated optical research for the next 100 years.

The 1672 paper was constructed as a Baconian story of core experiments conducted and results obtained. By contrast, the 1704 book took the form of an argument. In the *Optiks* Newton's rhetorical strategy was to present a mass of detailed experiments reported in virtual witness mode so that they could easily be replicated. The collection of hypotheses at the end of the book is separate from this mass of primary experimental data. This is sleight of hand because the hypotheses are the goal of the work, the experimental results the means for achieving that goal. The later version also demonstrates that an evolutionary argument is more persuasive than a revolutionary one. In 1704 Newton stressed the continuity of his work with ancient authorities from which the new work sprang, in contrast to the 1672 paper which had claimed a revolutionary break with the past. Brash arrogance proved less persuasive than anchoring new work in earlier achievement, accumulating a redundancy of evidence, and showing a degree of humility.

The detailed experimental reportage used by Boyle, and to a lesser extent by Newton, was later abandoned and is not the root of the modern scientific paper. Larry Holmes thought this might derive from the French *Academie des Sciences* in the late seventeenth century. In contrast to the Fellows of the Royal Society, French Academicians were salaried and professional natural philosophers. In the early days, they worked collaboratively. One such project was the 'History of Plants'. The initial report took the form of a critical argument rather than a story of detailed primary description of a series of experiments. The Fellows of the English Royal Society addressed a wider public and needed to persuade this wider audience of their achievements. French Academicians only had to address each other as members of a professional peer group, so did not need to describe their experiments in such detail.

The *Academie* abandoned its collectivist position at the end of the seventeenth century in favour of individual effort. Chemists working in this new mode presented their results in the annual *Memoires* from 1700 onwards, their papers being short and reporting limited investigations orientated towards special questions. A project might be reported in a series of papers, not collected into a comprehensive monograph as was the fashion elsewhere. Here the *Academie* once again set a blueprint for future science reporting. Negative experiments were not mentioned, laborious routes towards critical results not elaborated. Argument and story (discourse and report) were generally mixed together. Only enough information was supplied to allow those familiar with the procedures to follow what was going on. The French model, generated by and for an early professional cadre, looks like the precursor for communication among later professionals. Once again, Montgomery disagrees. He thinks the transition started in Germany in the early nineteenth century among newly professional German scientists reacting against an earlier approach to science known as *naturephilosophie*. But there is common ground in the idea that professional behaviour determined the form of professional communication.

SPECIALIZED PROFESSIONAL STRUCTURES BEGET SPECIALIZED PROFESSIONAL LANGUAGE

Early problems with the production of proto-learned journals like the *Philosophical Transactions* and their imitators and fakes were resolved by the early eighteenth century, but the publication of later generations of primary learned journals and monographs proved a problem because markets for professional science have generally been too small and too scattered.

The style of professional science communication has varied widely over time. Historians often do not agree on the purposes served by these different modes. But there are some historical trends, particularly the increasingly stereotypical form of the scientific paper, and the use of language suggesting that nature is telling the scientific story, not the scientist. Especially significant here is the passive voice, saying that experiments were done and results were found, but with the active experimenter strangely absent. The origins and problems with this and other norms of professional science writing are reviewed in the next chapter.

BIBLIOGRAPHY

Anon (2003). The internet in a cup. Coffee fuelled the information exchanges of the 17th and 18th centuries. *The Economist* (20th December), 48–50.

Atkinson, D. (1999). *Scientific Discourse in Socio-legal Context. The Philosophical Transactions of the Royal Society, 1675–1975*. Mahwah NJ: Lawrence Erlbaum Associates.

Broman, T. (2000). Periodical literature. In Fransca-Spada, M. and Jardine, N. (eds.). *Books and Sciences in History*. Cambridge: Cambridge University Press, Chapter 12.

Dawson, G., Noakes, R. and Topham, J.R. (2004). Introduction. In Cantor, G., Dawson, G., Gooday, G., Noakes, R., Shuttleworth, S. and Topham, J.R. (eds.). *Science in the Nineteenth Century Periodical. Reading the Magazine of Nature*. Cambridge: Cambridge University Press.

Fransca-Spada, M. and Jardine, N. (eds.) (2000). *Books and Sciences in History*. Cambridge: Cambridge University Press.

Gross, A. (1990). *The Rhetoric of Science*. Cambridge MA: Harvard University Press.

Gross, A., Harmon, J. and Reidy, M. (2002). *Communicating Science. The Scientific Article from the 17th Century to the Present*. New York: Oxford University Press.

Holmes, F.L. (1991). Argument and narrative in scientific writing. In Dear, P. (ed.). *The Literary Structure of Scientific Argument*. Pennsylvania: University of Pennsylvania Press.

Johns, A. (2000). Miscellaneous methods: authors, societies and journals in early modern England. *British Journal for the History of Science, **33***, 159–86.

Meadows, A.J. (ed.) (1980). *Development of Science Publishing in Europe*. Amsterdam, Oxford: Elsevier Science.

Medawar, P.B. (1969). *Induction and Intuition in Scientific Thought*. London: Methuen.

Rivers, I. (ed.) (1982). *Books and their Readers in Eighteenth-century England*. Leicester: Leicester University Press.

Rousseau, G.S. (1982). Science books and their readers in the eighteenth century. In Rivers, I. (ed.) *Books and their Readers in Eighteenth-century England*. Leicester: Leicester University Press, Chapter 8, pp. 197–225.

Shapin, S. and Schaffer, S. (1985). *Leviathan and the Air-pump: Hobbes, Boyle and the Experimental Life*. Princeton NJ: Princeton University Press.

2   Walk like an Egyptian: the alien feeling of professional science writing

Vernon, cowman, awkward in his washed-out boiler suit, goes forth from the cottage across the starlit yard to the hulk of the milking parlour. He can hear the cows fretting at the entrance as he throws the switches and the neon strips falter to life and the main pump hums up. Ten minutes later he opens the doors to his charges who stumble through to the relief of the milking stalls.

"Steady, steady, g'on, g'on, lummox, lummox, move over you lummox – steady now," restraining, directing beasts to stalls, "come on girl, come on", to a misdirected enthusiast then, "back, back, that's right my girl, that's right", in another adjustment of cow to stall, "g'on beauties, g'on," as the first eight fill the herringbone and sense the clamp of Vernon's suction caps, their damp breath clouding in the dawn air.

And so on, Vernon cajoling his cows through the two hour milking until they are all clomping back across the field towards the hay strewn in the upper pasture. The children have already left for school when he sits down for breakfast, idly scanning the paper.

"Well, Elizabeth, have you seen this?"

"What love?" replies his wife.

"Well I never did – says here," and Vernon scans the line with his finger, "Scientists at the National Dairy Laboratory have been working on a new way to make antibiotics and are forming a private company to develop their pioneering work. Herds of cows will produce milk containing antibiotic. The cows have been genetically altered by taking material from an antibiotic producing fungus. Scientists hope the modified milk will be a cheaper source of antibiotic than extracting it from the fungus."

Vernon shakes his head, "not sure I like the sound of that".

"Might get more money for milk though", says the practical Elizabeth, "pharmaceutical companies might pay more than supermarkets."

Threlfall slumps on the hideous armchair in what passes for an office 'converted' from a cupboard at the back of the lab, his mouth clamped round a cheddar and pickle doorstep. He shuffles the pages of the leftish redtop he still reads, a hangover from his student days as 'a man of the people'. He lights on the same article that Vernon read to Elizabeth three hours before.

"Hey, Harris."

"Yes boss," from the skinny youth delicately calibrating a temperamental instrument next door.

"Erinmeyer and Briggs are starting a spinout. Bastards never breathed a word to us."

"A spinout, how'd you know?" from Harris running his little finger through the line of dust on a casing flange.

"Says here, in the paper, NDL scientists start company getting antibiotics from cows' milk, must be them no?"

"Yes boss, sounds like it."

"But we don't like their methods or calibrations do we?" laying aside the doorstep in a welter of crumbs.

"No boss."

Threlfall thumbs through a small pile of printouts lurking on a desk top, part of his exquisitely tuned filing system.

"Here we are, Erinmeyer and Briggs, 'novel technique for measuring claxiform concentrations in protein containing solutions'." He turns to a subsection in the 'methods' entry and reads out.

"At clinically critical claxiform concentrations, readings taken using the methods of Driberg (1979), Fisher and Lockhead (1981, 83, 1990) and Marlberg (1992) show unacceptable variations (+/- 2 sds) compared with values obtained by the baseline procedure of Harding and Scott (1975). We believe our new technique which involves minimal tartrate substitution interferes with the initial benzyl group substitutions at the 3,5 positions which are the cause of the unacceptable variations in currently adopted procedures. We outline our reasons as follows, and blah, blah, blah they go on."

"Yes boss."

"They think with their method they've got a reliable way of measuring claxiform in milk."

"Maybe."

"Or maybe not as we, Harris, have every reason to suppose, providing you can get that machine working properly."

"Yes boss."

"So go to it," resuming the discarded doorstep. "When we've speeded up the Harding and Scott method it should be more reliable with milk estimates and wipe the grins off their faces. We don't believe they can get commercial levels of claxiform in cows' milk."

PROFESSIONAL SCIENTIFIC PROSE

These little scenarios contain three key pieces of text, Vernon governing his cows, the newspaper report of science news, and the extract from Erinmeyer and Briggs's scientific paper, notably more difficult to understand than the other two. In the past the language scientists used to write about science was similar to the language in newspapers and magazines. The peculiar language of modern scientific research is relatively new. It is not just that there is a lot of jargon and the topics are unfamiliar. There is something about the structure of the language of modern professional science that makes it hard to understand.

This can be measured objectively. Donald Hayes has compared samples of writing from scientific journals with other forms of writing since 1900. He uses a lexical analysis of word difficulty to compare articles against a 'standard' whose reading difficulty has been constant over the century; international English language newspapers. These newspapers give a constant score of zero. Texts that are more difficult to read are rated with positive numbers; those which are easier are negative. The linguistic extremes seem to be a particularly arcane paper published in *Nature* in 1960 (score +55.5) as opposed to farm workers talking to dairy cows (score -59.1), the mode of Vernon talking to his charges.

Hayes believes things are getting worse. In 1930, three of the primary magazines of science communication, *Nature*, *Science* and *Scientific American* all had lexical scores around zero, they were no more difficult to read than newspapers, but by 1990 *Nature* scored an average of +30, *Science* about +27, and *Scientific American* +10. The same trend appeared in learned science journals. For instance, *Astrophysical Journal* scored +3 in 1950 and +17 in 1990, *Genetics* scored +17 in 1950 and was nudging +30 in 1990, while *Cell* started at nearly +20 in 1974 and came close to +40 in 1990. Hayes has recently repeated his lexical analysis of *Nature* and *Science*. Both now have lexical scores of around +35, so things are getting more difficult.

What makes scientists' professional prose so hard to read? Some of the problem can be explained by increased use of jargon but a lot resides in the grammatical structure of the language in which science is written. Alan Gross argues that three of its most obvious grammatical features are the passive voice, extensive noun phrases, and over-description. All three seem to be there for rhetorical purposes, to help persuade the reader of the truth of what is being set out.

The use of the passive voice makes it seem that the report is what nature does, rather than the actions of the investigators and their interpretations of what nature does. This is the basic stylistic trick of writing up practical science that every school girl learns.

Her lab report entries might read, 'The choice chamber was set up according to the method of Smudge and Tomkins' and later perhaps 'The woodlice oriented to the damp and shaded side of the chamber'. These statements conceal the real events which she might more realistically have described as 'Steph and me spent most of the lesson setting up the choice chamber with the school technician. He'd read up what to do in an educational support manual but we didn't have any of the kit, so he rigged up a rough copy with stuff he did have in the prep room', and 'Maybe ten woodlice finally wound up on the damp and dark side with eight on the dry and bright side. Miss said we could call that a difference, if we had more time more of them would have gone to the dark side. Steph says woodlice are horrid little bleeders but I think they are well cool'. School science is, of course, a parody of the real thing but the essential point of using the passive voice remains the same, a lot of the personal, the social, and the messily contingent about gathering data are edited from all science reports with the passive voice.

Tortuous noun phrases are transitional terms through which raw data are converted into abstract concepts. The messy, confused, half-understood and inconsistent data at the experimental cutting edge are converted into fact and expressed as 'textbook' knowledge. Thus Lillie and Steph, in their later lives as practising scientists might say that woodlice had a 'low luminosity, high water saturation preference' to describe their tendency to huddle in dark, damp places.

Over-description is the piling on of methodological and descriptive detail, always composed in the passive voice and giving overwhelming technical information, although the experimenters themselves are still largely absent from the scene. The over-description has at least two rhetorical functions. It allows third parties to actually repeat the experiments and confirm that they give the results claimed by the author, and it also persuades readers who are not going to attempt such a replication that the events actually took place.

Apart from the big three, there are several other grammatical features characteristic of scientific papers. Halliday identifies seven more that make scientific prose hard to read. He believes such elaborate grammar is useful in professional communication because it enables scientists to make complex arguments with great economy. These grammatical features include the following.

Interlocking definitions

Scientific descriptive terms often have to be carefully defined. Very often, the definitions interlock; in other words a set of terms is introduced which only make sense when they are defined in relation to each other. Unless you understand all the terms, none of them make sense.

Technical taxonomies

Quite often in science terms are organized into a classification series. An example would be the definition of 'climate'. The different kinds of climate are defined by combinations of several types of factor such as sunlight, rainfall, altitude, geographic balance of land and water and so on. To make proper sense of a technical climate definition requires keeping in mind both the range of factors involved and the value of each factor expressed in that specific climate-defining term.

Special expressions

These are linguistic uses peculiar to science communication. For instance, scientific data are often presented in tables which readers are expected to interpret without any overt help from the text.

Lexical density

This is defined as the number of content (lexical) words per clause, and relates to the extensive use of noun-clauses. Generally, lexical density is low in spoken language and rises in formal writing. In science writing it can rise to extremely high levels. School textbooks often have clauses with eight or more nouns, while even relatively popular contemporary science magazines can rise to values of 13 or so. Such structures are efficient at conveying precise meanings in few words but are so dense that only several readings by someone familiar with the material can unpack the meaning.

Syntactic ambiguity

Scientific sentences often have a simple structure, but the dense noun phrases cannot be unpacked without prior knowledge of context and the linking verbs are often ambiguous.

Grammatical metaphor

Both lexical density and ambiguity arise from grammatical metaphor. This is defined not as the substitute of one word or phrase for another but where one grammatical structure is substituted for another. For instance, the noun phrase 'glass crack growth rate' substitutes for the more conventional phrase, 'how quickly cracks in glass grow'.

Semantic discontinuity

These are language constructions in which background information or assumptions have to be read in, to make sense of the text. If you are not familiar with the jargon and other current work in the field, even the clearest account will not make sense.

WHY IS PROFESSIONAL PROSE LIKE THIS?

While Halliday justifies the grammatical characteristics of professional science writing in terms of economy and brevity, Montgomery argues that the real reason for the weird grammar and jargon is to achieve exclusiveness; only the professional group trained in the language can understand what it says. This creates boundaries around professional practice and excludes amateurs. Plainer language could just as easily do the job, but it would not achieve the desirable goal of keeping non-professionals out. For Montgomery the passive voice is 'the scientific voice' and has the added virtue that its depersonalization implies universality, suggesting that science speaks with a single (and therefore authoritative) voice.

The scientific community itself lays the blame for increasingly unreadable papers at the door of jargon. The structure of Hayes's lexical instrument, LEX, seems to support this. The LEX score of readability assumes that it is easier to read text that uses familiar words. Hayes has a database of word use frequency (notice a three-word noun phrase slip in here, they can clearly be useful things), which he equates with familiarity. LEX scores increase with increased jargon levels. Scientific disciplines like immunology and cell biology are especially prone to coining new names for molecules and processes making them more difficult to read than the less jargon infested physical sciences. Thus leading physics journals such as *Physical Review D* or the astronomy publication *Icarus* both have relatively low LEX scores of +22.

If jargon is the key to unreadability, there does not seem much that can be done about it, although Judith Swan and George Gopen run workshops providing advice on how to make professional scientific writing easier to understand. They encourage scientists to put verbs close to the subjects to which they refer (rather than separating them with chains of subordinate clauses), to put any new information occurring in a sentence at the end of that sentence after stating the already known and familiar, and to ensure that there are bridges between sentences or paragraphs in which new concepts appear with previous ones which set out more familiar concepts. Consistent use of such rules can certainly help, but does not tackle the core problems of jargon and special grammar.

Modern scientific writing uses significantly shorter sentences with fewer clauses than pieces written before the mid twentieth century and Ceccarelli argues that these trends may compensate for the rise of jargon and kept lexical indices from climbing even higher. One ingenious scientist, Chris McCabe, who moonlights as a novelist, aims to improve standards of professional science writing by choosing examples of professional communication that seem to be effective in conveying meaning even though they are composed within the professional format. He aims to present them as benchmarks that others might emulate.

While scientific articles can be understood by the peer group of scientists for whom they are designed, there seems little doubt that professional scientific writing also sets boundaries round the profession. It requires long training and much time and effort to learn how to read and write the arcane professional science genre (a problem spreading to all academic writing in the social sciences and humanities as well). It may now have become impossible to write professional science that can be understood beyond the immediate peer group.

Greg Myers re-tells the famous story of F.J. Ingelfinger who, when editor of *New England Journal of Medicine*, got one of his journalists to rewrite a particularly obscure immunological paper as a news feature. He published both versions of the material side by side. He received two sets of letters in response. One group praised the journalistic piece for its clarity, but another group, all professional immunologists, complained that the popular version was harder to read. The reason for this is probably that scientists read papers with a huge amount of tacit knowledge which enables them to scan them quickly to see if they need to take note of anything. They will only read them thoroughly if they must, but actually won't unless they have to.

Charles Bazerman examined the reading practices of a sample of physicists. If they decided to read an article, they generally did not read it from beginning to end as lay people would. Lay people would probably try to read the paper as a linear narrative, but scientific papers are not structured like that. In many cases, scientists looked at the introduction and conclusions and perhaps scanned the illustrations, just to get a general idea of what the writer was trying to say. They only gave it more careful reading if it seemed immediately important to the work they were doing. Even when articles were read from start to finish following an author's arguments, the detailed maths was often skipped over and derivations simply assumed to be correct. If the new data or ideas could not be associated closely with what the scientists knew already, they found it difficult to know what they meant. In other words, if an article is the slightest bit outside their current field of interest, it is difficult for even professional scientists to read it. The writing can only have meaning if a tacit knowledge framework exists into which it can be fitted.

THE PROBLEM AGGRAVATED BY RUDENESS AND ARROGANCE

Another, more subtle problem with modern professional communication has arisen from a change of etiquette in research presentation in some disciplines. This may not make a research paper harder to understand, but disguises the tentative nature of new research findings, deceiving both professionals and lay people into thinking such new findings are more certain and reliable than is justified at an early stage.

In the seventeenth and eighteenth centuries, English natural philosophers were clear that they were making tenuous claims about which they had to persuade their audiences. Three centuries later some statements of tentative claims have been replaced by statements reporting new claims as fact. Montgomery argues that hesitancy in advancing new knowledge claims was abandoned as wasteful in the late nineteenth century because in the mature sciences where all readers are fellow professionals sharing the same values, there was no longer any need to persuade the audience. Various kinds of shorthand evolved to cut out the argument chains between data and theory which a non-expert would need to follow what was being claimed. If non-experts don't read research papers, the argument chains are no longer necessary. This focus on addressing only peers has sharpened since the 1920s and much professional science writing has taken on additional functions internal to the institution; fighting for status, for career position, and to obtain good supplies of students and/or grant money. The necessity for clear communication may have become less important. Hence Bazarman's physicists struggle to make proper sense of any paper outside their immediate fields.

The education scholar, Clive Sutton, argues that the language of scientific research should be interpretative and designed to persuade, only the language of established textbooks should be about labelling what is known and transmitting that established knowledge to students. According to Martin the main genre of a textbook is the report, which is defined as a logical presentation of information around a theme. The report genre is informative, is not cast as a story, and is marked by abstract descriptions of the behaviour of generic participants (classes, categories or groups) rather than linear narratives of events happening to individuals (as in a conventional story). Timeless verbs are used in the simple present tense, and there is a high frequency of 'being' and 'having' clauses. More advanced textbooks will have explanations, which Martin defines as a separate genre from the descriptive report. Explanatory texts have a higher percentage of action (rather than timeless) verbs and the actions are organized into logical sequences.

THE DAMAGE OF STATING NEW INTERPRETATIONS AS FACT RATHER THAN ARGUMENT

Exposition, defined as the development of an argument in favour of a position, is much rarer in science textbooks at all levels. Arguments tend to be missing from textbooks, because the body of knowledge described is unlinked from the tentative stories of knowledge claims of those who first generated it, and is now presented as factually certain. Therefore, no arguments (exposition) are needed and the stories of how the knowledge was developed (a form of narrative biography) are also missing. Sutton argues that scientists are now using styles appropriate to the transmission of established knowledge to make fresh claims. There is a tendency to assert rather than persuade, symbolically changing the knowledge status of research papers from acts of persuasion to transmission of established facts. Apart from anything else, this is bad scientific manners, but more seriously it misrepresents the essentially contingent nature of new research interpretations.

Perhaps the most interesting feature of science is how raw experimental data and tentative claims for new interpretations are transformed into statements of established fact and theory characteristic of textbooks. The most common view about how this happens is probably that the accumulation of more data supporting the new interpretation eventually confirms it. But this has not stood up to rigorous analysis by sociologists, philosophers and historians of science. The details of how this transformation takes place still remain unclear. It seems that scientists themselves (probably unwittingly) may be trying to short-circuit these complex issues by using a rhetoric of assertion of fact in place of persuasive argument for interpretation when they write research papers.

BIBLIOGRAPHY

Bazerman, C. (1988). *Shaping Written Knowledge. The Genre and Activity of the Experimental Article in Science.* Wisconsin: University of Wisconsin Press.

Bazerman, C. and Paradis, J. (eds.). (1991). *Textual Dynamics of the Professions. Historical and Contemporary Studies of Writing in Professional Communities.* Wisconsin: University of Wisconsin Press.

Ceccarelli, L. (2000). A scientific rhetoric. *Science,* **298**, 757.

Gross, A. (1990). *The Rhetoric of Science.* Cambridge MA: Harvard University Press.

Hayes, D. P. (1992). The growing inaccessibility of science. *Nature,* **30**, 739–40.

Halliday, H. A. K. and Martin, J. R. (1993). *Writing Science, Literacy and Discursive Power.* Brighton, Sussex: Falmer Press.

Knight, J. (2003). Clear as mud. *Nature,* **423**, 376–8.

McCabe, C. (2004). A mission to sex up scientese. *The Guardian,* Life Section, 5 February, 8/9.

Montgomery, S. (1996). *The Scientific Voice.* New York, London: The Guilford Press.

Myers, G. (1990). *Writing Science. Texts in the Social Construction of Scientific Knowledge.* Wisconsin: University of Wisconsin Press.

Russell, N. C. (1994). Sprechen sie sciencespeak. *New Scientist,* 10 December, 46.

Sutton, C. (1996). Beliefs about science and beliefs about language. *International Journal of Science Education,* **18**, 1–18.

3 The future's bright? Professional science communication in the age of the internet

Dr Esme Smith added the finishing touches to the Mark 6 version of her neuropeptide paper, pacing back and forth dictating and watching the words appear on her wall screen. Pausing, she passed a finger over her snazzy Hand Assistant to get the whole last paragraph on screen. Frowning slightly she read it through, glanced at her time bar, mentally rehearsed the chores she had to do before picking up the children (unusually Richard had to be in the office rather than the home console) and decided it would do. She swiped her finger again, checked the total sum in Euros, and sent Mark 6 into cyberspace.

She had put the first four versions on the private British science site, Impact One, but their charges were becoming excessive and the Nova Brainstem Foundation who funded her work refused to pay for it anymore. Impact One had a good reputation, most major players in her field were keyed in for on-the-hour alerts, and the Nobel Prize Winner submission index was high at 5.043, but she had become increasingly unhappy with the site, especially with the quality of review and post-review comments on the professional (peer) file. The Mark 1 version of the paper had been double blind (no one knew who had written it and reviewers were editor-selected and anonymous) but a reviewer had recognized who she was and used some hurtful put-downs. But overall she had scarcely altered the Mark 1 (Beta) paper and it appeared as Mark 2 under her name (with her Research Assistant and one of the Ph.D. students as co-authors).

Subsequent additions and addenda had generated Mark 3 and Mark 4. Esme was thankful for the modern practice of modifying existing material rather than writing new papers. It no longer made sense to salami slice results into serial papers to enhance output. Hyper-factorial bibliometric software could dice and slice even one or two papers into a rank value. After the Mark 4 version, Impact one raised their charges while allowing comments on the open (non-professional) commentary files from vicious members of neuro-patient activist groups.

So, when she had enough fresh material to generate Mark 5, she took the whole file across to the European Union public science site, European Agreement in Science (EAS). This site was more accommodating about amending the terms of agreement over the lifetime of the holding but, on the other hand, the site's overall impact factor was lower, although it was used more extensively for both pod casting and news caching, potentially giving her a higher public profile.

EAS acknowledged receipt of her files and Euros with the French accented male voice they tended to use with British submissions in 5.4 seconds. Even so, Esme thought this slow, the sheer weight of spam, wicki and blog filters now needed for sensitive e-communication was becoming excessive.

THE INTERNET TO THE RESCUE?

This scenario is futuristic but not that futuristic. It suggests that academic papers and the way they are traded are changing and will change more in the near future. Since there is no pressure on e-space, authors can write at greater length, include raw data files and describe the detailed genesis of their ideas for anyone interested enough to read them. Publishers already prepare materials for electronic dissemination and web cataloguing rather than manuscripts for print. Publishers are starting to provide versions of the paper for different readers; for instance, a scientific abstract, a news-release version, versions suitable to the needs of different professional reading groups, and so on. Many publishers are experimenting with open and invited review, the reviews to be included with the 'published' paper. Papers may grow and develop in response to open comment and perhaps get extended with new results and ideas, rather than fresh papers being written. This is the latest phase in the difficult story of professional communication in science. Scientists have historically been few in number, widely scattered and not especially affluent, all factors presenting headaches for scientific publishers.

The problem was partly resolved by the growth in science after the First World War and its acceleration during the 'golden age' of science after the Second World War between 1945 and 1975. University science grew fast and was generously funded. The infrastructure of laboratories, support staff, equipment and, most relevant here, libraries, grew dramatically. A commercial market of sorts now existed. Libraries could afford to buy specialized journals as an essential information resource for their scientists. While everybody accepted that such journals were expensive, the more astute publishing entrepreneurs built hefty profit margins on top, realizing that scientists would keep on demanding the journals, but would not themselves have to pay for them. To allow their scientists to stay competitive, university libraries were forced to pay extortionate prices for an ever-widening range of academic journals of increasing size caused by the ever more refined sub-specialization of scientific disciplines and increase in the number of scientists needing to publish.

The master at this technique of wringing huge profits from academic journal publishing in the UK was the late Robert Maxwell and Pergamon Press. Where he led, others followed. This created what academic librarians dubbed the 'Serials Crisis' of the 1980s and 1990s. Resources for science had stabilized yet journals kept on proliferating and increasing in price. Under conditions of financial stringency, libraries were forced to cut other essential services (like undergraduate textbooks and monographs, or staff or opening times) to keep the cuckoo of specialized scientific journals fed. There did not seem to be any way out of the trap.

The arrival of the World Wide Web started to change things. Mass electronic publication of scientific knowledge claims was now possible and, almost as soon as the World Wide Web was up and running, in 1994 publishers began to experiment with online journals. By the end of 1995, there were already over 300 online journals, although many were experimental and of variable quality.

By 1997, only a few mainstream academic journals were online but, once the trend had started, it could not be stopped. Science journals led the way because scientists need to have the latest information quickly and were among the first equipped with powerful enough desktop computers to make personal access to electronic journals possible. Academic journal publishers were forced online and all the big operators made the switch. By early 1999, Reed–Elsevier had more than 1200 journals online, Springer 360, and Academic Press 174. The situation had swung from passive resistance in 1995 to acceptance that any scientific journal without an electronic version was not going to survive in the twenty-first century.

In theory, electronic publishing can solve the Serials Crisis. It changes the whole nature and meaning of 'publication.' The capital-intensive processes of printing, storing and distributing paper versions of journals are removed. The electronic versions can be distributed everywhere and hard copies downloaded locally in libraries, offices and laboratories (although this simply shifts the direct costs of printing and storage to the users rather than the producers). However, neither users nor producers were able to cope with change at this speed. Most publishers continued to produce print versions of their journals and prevented libraries from taking the electronic version on its own by refusing to sell electronic licences unless the print versions were bought as well.

The nature and form of the 'academic paper' will be further influenced by the continued growth of pre-print archives. Paul

Ginsparg at the Los Alamos Physics Laboratory started the first of these archives in pre-Web days in 1991. The physics community had already developed a culture of communication by pre-print circulation to allow researchers access to material when conventional journals undertake peer review and prepare material for the press (which often takes several months or longer). The electronic system replaced hard-copy circulation and has grown steadily to the point where tens of thousands of papers a year are put up and made available free. A large number of the papers then appear in peer-reviewed journals, but by no means all. Most physics journals accept this practice and do not turn such articles down because they have already been published. Patrick Brown and David Lipman proposed a similar scheme for the life sciences in 1999, although it was not clear that biological journals would accept work that had been 'pre-published' and nor had the biological community any culture of communicating in this way through pre-prints.

THE INTERNET SPARKS A NEW PUBLICATION PHILOSOPHY, ESPECIALLY IN THE LIFE SCIENCES

The basic idea of public service e-publishing for biology was taken up by Harold Varmus, then Director of the US National Institutes of Health (NIH), who called for a single website, E-Biomed, to be responsible for all biomedical science publication. One of his objectives was to solve the Serials Crisis by cutting out commercial publishers and high journal subscription costs altogether. Publication of both un-refereed and peer-reviewed papers was proposed with authors retaining copyright of their material. The usual convention is for scientists to give the copyright of their papers to publishers in exchange for journal publication. This presented (and continues to present) problems for authors who want to make their work available in other forms; they cannot do it without the publisher's permission.

Varmus also suggested most of the novel possibilities for open review and paper update. While NIH was prepared to kick-start the process financially, it would not take on long-term responsibility and some alternative funding mechanism was needed. One possibility was public funding (unpopular in America) or page charges to authors for publication (unpopular if commercial publishers still take papers without charge). Initial responses from the scientific publishing communities to the Varmus plan varied from lukewarm to hostile. Some were concerned at the loss of journal diversity, others that it would soak up large sums of public money. The learned society, non-profit journal publishers were incensed because they were doing most of what Varmus proposed in response to market forces and technical change and were worried that loss of journal income would damage their positions.

But Varmus pressed on. The proposed site name was changed to PubMed and extended to embrace plant science and agriculture. Partly because of the strong American resistance to public funding, PubMed were forced to give a big role to the existing experts, the very commercial publishers whose sharp practices Varmus had set out to curb. There were worries about the distribution of un-refereed 'junk' science and concern about non-peer-reviewed clinical papers being available when they might prove unreliable guides to medical practice. The prestigious journal, *Proceedings of the National Academy of Sciences* agreed to appear on the (renamed) PubMed Central site, but only if all material on the site was peer reviewed.

PubMed Central (PMC) went live in February 2000 but at first few commercial or not-for-profit journals co-operated. Eighty-three life science journals signed up with an alternative site created by HighWire Press (a not-for-profit, established biomedical journal publisher) in March 2000. These journals made all their archive articles available free on the web, in some cases as quickly as one or two months after publication. PMC limped along and in 2001 was forced to relax its demand that publishers deposit the full texts of articles on the PMC site up to 1 year after initial publication. Instead, PMC would provide links to publishers' sites. The full texts would be available through PMC servers after a period of up to 1 year, which allowed commercial publishers to make a profit on their work while ensuring a free, long-term archive for the scientific community. This rather undermined PMC's original demand for free current science publishing.

The comparative failure of PMC stimulated more radical scientists to propose the Public Library of Science (PLoS), a central electronic archive where all published scientific articles should be deposited within 6 months of initial publication. Initially, it met the same backlash as the earlier PMC proposal. It still left publishers funding the initial business of publication and having to make a profit within 6 months, something to which they, not surprisingly, objected.

But the problem remains that science publication is not cost free. PMC and PLoS activists clearly believed publishers were making excessive profit, and that consumer pressure and boycott could reduce them. But some people still confuse the question of excessive profit with a naïve belief that the process can be made so cheap that no one needs to pay. That is simply not true and, if scientific papers are to be free at point of publication, funding will have to come from someone or somewhere if it doesn't come from subscriptions. Possibilities include levies to cover publication costs charged to government, research council or private funders of research, or that universities and other employers of scientists take on the responsibility. The only other possibility is that the authors themselves pay (which is exactly what happened in the days before organized commercial publication). If the scientific community does not pay for publication through journal subscription, it will have to pay through devices like page charges.

In 2002 PLoS announced its own, free at point-of-publication online publishing venture, hoping to fund the system by page charges to authors. By January 2003, there were plans for two new journals, *PLoS Biology* and *PLoS Medicine*, which would provide all their content free. PLoS could do this because it received a large grant from the Gordon and Betty Moore Foundation. The founders and their colleagues were aiming high, wanting PLoS journals to become leading journals in their fields, which would displace the equivalent journals produced by commercial publishers. Apart from the start-up grant, the journals can only be funded through author fees, initially set at about $1000 per article. Some research funding bodies are willing to pay these fees for scientists. For work not supported by trusts, councils or corporations, funding must come from universities, research institutes or the researchers themselves so, for purely economic reasons, especially for research in third world countries, many researchers will continue to publish in subscription journals.

By 2008 things at PLoS were not going all that well. The organization was kept afloat with large charitable donations, while author charges for its top ranking journals had risen to $2500 per article. PLoS introduced a less rigorous, 'light' peer-reviewed journal, *PLoS One*, which attracts more submissions at lower cost and where the only checks carried out on papers are for methodological soundness. While that may raise revenues, it is likely to impair the reputation of the brand. While PLoS has been making a lot of noise, the lower key successor to PMC, rebranded as *BioMedCentral*, has been quietly getting on with journal publication at the edges of science. It runs more than 90 peer-reviewed journals and began by charging a relatively modest fee of $500 for each article.

Funding bodies and parliaments are muscling in on the science publishing debate. The UK House of Lords Select Committee on Science and Technology published a wide-ranging report on science publishing in July 2004. It recommended that some independent research be conducted into the costs and benefits of different publishing models, that government support further experiments with the 'author pays' model, and that it encourage the half-way house pioneered by PMC where authors archive e-copies of any commercially published work on public or institutional websites (repositories) within 6 months of publication. The European Commission recommended much the same thing, that reports of all research funded with EU funds, even if published in commercial journals, should be e-archived for free public access. Not surprisingly, the open publishers welcomed it, while the commercial firms rehearsed reasons against it.

In the biomedical world two leading funding agencies, the American NIH and the British Wellcome Trust, were pioneers in requiring all their fund-holders to put copies of their papers on open access repositories within 6 months of publication. Learned Society publishers complain bitterly that they cannot recover their costs in 6 months, while others argue that there will be major disputes between commercial publishers and researchers because publishers, not authors, own copyright on their published papers and could prevent authors from archiving. In late 2004 the UK Government rejected all the recommendations of the House of Lords Select Committee about open access, both author pays and public archive repository. Nevertheless, by 2008 many academic journal publishers allowed their authors to archive their material for free access (usually on university repository websites) between 6 months and 1 year after initial publication.

There are also clear cultural trends emerging in scientific papers in the age of the internet and its search engines, reviewed by Linda Nordling. Paradoxically, the explosion in formal and informal web publication (home pages, blogs, social networks and so on) has produced a paralysis of access; no one has time to trawl through the material, leading to even greater pressure from researchers to get their papers into well-read and respected journals. Such pressures encourage researchers and journals to manipulate their impact scores, so that some journals now commission a series of commentaries on papers they publish, immediately generating countable citations. A further paradox is that, despite the explosion in information, published papers are citing ever narrower ranges of sources as authors focus down on reliable and trusted material.

Articles are also being written in more conservative prose so that titles, key words and so on are easily detected by search engines, so-called search engine optimization (SEO). This trend may reinforce the well-established exclusivity and low readability of scientific prose. Optimists believe that open access science publishing will eventually break this down as such publications integrate more closely with the rest of the web and search engines become more powerful. They also hope this will unlock the stranglehold that citation bibliometrics and impact factors have on scientific careers. If metrics become less important, then actual text content (what authors are claiming) may be restored to what should be its primary position.

THE FUTURE WILL BE MULTI-STRANDED

Electronic academic publishing and the associated culture of science are changing too fast for any conventional account to keep up. The gap between the imagined scenario at the start of this chapter and actual events towards the end of the first decade of the twenty-first century is closing rapidly. The pace of change demonstrates how central are the mechanisms of professional science communication to the cultural practice of science, and these associations between communication and the scientific institution are explored further in the next two chapters.

But the long history of technical change in communication suggests that, while a new platform can produce rapid cultural change, new platforms seldom completely displace old ones, rather they co-exist. Printing did not replace manuscript, film and radio did not replace print or theatre, television did not replace film, the internet has not replaced television or radio. The landscape may profoundly change, the new platform often both usurps and extends the cultural ranges and purposes of the old, but the older platforms persist, modifying and carving out new niches for themselves. I think we can therefore safely predict that, despite the upheavals caused by electronic journal publication, forms of print-based science publication will persist. There is unlikely to be a solely electronic future for professional science communication.

BIBLIOGRAPHY

BMJ (1997). The electronic future. What might an online scientific paper look like in five years' time? *British Medical Journal*, 20 December, **315**, 1692–6.

Brahic, C. (2002). Open access in biomedical publication. Unpublished Imperial College London M.Sc. dissertation.

Brumfiel, G. (2004). Biomedical agency floats open-access plan. *Nature*, 9 September, **431**, 115.

Butler, D. (1999). US biologists propose launch of electronic preprint archive. *Nature*, 14 January, **397**, 91.

Butler, D. (1999). The writing is on the web for science journals in print. *Nature*, 21 January, **397**, 195–200.

Butler, D. (2000). All parties keen to press on with Europe-based science website. *Nature*, 27 January, **403**, 347–8.

Butler, D. (2000). Souped-up search engines. *Nature*, 11 May, **405**, 112–15.

Butler, D. (2000). Biology back issues free as publishers walk HireWire. *Nature*, 9 March, **404**, 117.

Butler, D. (2003). Wellcome to fund publication in open-access journals. *Nature*, 2 October, **425**, 440.

Butler, D. (2003). Who will pay for open access? *Nature*, 9 October, **425**, 554–55.

Butler, D. (2004). Britain decides 'open access' is still an open issue. *Nature*, 22 July, **430**, 390.

Butler, D. (2005). Joint efforts. *Nature*, 1 December, **438**, 548–9.

Butler, D. (2006). Open-access journal hits rocky times. *Nature*, 22 June, **441**, 914.

Butler, D. (2008). PLoS stays afloat with bulk publishing. *Nature*, 3 July, **454**, 11

Butler, D. and Wadman, M. (1999). Mixed response to NIH's web journal plan. *Nature*, 6 May, **399**, 8.

Ewing, J. (2003). Open access will not be everyone. *Nature*, 9 October, **425**, 559.

Giles, J. (2004). Trust gives warm welcome to open access. *Nature*, 11 November, **432**, 134.

HMS Beagle (1999). http://www.biomednet.com/hmsbeagle/61/viewpts/synoposis, *Journals online. PubMed Central and beyond*, visited 30 September 1999.

House of Lords Select Committee on Science and Technology, *Tenth report*, http://www.publications.parliament.uk/pa/cm200304/cmselect/399/39903.htm (visited 25 October 2004).

Knight, J. (2003). Cornell axes Elsevier journals as prices rise. *Nature*, 20 November, **426**, 217.

Lawrence, S. and Giles, C. L. (1999). Accessibility of information on the web. *Nature*, 8 July, **400**, 107–9.

MacLeod, D. (2003). Publish and be free. *The Guardian*, Education Section, 17 June.

Marris, E. (2006). PS I want all rights. *Nature*, 13 July, **442**, 118.

Mellman, I. (2001). Setting logical priorities. *Nature*, 26 April, **410**, 1026.

Nordling, L. (2008). Web journals 'narrowing study'. Online publishing reduces academic research to little more than a 'popularity contest' critics warn. *The Guardian*, 28 October, Education Section, 8.

Ochert, A. (1999). Out of the morass. *Times Higher Education Supplement*, 8 January, 13.

Patel, K. (1999). Academics concerned about life science site. *Times Higher Education Supplement*, 3 September, 3.

Sequeria, E., McIntyre, J. and Lipman, D. (2001). PubMedCentral decentralized. *Nature*, 12 April, **410**, 740.

Wadman, M. (2001). Publishers challenged over access to papers. *Nature*, 29 March, **410**, 502.

Wray, R. (2004). Confused decision on science publishing. *The Guardian*, 9 November, 16.

Wray, R. (2006). Brussels delivers blow to Reed Elsevier. *The Guardian*, 19 April, 27.

4   Counting the horse's teeth: professional standards in science's barter economy

Karl Sabbagh tells the unhappy story of Professor J.W. Heslop Harrison FRS and his lapses from the professional standards of behaviour expected of a scientist. He came from humble beginnings, the son of an iron worker, and grew up in harsh conditions in the early part of the twentieth century. By dint of hard work he went to university and eventually became an academic botanist, specializing in the study of plant classification and distribution. In the 1930s when Heslop Harrison began his professional career, the Hebridean islands off the Scottish coast were largely unexplored. When he and others made scientific surveys on the islands, they discovered they had unique species and subspecies of plant and insect, some of which were new to science. These discoveries made Heslop Harrison's reputation. His richest site was the island of Rum, previously in private hands and not botanically examined at all.

At first, his discoveries attracted no suspicion. But by the end of the 1930s some of his claims were becoming bizarre. He was using them to support a hypothesis that the islands had escaped the last Ice Age which had buried the Scottish mainland under a massive sheet of ice. The final straw for a Cambridge colleague, John Raven (a classicist and amateur naturalist), came in 1941 when Heslop Harrison published two papers announcing the discovery on Rum of species previously unknown in Great Britain. After the war, Raven managed to join one of Heslop Harrison's expeditions to the island and see these wonders for himself. He was convinced that the specimens were not native, but had been transplanted from elsewhere.

Raven prepared a report in 1948 for leading British botanists. Everyone agreed that Raven's exposure was convincing. There was not much doubt that Heslop Harrison had planted the specimens on Rum, a clear case of fraud. But the report was never published and Heslop Harrison was not exposed. The decision not to go public was taken to protect his career and reputation. The professional group closed ranks to conceal misconduct, acting according to George Bernard Shaw's unkind jibe that much professional behaviour is a 'conspiracy against the laity'.

There are two rather serious moral failures here. A scientist has faked evidence for a hypothesis for which he did not have enough support and this was compounded by colleagues who knew what had happened but kept it secret. This all seems shocking because we are invited to believe that the scientific community is especially honest and upright. What is going on?

THE PIVOTAL STATUS OF THE SCIENTIFIC PAPER

Communication is at the heart of science, both in making claims to new knowledge, and then in transmitting the body of knowledge established from these claims. Journals, monographs and textbooks are essential for transmitting knowledge, while the scientific paper is particularly suited for making initial claims to new knowledge. The channels of science communication, therefore, play a major role in quality control and in this chapter we examine how the process of publishing scientific papers helps to ensure that science operates to high ethical standards. The scientific paper must first and foremost be an accurate and reliable record of the data from which new scientific interpretations or explanations are drawn. If, for any reason, the scientific community or the wider public cannot rely on the integrity of published records, the whole edifice of science is thrown into doubt.

Heslop Harrison like any other modern scientist presented his results in academic papers. But texts alone are not enough to convince us of the truth of claims made in them. We can only accept them if we trust the integrity of the authors; in this case scientists themselves. Generally, we do trust them to make truthful claims, although no one seems to manage them or to check independently on what they are doing. We have to rely on the scientific community's own professional values to assure the quality of their work. In the light of Heslop Harrison's moral lapses (and those of others) we need to examine carefully just what are these guarantees of integrity in science.

High-order voluntary behaviour (such as choosing to spend one's life in the study of science, for instance) tends to be motivated by intrinsic factors. For scientists, the key motivation is the satisfaction of personal curiosity through discovery and invention. Standard extrinsic satisfactions such as power, income, celebrity, or even a desire to help their fellow humans, do not seem to motivate scientists so much as they do members of other professions. Instead, their main extrinsic reward is recognition by the community of their peers. But internal purity of motivation and external recognition by peers are not enough to guarantee the trustworthiness of science. Scientific fraud exists, some scientists make dishonest or untrue knowledge claims.

Peer recognition for making original discoveries or devising new theories is necessary because only the peer group is competent to judge the value of the claims. The need to establish priority governs the publication pattern of scientific papers. Such publication does not lead to material gain; rather, the paper is a form of gift to the scientific community. The credit exchange system of science remains essentially feudal rather than commercial; the paper is not a product for sale. The key anthropological feature of gift exchange is that, because a gift is freely presented, accepting it implies a reciprocal obligation on the part of the receiver. This obligation is most commonly expressed in the mutual exchange of gifts within families, communities, or between societies or states. But the scientific paper does not invite a direct return in the form of papers back. What the scientific community returns instead is status. Scientists with the highest status are those who have published the most original work, the most productive claims to new knowledge.

GIFT EXCHANGE DEMANDS HIGH STANDARDS
OF MORAL BEHAVIOUR

Because a gift carries no formal right to a reciprocal return (even though one is expected), scientists generally cannot overtly accept high status and must deny that this is their main goal. Humility and self-deprecation are expected of even the most exalted practitioners (although arrogance and self-importance are often on display). By keeping transactions at this primitive level of gift exchange, moral control over science has to be maintained by its practitioners; scientists are personally and morally responsible for their own actions. They are not formally managed and do not enter into formal contracts to exchange a service or product for financial reward, the basis of most professional practice. There are clearly tensions between the ideals of a self-policing cadre exchanging gifts, and the behaviours and rewards appropriate to modern careers. Scientists do behave as self-interested individuals in making knowledge claims, although they must still stress their credentials as members of the scientific community dedicated to free exchange of information with no overt personal reward. They achieve this by embedding their work in established knowledge by making citations to previous master works, and in turn hope to be cited as major contributors in the ongoing development of knowledge.

The great American sociologist of science, Robert Merton, noted in a seminal paper published in the 1940s that scientists did not seem to work to any clearly stated professional code. But he argued that their behavioural norms could be inferred from observing their actions. He believed that scientists worked according to four ideals.

Universalism

The truth claims of science are tested against impersonal criteria. The claims should be independent of the personal or social attributes of the protagonist (in theory, it does not matter who proposes a new knowledge claim). Meritocracy should rule in science and there should be no social barriers to entry.

Communism

Scientific knowledge, once acquired, is owned in common by the scientific community. There is full collaboration and openness among scientists and new scientific knowledge is assigned to the scientific community as a whole. Intellectual property is given away in exchange for esteem.

Disinterestedness

Scientists are detached from their work in the sense that they should have no personal, social, emotional or financial commitment to the results. This enables them to maintain an objective distance and this ideal is important in minimizing fraudulent behaviour. Honesty is also encouraged by the extensive peer review that scientific papers undergo before they are published.

Organized scepticism

Science always questions its own output and that of other institutions.

Scientists themselves are naturally quite impressed by this set of ideals, but the extent to which scientific behaviour is actually constrained by them is open to debate. The existence of professional standards is only one of the reasons we are invited to treat scientific claims with special respect. Also invoked are the especially rational nature of scientific thought and the ability to check the underpinning of knowledge claims by replicating observations and experiments, all of which are dependent on the existence of formalized networks of professional science communication.

UNINTENDED CONSEQUENCES OF MERTONIAN IDEALS

The most successful scientists are those who discover important ideas first. If two or more individuals or teams are moving towards a significant discovery, the stakes are high because all the credit will go to those who announce the discovery first, there is little reward in science for coming second. Merton argued that this explained the virulence of priority disputes in science, such as the famous spat between Newton and Leibniz over who first invented the calculus. This need to be first must surely stretch the concept of the common ownership of scientific knowledge to the limit and tempt people to bend the professional and ethical rules to gain advantage. There are too many ambitious juniors pushing for too few established academic posts and many scientists exist in a competitive snake-pit, constantly applying for short-term grants to survive. Getting a long-term, stable job calls for political, rhetorical and manipulative skills of a high order. As the late veteran science watcher John Ziman remarked in a commentary in *Nature* in 1999, 'What price now those noble (Mertonian) norms? Tied without budgets into a system of projects and proposals, budgets and assessments, how open, how disinterested, how self-critical, how riskily original can one afford to be?'

There may therefore be strong pressures on scientists not just to bend the conventions of professional behaviour but to abandon them. Scientific 'misconduct' of various kinds may be increasing, and well-publicized recent cases of scientific fraud lead many to assume that this is the case. However, no one really knows how much dishonesty there is in science now, and we have little idea how common it was in the past.

In the first place it is not easy to define exactly what is meant by misconduct in science. In the experimental sciences, the acceptable 'processing' of raw data varies widely between disciplines. At the practical level, some people, such as Kealey, argue that misrepresenting data is built into the way undergraduate students are taught to do practical work while others, such as James, claim that fraud is the inevitable by-product of taking risks to gain insight in a creative way. The key test for misconduct must be intention. Did a scientist intend to deceive his/her peers about the validity of his/her knowledge claim, or was he/she simply mistaken or over-enthusiastic? The problem lies, as in the law courts, in establishing such intention.

The US National Institutes of Health (NIH) has an Office of Research Integrity (ORI) which defines misconduct as 'fabrication, falsification and plagiarism (FFP)'. Scientists must not make up data (fabrication), present a false impression of the data they have obtained (falsification) or steal data from other people (plagiarism). Fictitious and stolen data do not seem to present any ethical problem. If either or both of these can be demonstrated, any perpetrator is going to have a hard time arguing that their actions were not dishonest. Falsification is much more difficult to prove because standard conventions of data selection can be exploited to give a deliberately false impression.

Clearly, journal editors, editorial boards and referees involved in the formal paraphernalia of peer review have a duty to look out for dishonest reports, although they are not that easy to spot. Unless the authors themselves confess, or independent evidence emerges, there is little editors can do, even if they are suspicious, although as all learned publication becomes electronic, anti-plagiarism software is being used by editors to spot that particular form of dishonesty, and has been useful in detecting self-plagiarism (authors making essentially the same claim in different places and at different times). Editors who use plagiarism-detecting software have shown that in many fields there is a persistent rump of plagiarized papers, often from non-English speaking authors who justify their behaviour on the grounds that they are plagiarizing in order to improve their writing of professional scientific text in English.

To the question 'how much scientific misconduct is there?', the only honest answer is that we do not know. Formal investigations of misconduct suggest it is rare. For instance, in the 4 years 1993 to 1997, the American ORI of the NIH received 1000 allegations of misconduct and investigated 150 of them. In these cases it found

76 researchers guilty of misconduct, 80% of whom had falsified research data. Denmark has had a similar committee since 1992, but had considered just 7 cases and substantiated only 4 up to 2000. This has led many people to embrace the 'few rotten apples' view of unprofessional behaviour. Most scientists are upright and honest but there are, it must be admitted, a few rogues who let the side down. Such rotten apples must be quickly extracted from the barrel of otherwise sound fruit, ideally using 'private' investigation and disgrace, with as little fuss as possible so as not to alarm funding bodies and the public.

Some scientists are reluctant to admit that those who commit fraud are rogues. The great British immunologist–philosopher, Peter Medawar, believed that fraud must be the consequence of over-enthusiasm for one's own ideas, a conviction that these ideas must be right. There is therefore a temptation to commit fraud in the certainty that real data to support a hypothesis must eventually emerge. Perhaps only an upper middle-class Englishman of impeccable manners could have been so sure that everyone had the same high standards as himself. Medawar simply could not understand how anyone trained in the professional norms of science could be dishonest or nakedly careerist.

But other evidence suggests that dishonesty in science is more ingrained. In 1993, Swazey published the results of a large survey in *The American Scientist* among graduate students and academic staff on misconduct in science and found plenty of evidence of dishonesty. Most seriously, 9% of respondents said they were aware of plagiarized or fabricated results within their faculties. Soon afterwards, an MIT report about its own undergraduates showed that 83% confessed to dishonest behaviour, including plagiarism and misusing data. We should not perhaps take too much notice of this result. As Kealey pointed out, undergraduate teaching would not work unless staff and students colluded in a fictional charade about what they were doing in practical classes, and it may have little implication for the honesty of those who go on to do actual research.

In a huge survey of over 3000 American early and mid-career scientists in 2005, Martinson and his colleagues also found an alarming amount of bad behaviour but considered it to be an underestimate because those with something to hide were unlikely to have responded to the survey. While outright fabrication, falsification and plagiarism were rare, behaviours like overlooking others' flawed data, changing elements of a study in response to funding source pressure, dropping observation points because of a 'gut feeling' that they were wrong, and inadequate record keeping, all seem rather common. The authors subscribed to the view that the pressure to behave badly came from over-severe competition for scarce resources.

More evidence keeps emerging that dishonesty in scientific research is not as rare as it should be. In 2008 Titus and her colleagues noted that, while the American Office of Research Integrity (ORI) conducted an average of 24 investigations each year into institutions where dishonesty was suspected, this is probably a massive under-measurement of the extent of the problem. They conducted a survey among over 2000 researchers of all grades funded by the American Department of Health and Human Sciences and found strong evidence of 201 serious cases of scientific misconduct over the 3-year period from 2002 to 2005.

If these data were representative of research scientist behaviour overall, the team estimate that there are over 2000 serious instances of scientific misconduct every year, implying that about 3% of the research community are dishonest (which while less than the 9% more crudely estimated by Swazey in 1993 still represents a serious problem). They suggest that the mismatch between institutional reports, ORI investigations and the 'true' levels of dishonesty arises because institutions have too many vested interests in sweeping these problems under the carpet, chiefly loss of reputation and research income which benefits the institution over and above the direct costs of grant-holding scientists. Dishonesty is not confined to junior ranks, indeed it may be at its most serious among team leaders who thus provide role models of how calculated and cautious dishonesty may constitute acceptable professional behaviour.

Things become even more reprehensible if leaders seem to protect themselves from accusations of dishonesty by blaming junior team members. For instance, Homme Hellinga, a leading biochemist involved in the synthesis of active enzymes from inactive protein molecules, accused one of his doctoral students of presenting false results when it emerged that the activity of one of his 'novo' synthesized enzymes was probably due to contamination with naturally occurring enzyme. Hellinga's student claims that her results were always unstable and contradictory and that she was unsure of what they meant, but claims Hellinga went ahead with an announcement of successful synthesis and only presented the best data in the published work. Hellinga claimed that he was unaware of their poor quality and blamed the student for giving him a false impression.

THE VIRUS OF DISHONESTY IS IN THE PHYSICAL SCIENCES AS WELL

Most concern about fraud has been in the life sciences. The physics community has always thought it had higher ethical standards, with precision measurements that are easily replicable, and the habit (at least in big particle physics) for large teams to be involved in experiments and interpreting results. But any complacency was blown away by a scandal emerging from one of the world's leading solid-state physics laboratories, Bell Labs of New Jersey. An investigating committee in October 2002 found the young German physicist Jan Hendrik Schon guilty of falsifying or fabricating data in 16 papers (from a total of 25 that were investigated).

This case is all the more astonishing for the prominence of the work. Schon went to Bell Labs from Germany in 1998 having completed a Ph.D. on building novel junction devices for semiconductors in solar cells, although he failed to get an actual system to work. Once at Bell he immediately impressed his supervisors and worked on a range of related cutting edge technologies. Schon published on a truly heroic scale, 74 papers in 2½ years, 15 of them in the maximum impact *Nature* and *Science*. Because fraud has never been seen as a significant issue in physics, neither the huge output of papers nor the replication failures initially attracted suspicion. People assumed that Schon was using a form of legitimate gamesmanship and withholding small amounts of vital information to hold up competitors (which interestingly is not regarded as unethical by the physics community). Post-exposure, several labs have tried to replicate his results without success.

Only when people at Bell Labs noticed that graphs published in two different papers were identical did anyone become suspicious. Schon admitted cheerfully that he had made an 'honest' mistake. But closer examination of more graphs aroused further suspicion; some of them fitted theoretical predictions far too closely. It was hard to believe they were generated from genuine experimental data and indeed they weren't. Schon admitted to applying mathematical functions to make curves look more realistic. He confessed to making presentation mistakes but insisted that the scientific effects he observed were real.

The case has stimulated three key questions, what was Schon's motivation, how did he expect to get away with it, and how did professional 'checks and balances' take so long to spot the problem? To the first there is no clear answer, although Schon's attitude may reflect that attributed to fraudsters by Peter Medawar; an excessively optimistic belief in the truth of his own theories. On the second, a number of unsavoury allegations have been circulating that *Nature* and *Science* behaved like competitive tabloids looking for scientific scoops and their peer review standards declined as a consequence, something both journals deny. The other foci of blame are Bell Labs management and Schon's co-workers. It seems there were no mechanisms for monitoring or investigating such cases while all his significant results were recorded when no one else was present. This suggests that labs and funding bodies in the physical sciences may have to develop tougher regulation over research in the same way the life sciences are sharpening up their checking procedures.

WIDESPREAD EVIDENCE OF FRAUD WOULD UNDERMINE THE AUTHORITY OF SCIENCE

Circumstantial evidence that scientific fraud may be on the increase must call into question whether the traditional belief that rigorous training and enculturation into the self-regulating institution of science, with peer review of papers as a failsafe procedure to detect dishonesty, is adequate any more. If the practice is growing because of competitive career pressure, pure science may no longer be able to rely on standards of personal trustworthiness and honesty to guarantee the integrity of the system. It is also hard to see how the machinery of professional communication, from traditional human peer review to elaborate electronic anti-plagiarism software, can detect scientists who make up or modify their data to create a false impression, or in the most pernicious cases commit deliberate fraud. The scientific community may have to contemplate introducing tighter external administration or management of scientific activity. Since peer-reviewing papers for introducing new knowledge is part of the traditional gift-exchange and self-regulating norms of science, any change towards more rigorous external management may well eventually undermine it as the standard method of making new knowledge claims in science.

BIBLIOGRAPHY

Abbott, A. (2002). Rising star crashes back to Earth. *Nature*, 3 October, **419**, 420–1.

Abbott, A. (2003). Ethics panel attacks environmental book. *Nature*, 16 January, **421**, 201.

Anon (2008). More than one bad apple. *Nature*, 16 October, **455**, 835.

Ayes, C. (2002). World's tiniest computer vanishes without trace. *The Times*, 28 September, 3.

Ball, P. (2003). Physicists fail to find saving grace for falsified research. *Nature*, 27 February, **421**, 878.

Briefing (1999). Science comes to terms with the lessons of fraud. *Nature*, 4 March, **398**, 13–17.

Brumfiel, G. (2002). Time to wise up? *Nature*, 11 July, **418**, 120–1.

Brumfiel, G. (2002). Misconduct finding at Bell Labs shakes physics community. *Nature*, **419**, 419–21.

Butler, D. (2008). Entire paper plagiarism caught by software. *Nature*, 9 October, **455**, 715.

Check Hayden, E. (2008). Designer debacle. A high-profile scientist, a graduate student and two major retractions. *Nature*, 15 May, **453**, 275–8.

Collins, H. M. (1992). *Changing Order. Replication and Induction in Scientific Practice*. Chicago: University of Chicago Press.

Dalton, R. (1999). NIH office plans research on misconduct. *Nature*, 8 July, **400**, 99.

Dalton, R. (2002). 2002 in context. *Nature*, 19/26 December, **420**, 728–9.

Farrar, S. (2002). For whom the Bell tolls? *Times Higher Education Supplement*, 8 July, 12.

Feder, N. and Stewart, W. W. (2008). Integrity: juniors see leaders gain from calculated dishonesty. *Nature*, 31 July, **452**, 574.

Giles, J. (2004). Plagiarism in Cambridge physics lab prompts calls for guidelines. *Nature*, 1 January, **427**, 3.

Giles, J. (2005). Taking on the cheats. *Nature*, 19 May, **435**, 258–9.

Giles, J. (2006). The trouble with replication. *Nature*, 27 July, **442**, 344–7.

Hagstrom, W. O. (1982). Gift giving as an organizing principle in science. In Barnes, B. and Edge, D. (eds.). *Science in Context: Readings in the Sociology of Science*. Milton Keynes: Open University Press.

James, W. H. (1995). Fraud and hoaxes in science. *Nature*, 12 October, **377**, 474.

Kealey, T. (1997). No sleaze please, we're scientists. *The Guardian*, 27 March, Online section, 14.

Martinson, B., Anderson, M. and de Vries, R. (2005). Scientists behaving badly. *Nature*, 9 June, **435**, 737–8.

Medawar, P. (1991). *The Threat and the Glory*. Oxford: Oxford University Press.

Merton, R. K. (1973). Institutionalized patterns of evaluation in science. In Merton, R. K. *The Sociology of Science*. Chicago: University of Chicago Press.

Minkel, J. R. (2002). Reality check. Alleged fraud gets physicists thinking about misconduct. *Scientific American*, November, 10–11.

Morris, E. (2006). Should journals police scientific fraud? *Nature*, 2 February, **439**, 520–1.

Sabbagh, K. (1999). *A Rum Affair*. London: Penguin.

Titus, S. L., Wells, J. A. and Rhoades, L. J. (2008). Repairing research integrity. *Nature*, 19 June, **453**, 980–2.

Ziman, J. (1999). Rules of the game of doing science. *Nature*, 19 August, **400**, 721.

Zinsberg, D. (1994). A big stink in the labs. *Times Higher Education Supplement*, 14 January, 7.

5 Separating the wheat from the chaff: peer review on trial

New times call for new men. The economy of computer and communication technologies has spawned new millionaires. Like successful businessmen of previous generations, they have turned to philanthropy and are giving their money away to good causes. In the past, if such philanthropists invested in science or technology, they had projects evaluated by the traditional process of peer review. Proposals were considered by panels of scientists specialized in the fields concerned.

But the new silicon millionaires do not favour this model. They want things to be riskier and more like their own business practice. They select areas of science that interest them personally (often biomedicine or neurophysiology) and target funds there. They often hire a leading expert in the chosen field as a technical advisor to network with other field leaders and identify people with interesting ideas whom they encourage to apply for funds. They are trying to spot winners, with the inevitable fall-out of failed projects hopefully counterbalanced by enough successes. The system has an element of peer review (opinions of field leaders are sought) and some early promise in track record is necessary, but much more emphasis is placed on searching out promising innovators to make applications that look like business plans. The millionaires make quick and less bureaucratic decisions than conventional funding agencies using traditional peer review, although the risks of failure are higher.

These new philanthropists are not the only ones questioning peer review as a gold standard in quality control in choosing projects to fund. The dissatisfaction with peer review runs deeper and some people are calling into question the whole system of quality control in science based on review and its modifications.

PEER REVIEW AS THE CORNERSTONE OF QUALITY CONTROL IN SCIENCE

Academic papers published in journals are the main vehicles scientists use to make new knowledge claims. A decision by a journal editor on whether to publish a particular paper depends on peer review by fellow scientists of the value of the claims being made. Peer review and variations on it are also used to judge the potential value of future research in applications made to funding agencies. These processes are central to the 'professional' operation of science. The scientific community itself decides what science should be done, what scientific knowledge is valid, and these decisions are mediated through the elaborate mechanisms of professional science communication.

Systems of evaluation, of which peer review is an example, work best if there are clear objectives against which to judge success. For basic research this is difficult because the ultimate objective, 'new knowledge', is unpredictable. So, how are good scientists selected and monitored, and what characteristics make them successful? Virtually every performance indicator and management mechanism in science is a variant on peer review. Its most familiar expressions include: voting for higher membership grades of learned societies, refereeing of papers before publication in learned journals, choosing individuals for the award of prizes or honours, counting citations to assess impact (the more an author's work is cited by others, the more this author must have influenced them, which implies that this work is good), and the review and evaluation of proposals to carry out future research made in applications for financial support.

Most of these are historical judgements, with the exception of the review of future research proposals. Peer review may be at its least reliable in this latter context and its use in journal refereeing may scarcely be better. The quality of judgement might increase the greater the amount of data there is to go on, but the deliberations of the Committee for the award of Nobel Prizes (which makes its decision on the track records of nominees) do not inspire confidence even in the quality of such historical judgements. The records show such judgements to be rife with political horse-trading and personal and institutional bias.

Bibliometrics

There has been considerable pressure from civil servants, politicians and businessmen to use citation counting (bibliometric analysis) instead of peer review because it allows non-scientists to join the evaluation game without knowing anything about the work being considered. There are simply numbers to compare. The Bibliometric School validate their procedures by showing how closely their conclusions about quality match those derived from conventional peer review. However, showing that bibliometric measures correlate with peer review says little about what is actually being measured. For instance, can we say how the citation pattern for a given paper reflects its quality? Harry Collins was among the first to suggest that the connections may not be obvious. He strings out a long list of reasons why papers might be cited and not all of them are related to the quality of the work reported. The reasons may have more to do with the cultural conventions of the scientific community, some of which have nothing to do with judgement of good or bad science. People have questioned the basis of citation data and shown that errors occur with important bibliometric indices such as journal impact factors. These are measures of how important journals are to the scientific community, judged on the basis of how often papers published in these journals are cited by papers published in other journals, also ranked by impact.

Despite these doubts, publishing in top journals with the greatest impact factors is now so important in science career development that huge amounts of energy are spent trying to get papers into target journals. Errors constantly creep into the bibliometric calculations of impact factors and into the raw data upon which they are based, and with funding agencies and promotion panels taking more notice of citation patterns and impact factors, the potential for mistakes in allocating resources and credit may be serious.

Ian Sample presents data showing that many leading world scientists (as judged by other criteria) are also in the top 50 as measured by citation counting bibliometrics. But the data are biased towards American male-authored biology papers because this is the profile of the writers of the greatest volume of papers. Any high-flying, female, non-American, physical scientist will find it harder to figure in the index. Most of the top cited individual papers describe useful experimental methods, even when authored by scientists with reputations for making new scientific knowledge claims. This implies that the 'best' science (as judged by bibliometrics) consists of biological methods work by male scientists from American laboratories, a conclusion which seems inherently unlikely.

Peer review of academic papers

Peer review of papers submitted to journals produces judgements of the quality of work soon after it has been done. Pioneering work by Pearlman and Dean suggests that scientists consider five factors as 'biases' in the process, although that only has meaning if objective standards of quality actually exist. The 'biases' are that institutional journals favour authors connected with the institution; reviewers prefer papers that confirm status quo in method, content and approach; they prefer papers from people who produce work similar to their own; they are heavily influenced by the status of the institution of the author; and they find faults rather than virtues. Furthermore, reviewers seldom agree, casting more doubt on the existence of any consistent set of quality standards. This puts journal editors in a potentially powerful position because they can resolve peer review differences in whatever way they wish, although anecdote suggests they are actually quite cautious. But in extreme cases, this editorial power could negate peer review altogether, rendering the whole laborious process pointless.

However, other evidence suggests that editors do try to balance the best interests of potential authors with the expectations of the scientific community. The three factors which dominate editorial decisions on what to publish in rank order are: firstly the author's grasp of experimental design and sophistication of methodology, secondly the theoretical relevance and creativity of the author's ideas and thirdly the social value of the author's findings. Further evidence of the dominance of practical issues in editorial thinking comes from the self-reflection of a medical journal editor (T.P. Strossel) selecting work for his journal, *The Journal of Clinical Investigation*. Less than 2% of all submitted papers were accepted without amendment in a sample year, 1983. The rest were rejected or only accepted after revision. Throughout, the emphasis in the various reasons for rejection was the amount and quality of experimental data. This reflects the ongoing influence of the original Baconian insistence on observation and experiment as the root of natural philosophy, and that the interpretation and argument built on the results is clearly dependent on them.

Journal editors are therefore obsessed with the mechanics of experimental practice although Sternberg argues that papers of high intellectual importance (and the ultimate point of science is to generate intellectual interpretations and explanations, not to generate data) do not necessarily have high standards of experimental design or execution in terms of data quality. Strossel polled a panel of 15 previous editors of the *Journal of Clinical Investigation* about the quality of the output in the journal in the sample year 1983. They reckoned about a third of the papers were excellent, a rump of just over half were competent, appropriate for publication but not very inspired, while some 15% should not have been published at all. Another classic early piece of research on peer review by Peters and

Ceci took 12 previously published papers, invented new names and institutions for them, and then resubmitted them for publication. The results were revealing; many of the papers were rejected, sometimes from the journals that had previously published them.

But these comments about the failure of peer review to recognize the best scientific work may be unfair. Its institutional task may be less elevated, perhaps simply to guarantee baseline competence; identifying the starters in the race for scientific merit rather than picking winners. It may just certify that published work reaches a minimal standard. More pessimistically it seems that, despite the time-consuming checks and balances at the heart of journal peer review, much published science is mediocre stuff, although some argue the wastage may be an inevitable overhead for the nuggets of high-quality science; a necessary spoil-tip from the scientific gold mine.

Pure science undermined by commercial funding pressures?

The increasing level of commercial funding of basic research means that it can no longer be considered disinterested in a Mertonian sense because the outcome of the work has implications for firms putting up the money and recipient universities have strong financial interests in research income. Many academic journals respond to this problem by making authors reveal the sources of their funding. For example, it makes sense to know, in evaluating medical research on the effects of smoking, if authors are funded by the tobacco industry. But things may already be out of control. Medical agencies working for pharmaceutical companies now generate ghost-written articles for submission to biomedical journals, reviewing research in a way favourable to company interests. They then get bona fide researchers or clinicians to put their names to the work, often for a fee. The ghost-writer and pharmaceutical company involvement are concealed from the journal editors and the paper appears under the name of the bona fide researcher. By their nature, the extent of these practices is unknown, but they represent a serious threat to the integrity of biomedical science in clinical context.

More evidence of such unethical practices has emerged as a by-product of the publication of internal documents from the pharmaceutical company Merck after a lawsuit brought in the US to force it to withdraw its painkiller Rofecoxib (Vioxx). Analysis of these documents by Ross and colleagues and by Psaty and Kronmal reveal circumstantial evidence of ghost-writing by apparently independent academic scientists, whose only contributions to published papers seems to have been some light editing. Too many researchers who receive support from industrial interests fail to record their income from these sources, leaving themselves open to accusations of corruption if their research publications relate to those industrial interests. In America, Senator Charles Grassley has been on a mission to expose such behaviour among leading psychiatrists and pharmaceutical companies marketing psycho-active drugs. Peer review on its own clearly cannot provide much of a defence against malpractices like these.

Peer review in grant application: its most
unsatisfactory use?
In grant applications for future research the most discussed systems of peer review are those of the American National Institutes of Health (NIH) and National Science Foundation (NSF), although similar agencies in Britain and Europe use the same principles. Researchers prepare a proposal for a project on paper, which is sent to the central secretariat of the grant body, which commissions written peer reviews of the proposal. After review, the proposals are discussed by a committee to decide which ones to fund.

There is widespread dissatisfaction with the system. The main charge is that it favours institutional and personal elites, 'old-boy networks' or 'cronyism' of various types. There has been a groundswell of opinion that the procedure simply does not make the best funding choices. Among the criticisms are the high-mindedness expected when reviewers are themselves after the same pot of gold, that grant managers can easily 'pack' the reviewers for a proposal to produce a thumbs-up or thumbs-down as desired, and that it wastes too much valuable time that scientists could better spend actually doing research. It is also said to disfavour innovation because of the 'orphan' nature of inter-disciplinary proposals and the reluctance of people to expose their best ideas to rivals. There is also little evidence that the ability to make a good proposal on paper correlates with the ability to carry it out.

Critics of the system like Rustrum Roy have long argued that grants should be awarded on the basis of applicants' previous track record, not on peer review of each new proposal. Track record is a historically validated measure of worth anchored in previous achievement and seems inherently sounder than guessing the value of a proposal in isolation. But there are arguments against past achievement as a reliable measure of future prospect. It might lead to discrimination against younger scientists without such achievement although younger researchers may have more innovative ideas. If peer review does not really measure quality, quality selection may occur elsewhere in the scientific institution, perhaps within the social organization of the core elite.

Where do scientific value and quality lie?

In her book, *Scientific Elite. Nobel Laureates in the United States*, Harriet Zuckerman investigated master–apprentice relationships between different generations of elite scientists. The chance of a bright young scientist becoming a member of the super-publishing, well-resourced elite is closely tied to the status of the supervisors with whom he/she chooses to serve in doctoral and post-doctoral apprenticeship. Good apprentices know how to persuade good masters to take them on. As to what is transferred between master and apprentice, that remains controversial. Zuckerman thinks it is socialization into the cultural conventions of elite science rather than any specific knowledge transfer or technical know-how. Standards of scientific performance and taste seem to be transferred from elite masters to apprentices, one of the few instances where issues of value and quality are made explicit. Zuckerman argues that elite scientists exert scientific taste by choosing important problems and knowing what are elegant solutions. Within the scientific community, masters 'look after' favoured apprentices with co-publication arrangements, introductions and recommendations to the right people and so on.

Alvin Weinberg is another commentator who has had much to say about mechanisms for measuring quality in basic science. He is best known for discriminating between internal and external criteria of value judgement. The internal factors are efficient conduct of research, procedural rules and customs embedded in experimental design, practice and interpretation, evolved from long 'craft' practice. The external criteria are technological, social and scientific merit. Weinberg defined scientific merit in terms of the impact of research in one field on surrounding scientific fields, since he believes explanatory unity to be the prime goal of science. On his criterion, molecular biology has high scientific merit because of the influence it has had on surrounding fields. Weinberg elaborated his original ideas by distinguishing between two aspects of the internal criteria in science judgement which he calls 'administration' and 'practice'.

Administration is deciding what to do, practice is getting it done. Peer review seems to be geared to matters of practice, carrying out experimental work correctly, drawing defensible conclusions from it and the like, while matters of administration (the point and meaning of the work) go by default. Yet it is just these questions of choice of problem that seem to distinguish the elite from the rest. Weinberg argues that choice of problem is the basis of good scientific taste, which is otherwise seldom made explicit. It is the 'taste' of individual scientists that lies at the heart of scientific quality and value. Weinberg, like Zuckerman, says this is seldom made explicit; it simply resides with the elite.

This view is probably too simple because the notion of a self-perpetuating elite with exquisite scientific taste does not cope well with innovative marginality. In many cases, key new ideas or scientists have come from places which are, academically speaking, the outer darkness, although they may represent 'special' cases of innovation dependent on forging new sub-fields where there are no existing experts. The simple notion of good individual taste may also be inadequate because it allocates credit to individuals, when science is a team effort. The automatic allocation of credit to team leaders may be reaching scandalous proportions. Junior team members, students and post-doctoral researchers often have their credit ruthlessly taken from them by leaders, but find it hard to protest because their career development depends on references. No junior can afford to upset their leader by claiming credit for him/herself if this would destroy their career.

Unlocking evidence of institutional sexism

Wenneras and Wold undertook a comprehensive analysis on peer review in grant application, published in 1997. They investigated procedures used by the Swedish Medical Research Council (MRC) in awarding post-doctoral fellowships. They wanted to find out if sex discrimination in the award of grants accounted for the absence of women in the middle and upper ranks of the biomedical research community. The Swedish MRC uses a complex evaluation procedure, which translates written comments on proposals into numerical scores and grant decisions are taken largely on the basis of these numerical summaries. Wenneras and Wold found that all female applicants were consistently underscored compared with male applicants. They evaluated the parameters underlying these scores and could not find any grounds other than gender for this difference and concluded that the procedures are innately sexist.

The lower female scores might have been because the research fields of female applicants had lower priority, or the female applicants all came from low status institutions. But analysing these possibilities still revealed gender as the most influential factor. The bias against women was only compensated if they had affiliation links with members of the review panel. The study therefore suggests that institutional sexism and nepotism are rife in review procedures. The Swedish MRC was genuinely shocked by these findings and introduced procedures to try to correct them.

Ten years after Wenneras and Wold, data published by Sherry Towers in 2008 seem to reveal a comparable situation in particle physics. She analysed data on the productivity of post-doctoral scientists associated with the DZero particle detector at the American Fermilab as measured by how many internal reports each researcher produced. This suggests that women are both over-committed to 'service work' on maintenance of instruments (which does not lead to published papers) and are more productive in generating internal papers than men. Yet women are given fewer opportunities to present their work at conferences. Such presentations are essential in raising young researchers' profiles. This lack of presentation opportunities seemed to lead to fewer women obtaining academic posts than males with similar or less productive profiles. An element of institutional sexism therefore seems to be built into the organization of at least this major physics site.

PEER REVIEW IS DEAD: LONG LIVE PEER REVIEW
Analysing the products and patterns of professional communication has revealed cultural flaws in the institution of science; for instance, in bibliometric distortions and institutional sexism and nepotism. It demonstrates once again just how central are communication systems to the institution of science. This review of the workings of peer review clearly shows that all is not well, which has led to increasing dissatisfaction with the practice and calls for its reform or abolition. The arrival of the internet is loosening things up, and in grant evaluation more attention is being paid to research project choice in response to forces from outside science. One of these is popular taste and demand (as we will explore in Part II), a trend that scientists naturally tend to mistrust because it downgrades their professional status as judges of their own activities. But the application of external controls might lead to a fairer deal for the scientific community as a whole, rather than perpetuating the privileges of internally determined elites. It might also show that external management can be an alternative to peer review in quality control. But peer review has proved remarkably robust in the face of criticism in the past and may well survive more

or less intact in the future because, like democracy, it may turn out to be the best option from a pool of flawed choices.

BIBLIOGRAPHY

Adam, D. (2002). The counting house. *Nature*, 14 February, **415**, 726–9.

Adam, D. and Knight, J. (2002). Publish and be damned.... *Nature*, 24 October, **419**, 772–6.

Ball, P. (2006). Prestige is factored into journal ratings. *Nature*, 16 February, **439**, 770–1.

Barnett, A. (2003). Revealed: how drug firms 'hoodwink' medical journals. *The Observer*, 7 December, 15.

Boseley, S. (1998). Medical studies 'rubbish'. *The Guardian*, 24 June, 5.

Braben, D. (1996). The repressive regime of peer-review bureaucracy. *Physics Review*, November, 13–14.

Braben, D. (1994). *To be a Scientist*. Oxford: Oxford University Press.

Brumfiel, G. (2008). Data show extent of sexism in physics. *Nature*, 24 April, **452**, 918.

Campanario, J.M. (1995). Commentary. On influential books and journal articles initially rejected because of negative referees' evaluations. *Science Communication*, **16**, 304–25.

Collins, H. (1992). *Times Higher Education Supplement*, 10 October, 15.

Cressey, D. (2008). Merck accused of disguising its role in research. *Nature*, 17 April, **452**, 791.

Dalton, R. (2001). Peers under pressure. *Nature*, 13 September, **413**, 102–4.

Davis, S.C. (2004). An unbiased teacher? Scientists' views on the ethics and value of pharmaceutical industry driven medical education. Unpublished M.Sc. Dissertation, Imperial College London.

Elliot Major, L. (1998). Safety standard under fire. *The Guardian*, Higher Education Section, 7 July, xxiii.

Fugh-Berman, A. (2005). Not in my name. *The Guardian*, 21 April, Life Section, 9.

Giles, J. (2006). Stacking the deck. *Nature*, 16 March, **440**, 270–2.

Gura, T. (2001). Biomedical philanthropy, silicon valley style. *Nature*, 8 March, **410**, 140–3.

Jackson, D.N. and Rushton, J.P. (eds.) (1987). *Scientific Excellence, Origins and Assessment*. California: Sage Publications.

Jasanoff, S. (1985). Peer review in the regulatory process. *Science, Technology and Human Values*, **10**, 20–32.

Lawrence, P.A. (2003). The politics of publication. *Nature*, 20 March, **422**, 259–61.

Lock, S. (1991). *A Difficult Balance, Editorial Peer Review in Medicine*. London: BMJ Publishing Group.

Merton, R. (1988). The Matthew effect in science, II. Cumulative advantage and the and the symbolism of intellectual property. *Isis*, **79**, 606–23.

Monastersky, R. (2005). The number that's devouring science. *The Chronicle of Higher Education*, 14 October (accessed as e-site The Chronicle: 10/14/2005).

Pearson, H. (2006). Credit where credit's due. *Nature*, 30 March, **440**, 591–2.

Peters, D. P. and Ceci, S. J. (1982). Peer review practices of psychological journals: the fate of published articles submitted again. *Behavioural and Brain Sciences*, **5**, 187–255.

Psaty, B. M. and Kronmal, R. A. (2008). Reporting mortality findings in trials of Rofecoxib for Alzheimer's Disease and cognitive impairment: a case study based on documentation from Rofecoxib litigation. *Journal of the American Medical Association*, **299** (15), 1813–17.

Revill, J. (2005). How the drugs giant and a lone academic went to war. *The Observer*, 4 December, 10–11.

Ross, J. S., Hill, K. P., Egilman, D. S. and Krumholz, H. M. (2008). Guest authorship and ghost writing in publications relating to Rofecoxib. A case study of industry documents from Rofecoxib litigation. *Journal of the American Medical Association*, **299** (15), 1800–12.

Roy, R. (1984). Alternatives to review by peers: a contribution to the theory of scientific choice. *Minerva*, **XXII**, 316–28.

Sample, I. (2003). The giants of science. *The Guardian*, 25 September, Life Section, 4–6.

Smith, R. (1997). Peer review: reform or revolution? Time to open up the black box of peer review. *British Medical Journal*, **315**, 759–60.

Sternberg, R. J. (1988). *The Nature of Creativity*. Cambridge: Cambridge University Press.

Strossel, T. P. (1985). Refinement in biomedical communication. A case study. *Science, Technology and Human Values*, **10**, 39–43.

Taylor, R. and Giles, J. (2005). Cash interests taint drug advice. *Nature*, 20 October, **437**, 1070–1.

Travis, G. D. J. and Collins, H. M. (1991). New light on old boys: cognitive and institutional particularisation in the peer review system. *Science, Technology and Human Values*, **16**, 322–41.

Towers, S. (2008). A case study of gender bias at the postdoctoral level in physics and its resulting impact on the academic career achievement of females. *arXiv: 0804.2026v3* [*physics.soc-ph*], 19 April.

Watts, G. (2000). Are peers prejudiced? *Times Higher Education Supplement*. 12 May.

Weinberg, A. (1984). Values in science: unity as a criterion of scientific choice. *Minerva*, **XXII**, 1–12.

Wenneras, C. and Wold, A. (1997). Nepotism and sexism in peer-review. *Nature*, 22 May, **387**, 341–3.

Zuckerman, H. (1977). *Scientific Elite. Nobel Laureates in the United States*. London: Collier Macmillan.

Part II Science for the public: what science do people need and how might they get it?

6 The public understanding of science (PUS) movement and its problems

Daisy the cat had a pretty good life all things considered, finally fading away when she was nearly 22 years old. Five years earlier she had urinary problems and we took her to the vet. Tests suggested she had partial kidney failure and the vet recommended special diets but Daisy refused to touch them. We gave up and let her eat what she liked and she lived on happily until her last few frail months. We buried her in the garden, the spot marked by a jovial, pipe-smoking concrete gnome.

The vet who diagnosed Daisy's kidney problems was a young and modern man. Veterinary practice is firmly based on scientific understanding and the vet told us a science story, explaining renal physiology and what had gone wrong and how a change of diet might help. I used to teach physiology and I think he gave an accurate 3-minute lecture. But most pet owners don't have past lives as physiology teachers, so the intense lesson would mean little to them. The information only makes sense if the listener already has a good grounding in the area; some familiarity with the vocabulary and concepts. Otherwise, while the lesson is delivered in good English, it conveys no real meaning. What we really needed was prognosis; how serious is this condition, how life-threatening or shortening is it likely to be, what happens if she doesn't like the diets, is she now or likely in the future to be in pain? But on these matters the vet was silent, and as he had other patients barking and mewing outside there was no time to ask him.

The prognosis we wanted is more uncertain than the science lecture he gave and I think the vet preferred to impart reliable information than make vague statements. But, despite all the advances in scientific diagnosis, I doubt that advice about the care of ageing cats with kidney failure has changed much over recent years. Yet communicating the science of veterinary medicine has become a priority (to command respect and bolster authority), while the advice from which owners and their pets would really benefit may be going by default.

It is not only vets and doctors who are communicating science. Scientists also feel increasingly obliged to describe their work in popular terms. While their motivation may be different, the outcome has been similar; the public does not seem to understand what they are saying. The non-communication between vets and pet owners is repeated when scientists try to explain what they do (and why they do it) to lay audiences, because of tensions over what ought to be communicated, and for whose benefit the communication is taking place.

The contemporary impetus for scientists in the UK to tell the public more about their work has come from the scientists rather than from the public. It is done to foster the social contract between publicly funded scientists and the people who ultimately pay for them: taxpaying voters. If there is to be a consensual social contract, both parties, scientists and the public, must feel that science is of benefit. Some scientists have taken this to mean that the public has a duty to learn and understand what scientists are doing. But the social contract implies that the public also has a right to influence what science is done, and that scientists should engage with the interests of the public, often different from what interests scientists. These questions of what science to communicate, to whom, and with what effects for all parties, have turned out to be contentious.

COPUS AND THE SCIENTIFICALLY ILLITERATE PUBLIC
Recent concern among the UK science community with 'public understanding of science' dates from 1985 and a Royal Society committee

report (chaired by Sir Walter Bodmer), *The public understanding of science*. This report identified clear public ignorance of scientific facts and theories and argued that this reflected a lack of public approval for science. The committee advocated that more communication of science to the public should take place.

Any contract is an agreement between the parties who commission a service and those who provide it, and the commissioners usually monitor progress through various channels. Quite a number of such channels were already in place for science before the Royal Society suggested more communication with the public. For instance, the ethos of pure science demands that researchers openly publish their results, although the volume of scientific papers, specialized language and inaccessibility of journals conspire to make direct public access to science difficult. Publicly funded researchers make constant reports to their immediate supervisors, senior civil servants, research councils, parliamentary committees and government ministers. But, the defect of these communication channels is that they are private between consenting technocrats, and the public has little access to them.

Strangely, the public was not the contracting party most alarmed by failures of monitoring and communication, it was the scientific community who felt they were inadequate. In the mid 1980s that community was feeling hard done by; there had been stagnation in public funding for research over the previous 15 years and scientists were unable to convince government that this was a bad thing, that less science (with potential benefit to society) was being done than ought to be done.

Since governments determine public science funding and Western governments are democratically elected, one way to put pressure on government would be to persuade voters that science should be more generously supported. A public better informed about the wonders of science would surely appreciate its value and support the scientific community? The authors of the report did not see that the opposite might happen: a better-informed public could be a more critical public, asking more searching questions about what scientists were doing and why they were doing it. Indeed, longitudinal surveys of public responses to science in America already showed that lack of understanding of science was no barrier to support for it. Despite the fact that only a minority of American adults describe themselves as scientifically literate, surveys repeatedly show that most Americans are interested in science and technology, believe science and technology have improved their lives and continue to support government funding for it.

The Bodmer Report argued that a lack of public understanding of science had three undesirable consequences. A lack of trained scientific and technological personnel might slow economic progress; a populace with no science knowledge could not take informed democratic decisions about issues involving science; and a scientifically ignorant public is a culturally deprived public; it misses out on the pleasures and insights that a deeper understanding of science can bring.

By the early 1990s, various bodies representing UK science, including the Royal Society itself, the British Association for the Advancement of Science and the science and engineering research councils were sufficiently enthusiastic about the report to fund schemes to encourage scientists to improve communication of science to the public. These included setting up a permanent Royal Society Committee on the Public Understanding of Science (COPUS) with a budget for public understanding initiatives and projects, and British Association for the Advancement of Science Media Fellowships. The latter allowed scientists to spend periods as interns in media organizations finding out how journalists work so that, on return to their laboratories, they could become more effective communicators. The research councils set aside small percentages of their budgets to encourage scientists to communicate their work to the public and John Durant (newly appointed Assistant Director at the Science Museum) took up an adjunct post at Imperial College London as the first UK Professor of Public Understanding of Science in 1991.

Durant set out why the 'public understanding' agenda was important in an article in *Science and Public Affairs*. He put forward similar cultural, practical and political arguments to those in the Bodmer Report. His cultural point was that science is the most significant success of modern Western civilization. Science had been culturally important in the past because it had philosophical or theological implications such as 'where did the universe and the human species come from and what purpose do they serve'? Astronomy, cosmology, natural history and evolution remain the most popularized sciences, reflecting this long association with philosophical and spiritual concerns.

Durant's practical argument was that we live in technology-based societies, which require us to grasp how things work and the science that lies behind them. But strong counter-arguments exist to this position. Firstly, it is not true that technology is solely dependent on underlying science; technological development is much more than applied science. Secondly, the uses to which technologies are put have as much to do with cultural value as with their technical base. Thirdly, the science needed to discuss issues like public health or appliance safety is of the most basic kind, easily grasped by nearly everybody without a need for deep understanding. Fourthly, if there was a demand for scientifically competent employees, market pressure would reflect this with rising status and pay for scientists and technologists. Until recently in the UK there has been little evidence of such demand, although slowing Western economic growth after the deregulation and globalization which began in the mid 1980s may prompt a sharp change in attitude. The Council for British Industry (CBI) pleaded loudly in August 2008 for a large increase in the numbers of students taking science and technology degrees.

Durant's political argument was that, in democracies where issues have scientific or technological dimensions, citizens cannot take rational decisions unless they understand the science involved. This is the British version of the older American 'scientific literacy' position. However, it is hard to see exactly what the concerned citizen needs. Given that issues crop up from many different scientific areas, how can the citizen ever learn all the science he/she might need to know? Does he/she need to know a body of scientific facts or would a grasp of the methods and processes of science be better? If the latter, what understanding of these methods is appropriate; a grasp of experimental and observational procedure perhaps, or of philosophical questions of theory choice, or the sociology of professional practice and cultural context, perhaps restricted (as the sociologists Collins and Pinch suggest) to scientific controversies?

There is no universally agreed methodology of science and no core body of scientific knowledge upon which the ordinary citizen can draw. In any case, as Durant concedes, political decisions and moral judgements are matters of value, not the matters of fact with which science deals. His examples of environmental debates are illuminating. He asks what ordinary people are to make of advertisements run by British Nuclear Fuels in favour of nuclear power as opposed to those run by anti-nuclear campaigners like Greenpeace, when both routinely carry scientific data in support of their opposing positions, often using the very same data. In practice, more scientific knowledge does not help because the science itself may be too uncertain. The multiple interpretations that can be taken from the data are not resolvable scientifically because the science, to use Funtowicz and Ravetz's terminology, is 'post-normal' and more uncertain than the political and social frameworks in which decisions involving science have to be taken.

SCIENTISTS' SCIENCE: THE WRONG SCIENCE
FOR MUCH OF THE PUBLIC?
What characterizes both the British Public Understanding of Science and the American Scientific Literacy movements is that they are framed in the interests of scientists who feel that the public are ignorant about science and that such ignorance is a bad thing. The proposed solution is for scientists to spend more time informing the public about what they do. The public understanding agenda

was therefore set up using an overtly 'cognitive deficit' model of communication. Since surveys show the public does not know much science (in the sense of textbook facts and theories), the scientific community should therefore tell them about these missing facts and theories, as often as possible, using all available media and opportunities.

Such a model makes perfect sense for preaching to the already or part converted. There are reasonably large numbers of ordinary people on both sides of the Atlantic who are deeply interested in science. They benefit from an increasing availability of popular science in the media. But the scientific community's PUS agenda aimed to reach those who were not already interested in science. A straightforward agenda of popular communication of textbook science and reports from the research front may not work. This material fascinates scientists but does not necessarily interest anyone else. Competitive exercises like the UK's 'Fame Lab' initiative may therefore have only limited success. Fame Lab invites young working scientists to explain what they do as excitingly as possible to judges who choose what they believe are the most dynamic presenters. This probably misses the point; the problem does not lie in how science is presented but rather in what science is presented and in what context.

Research in the early 1990s had already shown that public communication of scientific or technical information in cognitive deficit mode was seldom satisfactory. Irwin demonstrated that communication to at-risk public groups about industrial hazards in emergencies is extremely poor. The information is seldom couched in terms to which the target audience can relate. It would be better set up within the cultural framework of the audience, not within the concerns of industrial technologists. Such communication often uses inappropriately technical language and fails to express warnings in terms of public benefit rather than in terms of those of the warning institutions. In the parallel case of biomedical information provided by doctors to patients (or vets to pet owners), patients often find little of value in what they are told. Patients learn more valuable things from other patients or their carers who share their concerns and cultural context.

The practical lesson is that any professional group with a technical message must understand the cultural milieu of the receiving audience and tailor the presentation and content of the message to that milieu. The political lesson may be that, to an extent, the social contract between scientists and the public has broken down and science has become divorced from the concerns and interests of the people whose taxes pay for it. The scientific community needs to understand more of what the public see as important issues and address these more directly. Some radicals go so far as to advocate what Irwin calls 'Citizen Science', in which the public contributes to science through extended peer review. However, there is a counter-argument that science should not respond directly to current public need. It is often not possible to solve problems with present scientific knowledge and progress in pure science may produce insights that will help to solve a currently intractable problem. This is the argument that scientists have always used to undertake pure science of interest to them; that it will ultimately yield useful consequences. Resources spent on pure science now are an investment for greater (if unspecified) benefits in the long run. The argument clearly has merit, but the principles of democratic oversight suggest that research entirely determined in the interests of scientists may not necessarily be the best option.

PROBLEMS ARISING FROM A COGNITIVE DEFICIT COMMUNICATION MODEL

Early in the debate over public understanding, the sociologist Mike Michael made a useful distinction between 'science-in-general'; reliable, textbook science, and 'science-in-particular'; science applied to people's everyday situations. Science in the first category is authoritative and isolated from social and political effects, while, in the second, knowledge is useful for ordinary people in their personal lives. In that context, textbook science often loses its Olympian detachment and can fail. The abstracted, verified scientific principles may either not work in particular cultural contexts, or may need to be investigated in particular local conditions. Despite these local failures, people continue to regard textbook science (science-in-general) as worthy of respect because science still carries great authority with the lay public, despite the PUS fear that it does not.

One area where there has been considerable debate has been the perception of risk. People do not understand risk in a statistical sense. The sociologist Brian Wynne argues that the public cannot be expected to understand the mathematics of risk, it is a complex technical matter, and no helpful attempt at popular communication will work. Members of the public do nevertheless make evaluations of risk, but on the grounds of what trust they place in the 'authorities' making the risk assessment. Technical issues are properly the job of experts. Wynne argues that judging the trustworthiness of the institutions and people making the risk assessment is the rational thing for the public to do. Scientists should be glad that 'science-in-general' is a major source of trust, but be more sensitive to the fact that it often needs severe mediation to have value in a local context.

In a classic case study Wynne analysed the Cumbrian sheep-farming community's experiences of expert technical advice following the Chernobyl nuclear reactor accident in May 1986. The incident led to caesium isotope fallout on upland Cumbrian pastures, which found its way quickly into the wool and flesh of grazing sheep, making them unfit for human consumption. Early scientific advice suggested the long-term risks from this fallout were low and would disappear in a matter of weeks. But in practice it persisted for months and in some cases years. Local conditions were such that fallout predictions based on laboratory experiments did not apply. It took time for scientists to work out what was going on and make a more accurate assessment (that the risk was long term and persistent), and they also failed to make use of local expertise, which might have led either to the answer more quickly, or to formulating more useful advice about processing livestock tailored to local circumstances.

Scientists initially gave advice based on unjustified confidence in textbook 'science-in-general'. Official control measures on sheep farming made in the light of changing scientific assessment caused deep resentment. Government scientists made few attempts to learn from the local experts in geography, geology and land management: the farming community itself. Ignorance of such matters by officials earned contempt from farmers. This inability of the two groups to make use of each other's expertise is a classic example of a failure of communication, the root cause lying in the different mind sets and cultural contexts of the two communities. Effective communication demands that each become familiar with the other's interests, and that takes time. This is a general lesson for science communication in both the professional and the popular contexts; nothing effective can be conveyed unless mutual accommodation is made between the cultural worlds of the different communicating groups.

For some farmers, as Meikle reports, this story was still running 20 years later. There were still nearly 400 farms where sheep still picked up unacceptably high levels of caesium in 2006, over 350 in Wales, 10 in Scotland, and 9 in Cumbria. A public understanding agenda based on people knowing and understanding more 'science-in-general' does not work in situations like this. Established science might, paradoxically, gain more respect if it confessed that, at the local level, it was not sure of itself, but nevertheless could show how sophisticated it was (in detective mode) at unravelling an accurate explanation from the welter of social and cultural distractions.

David Layton's educational team published case studies supporting many of the objections to deficit model science communication made by sociologists like Wynne, Michael and Irwin. They asked members of public subgroups what they thought science could do for them, not what scientists thought they ought to know. One of their case studies was on parents of children with Down's syndrome. The medical establishment informs parents about the chromosomal origin of this disorder. But for most parents this is irrelevant because it has no bearing on the practical problems of caring for a Down's child. They need information on clinical, social and other aspects of the condition. Not only may this 'knowledge-in-particular' be hard to come by, but parents often cannot even articulate what they need to know to begin with. Eventually, most parents were able to cope with the situation, although the care regimes they came up with varied enormously. Many people devised perfectly good care methods based on increasing experience without any grasp of science or much clinical or social advice. Where therapies or procedures were recommended as a result of scientific investigations, parents complained that no one could give a clear indication of their efficiency (the uncertainty of prognosis again).

Genetic counselling produced a mixed response, while ancillary professionals like health visitors, speech therapists, physiotherapists and social workers had very patchy effects. By contrast, self-help groups proved extremely valuable; audiences themselves are the best at working out what they need and how to get it. The lesson is that medical and scientific professions should try to discover what patients and the public actually need to know, not just provide information from their own clinical and scientific agendas. Down's syndrome parents could not make use of scientific and medical knowledge, while medical and social professionals failed to learn much from the parents which could have led them to offer more useful advice, and perhaps redirected their research towards work of greater practical value.

STRUGGLING TOWARDS A BETTER COMMUNICATION
MODEL: THE SCIENCE SHOP MOVEMENT AND
THE VALUE OF MEDIATION BETWEEN MIND SETS
The different contexts within which scientists and publics operate are a major problem for popular science communication. One device for overcoming them is the science shop, an idea from the Netherlands of the early 1970s designed to provide a point of interchange between experts and community groups who did not know how to tap into them. The British educational charity, the Nuffield

Foundation, funded two experimental science shops in the UK, the Northern Ireland Science Shop in Belfast from 1989 and the Merseyside Science Shop (later renamed 'Interchange') in Liverpool in 1990, making use of local universities. Typical problems brought to science shops might be a village group concerned about large-scale tourist development seeking help in evaluating planning changes, a tenants' group concerned about the cost of heating their flats wanting an independent assessment of an official report, or a community group needing to know whether soil was contaminated as a result of industrial activity. In most cases (as we might predict) the client problem was not well articulated or in a form that someone in a university could set about solving. The cultural frameworks of lay groups and academic specialists are too far apart. The science shops therefore act as points of access for community groups to mediate and translate between the clients and the academic experts.

Irwin evaluated the two British centres in their first 5 years and showed that most of the parties found benefits from them. The client groups were most in favour, they had their problems clarified and received expert feedback focused on their particular needs. Students who had undertaken project work based on science shop requests also reported a high level of satisfaction, while the least satisfied people were the academics. The effort needed to re-formulate their expertise to the needs of the client group (knowledge-in-particular) was often great and, in the framework of their careers, community work carries no kudos.

The science shop movement has since had mixed fortunes but Hellemans reports that the movement is rediscovering its radical roots. The survivors have formed the International Science Shop Network (ISSNET) funded with European Commission money. Its leaders believe the movement can influence the direction of science, re-orientating it to research of more direct public use. By 2005 there were 60 shops worldwide, but difficulties with the status of academic work done for science shops remain a problem. Nevertheless, the EU sees huge public understanding of science potential and that the shops could encourage new types of student to take science degrees.

WHERE DOES THIS LEAVE US?

Popular science about significant ideas and new breakthroughs is of interest to a significant minority of the public who are fascinated by science. This group has appreciated the greater range of popular books, articles, broadcast programmes and museums and exhibitions about science, which may have come about as a result of PUS agitation. But, this cornucopia has not really reached the larger sections of the public who have no interest in science, but who might nonetheless benefit from scientific knowledge and expertise if they realized it could be of value to them. Throughout the 1990s, evidence accumulated that a deficit approach of top-down popularization of establishment science was not reaching these wider audiences. The rhetoric, if not the substance, has therefore changed in the twenty-first century. The need for dialogue and a degree of mediation between experts and publics has been recognized and the ugly duckling of PUS transformed into the swan of Public Engagement with Science and Technology (PEST). PEST may be an improvement but tensions persist over who is communicating what science, for whose benefit, as we shall see in the next chapter.

BIBLIOGRAPHY

Collins, H. and Pinch, T. (1993). *The Golem. What Everyone Should Know About Science*. Cambridge: Cambridge University Press.

Durant, J.R. (1990). Copernicus and Conan Doyle or why should we care about the public understanding of science? *Science and Public Affairs*, **5**, 7–22.

Durant, J.R., Evans, G.A. and Thomas, G.P. (1989). The public understanding of science. *Nature*, **340**, 11–13.

Funtowicz, S. and Ravetz, J. (1990). Post-normal science: a new science for new times. *Scientific European*, October, 20–22.

Hellemans, A. (2001). After years of decline, non-profit consultancies – science shops – are starting to re-invent themselves. *Naturejobs*, special report (5 July), 415–16.

House of Lords, Select Committee on Science and Technology (2000). *Third Report. Science and Society*, 23 February, http://www.parliament.the-stationery-office.co.uk, visited 4 May 2000.

Irwin, A. (1994). Science and its publics: continuity and change in the risk society. *Social Studies of Science*, **24**, 168–84.

Irwin, A. (1995). *Citizen Science*. London: Routledge.

Irwin, A. (1995). *Science at the service of the community? The Nuffield Foundation Science Shop initiative. A report on the Northern Ireland Science Shop and the Mersey Science Shop/Interchange*. London: Nuffield Foundation.

Layton, D., Jenkins, E., Macgill, S. and Davey, A. (1993). *Inarticulate science? Perspectives on the public understanding of science and some implications for science education*. Driffield, East Yorkshire: Studies in Education Ltd.

Leydesdorff, L. and Ward, J. (2005). Science shops: a kaleidoscope of science-society collaborations in Europe. *Public Understanding of Science*, **14**, 353–72.

Meikle, J. (2006). Sheep farms under curbs see no end to Chernobyl fallout. *The Guardian*, 13 April, 17.

Michael, M. (1992). Lay discourses of science: science-in-general, science-in-particular, and self. *Science, Technology and Human Values*, **17**, 313–33.

Miller, J. D. (2004). Public understanding of, and attitudes towards scientific research: what we know and what we need to know. *Public Understanding of Science*, **13**, 273–94.

Worcester, R. M. (2002). Public understanding of science. *Biologist*, **49**, 143.

Wynne, B. (1991). Knowledges in context. *Science, Technology and Human Values*, **16**, 111–21.

Wynne, B. (1992). Misunderstood misunderstanding: social identities and public uptake of science. *Public Understanding of Science*, **1**, 281–304.

7   Public engagement with science and technology (PEST): good principle, difficult practice

A GARDEN IN SUBURBAN HERTFORDSHIRE, JANUARY

Stage whisper, "There's a greenfinch!" from Emma.

"Oh kid sister, I don't think so," from Rob the worldly-wise 12-year-old.

"I'm sure it is," from Emma louder.

"Hush up Emma, you've frightened it," from dad, "It's flown off."

"Not a greenfinch though dad, eh – Emma gets so excited."

"Rob, I think she was right, mark it on the chart."

Rob tried to ignore his sister's sarcastically extended tongue, realizing for the first time just how cold he was, notwithstanding two sweaters, windcheater and bobble hat after standing still for three-quarters of an hour behind a bush. He had spotted the first robin and the only coal tit, but yielding the most exotic tickbox of the afternoon to Emma was almost too much to bear.

A KITCHEN TABLE IN RURAL SOUTH DEVON, JULY

Len: "I ought to walk as far as the copse more often."

Jo: "Only if you're careful, the ground's uneven and you nearly fell last week."

Len: "Don't fuss, I was fine with the new stick. Best thing though was a definite stag beetle on that pile of old logs by the lightning oak. That's the second this year."

Jo: "Isn't it three or four? Didn't Matt see some when he was here?"

Len: "I'm not sure with young Matt, he's claimed to have seen an eagle in the garden before now, I think maybe he saw

Cockchafers because there were lots of them flying in the evening when he was here. Think I'll censor his returns and stick with the ones I've seen."

MARJORY ON THE MOBILE PHONE TO KATE IN LEICESTER TOWN CENTRE, JUNE

"Thanks for the last newsletter Kate, I see you mentioned the shenanigans round our box."

"It's an interesting story so it makes the papers! There haven't been many second occupations this year. How do you think they are doing?"

"It's a bit quiet to be honest luv. I'm not sure anyone's still there or maybe the babies are dead. Perhaps you should come and check for yourself. I don't like to touch anything."

"All right Marjory I'll pop in tomorrow if you'll be there in the morning."

"Yes dear, all morning – checking what the other sparrows are doing. Being in this survey makes looking at these little chaps very interesting."

These are three banal conversations that might have occurred on three scientific natural history surveys, which used ordinary people to monitor changes in populations of wild animals. Lindsay Tufft investigated such lay participation in scientific surveys and these extracts relate to specific projects. The first is the Royal Society for the Preservation of Birds (RSPB) Big Garden Watch, which checks the frequency of 15 marker bird species in 1-hour observation periods on the last weekend in January, an annual event that attracts hundreds of thousands of participants. The second is the national stag beetle survey using lay observers, which showed that, while these beetles are common in Dorset and Somerset, they only spread into Devon along the south coast. The third is Kate Vincent's field work on sparrow biology in Leicestershire undertaken as a Ph.D. student at De Montfort

University. She asked members of the public to put up nesting boxes in their gardens and help her observe the behaviour of the inhabitants.

These are all examples of lay engagement with science through participation with professional scientists. Some were already natural history enthusiasts enrolled in organizations like the RSPB, others were drawn in by personal contact or in response to local advertisements. This is a special (and specialized) example of public engagement with science. These lay-assisted surveys have been called 'citizen science' but in a rather different sense to Irwin's call for public engagement.

What is missing from these examples is any sense of true dialogue between the scientists and their lay assistants. In the surveys that Tufft analysed, lay observers contributed comparatively little to the formulation and direction of research, although Kate Vincent did accept that input from her observers enriched her ideas. This kind of public participation with science certainly addresses the core public understanding agenda; it succeeds in stimulating some people with no previous overt interest in natural history or science to take part in professional work. However, the degree of engagement is limited because the lay participants have no say in the organization or purpose of the surveys, and are engaged on professional terms with the mind set of the academic researchers.

DIALOGUE AS THE BASIS FOR ENGAGEMENT

To be of real value in a public policy or consumer context, scientific knowledge has to be re-framed to engage audiences in terms specific to their culture and understanding, not in terms of those of the scientific community. The only way that scientists can make themselves aware of these public contexts is through dialogue and conversation with their potential audiences. Fifteen years after the publication of Bodmer's *Public Understanding of Science* report in 1985, the UK Government and the scientific establishment began to accept the need for science communication to be framed in audience terms. The breakthrough was symbolized by the Third Report of the House of Lords Select Committee on Science and Technology, *Science and Society*, published in February 2000.

The Committee recognized that most scientific issues of public concern have moral, social and ethical dimensions and that people's attitudes towards science are underpinned by the values they hold. The Committee noted that 'Policy makers will find it hard to win public support on any issue with a science component, unless the public's attitudes and values are recognized, respected and weighed' (Summary p. 2). The Committee also argued that trust in science, especially when dressed in industrial or government clothing, had broken down creating a mood for consultation and dialogue. It therefore called on government departments concerned with science and the scientific research councils to encourage more active popular communication and to improve the training of scientists to undertake it.

The Committee recommended a tranche of procedures to improve openness and reveal the sources of funding or other support received by scientific advisors. While it still believed that scientific quality was best assured by professional peer review, it argued that more should be done to involve stakeholder (and wider) publics in agenda setting. The Committee heard a great deal of complaint from scientists about the misrepresentation of science by the media and it did accept some of the scientific establishment line on this, supporting the pompous guidelines to editors put out by the Royal Society calling for 'factual accuracy and balance in media coverage of science' (Summary p. 7). But it was also aware that much of the problem lay with the scientific establishment's attempt to control the media agenda, rather than seeing that it must learn to work by media rules. On balance, the Committee's report was a well-argued call for significant changes in the 'social contract' between science and society.

The report made use of a survey of British public attitudes towards science and technology undertaken at the behest of the Science Minister in the Department of Trade and Industry. The results showed considerable public interest in science and approval for those aspects of science that enhanced the quality of people's lives. Detailed analyses of the responses allowed researchers to recognize attitudinal groups with respect to science. Just over half the total was broadly supportive of science, and of scientists, and they were happy with the regulation and direction of science, while just under half expressed varying degrees of doubt. As so often before, despite survey data showing public ignorance of scientific knowledge, there is no evidence that this translates into significant public mistrust of science.

The government took comfort from this majority in broad support of science. The Office of Science and Technology (OST) commissioned another report on 'Science in Society' in 2005, which showed that things had stayed broadly the same. Over 80% of the sample felt that science made a positive contribution to society (although there were severe caveats over things like genetically modified crops) and more than half claimed to have taken part in a science-based non-work activity in the previous year. The overall level of trust in science and scientists had increased, but repeated previous survey differences in the trust in different categories of scientist. Only 40% felt confident that they understood enough science while 80% supported public consultation about scientific matters, although most of them thought such consultation made no difference to policy. A majority believed they were public relations exercises unrepresentative of public opinion. More than in previous surveys believed that the media sensationalize science.

These results suggest that scientists and engineers still have authority and are widely trusted, although some people have reservations about how science is used and are worried that machinery to regulate it does not work. A majority felt that scientists did not listen enough to what ordinary people think.

Since the House of Lords Report in 2000, the rhetoric of science communication has moved strongly from deficit (PUS) to dialogue (Public Engagement with Science and Technology, PEST), from understanding to engagement. The lesson has been learned that public engagement requires mediation, re-expression or translation of scientific issues into contexts that mean something to audiences. But, evidence also suggests that the change has not altered the fundamental rules of engagement. Dialogue and engagement are being designed to produce the same public outcomes as PUS; public approval for current science and the scientific community, now reinforced by active government participation.

The PUS agenda was originally intended to get the public to put pressure on government to provide more support for science; the scientific community and government were are loggerheads. The situation in the 1990s and into the twenty-first century has changed; UK government support for science (especially science with obvious technological and economic benefits) is now a central element of industrial policy. The science community's need for resources meshes smoothly with government need for public acceptance of what it sees as valuable technologies (such as genetic modification of crop plants) to which the public has been so far resistant. Science and government are now engaged on a mission to obtain compliance for their joint agendas. But, the real benefit and value of dialogue is that both sides should listen to each other and modify their behaviours accordingly. It is not just for the public to comply, but for science and the state to listen and learn about public needs and desires; that is the only way to retain an effective social contract. Actually, the overwhelming evidence is that the contract is fine from the public side, as far as the public understands it. But it does not necessarily lead to the positive results that government and scientists want, hence the continuation of the story that the contract is broken and needs fixing through an intense communication agenda. But still missing are the more democratic principles of public engagement with the social contract, greater in-depth understanding and compromise on both sides for nurturing and developing it.

DIALOGUE: TURNING PRECEPT INTO ACTION

While the principle of dialogue can be clearly articulated, turning that principle into practice is harder. Some organizations undertook dialogue-based activities before the House of Lords Report appeared; for instance, in London the Natural History Museum Darwin Centre and Science Museum Dana Centre. In the Natural History Museum real taxonomists have their laboratories housed in the Darwin Centre and make use of the 'spirit collection' of alcohol-preserved specimens on a daily basis. Museum visitors are encouraged to come into the public space on the ground floor of the Darwin Centre, to view the specimens through glass panels, to listen to presentations from scientists and to quiz them about their activities. Such public access to scientists should encourage dialogue between the scientific community and the public, although it was not part of the original thinking for the space, which was designed to overcome internal estate and managerial problems.

By contrast, the Dana Centre at the Science Museum was deliberately engineered as a space for interaction, indeed for potential confrontation, between scientists and public audiences. The Centre is used for public debates concerned with controversial aspects of science and its consequences. These debates mainly engage stakeholding interests and activist pressure groups rather than members of the general public. Sarah Davies carefully analysed some of these Dana Centre activities to see how far they allow dialogue where lay concerns are not subordinated to professional science agendas. The number of dialogue events is increasing, but it is difficult to evaluate how effective they are, although some of them certainly foreground the attitudes of stakeholders (if not the public) rather than scientists. The Dana Centre sponsors some events where mainstream science is brought up sharp by confrontation with different public attitudes, but this does not perhaps happen often enough. For instance, the Centre organized a conference of neuroscientists and science journalists to discuss what issues the public are likely to raise over progress in brain sciences. Steven Rose observed that any optimism that the event would be a celebration of progress and benefits from science was deflated by the issues that emerged as public concerns; the increasing medicalization of human social behaviour and the dangers of behaviour-changing drugs.

This is an example of the second principle of public engagement work: the scientific community confronted with the public's concerns about the consequences of new scientific knowledge. The scientific community and the government still seem to want only appreciation and wonder, they are less keen to encourage critical evaluation of science or genuine moves by the scientific establishment to listen to public concerns and modify its aims and objectives accordingly. There still seems to be a democratic deficit at the heart of the PEST agenda.

A great deal of the PUS/PEST movement's work is in educational mode, aiming to add to, or substitute for, science taught in schools. Two leading players have been science museums and science centres. Both are constructed in a top-down, science education mode, and both may fail to the extent that they expect formal learning from informal visits. The interactive science centres may be too games-orientated to produce useful learning about science. A better option might be to have more human guidance through traditional museum exhibits using teachers, explainers or actors. There is also evidence that audience participation and learning are maximized by group visits, where visitors discuss what they are seeing and experiencing.

Christian Heath's team argue that computer-based interactive displays in museums and science centres seem to reduce such discussion because they focus too sharply on individuals engaging with activities designed to produce learning by following an organized strategy. In practice, few visitors do this. Instead, people simply push buttons and look aimlessly at the responses as pure entertainment. Rachel Souhami argues that science centres and museums are finding it hard to work out how to move from simple learning and display to create dialogue and show how science is embedded in a cultural context. Others argue that museums are sinking beneath the weight of their accumulated collections of objects, with no proper resources to conserve, display, catalogue or research them.

There are other types of collection and display sites with strong educational/public understanding associations; zoological and botanical gardens. Zoos have re-invented themselves from displays of taxonomic diversity to centres for the study of animal behaviour and sites for endangered species conservation. Botanic gardens are traditionally less visible and less controversial, but Tim Smit's Eden Project in reclaimed china clay workings in Cornwall has become well known. The site allows visitors to immerse themselves in natural and agricultural plant ecosystems, relating ecological and agricultural science firmly to human culture and the arts. Its founder wants to educate, inspire and change people's attitudes and actions. This is not the virtual interaction of the computer screen but the real interaction of being in versions of actual ecosystems from across the globe, a massively expensive but probably an effective form of experiential learning.

REAL DIALOGUE AND POSSIBLE DEMOCRACY?

The logical outcome of serious conversation about science between the public, the scientific community and the political establishment, is that public opinion should have an impact on what scientists and government do, a version of Irwin's 'citizen science'. One of the PUS/PEST establishment's looser cannons, Lord Robert Winston, dared to stick his head above the parapet to suggest that dialogue with the public might influence what scientists did. The response was a cacophony of protests from leading members of the scientific community, who thought the idea either dangerous or ridiculous, while Winston's subsidiary argument that some scientists were tainted by too close an association with government was strongly attacked by both politicians and science spokespeople. It is clear from these responses that there is still a long way to go in convincing the main PUS/PEST constituencies, scientists and science communicators that more sophisticated approaches to communication are desirable and necessary.

The left-wing UK Think Tank, Demos, produced a report, *See Through Science*, advocating a genuinely responsive dialogue with the public, preferably early on in the development of any new science or technology (referred to as upstream consultation), so that public engagement can help determine policy. Demos advocated this approach especially for nanotechnology, the next innovation that everyone fears will go the same way as the genetic manipulation of organisms (GMO) debate, where the British public rejected GMOs despite strong government and scientific support. Following an earlier Royal Society Report on the potential risks of nanotechnology, Demos called for public engagement early on and a proper commitment from government to listen to public concerns.

The report certainly sent out the right signals, but doubts arise because once again the establishment is setting the agenda. At this early stage public awareness of nanotechnology may be too low for constructive dialogue. How the public reacts once nanotechnology moves from speculation and minor applications to real significance is unpredictable and therefore impossible to plan in advance. It still looks as if the instigators of the communication are aiming at public compliance with the industrial use of nanotechnology, rather than engaging in a genuine debate over the issues as they rise into public consciousness and responding to the concern or support which eventually arises.

CAFÉS SCIENTIFIQUES AS DIALOGUE EVENTS

The Café Scientifique is essentially a French idea, springing from an older Café Philosophique tradition where professional philosophers discussed issues with lay audiences in informal environments. The first Café Scientifique was set up by French physicists in 1997, while the first cafés appeared in Britain in 1998 organized by Duncan Dallas and friends in Leeds and Nottingham. At an international forum for Café organizers and enthusiasts held in Newcastle in 2004, there were representatives from 11 countries and, between them, France and Britain organized about 70 events a year.

Café Scientifique meetings are held in bars and cafés, usually with groups of up to 50 people. The discussions are initiated by an 'expert' who gives a short presentation as a basis for subsequent discussion. The British movement is deliberately democratic, aiming to put scientists into face-to-face contact with people who otherwise have little access to scientific culture. The lay audience and the speaker are considered equals and the agenda is not educational; rather, the audience is encouraged to question scientists about their motives, funding and career structure. They are perhaps the scientific equivalent of book clubs, discussion groups organized by enthusiasts for other enthusiasts. For some, this 'in-crowd' feature is a problem, they claim cafés scientifiques cannot reach those who are not already engaged, but countering that is the argument that the events are often run in towns without universities or museums, where they may have significant educational impact.

ECOTOURISM

Bird-watching, rock-pool dabbling, flower identification and so on are popular activities that can be tapped by professional biologists, who make use of amateur enthusiasm to conduct survey work at minimal cost, as we saw at the start of the chapter. Environmental organizations can now mobilize large numbers of amateur enthusiasts into environmental activism. Many conservation issues are prominent in parts of the world which attract extensive tourism.

During the 1990s conservationists began to see that science is only one input into solving environmental problems. They can only be successfully dealt with in tourist areas in terms of the cultural needs of human communities. In lessons that the scientific community might take to heart, technical conservation efforts must be tuned to the cultural and economic needs of local communities. Practical moves in this direction have produced ecotourism. One firm that organizes ecotours, Earthwatch, matches volunteers to scientists in exotic locations who need some observational or other work done. The point of this from a science communication perspective is that science will be a much more effective resource for solving conservation problems in tourist areas, the more it is mediated through communication between scientific culture, the cultural expectations of tourists and the local economic and social cultures at the destinations.

Brumfiel notes that astronomy shares with natural history a background as an open activity. This changed during the twentieth century as instruments for professional observation became too sophisticated for amateur use. But the situation has reversed recently because top-of-the-range amateur equipment is sufficiently good for dedicated amateurs to once again make professional level observations. A minority among the armies of amateur sky watchers now contribute to astronomy and this has generated tensions. Some professional astronomers want to mobilize this amateur expertise for their own ends, but others resent amateur intrusion and the possible siphoning off of scarce research funds. Successful amateurs can find themselves cold-shouldered by the professionals while, on the other hand, many hi-tech amateur enthusiasts are only interested in the technology and do not want to collaborate with professionals. Engaging amateurs and professionals in productive collaboration presents the problems of matching interests and mind sets, which we have noted before.

EDUCATIONAL ENGAGEMENT: MEDICAL SOAPS IN THE DEVELOPING WORLD

In Britain in the 1940s and 1950s, the radio soap opera *The Archers* played a significant role in alerting the farming community to new ideas, new techniques and new markets after the Second World War. We no longer expect our soap operas to provide educational messages but the situation in the developing world is different. Ebert describes a Vietnamese radio drama based on *The Archers*, which has proved effective in teaching farmers the elements of sustainable agriculture and has won a World Bank prize. International agencies are starting to explore the value of 'edutainment' in more developing world contexts. A radio drama in Somalia encouraged 30 000 people to sign up for literacy courses, while in India 200 000 people sought help with leprosy after a drama in which it was made clear that the disease was treatable.

Another exercise of this type is the BBC World Service Trust initiated Cambodian drama, *Taste of Life*, whose story lines will involve medical dramas with embedded advice on disease prevention, especially of HIV/AIDS. The soap's fictional tropes allow the programme to achieve greater reach than a conventional educational documentary. Since Cambodian television consists almost entirely of quiz and karaoke shows, it is expected that these stories will have powerful effects. However, problems can arise with dramas like these because of tensions between public and private sponsorship, issues of inappropriate product placement, and with the question of overt Western values because the shows are based on Western models and made by Western companies.

WHERE DOES THIS LEAVE US?

The rhetoric of science communication has moved firmly in the first decade of the twenty-first century from Public Understanding (PUS) towards Public Engagement (PEST). To an extent, the structure and purpose of science communication has also changed, although the point of the activity so far as the establishment (the scientific community and the state together) is concerned has remained the same, ensuring public appreciation of science and compliance with government desire to encourage high technology industrial development. Underlying both activities is the feeling that something has broken in the social contract between science and society, which needs fixing. But the overall evidence suggests that this contract (in terms of public trust and support for science) is fully functional.

In practice, public engagement has turned out to mean a number of related, but different things. There is lay participation in scientific research through activities like ecotourism, domestic natural history surveys and astronomical observation. There is the use of a variety of methods in museums and broadcasts to produce and maintain close attention to educational messages about science itself, its social context or in health or environmental policy. Engagement through dialogue has been explored as a more effective way of obtaining public approval for science policies than was being achieved through a deficit agenda of lecturing about science. And finally, there has been some small movement towards accepting the logic of genuine dialogue and conversation about science and policy, that various social contracts could be re-negotiated, so that greater public monitoring and engagement would provide genuine public input in formulating science policy. Such democratic idealism is explored in the next chapter.

BIBLIOGRAPHY

Anon. (2004). Going public. *Nature*, 21 October, **431**, 883.

Anon. (2004). The rise of café culture. *Nature*, 17 May, **429**, 327.

British Association for the Advancement of Science (2003). *Science in Society. Advice to the OST from the BA*. London: BA Website (visited 25 June 2003).

British Association for the Advancement of Science (2003). *Science Communication Conference 22/23 May 2003*. London: BA Website (visited 1 August 2003).

Brumfiel, G. (2003). Night club. *Nature*, 13 November, **426**, 116–7.

Burnie, D. (1994). Ecotourists in paradise. *New Scientist*, 16 April, 23–7.

Cotton, C. (1998). Environmental education and interpretation in nature based tourism. Unpublished M.Sc. dissertation: Imperial College London.

Dallas, D. (1999). Science in culture. The café scientifique. *Nature*, 13 May, **399**, 120.

Davis, C. (2002). The ubiquity of antiquity. *Times Higher Education Supplement*, 11 January, 17.

Davies, S.R. (2007). Scientists and the public: studies in discourse and dialogue. Unpublished Ph.D. thesis: Imperial College London.

Demos (2004). Media public debate needs to move upstream. London: Demos website, http://www.demos.co.uk/media/pressreleases/pressreleases 2004 ... (visited 26 October 2004).

Durant, J.R. (2002). The gravity of the centres. *Guardian*, Online section, 21 February, 11.

Ebert, J. (2005). Soap opera reaps prize for its clean message. *Nature*, 9 June, **435**, 723.

Evans, S.M., Foster-Smith, J. and Welch, R. (2001). Volunteers assess marine biodiversity. *Biologist*, **48**, 168–72.

Fazackerley, A. (2003). Critics lambast Winston's ideas. *Times Higher Education Supplement*, **12** December, 213.

Giles, J. (2004). Pop science pulls in public as café culture goes global. *Nature*, 27 May, **429**, 332.

Goodwin, H. (1995). Tourism and the environment. *Biologist*, **42**, 129–33.

Haag, A. (2005). A trip of a lifetime. *Nature*, 23 June, **435**, 1018–20.

Heath, C., van Lehn, D. and Osborne, J. (2005). Interaction and interactives: collaboration and participation with computer-based exhibits. *Public Understanding of Science*, **14**, 91–101.

House of Lords, Select Committee on Science and Technology (2000). *Third Report. Science and Society*, 23 February, http://www.parliament.the-stationery-office.co.uk, visited 4 May 2000.

Karpf, A. (2002). Hands on museums: just the place to switch minds off. *The Guardian* G2 section, 12 March, 7.

Kerr, A., Cunningham-Burley, S. and Amos, A. (1998). The new genetics and health: mobilizing lay expertise. *Public Understanding of Science*, **7**, 41–60.

McHugh, S. (2002). How do we turn the doing into the communicating? – a study of two projects allowing access to museum science. Unpublished M.Sc. dissertation, Imperial College London.

Miller, J.D. (2004). Public understanding of, and attitudes towards scientific research: what we know and what we need to know. *Public Understanding of Science*, **13**, 273–94.

Monroe, J. (2004). Soap and charity. *The Observer*, 8 August, 6.

Mori (2005). *Science in Society. Findings from qualitative and quantitative research.* Conducted for the Office of Science and Technology, Department of Trade and Industry. London: DTI, March.

Moss, S. (2004). And now for the scientific bit. *The Guardian*, Life Section, 1 July, 10.

O'Brien, H. (2006). Brave new world. *The Guardian*, Education Section, 5 September, 3.

Office of Science and Technology Press Release (2000). *Advancement of Science: announcement of public attitude to science and technology survey by Lord Sainsbury at the Wellcome Trust.* London, OST, 20 March.

Office of Science and Technology (OST) and the Wellcome Trust (2001). Science and the public: a review of science communication and public attitudes towards science in Britain. *Public Understanding of Science*, **10**, 315–30.

Parry, W. (2006). Paradise revisited. *Biologist*, **55(2)**, 66–71.

Rose, S. (2003). Rings around the mindfield. *The Guardian*, Life Section, 22 May, 6.

Rowe, G., Horlick-Jones, T., Walls, J. and Pidgeon, N. (2005). Difficulties in evaluating public engagement initiatives. *Public Understanding of Science*, **14**, 331–52.

Shapin, S. (1996). Science and the public. In R. Olby *et al.*, *The Companion to the History of Modern Science*. London: Routledge, Chapter 65.

Souhami, R. (2006). A very public engagement. *Museums Journal*, August, 26–9.

Tufft, L. (2002). The lay public in science. A model for the systematic use of lay public knowledge in the generation of scientific knowledge. Unpublished M.Sc. dissertation: Imperial College London.

Wellcome Trust (2001). *Science and the public. A review of science communication and public attitudes to science in Britain*, http://www.wellcome.ac.uk/eu/1/mismiscpub.html, visited 12 March 2001.

Wellcome Trust (2001). *The role of scientists in public debate, research conducted by MORI for the Wellcome Trust, Dec 1999- March 2000*, http://www.mori.com/polls/2000/pdf, visited 12 March 2001.

Wilsdon, J. and Willis, R. (2004). Technoprobe. *Guardian Online*, 1 September, http://society.guardian.co.uk/societyguardian/story/, 1294106, 00.html, visited 26 October 2004.

8 Citizen scientists? Democratic input into science policy

Several 'ordinary people' filed into a conference room in London in June 1998 and took their places behind a table separating them from media and academic folk occupying rows of seats. They were shepherded in by Dr Tom Wakeford, then of the University of East London, although he was careful not to speak too much at this press conference. As far as possible, presentations were given and questions answered by the people behind the table. We were witnessing an early example of a political device that has become more common in the twenty-first century; a citizens' jury. This one was convened to consider an issue with wide scientific implications; the future of food.

Tom Wakeford had facilitated the jury which was overseen for fairness by an advisory panel of stakeholders, representing a range of interest across the theme. The stakeholders were the Consumers' Association, the John Innes Food Research Centre, the National Farmers' Union, Sainsbury's, the Soil Association, the Transport and General Workers Union, and Whole Earth Foods. Attempts were made to find representatives from the biotechnology industry but apparently no one would take part.

The 12 jury members were chosen from people in a Brighton suburb, drawn from a pool of 2000 and offered £150 to participate in ten weekly deliberation sessions held in the function room of a local pub. Four principal technical witnesses for the jury to consult were chosen by the stakeholders. The jury called for three more witnesses. The jury's draft ideas were considered in an expert seminar of people appointed by the stakeholders. The jury then prepared its report, which was amended as necessary at its final meeting.

The jury reported that it was unhappy with the state of agricultural production and food manufacture, distribution and sale. They did not like the widespread use of agrochemicals and wanted more encouragement for farmers to move into organic production. They wanted to reduce the price differentiation between organic and conventional food but were unclear how to do this. They also felt that consumer groups should be represented on the then newly proposed Food Regulatory Authority.

The jury was also opposed to genetically modified (GM) food, wanted any such produce clearly separated from 'standard' material, and believed strongly that GM produce should be clearly labelled. They did not trust the agrochemical companies and food manufacturers and wanted to return to local food production and processing with retail moved from big, out-of-town supermarkets to smaller, in-town stores. It seemed to me attending the Conference that they had not been offered much economic advice. The proposals had a distinct feel of unreality because there was no comment on costs.

THE SCOPE OF SCIENCE POLICY

Citizens' juries are one of a series of mechanisms devised over the past 30 years to allow ordinary people to influence social and technical policy issues. Conventionally, such matters are considered so specialized that only experts are qualified to advise politicians. There has been a slow acceptance of the democratic principle that those affected by such policy decisions should contribute to them. Even highly technical decisions have human and ethical dimensions in which lay people's views are important, and they should be able to question and monitor technical experts about such decisions.

Our concern here is with democratic input into 'science policy', although this term is rather difficult to define. It includes all government (public) decisions on action and expenditure about issues involving science and technology. Such decisions are made in at least three contexts. Firstly, there is government policy for the support of basic (or 'fundamental' or 'blue-skies') scientific research. How much money should be spent in total, on which activities should it be spent and what administrative mechanisms are necessary for initiating and overseeing expenditure?

Secondly, there is publicly funded research and development, which government departments find useful for better carrying out their functions. Decisions tend to be technocratic, in some cases because they are secret (in defence or nuclear energy, for instance) and in others because they are boring. Only when things go wrong is government department science exposed to public gaze as it was, for instance, when the UK Department for Environment, Food and Rural Affairs (DEFRA) found its internal research policies and attitudes severely questioned during the major Foot and Mouth disease outbreak in 2001.

Thirdly, there is coordination of decisions by different government departments to ensure that the expected benefits outweigh potential risks. Science policy in this third sense of balancing the risks and benefits of public decision-making has proved contentious. Powerful special interest groups (famously such organizations as Greenpeace and Friends of the Earth) have acquired virtual establishment status. These NGOs expect to take part in policy discussions as prominently as 'official' organizations such as universities, professional bodies or civil servants.

Environmental activists and policy makers use scientific data extensively even though environmental decisions are often matters of moral philosophy; concerned with the relationships which man ought to have with the natural world. The sociologist Stephen Yearley believes that both the government and environmental groups such as Friends of the Earth rely too heavily on science. Environmentalists do this because they have observed that technical arguments (drawing on the positive authority of science-in-general) are more persuasive to their 'enemies' (government agencies, business and developers) than spiritual or moral ones. Players on both sides of the environmental game often argue for more ecological research to improve policy decisions, although this cannot stand alone, but must be incorporated into the economic, social and ethical dimensions that dominate these decisions. The scientific community has a vested interest in calling for more research, so in this context its participation cannot be considered neutral. Overuse of the rhetoric of scientific authority in policy disputes is unwise because it can be undermined by cross-examination from opposing policy stakeholders.

For instance, when the American Environmental Protection Agency (EPA) called for draconian emission control from factories in the early 1970s, American industry vigorously disputed the scientific grounds for the imposition of controls. There was a series of landmark legal cases where scientific evidence was exposed to savage interrogation about its reliability. Both sides could always find expert scientific witnesses who could justifiably support any chosen position, because standards of proof, neutrality and authority in science are more flexible than is usually claimed. In practice, scientific interpretation and explanation are always open to question; for instance, the case of the extrapolation of rat toxicity tests to humans. This extrapolation is always open to question on the grounds of biological differences between rats and humans. But it is only likely to be questioned in practice if one of the parties in a dispute is strongly disadvantaged by evidence from research on rodents.

While scientific evidence and expertise are certainly desirable and even necessary, they are not sufficient for making technical policy decisions. In areas of strong controversy, science (whose main claim to influence is its command of objective, factual truth) is often seen as politicized; being in the service of economic and political authorities so that its factual claims are undermined. As with risk perception, the public response here is not to evaluate the science itself, but the authority and reliability of its source. The public correctly believes science is a specialist matter, but is more aware than some scientists that, outside the laboratory, science can neither be separated from the wider contexts in which it is embedded nor does its authority necessarily apply in local circumstances.

CAN NON-EXPERTS CONTRIBUTE TO TECHNICAL DECISION MAKING?

The American scientific literacy movement arose from the belief that elected representatives and 'opinion-formers' in the professions and the media should understand all the issues involved in technical decision taking. Only if these leaders are competent can ordinary voters trust them to cross-examine technocrats about what they are doing on the people's behalf. The public understanding movement in the UK has something of the same ideology modified initially, as we have seen, by close association with the scientific community's need for more funding. The logical outcome for both movements is to find communication mechanisms where the voices of ordinary people can be heard in government on scientific and technical matters.

Western states are generally representative democracies, designed to retain the principle of self-government in populations too large for everyone to vote on political decisions. In ancient Greek City States, self-government meant that all citizens eligible to vote were entitled to listen to debate and cast their votes to collectively decide public policy. In representative democracies, elected representatives undertake voting on policy matters on behalf of the population as a whole. But the process of overseeing government is not left entirely in the hands of representatives in the gaps between elections. There are a variety of mechanisms to gauge the strength of public concerns and attitudes on policy issues and feed them back to politicians. The media act as a major voice of such opinion, buttressed by opinion polls and market research. Special interest groups lobby parliament and try to influence media coverage of the matters with which they are concerned, while individuals can consult their representatives (Members of Parliament in the UK) about matters of concern by writing letters or consulting them at their 'surgeries'.

But, despite these checks there is a tendency for technical experts to dominate policy decisions. This anti-democratic trend is compounded by the increasing complexity of policy issues. But the situation might be considered particularly serious on matters involving science and technology, clustered particularly around environment and health. These include environmental pollution, conservation, climate change, health and safety at work, agricultural production, food safety and public health. In all cases it is necessary to decide what risks society is prepared to take with new phenomena (such as therapeutic and preventive drugs, genetically engineered organisms in the environment and the like) compared with the benefits that they might bring. Enthusiasts for democratic participation have therefore devised a number of mechanisms by which public interest can influence public policy over and above the opportunities to change whole governments at general elections.

DEMOCRATIC MECHANISMS WHICH ENHANCE THE INVOLVEMENT OF ORDINARY PEOPLE IN POLICY DECISIONS

Referenda

Here a policy question is framed in yes or no format and put to a universal vote. In most states over-use of referenda is thought to undermine the principle of representation. In the UK, for instance, referenda are confined to high level constitutional issues such as joining the European Union or deciding on various forms of regional government in Scotland, Wales and Northern Ireland. However, one European country, Switzerland, does make extensive use of referenda, usually holding several every year. In the early summer of 1998, it held a famous referendum on whether its universities and pharmaceutical companies should be involved with work on genetic engineering. Despite strong lobbying in its favour, a motion to restrict research on genetic manipulation was defeated, although subsequent referenda and case law have complicated the issue.

Scenario workshops

These are usually held for local technological issues. A group of experts debate different scenarios associated with a new development with local groups. The technocrats gain better understanding of how the policy they propose will affect the local community.

Deliberative opinion polls

This procedure is often televised. A statistically representative sample of a local population discusses a well-defined policy issue with technocratic experts and then votes on the issues raised to gather a feeling for majority opinion.

Electronic consensus building

The issues for debate are put up on the internet and open to discussion and deliberation across frontiers. Respondents can influence the parameters for discussion and the context and can decide to take a vote at any stage of the proceedings.

People's Panels

This device is now used by the UK Government for sampling opinion on a variety of policy issues. Currently, the British People's Panel consists of 5000 individuals recruited to be representative of the country. Members of the Panel make themselves available for focus group meetings, deliberative conferences and in-depth interviews.

Citizens' juries

Here, ordinary people discuss the implication of a policy initiative. Groups of up to 25 individuals participate and their conclusions allow policy makers to gain a view of informed public opinion on an issue. Such information can seldom be obtained by questionnaires or opinion polls, which rarely expose the reasons why people hold the opinions they do.

Consensus conferences

Consensus conferences began as extensions of policy making in expert technology assessments. From the mid 1970s in America 'consensus development conferences' were organized by the National Institutes of Health (NIH) to assess new medical treatments for clinical practice. The thinking behind the early conferences was that, since medicine was based on science, variations in clinical practice must be due to failure to implement the latest scientific ideas. But regional and institutional differences in practice were much wider than had been expected and not resolvable with updated scientific knowledge. Medical practice was found to depend as much on medical values as on scientific facts. The consensus discussions helped different schools of thought understand each other, but since values underlay everything, the final court for decisions must be society in which medicine is practised and from which doctors take their values. Technical matters of clinical treatment are therefore matters of public interest, leading to moves to incorporate lay views into medical consensus discussions.

THE CONSENSUS CONFERENCE IN PUBLIC POLICY MAKING

In the mid 1980s, the newly constituted Danish Board of Technology used the American NIH consensus conference as a template for public involvement in technology policy. The Board of Technology provides technical and scientific advice to the Danish parliament and facilitates public debate about technology. It began by copying the public consultation element from the medical consensus model and substituted one expert panel with a panel of ordinary people. The format then evolved into an interrogation of a group of technical experts by a panel of ordinary citizens. The citizen panel then discusses the issues and prepares an agreed report for the Board which feeds it to the Danish parliament. The final outcome is intelligible in lay terms and focuses the debate on the impact of technology on people and society, rather than being framed in the mind set of experts and politicians.

Consensus conferences are convened round novel or controversial issues. A lay panel, recruited by local newspaper advertisements, learns about the topic in a preparatory weekend and formulates a set of questions to be answered by appropriate experts in front of an audience of more lay people who may also contribute to discussion and debate. The panel participants should be 'non-expert', although this is hard to define since lay people with a special interest in a topic (patients of a disease being discussed for instance) do take part. The group prepares a single report, which must be a consensus, no minority reports are allowed. Ideally, reports receive wide media coverage and are considered by parliamentarians and policy makers.

The Danish conferences are based on a long tradition of public consultation on public policy issues; a tradition entirely absent in the UK. Conferences take a considerable amount of organization and their cost is high. Lay members do become better informed and their opinions change as a result of debate, although their fundamental values seldom alter. The impact of conferences is hard to measure even in Denmark, but there are examples of demonstrable effects. Following the 1989 conference on food irradiation, the Danish parliament decided against irradiation except for dry spices and, after the Human Genome Mapping conference in the same year, came out against genetic testing for employment recruitment, or insurance claims, and the government framed legislation to outlaw these practices.

The consensus conference spread to the Netherlands and the UK in the early 1990s and a pilot consensus conference on plant biotechnology was held at the Science Museum in the UK during July/August 1994. There was suspicion that this conference might not be concerned with participation at all; some felt it might follow the 'public understanding' agenda of the biotechnology industry, designed to obtain acceptance of the use of genetically modified products. The environmental lobby worried that the panel members might have been chosen for sympathy with industrial biotechnology, although this does not seem to have happened. The final report was a genuine lay attempt to come to grips with the issues. The consensus was certainly not as critical of the industry as the environmental lobby wanted and various politicians poured scorn on the panel's efforts, suggesting that its lack of technical expertise meant that it could not reach valid conclusions.

A second large British consensus conference was organized in 1999, the UK National Consensus Conference on Radioactive Waste Management, aiming to resolve the long-standing controversy over how to dispose of nuclear waste. There were 'issues' among stakeholders, contributors and pressure groups about the neutrality and range of pro and anti-nuclear experts available, and about the extent to which the lay panel could consider the disposal problem in isolation from, or in relation to, the future of nuclear power. The report that emerged was a hybrid mix of agreement with points on both sides of the waste disposal argument. As with the biotechnology conference, there was no obvious political framework for incorporating the results in political action.

The UK Government is moving slowly towards public consultation on policy, although it tends to preset the agenda to prevent anything very radical from emerging. The Office of Science and Technology (OST) has a 10-year vision of scientific investment to create industrial wealth and wants to avoid public controversy that might interfere with the programme. It wants to use public consultation to defuse protest and encourage approval of government policy. The Council for Science and Technology (CST) is also clear about this. While it recommends that government undertakes more public dialogue, it sees the purpose of dialogue as informing, not determining, policy. Not surprisingly, when the CST then commissioned research into what participants felt about taking part in consultations, they were disillusioned about whether they had made any difference and displeased that no one thought it worth evaluating public consultation exercises to assess how useful they had actually been.

THE CITIZENS' JURY IN PUBLIC POLICY MAKING

The consensus conference is said to suffer from a number of democratic 'deficits', including the fact that participants rely on experts chosen for them, they do not often see experts contradicting each other, and nor do they have any input into the format of the conference (they have little to do with the agenda, the house rules, or the decision-making procedure). Citizen's juries are said to overcome these problems.

Citizens' juries provide policy makers with the informed opinions of representative groups of citizens. Jury members are given the chance to spend some time considering a policy issue in depth with the benefit of access to a range of expert witnesses speaking for various stakeholders. At the end, the jury produces a report and makes recommendations. Tom Wakeford argues that, unlike opinion polls or focus groups, citizens' jury participants represent their own views rather than responding to the agendas of consulting organizations. But, since there are no formal channels for taking notice of the juries' views in the UK, their influence on policy making is negligible.

Citizens' jury members are selected at random, usually from the electoral register (rather than being advertised for) and are paid to attend meetings. The information they receive comes from several points of view, usually via witnesses whom the members themselves cross-examine. These witnesses are chosen either by agreement among representatives of supervising stakeholder organizations and/or by the jury members themselves. Unlike the consensus conference, the participants are not obliged to come to a single set of agreed conclusions; the views of minorities are recorded.

We have already seen the outcome of one jury's deliberations on the future of food in the chapter scenario, and another UK citizens' jury was held on Nanotechnology in 2005. Stakeholders in nanotechnology worry that this emergent technology will encounter the same public resistance as genetically modified crops. A group of nanotechnology scientists from Cambridge collaborated with Greenpeace and *The Guardian* newspaper to set up a citizens' jury to explore the issues; Nanojury UK. Uninformed about the technology to start with, the jurors took a variety of positions on the risks and benefits from what they heard. In the end, they recommended greater transparency in research, greater emphasis on health, equity and environmental protection, and that all small nano-particles should be treated as new substances and thoroughly tested before release. In other words, they took a moderately supportive view of the technology, but needed assurance that there would be adequate regulation to prevent anything going wrong. Macoubrie reports that early survey analysis on nanotechnology in America has been less positive. Researchers found widespread mistrust of the government in managing risk which the public extrapolates to risk in nanotechnology. Since previous episodes of big technical breakthroughs were initially poorly understood and then apparently mismanaged, they fear the same thing will happen with nanotechnology.

MORE ELABORATE CONSULTATIONS IN CANADA,
THE UK AND AMERICA

While public consultation is not common in the UK, it is more widespread in other countries. In Canada, for instance, Allspaw describes how Health Canada conducted an extensive consultation exercise on the subject of Xenotransplantation (the grafting and transplanting of tissues and organs from animals to humans) in 2001. The methods used in the consultation included telephone surveys, a website survey, a postal survey of identified stakeholders, and a series of citizens' jury-style forums where opinion was sampled before and after a series of educational sessions on the topic. These forums generated what Health Canada called 'informed citizens' as opposed to ordinary citizens polled by phone and website who were designated 'uninformed'. The forums of informed citizens were generally less happy to support animal trials with xenotransplants than ordinary citizens; another classic case of knowing more about an issue leading to negative feelings about it.

The deliberation was immediately attacked by the pro-xenotransplantation community because the results were not what they wanted. The non-statistical nature of the forums, the issue of the extent to which the forum members were properly informed, and whether the public was sufficiently concerned by the issue, were all raised by those who want control of xenotransplantation relaxed. The consultation did not lead to the hoped-for go-ahead for experimental work, leaving the professionals uncomfortable, approving of public consultation in principle but objecting to the outcome. The British Government and scientific community seem to be of the same mind, unable to believe that technical knowledge of innovation might lead to caution rather than support. There is disappointment that the 'wrong' results are delivered, which leads to extensive manipulation of expectations to try to massage them.

For instance, Irwin analysed a British Government public consultation on 'Development in the Biosciences' held between late 1997 and early 1999, which used qualitative consultative work-shops combined with quantitative surveys of people drawn from the government's 'people's panel'. This consultation was conducted in haste because the report's findings had to be incorporated into government action in regulating biotechnology, for which a parliamentary agenda and timetable had already been set. From the start, the agenda was driven by government framing the consultation entirely in terms of regulation and belief that matters of scientific fact could be considered in isolation from their cultural context and inde-pendent of what people already knew and thought about the issues. There was no understanding that the scientific facts themselves cannot be separated in the public sphere from social, cultural and political contexts, while it was felt that a quantitative survey should be more persuasive than evidence from qualitative workshops. This central government-framed, science-dominated model prevented the exercise from being, in any proper sense, deliberative with public input having any real impact on policy.

More elaborate consultation processes keep cropping up, although the status of any decisions made or advice offered remains equivocal. For instance, the UK Engineering and Physical Science Research Council (EPSRC) funds a project called *SuScit* (Citizen science for sustainability), which is conducting citizens' workshops in three low income communities to identify their environmental and sustainability research needs. Another example is a report on the future of Brain Science from the Foresight team at the Office of Science and Technology (OST), where a public consultation exercise was run on questions raised by future applications of brain research to behaviour. Participants were clear that individual rights to free choice were more important than society's rights to be protected from dangerous individuals, did not support pharmacological interventions to alter behaviour (preferring education as a mechanism of prevention), and did not want drug treatment of individual behavioural conditions, even if community safety was threatened. In other words, people do not like the idea of chemical coshes, being innately distrustful about who would make decisions to use them and on what grounds. This is not perhaps what pharmaceutical companies and government looking for new solutions to intractable problems wanted to hear.

WHERE DOES THIS LEAVE US?

The most elaborate and potentially most effective public consultation devices, citizens' juries and consensus conferences, are expensive to organize and, in the UK at least, of doubtful value because there is no political machinery for feeding the results into policy. The potential of such activities for real democratic input, for producing 'citizen science' is missed, perhaps deliberately by governments and technocrats uncomfortable with lay participation in what they continue to believe are wholly technical issues.

Experience with consulting, public engagement and public understanding repeatedly shows that, in the public policy domain, scientific and technical issues are never seen in isolation. The state and other sponsoring interest groups are repeatedly surprised when the consultation which they sincerely believe will lead to approval, instead finds resistance or distaste. The reasons for this seem clear. Resistance or distaste are seldom (if ever) built on ignorance and cannot be overcome by explaining the factual or theoretical science more clearly. People always consider science or technology policy in the context of their culture and beliefs. In the classic case of UK resistance to GM crops, for instance, teaching people more about the science of genetic manipulation was not persuasive because the objection was not to the science or technology as such, but to the place of these innovations in wider public culture. Only changing that culture can change attitudes towards these crops, not the scientific facts themselves. This is at least partly because, in wider culture, these facts never speak for themselves; in the public context they are always embedded or interpreted in wider cultural, social or political terms.

Science in the public domain is therefore always a different beast from professional science. If professional scientists, or those interested in developing the consequences of scientific knowledge, want to influence the public (for whatever purpose), the science must be mediated or transformed. Even in the most straightforward cases of popularization of science to those already enthusiastic about it in books, television or film, framing the material as a textbook style description or explanation is less persuasive than an expository framework (explanations incorporated into an argument to resolve a conflict), or within conventions of narrative borrowed from literature or fiction. The popularization of science as an especially clear or simplified lecture seldom works, except for the relatively small group of lay people interested in science for its own sake.

This leads us to the issue of science education. If popularization cast as a lesson seldom works, do lessons work as educational devices on their own terms? This is a difficult question. It demands some attention to teaching and learning, and to how difficult it is to teach professional-type science to anyone apart from small groups of highly motivated students. Despite the objections of teachers and scientists who believe that all pupils have the right to encounter work leading to professional level science, evidence suggests this is not possible. The majority of pupils probably need a different kind of science education, 'science for all' or 'science appreciation' in which elements of science are interpreted in terms of more familiar contexts. Seeing science in a wider context is the remit of the best PUS/PEST thinking and, not surprisingly, a new kind of school 'science for citizenship' is being rolled out in school science education. Science education therefore needs a chapter to itself.

BIBLIOGRAPHY

Adam, D. (2001). When the going gets tough … *Nature*, 24 August, **412**, 472–3.

Allspaw, K. M. (2004). Engaging the public in the regulation of xenotransplantation. Would the Canadian model of public consultation be effective in the US? *Public Understanding of Science*, **13**, 417–28.

Anon (March 1998). *Citizen Foresight. A Tool to Enhance Democratic Policy Making*. London: London Centre for Governance Innovation and Science and The Genetics Forum.

Anon (June 1998). *The Future of Food*. Report of the Citizens' panel on the future of agriculture and the food system.

Borger, J. (1999). How the mighty fall. *The Guardian*, 22 September, G2 Section, 2–3.

Council for Science and Technology (March 2006). *Policy Through Dialogue: Informing Policies Based on Science and Technology*. London: OST.

Hartel, R. (1998). The Swiss gene-protection initiative, 'Notes of a Monday morning quarterback'. Unpublished M.Sc. dissertation, Imperial College London.

Irwin, A. (2001). Constructing the scientific citizen: science and democracy in the biosciences. *Public Understanding of Science*, **10**, 1–18.

Joss, S. and Durant, J. (eds.) (1995). *Public Participation in Science. The Role of Consensus Conferences in Europe*. London: Science Museum.

Macoubrie, J. (2006). Nanotechnology: public concerns, reasoning and trust in government. *Public Understanding of Science*, **15**, 221–41.

Office of Science and Technology (2005). Foresight Brain Science, Addiction and Drugs Project. *Drugs Futures 2025 Report*. London: OST.

Padilla, A. and Gibson, I. (2000). Science moves to centre stage. *Nature*, 27 January, **403**, 357–9.

Parry, V. (2005). The people have spoken. *The Guardian*, Life Section, 21 July.

Sample, I. (2005). It's good to talk. *The Guardian*, Life Section, 28 July, 6.

Sample, I. (2005). Citizen's jury delivers verdict on safety. *The Guardian*, 22 September.

Stewart, J., Kendall, E. and Coote, A. (1994). *Citizens' Juries*. London: Institute of Public Policy Research.

SuScit website, http://www.suscit.org.uk/news/, visited 19 May 2006.

Trewavas, A. (1999). Much food, many problems. *Nature*, 18 November, **402**, 231–2.

Wakeford, T. (2002). Citizens' juries, a radical alternative for social research. *Social Research Update*. Guildford: University of Surrey. http://www.soc.surrey.ac.uk/sru/SRU37.html.

Whitehead, T. (2005). Inform and involve: putting science at the heart of society. Talk at the Science Communication Conference in London, 24 May.

Wilson, W. (1998). What's in a name? Analysis of the Swiss Gene protection/ban initiative. Unpublished M.Sc. dissertation, Imperial College London.

Wooding, S., Scoggins, A., Lundin, P. and Ling, T. (2005). *Talking Policy: An Examination of Public Dialogue in Science and Technology Policy*. Cambridge: Rand Europe.

Yearley, S. (1995). Science policy and the environmental challenge of modern science. In Hornig, C. (ed.). *Science and Technology Policy. An International Perspective*. London: The British Library.

9 Teaching and learning science in school: implications for popular science communication

"The trouble is", said Andrew spinning on his chair and poking me with the end of his pencil, "you still think of energy as caloric, don't you?"

"Caloric?" I spluttered, puzzled and digging deep into the murky recesses of my knowledge of ancient chemical theories – phlogiston? No not phlogiston – caloric, desperate scramble to recall, "Isn't that some sort of stuff?"

"Yes, energy as stuff flowing like ethereal water. That's why you are confused about fuel and energy – it's all caloric to you!"

Properly trained chemist that he was, Andrew was right and here was I, a science curriculum developer, caught out in an embarrassing confusion about something central to the understanding of pretty well all science, I had been using an incorrect concept of energy for decades. But I had two lines of defence, one rather feeble, that I was a biologist and only ever learned enough chemistry to get by, and the other that endless educational research papers have shown that most students misunderstand most science most of the time, and too many of them never overcome the problem. I was clearly one of these unfortunates.

But I had got on quite well because, to the extent that I needed 'energy' in biology, a caloric concept did a serviceable job. Was I as confused and partial in my understanding of everything? As far as I could tell: no. With theoretical concepts central to the science I was supposed to understand, genetics and evolution theory, for instance, I hoped my grasp of fundamentals was stronger.

I knew that other people for whom genetics was not central held essentially folk-genetic ideas. My father, a design engineer, dabbled a bit in biological ideas and only half understood them. But it did not really matter, to understand to the extent that interested him, his pre-Mendelian ideas did the job. My ignorance of the full Monty of chemistry and my father's half-baked genetics would have been fatal flaws if these concepts had been central to our professional practice, but they weren't. We fired on two cylinders and got by on half a loaf. But the purist tendency in science education does not think this is good enough; they want the whole loaf or nothing.

I would argue that my position (and that of my father) is more realistic, certainly for popularizing science and for science education for the majority of children who never want to become professional scientists. I would even argue that, if children go into technical professions, failure to grasp full-cream science may not matter; the key ideas are routinely simplified to approximate working assumptions in many technical careers, where most of the fundamental science is 'black-boxed'. Practitioners make use of the outcomes of science but do not themselves see anything but a black box from which the outcomes derive.

As we have seen, the stimulus for the current UK PUS and PEST movements came from the scientific community. The public was ignorant of science, this was a bad thing, and the solution was for scientists to do more communication. The mission was overtly educational, public audiences should be taught some science to narrow the 'cognitive deficit' between the understandings of science among experts compared with lay people. We have argued that this model of communication is misconceived because it privileges the scientific community agenda at the expense of equally important public concerns. But it may also be misconceived if scientists believe it possible to convey understanding of science to a majority of people.

Science teaching is the oldest form of science communication and a large amount of research has been done on all aspects of it. There are surely some lessons that could be applied to the popular communication of science? Before suggesting what these might be, we need to examine a potential difference between children and adults; children are not just smaller people, their brains may be configured differently so that they may think differently from adults.

THEORIES OF MENTAL DEVELOPMENT IN CHILDREN

Learning in both children and adults depends on the same set of mental skills; memorizing, perceiving, attending (being sufficiently motivated to devote time and energy to learning), and refined use of language, both orally and in reading and writing. Do such skills develop uniformly as children's brains grow in complexity, or does mental development occur in stages so that certain levels of maturation must be reached before some types of understanding can occur? In either case, can these mental skills be enhanced and developed by intervention and training?

There seem to be three classes of answer to such questions. In two cases the child's brain is considered to be different from that of the adult. In one, the development of the adult brain is thought to be to an extent spontaneous, in the other, the transition requires extensive contact with, and instruction from, competent adults. In the third case, the child and adult brains are not thought to be qualitatively different, the maturation process is simply the result of a bigger brain with more connections being able to process more information and draw on more experience.

Jean Piaget

The Swiss psychologist Jean Piaget championed the first case: the child's brain was different from an adult's brain, but maturation transparent; they are interpreted in the light of values and attitudes. In many cases it is hard to pick out the changes which are important in the interpretation of an experiment from more dramatic but irrelevant changes, or indeed to become totally distracted by the form and behaviour of the apparatus itself.

It seems that children continue to interpret demonstrations and experiments according to their existing lay ideas, even when heavily steered towards the scientific interpretation by a teacher. Lay interpretations prove remarkably resilient, and there is ample educational research that demonstrates that many students, even those studying science at university, do not understand scientific theories. One way the constructivist school tries to overcome these learning problems is to encourage discussion of pupil-generated 'wrong' concepts in comparison with scientifically correct ones, getting pupils really thinking about the issues and rejecting common-sense interpretations to accept the scientific one. Children certainly can, and do, learn to reframe their lay interpretations to the scientific, and some aspects of education help them do it. Critical discussion of different interpretative ideas may be a good (if time-consuming) way to achieve this. However, Piagetian or Russian school science educationists might argue that these methods work because they encourage cognitive conflict (Piaget), or develop verbal fluency (Russian school).

INTERVENTIONS AND ALTERNATIVES

Since the introduction of the UK National Curriculum, all children have had to do science up to GCSE at age 16, but the number of children choosing to specialize further in science has not increased. For followers of Piaget, the miserable outcome of all this additional teaching of science has a simple explanation. Success with science depends on formal-operational thought. Clearly, if children of 15 or 16 have not successfully made the transition from concrete-operational to formal-operational thinking, science (and a lot of other subjects too) will remain incomprehensible. Several teams in the UK and elsewhere, thinking along Piagetian lines, have devised interventions designed to stimulate the cognitive conflict that Piaget argued was essential for the development of formal-operational thought. One example is the Cognitive Acceleration through Science Education (CASE) programme devised in the 1990s at King's College London.

CASE intervention sessions slot into science lessons from age 11. The main point is to deliberately engineer cognitive conflict, a situation where pupils cannot explain new events by concrete thinking. Since students do better if they reflect on how they learn (meta-cognition), teachers using CASE materials are also trained to encourage this by asking individuals and groups to explain what they found difficult and how they overcame it. To undertake such meta-cognition, children must be able to use language in a sophisticated way. Teachers are also encouraged to build bridges between these special 'thinking' sessions and the regular science curriculum and to students' everyday lives.

In pilot schemes, test pupils received 2 years of 'thinking science' sessions, while matched control classes did not. GCSE performance was assessed in maths, English and science and pretty well all the intervention groups showed significant examination improvements compared with control groups. The designers of the scheme believe this showed acceleration from concrete to formal-operational thinking, induced by deliberate cognitive conflict. Those less happy with the idea of Piagetian mental stages point out that the CASE exercise involves many other critical differences between intervention and control groups, such as the encouragement of meta-cognition and associated development of language skills. As we have seen, such open-ended discourse and linguistic fluency are considered key learning development skills by other schools of educational thought.

Other alternative approaches to science education have followed Richard Gregory's belief in science for all: science appreciation. The most recent manifestation is derived from the public understanding, engagement and science literacy thinking for adults.

Adult citizens are encouraged to appreciate the cultural value of science and to understand science to the extent that it is helpful for taking democratic decisions in an increasingly technological society. The same principles have been applied to the UK school science curriculum.

Such courses have been introduced at both ordinary and advanced levels in the UK, making a virtue of discourse and linguistic skills-led learning techniques that are suitable for understanding the place of science in ethical and political decision making, and which also seem central to learning the methods and content of science as well. The introduction of these courses has proved contentious; teachers are not always confident at dealing with 'science in society' issues and many feel uncomfortable that large numbers of children could miss the chance to specialize in the sciences because these courses do not prepare them adequately for advanced science study. The government has muddied the waters because it believes that the public understanding/engagement approach will also solve the problem of too few students taking up advanced science, whereas advocates for the public understanding approach have always argued that advanced participation in science demands more specialized science courses, which should continue for those motivated to take up science.

COMMUNICATION IS THE KEY?

But the key to improving science education at all levels and in all contexts may be structured development of communication skills. Nearly every educational theory has, lurking near its core, a concern with the fluent use of language. The ability to use language to comprehend instruction, work out meaning and articulate a coherent discourse about what has been learned is critical. Being linguistically articulate may be a necessary prerequisite for intelligent thought in science (and other intellectual domains). Fluent use of language and delight in listening to language and reading seem to be prerequisites for effective advanced learning.

All children are able to hold elaborate conversations with each other and with adults provided these are strongly interactive, composed of short dialogue turns, and conducted face-to-face, so that linguistic content is supported by non-verbal cues that reinforce meaning. But only a minority of children are able to narrate or argue in long presentations free of turns and non-verbal cues, and to understand and relay complex verbal instructions. Such oral fluency correlates closely with abstract reasoning ability. It seems feasible that the development of high-level oral fluency is the basis for formal-operational thinking.

Children's abilities to speak in continuous narrative can be improved by making them listen to stories before telling stories themselves, and there is evidence that they are often limited in their linguistic development because teachers ask closed questions which fail to encourage discussion. Closed questions (demanding a single right answer) do nothing to encourage speculation, reasoning or hypothesis generation, which are all essential mental skills for high-level learning. Such open-ended discourse by learners inevitably produces error on the way towards correct interpretations, and working through such mistakes is essential for learning. But, in many school situations, fear of making mistakes dominates the strategies of most children to the exclusion of much else. Holt notes drily how primary school children daydream in class until the spotlight turns on them and then use a mass of prevaricating and evasion strategies to conceal ignorance and avoid mistakes until the spotlight leaves them and turns on someone else.

John Hurley argues that emphasis on communication is important, right up to the top of science education. American college entrants have to undertake communication aptitude tests and take communication modules as undergraduates. One American university chemistry department has records of the entrant and undergraduate performance of all their students over several decades. A proportion of those students went on to doctoral research and a smaller proportion still became research scientists in their own right.

The single feature of their entrance and undergraduate performance that predicted later research career success was performance in communication modules. The best communicators turned out to be the best researchers.

LESSONS FOR ADULT SCIENCE COMMUNICATION

The main lesson must be that communicating science at a professional level is not a realistic objective for popular science communication. In previous chapters we have seen that communicating 'scientists' science' has been criticized for a variety of sociological reasons. The difficulties in developing abstract thinking for science reinforce the point that trying to teach such science to a lay audience is unlikely to work. The amount of teacher-mediated intervention necessary for effective learning of school science should daunt any popularizer bent on trying to communicate professional level understanding to lay audiences.

The educational evidence suggests that only a minority of school students will ever be able to engage with science at a level leading to professional competence. The rigour of Armstrong and Nuffield 'pupil-as-scientist' educational schemes is only useful to an academically motivated subgroup. There seems little alternative, if most school children and students are to gain much of value from school science, to science appreciation programmes which try to embed science in social and moral contexts. The PUS/PEST agenda has had a positive influence on twenty-first-century rethinking of the older 'science for all' or 'science appreciation' approaches to school science education and has adopted the contextual, ethical and democratic elements implied (but not necessarily recognized) in adult PUS/PEST. Only time will tell if a population exposed to this approach as children (if these schemes survive), will find that they engage better with contextual and democratic aspects of science when they are adults.

The detached, logical abstract thought judged essential for the practice of science is not necessarily a focus for most people.

Indeed, one theory of mental development (information processing) downplays the value of such thought in both child and adult learning. The re-introduction of school science appreciation curricula on the scientific literacy and public understanding models accepts that, for most people, science is most valuable in context, not isolation, and that the rigours of the scientific method are not useful to them. Emphasis on a professional science approach for most children learning science, or for adult science communication, therefore, seems inappropriate.

BIBLIOGRAPHY

Adey, P. and Shayer, M. (1993). An exploration of long-term, far-transfer effects following an extended intervention programme in the high-school science curriculum. *Cognition and Instruction*, **11**, 1–29.

Black, P. (1998). Formative assessment, raising standards inside the classroom. *School Science Review*, **80**, 39–52.

Black, P. and Harrison, C. (2001). Feedback in questioning and marking: the science teacher's role in formative assessment. *School Science Review*, **82**, 55–61.

Brook, A., Driver, R. and Johnston, K. (1989). Learning processes in science: a classroom perspective. In Wellington, J. (ed.). *Skills and Processes in Science Education. A Critical Analysis*, Chapter 4. London: Routledge.

Claxton, C.S. and Murrell, P.H. (1987). *Learning Styles. Implications for Improving Educational Practice*. ASHE-ERIC Higher Education Report 4.

Gooday, G. (1990). Precision measurement and the genesis of physics teaching laboratories in Victorian Britain. *British Journal for the History of Science*, **23**, 25–31.

Hand, B. and Prain, V. (1995). Using writing to help improve students' understanding of science knowledge, *School Science Review*, **77**, 112–17.

Holt, J. (1983). *How Children Learn* (revised edition). London: Penguin.

Holt, J. (1993). *How Children Fail (revised edition)*. London: Penguin.

Jenkins, E. (1989). Processes in science education; an historical perspective. In Wellington, J. (ed.). *Skills and Processes in Science Education. A Critical Analysis*, Chapter 2. London: Routledge.

Luria, A.R., trans. Lopez-Morillas, M. and Solotaroff, L. (ed. Cole, M.) (1976). *Cognitive Development. Its Cultural and Social Foundations*. Cambridge MA: Harvard University Press.

Macaskill, C. and Ogborn, J. (1996). Science and technology. *School Science Review*, **77**, 55–61.

Makins, V. (1993). *50th Anniversary Report*. London: The Nuffield Foundation.

Millar, R. and Osborne, J. (eds.) (1998). *Beyond 2000. School Education for the Future*. London: Nuffield Foundation.

Millar, R., Osborne, J. and Nott, M. (1998). Science education for the future. *School Science Review*, **80**, 19–24.

Nott, M. (1997). Keeping scientists in their place. *School Science Review*, **78**, 49–60.

Osborne, J. and Collins, S. (2000). Pupils' and parents' views on the school science curriculum. *School Science Review*, **82**, 23–31.

Osborne, J., Erdman, S., Simon, S. and Monk, M. (2001). Enhancing the quality of argument in school science. *School Science Review*, **82**, 63–70.

Perks, D. (ed.) (2006). *What is Science Education For?* London: Academy of Ideas Ltd.

Wood, W. (1998). *How Children Think and Learn. The Social Contexts of Cognitive Development*. Second edition. Oxford: Blackwell.

Part III Popular science communication: the press and broadcasting

10 What every scientist should know about the mass media

The Beijing Olympic Games opened in August 2008, the culmination of a year-long news agenda following China's bid to mount a great sporting event to symbolize its arrival on the world stage. When the games finally started with a spectacular ceremony, the world expected to settle down to 3 weeks of benign Corinthian rivalry.

But the world is an unpredictable place. Just as global media attention was focused on Beijing, a hot war erupted on the southern borders of Russia and, for several days, vicious fighting broke out between Russia and the Republic of Georgia. Television pictures of synchronized ranks of Chinese drummers and dancers were rapidly replaced by rumbling tanks, reporters in front of bombed-out flats with grief stricken civilians mourning their already dead, Russian planes banking steeply with exhaust gas streaks as rockets crashed to Earth; all the shocking and yet familiar imagery of medium-level conflict. This sort of thing is always with us; it comes from Palestine, Lebanon, Iraq, Afghanistan and occasionally from places like Georgia.

Modern communication technology and efficient corporate media organization meant that pictures and reports of the fighting were beamed into homes and onto news-stands across the globe within hours of the conflict starting. The coverage was staggeringly comprehensive; reports came in from both sides and from a wide range of sites. The international mass media pulled out all the stops to inform the global audience of what was going on, the long-planned media assault on the Beijing games was disrupted and resources re-deployed at staggering speed. But such rapid reaction has a downside.

The global audience hardly knew where Georgia was and viewers and readers knew nothing about the 15 years of cultural and political rumbling in which newly independent Georgia, breaking away from Imperial and Soviet Russia, had been grappling with the problem of a population of ethnic Russians who preferred to be part of Russia rather than Georgia. The Georgian President, buoyed up by contacts with the West, put troops into one of these Russian-dominated regions, South Ossetia, to assert Georgian control, knowing that this might provoke a Russian response but gambling that his Western friends would help. In practice, nearly all his optimistic assumptions turned out to be wrong and a nasty little war with long-term global implications was the result.

To make sense of the dramatic coverage of the war, the viewer or reader needed to know the political background. A week after the war began, from diligent reading of lengthy news feature articles in the quality press, some members of the audience were up to speed on the outline of events. But the subtleties and refinements were still passing us by. With no previous knowledge and limited time available to learn up the background, few ordinary people were able to understand what was going on. The war in South Ossetia demonstrates clearly the chief strengths and weaknesses of mass media. They are quick with news of events but slow in the explanation and interpretation of events.

THE MASS MEDIA FRAMEWORK IN DEMOCRATIC SOCIETY

Politics is the business of organizing public life. The mass media are major avenues of communication and therefore part of the apparatus of politics. In democracies communication in the 'public sphere' is important because voters can only make sound decisions if they are well informed about public issues. Most people learn about wider society through the media. Newspapers, radio and television are bridges between wider social reality and the necessarily limited experiences of individuals. There are a variety of metaphors for this mediating role; window, mirror, filter, signpost, interpreter, platform or barrier, suggesting a wide range of potential interpretations of the role of mass media in society.

Given this importance of mass media, it is valuable to understand the implicit rules (norms) that govern its behaviour. A reasonable place to start is the 1947 US Commission on Freedom of the Press. This upheld the principle that the press in a democratic society should be free from government or other regulation but that there have to be limits to freedom of expression; the press must demonstrate social responsibility. The emphasis on social responsibility implies that media companies or corporations cannot just operate as commercial enterprises on market principles; they are forms of public trust with obligations beyond commercial success.

While mass media have a primary role in reporting public and political events, news media have always had to entertain as well, producing non-news material of interest to readers and viewers. To the extent that readers and viewers have only limited interest in news as such, these popular entertainment elements are important in building media audiences. If press freedom is interpreted only in terms of the freedom to use capital to make and sell a product for a profit, the emphasis on entertainment may become overwhelming and there will be little protection for diversity of political and social expression. This is especially true in mature markets where ownership of media companies settles into the hands of a small number of big organizations. The notion of a free press cannot just be subsumed within commercial or market freedom. The idea of public trust means that there must be positive encouragement of media diversity and a duty to devote space to politics.

Most social democracies therefore try to restrict cross-media ownership (print corporations should not own too many broadcast companies, for instance) to prevent loss of platforms for the expression of diverse opinion. Media concentration always raises worries about reduction in the content, quality and choice of both news and entertainment. Concentration of media ownership threatens the idea of a socially responsible free press and many believe that diverse opinion can only be achieved with diverse ownership of media outlets. Thus the media scholar Dennis McQuail argues that governments must make positive moves to replace large media corporations with multiple, small-scale, local media, responsive to community demands. He argues that playing by the rules of the free market is not a good mechanism for ensuring a free press. Other commentators such as Ian Hargreaves (British newspaper editor turned media academic) are also uneasy about purely commercial media markets and want journalists and editors to set themselves standards and attitudes 'above' the pursuit of sales.

THE NEWS GENRE AND NEWS VALUES

Implicit in this thinking about freedom of the press is the primacy of its political role. This means that, even in media where entertainment is a major component, reporters and editors still operate in a news culture. News and news values remain central features of most periodical and broadcast operations.

It is difficult to define 'news'. In the 1940s Park compared news with history (since both are accounts of past socio-political events) and extracted features which he thought characteristic of news. These included the idea that news is about recent or recurrent events and is unsystematic, dealing haphazardly with discrete events. It is not the primary task of news media to interpret, explain, or put material into a wider context. News is perishable; it lasts only so long as events themselves are current and as long as the events reported as news tend to be unusual or unexpected. News events have 'news value', a property which involves subjective judgements about likely audience interest. News is mainly for orientation and attention-direction and is not a substitute for knowledge, and news is, to a large extent, predictable. This list contains one very loose concept, news value, and one paradox, that news (despite being about the unexpected) is predictable.

Galtung and Ruge in the 1960s, in a classic study of Norwegian newspapers and their coverage of foreign news, provided further insight into news values extending and confirming Park's analysis. News media have a preference for reporting events that fit advance audience expectations (events which are consonant with past news). There is a bias towards the unexpected and the novel but always within the limits of what is familiar, a wish to continue with events already established as newsworthy. Foreign news interest is heavily influenced by a country's trading partners and international treaty obligations.

The existence of this set of news values provides editors with a set of cultural algorithms. Their decisions are subject to the ideology of news value because otherwise they could not take necessarily rapid decisions. Since different organizations consistently respond in a similar way to the same events, this suggests that a strong set of common professional values is involved. News is socially constructed according to the schemes of interpretation and operating assumptions of news institutions. News is predictable for fairly obvious reasons: the presence of reporters and facilities for recording and transmitting events plays a major part.

All other things being equal, geographically close events are covered before those from further away, and areas where news is thought likely to happen are covered continuously by resident reporters, making it increasingly likely that there will be more news from such areas. News events are often pre-defined and planned, and positions taken about what to 'expect'. To allow for such pre-definition, editors and journalists cultivate close contacts with sources and, even if an event does not turn out as expected, it may be covered as closely as possible to the form that was predicted.

Nonetheless, it is still true that the most newsworthy stories are unplanned and happen at unexpected locations. As our scenario illustrated, while news organizations are geared up for the entirely predictable (the Beijing Olympics), they can respond instantly to the unplanned in an unexpected place: a war in Georgia.

The demand for consistent supplies of news and entertainment to fill media can lead to a close (often over-close) relationship between reporters and their sources. This greatly improves the planning of supply of news, despite the fact that it conflicts with the media's ideology of novelty, spontaneity and creativity. Some organizations are much more powerful as suppliers of news than others and the interests of some suppliers are so dovetailed to the news organization that assimilation (or virtual collusion between source and supposedly independent reporting) occurs. A great deal of news derives from public relations (PR) agencies. These agencies are very effective at placing stories, despite claims by journalists to resist them. In practice, journalists make a great deal of use of information releases from 'official' sources, mediated through such agencies.

THE PERVADING INFLUENCE OF MEDIA LOGIC

Information flows through media organizations in huge volume; there is far more than can be turned into news or entertainment. Therefore, there are filters at work, discarding a great deal of material and modifying severely what passes through. On the whole, these day-to-day decisions about content have little to do with the needs of the audience or the commercial imperatives of owners. In association with news values, media organizations develop specific rule-of-thumb procedures and conventional shortcuts, sometimes summarized as media logic, the main features of which are as follows.

Space and airtime are always limited

All reporters have to compete for space and time with equally 'newsworthy' stories. All reporters fight most fiercely with their own colleagues to get stories past their editors and into print, sound or vision. Television news slots are often 90 seconds or 2 minutes long, and the material has to be filmed and edited with a script of 150 words at the most. All this is done against tight deadlines that allow little space for proper investigation.

The ethos of journalism still revolves round hard news

Hard news of current dramatic events is still the most respected media material. Explanation and analysis need feature articles, which require time for investigation and research. Many media organizations do not have the resources to support such activities and many journalists, trained in the hard news school, are temperamentally disinclined to do explanatory work. The credit ethos for journalists favours the person who 'breaks' the story, rather than the one who analyses it. This failure to explain and set things properly in context, well established by Park in the 1940s, is a critique of all media behaviour made (with justification) by many radical media critics.

Tight deadlines encourage dependence on pre-digested material

This pre-digested material consists largely of press conferences and releases. Many journalists use too few sources, or when they use more with which they are unfamiliar, accept what they are told uncritically and become too friendly with them.

Editors have a huge influence on all news reporting and feature sections

They assign reporters, decide which stories to run, write (or approve) headlines and may well cut or rewrite copy according to their preferences (and exert similar influences in the case of broadcast news). Reporters therefore tend to work for their editors and their known prejudices and tastes, rather than for the public who technically are their audience.

Working journalists tend to think of media as windows on to society, or mirrors reflecting it back, but academic theorists see media actively filtering, screening and interpreting the events upon which they report. This is partly a consequence of news values and media logic and partly a product of agenda setting by powerful groups. These groups can determine which real-world events are turned into news. Thus research by Justin Lewis (of the Cardiff School of Journalism) shows that media coverage of international terrorism has been at higher levels since the events of 9/11 in 2001 than at any time in the previous 15 years. But this does not reflect the actual extent of international terrorism, which has been declining steadily (with the exception of the 9/11 blip) since the mid 1980s, when the combined efforts of international terror groups produced more than 600 terrorist events per year. By 2002/03 this had fallen to 200 events a year. The media coverage therefore more closely reflects a political agenda-setting rhetoric (media as filter or interpreter) rather than reporting the objective rates of international terrorism (media as window or mirror).

NEWS VALUES AND MEDIA LOGIC; A LETHAL CONSPIRACY AGAINST UNDERSTANDING?

Park, Galtung and Ruge, and others long ago established that it was not a professional norm of news media to interpret or explain events; they work on the assumption that the audience understands the context of events reported. Given the complexity of the modern world, this absence of any duty to explain makes one uneasy. Some critics of media go further and suggest that professional news values and media logic actively prevent the audience from understanding social reality. Things may be especially bad on television. Media logic dictates an emphasis on pictures beamed out as soon as possible from visually dramatic news events. As we have seen in the scenario, the background the viewer needs to make sense of the visual drama is not covered because it requires explanation, which is best developed linearly by spoken word or text. It is hard to make a good, visually interesting television 'essay' quickly. There is a genre that tries to achieve this, the current affairs film but, by the time such a programme has been made, events have often moved on.

These problems with television news in the UK have been discussed for a long time. Particularly voluble criticism came from the then young broadcasting Turks, John Birt and Peter Jay, in a series of articles written in the mid 1970s. To use John Birt's phrase at the time, television news was structured to produce a 'bias against understanding'. When Michael Checkland was appointed Director General of the BBC in 1987, he hired John Birt as Head of News and Current Affairs. Birt himself then went on to become Director General after Checkland, until replaced by Greg Dyke in 1999. Throughout the 1990s, Peter Jay was also at the BBC as its Economics Editor, so the two ex-young Turks who had claimed television news had a bias against understanding found themselves in charge of the largest television news gathering organization in Europe and set about reforming it with their 'mission to explain'.

News bulletins at the BBC became more focused, with fewer items per programme and more background and context, while current affairs were separated into specialized strands. The changes increased viewing figures; they were popular. But many BBC journalists disliked them, claiming that the new approach, especially towards the current affairs film, might be worthy but was also dull. The spark and originality had gone from news-based documentaries, together with committed polemical journalism, which had been a hallmark of much previous work. It was this decline of current affairs films which most distressed critics of the Birt era at the BBC. They argued that he failed to understand the extent to which such programmes need a strong story framework and, by ignoring narrative at the expense of explanation, the whole genre was emasculated.

Research by members of the Glasgow University Media Group (long-term critics of the failures and distortions of news broadcasting) demonstrated that television news immediately after the Birt regime did not explain the complex events in Israel during the Palestinian intifada, and maintained that television news is consistently biased against the Palestinians.

In 2004 the Group published an analysis of a 3-year research project into the treatment of Israeli–Palestinian conflicts on British television news. They looked at the situation from three angles: what the news items contained; what constraints the news generators (producers and journalists) worked under; and what a large sample (800) of viewers made of it. They demonstrated the greater emphasis and construction of news on the Israeli side of the argument (Israel's security and survival are threatened by terrorist actions from hostile neighbours) than that of the Palestinians (resisting a brutal military occupation by invaders who stole their land). Viewers whose only knowledge of the situation came from television confessed deep confusion because enough history and context are never provided. Television journalists complain that they are not allowed to provide such explanations because of editorial demands for action and strong visuals.

For the Glasgow Group this is an open-and-shut case of broadcasting organizations' failure to explain, and of virtually deliberate distortion. However, this analysis in isolation may give an unfair picture of public ignorance (the public might show just as much confusion about other foreign news stories), while the failure to explain, and the 'bias', may be products of political agenda-setting as much as media failure. In the latter case the Group would still have a strong case against the media for failing to critique such political framing. Another recent analysis (by Cardiff School of Journalism again) of media coverage of conflict, this time the coverage of the Iraqi war by journalists 'embedded' with British and American troops, shows that, while reporters were not guilty of being manipulated by their military minders, they did operate within a pro-war agenda and used plenty of over-sanitized visuals provided or sanctioned by military sources. Viewers were irritated by this superficial approach and expressed a strong desire for a better grasp of the situation, especially from the Iraqi point of view.

News culture is dependent on both audience and journalists being familiar with the context of events. No one who does not already understand the context is going to learn enough from the news alone. Citizens in democracies have a responsibility to inform and educate themselves through other means about issues as they become politically or socially relevant.

THE TENSION BETWEEN SERIOUS NEWS AND POPULAR ENTERTAINMENT: THE 'DUMBING DOWN' OF THE MEDIA

A 'free' press in a market-orientated social democracy faces constant tension. Commercial pressures mean media organizations must make a profit. If the audience does not find the reporting and analysis of news sufficiently interesting, they will not buy or view that media outlet. Under these circumstances, the key moral virtue of a free press, the expression of a range of cultural/political views, will tend to decline as media seek other material with which to entertain the audience and keep sales up.

In some democracies, notably the UK, the commercial media operate in competition with Public Service Broadcasting (PBS), organizations not funded by commercial income, but through some public mechanism such as the universal licence fee on all television-owning households, which funds the BBC. PBS broadcasters have statutory duties to represent diversity, report in a fair and balanced way, and produce a minimum amount of serious material such as news, documentary, quality drama and so on. But PBS organizations have to compete with the commercial media for audience share and, if audiences lose interest in serious issues, PBS broadcasters increase the proportion of cheaper and entertaining output to keep viewing figures up. Despite the moral duty to provide what the audience ought to have, they feel compelled to supply what the audience want. For those who believe that free and serious public media are vital for active democracy, the narrowing down or trivialization of the news agenda, or the reduction of serious content overall are seen as dangerous, summed up by the accusation that the mass media are 'dumbing down'.

Thus it is claimed that many newspapers are degenerating into purveyors of scandal, while 'serious' coverage has decreased. The emphasis on entertainment and the lives of celebrities has gone up, as has the space devoted to 'lifestyle' (travel, food, drink, housing, gardening, interior design, fashion, and both popular and serious culture) at the expense of political news and analysis.

One could interpret these changes in several ways. It might be caused by pressure to maximize income by the easiest means, or it could be argued that changing media logic is responsible. On a less conspiratorial reading, the changes in form and content of mass media may reflect changes to our cultural values. Now that we are relatively rich, we are more concerned with rewarding ways to enjoy our wealth (hence the rise of lifestyle journalism). Many people now feel that politics is about managing economic and political systems upon which we now are all agreed, providing a perfectly sound cultural reason why political discourse takes less of our attention.

On UK television the increasingly commercial and free market spirit, which began in the 1980s, is said to have reduced quality by undermining the public service ethos, which previously dominated both the BBC and ITV. Television executives have chased ratings to maximize income and popularity, quality television has been replaced by 'tabloid' television with a decline in the serious agendas of news, politics, documentary and drama and an increase in game shows, docusoaps and reality television. The public service and democratic functions of journalism have been reduced or subsumed. Many commentators regard this regularly documented 'dumbing down' as both a fact and a problem.

There are counter-arguments. People now have more access to information that feeds more easily into the most important forum for decision making: people's own families and social circles. The greater range of broadcast channels and topics can enhance public appreciation of previously neglected minorities. In any case everyday life has always been more important to most people than issues of politics or governance. It could be argued that the high-minded view of the purpose of broadcast journalism espoused by many of the exponents of the 'dumbing down' thesis is unreal. The popularization which the elite perceive as trivializing may actually be more inclusive and agenda broadening. There is every reason to suppose that popular media have a duty to provide popular culture.

There is clearly unequivocal evidence that mass media content is changing, even though there is sharp disagreement about its cause and consequences. Realistically, it has to change. The culture of the societies upon which it reports is changing fast, as is the relative power and influence of markets, media platforms and the advent of new media. Such changes are significant for all specialized subjects and interests seeking media representation, no less for science than for anything else.

THE LESSONS FOR MEDIA SCIENCE COMMUNICATION?

We will explore these lessons more thoroughly in Chapter 13. But it is already clear that the mass media operate on different principles and hold different values from many of the institutions, including science, on which they report. It is naïve for scientists to see 'misrepresentation' as a problem peculiar to them. To the extent that media values are imposed on all stories in the media, all public institutions resent the degree of filtration and mediation to which their actions are subjected. They all resent the media emphasis on audience interests, rather than on those of the institutions themselves. It is not just frustrated political parties who rage against not being able to 'get their message across'. Because the media have to react to cultural and social changes across the whole of society, their own norms and values are not as stable as those of some institutions (and science perhaps is particularly conservative in this respect). So, institutions face a daunting challenge in achieving favourable public exposure for the things they want mass audiences to hear. Optimistically (for science), there is evidence that some institutions in science are successful at riding media agendas to their own advantage.

BIBLIOGRAPHY

Barnett, S. and Gaber, I. (2001). *Westminster Tale: The Twenty First Century Crisis in Political Journalism*. London: Continuum.

Barnett, S. and Seymour, E. (1999). *A Shrinking Iceberg Travelling South ... Changing Trends in British Television: A Case Study of Drama and Current Affairs*. London: Report for the Campaign for Quality Television Ltd.

Barnett, S., Seymour, E. and Gaber, I. (2000). *From Callaghan to Kosovo: Changing Trends in British Television News 1975–1999*. London: University of Westminster Report.

Boyd-Barrett, O. and Braham, P. (eds.) (1987). *Media, Knowledge and Power*. London: Routledge.

Curran, C. and Seaton, J. (2003). *Power without Responsibility. The Press and Broadcasting in Britain*. 6th edition. London: Routledge.

Davies, N. (1999). Getting away with murder. *The Guardian*, 11 January, Media Section, 4–5.

Downing, J., Mohammadi, A. and Sreberny-Mohammadi, A. (eds.) (1995). *Questioning the Media. A Critical Introduction*. 2nd edition. London: Sage Publications.

Hargreaves, I. (2003). *Journalism. Truth or Dare?* Oxford: Oxford University Press.

Hencke, D. (2001). No news is bad news. *The Guardian*, G2 Section, 5 March, 16–17.

Inglis, F. (1990). *Media Theory, An Introduction*. Oxford: Blackwell.

Lambert, R. (1999). Press in peril. *The Guardian*, 4 January, Media Section, 20–21.

Lewis, J. (2003). Facts in the line of fire. *The Guardian*, 6 November, 25.

Lewis, J. (2004). At the service of politicians. *The Guardian*, 4 August, 19.

Lloyd, J. (2004). *What the Media are Doing to our Politics*. London: Constable and Robinson.

Macnab, G. (2003). Keep it real. *The Guardian*, G2 Section, 27 March, 14–15.

Marr, A. (2004). *My Trade. A Short History of British Journalism*. London: Macmillan.

McNair, B. (2003). *News and Journalism in the UK*. 4th edition. London: Routledge.

McQuail, D. (2005). *Mass Communication Theory; An Introduction*. 5th edition. London: Sage Publications.

Mosey, R. (2004). The BBC was no cheerleader for war. *The Guardian*, 27 July.

Philo, G. (2002). Missing in action. *The Guardian*, Education Section, 16 April, 10–11.

Philo, G. (2004). What you get in 20 seconds. *The Guardian*, 14 July, 19.

Silverstone, R. (1999). *Why Study the Media?* London: Sage Publications.

Wells, M. (2002). TV news biased against Palestinians, says study. *The Guardian*, 16 April, 4.

Wells, M. (2003). Where the writer is king. *The Guardian*, Media Section, 27 January, 6–7.

Williams, R. (1984). *The Long Revolution*. London: Penguin.

11 **What every scientist should know about journalists**

Journalists, like scientists, are morally obliged to tell the truth. But the truth is slippery stuff. It seems to go without saying that facts must be reported accurately but it is much harder to make a clear judgement about the 'truth' of interpretation, which depends on who is interpreting events for whom. We all know that my terrorist can be your freedom fighter. But, sometimes even the facts don't have to be objectively true for an interpretative truth to emerge.

For instance, what should we make of the American school of 'new' or 'Gonzo' journalism espoused by American figures such as Norman Mailer, Truman Capote, Hunter S. Thompson and Tom Wolfe? All these writers reported and interpreted real events at book length, spending time with the people and institutions upon which they were reporting but writing things up with a variety of narrative, plot and character techniques drawn from fiction. In Park's early work on news, he defined it by comparing it to history, which he regarded as a different genre. The new journalists might argue that this distinction is false, that what they are doing is contemporary history. Convention says this is not news, but 'new' journalists argue that this is still journalism but now trying to explain events as well as report them. For clear and stimulating interpretation, events may need to be re-ordered or dressed in fictional clothes.

And what of young Stephen Glass, cub reporter on the radical American news magazine, *New Republic*, dismissed from his post in 1998? Glass specialized in writing slice-of-life features about American subcultures, all apparently verified by websites, voicemail messages, reporter's notes and so on. Yet on analysis nearly everything he wrote turned out to be fiction, the stories and all the supporting evidence were fake. Glass has never explained himself so we do not know his motives. This looks like fraud just as morally unjustified as fake data and experiments in science. And yet ... .

Fiction is not always intrinsically untrue. Many canonical works of fiction distil a filtered copy of the real world, which may be as valuable as a report from the real world in the sense that the fictive interpretation can be just as valid as factual interpretations. Perhaps Glass was aiming to build truthful interpretation of his subject groups through fictive techniques? Or, then again, he could just have been lazy and exploitative, or have set out deliberately to deceive for the thrill of it.

What about the iconic rescue of the American GI, Jessica Lynch, from an Iraqi hospital behind enemy lines by American Special Forces in the 2003 Iraq War? The American military released dramatic video footage of forces overrunning the hospital and rescuing the wounded Lynch. The military story was of her mistreatment by the Iraqis from whom she was dramatically rescued. Eventually, a counter-story emerged. She had been hurt in a road accident involving American vehicles; the Iraqi medics had treated her well, and were trying to return her to the Americans when they were shot at for their pains. The military version of the story was 'spun' and showed American troops in a heroic light when America was making slow progress and public opinion about the rightness of the war was shifting. It looks like naked propaganda; truth is always the first casualty of war. And yet ....

While this construction may have been blatantly rigged, by their nature, events in conflict are confused. The 'new' journalism of Wolfe and Thompson was born partly from frustration with the confused reportage from the Vietnam

War. A great deal of the news reporting of conflict does need 'correcting' in the light of later evidence and better understanding. While the Lynch story is at the unacceptable end of the spectrum of problems arising from reporting war, its origin could have been honest misinterpretation.

THE FOOT-SOLDIERS OF THE MASS MEDIA: WHAT DO JOURNALISTS DO AND WHAT OUGHT THEY TO DO?

McQuail has tried to summarize what a professional journalist should be, accentuating objectivity and neutrality as key attributes, with good skills at attracting attention and assessing public taste. But there does not seem to be a body of journalistic knowledge and nor are attributes like freedom, creativity and a critical approach compatible with the bureaucratic regulation of professions dependent on specialized knowledge and expertise.

Yet journalists are socialized into their trade carefully (even if the methods are informal). Once socialized, most journalists and editors feel free to choose stories without interference by senior management. The social characteristics of journalists are important because these may reasonably be thought to influence their professional behaviour. In the US journalists have long been secure, with middle incomes and average social backgrounds with an elite layer who are much wealthier; generally white, male and agnostic, and coming from the same social strata as those in charge of the economic and political systems. In the US, women entered journalism extensively in the 1970s and 1980s, but ethnic minorities less so. Most American journalists have a university education in a subject relevant to journalism, or even hold a degree in it. Journalists have always taken themselves more seriously in America than they have in the UK.

In the UK, both newsrooms and print shops were, until recently, controlled by powerful unions able to impose their own patterns of apprenticeship on new entrants. Newsrooms were dominated by the National Union of Journalists (NUJ), which enforced a craft apprenticeship pattern of entry, ensuring that a variety of people with different social backgrounds became journalists. Most journalists in the UK saw themselves practising a trade, not belonging to a profession. But all that has changed. Computerization has destroyed the power of the old print unions, and the influence of the NUJ has been reduced in the nation's newsrooms. Partly as a consequence, the social composition of the community is changing. Journalism in the UK, as in the US, is becoming a thoroughly middle-class profession. Forty-nine per cent of British journalists are graduates and, as in America, increasing numbers of women are entering the profession. In the mid 1990s they were packed at the bottom end of the age range but by 2002 more than 50% of jobs were held by women. By that date, the British journalist community had become overwhelmingly white, middle-class, and graduate.

HOW SHOULD JOURNALISTS BEHAVE?

The ethical journalist

Professions like medicine and law have classically been self-regulating with codes of behaviour (essentially sets of moral principles) devised and policed by the professions themselves. Clients must trust professionals to have reputable knowledge and skill and to use these in clients' interests because clients cannot judge this for themselves. A professional behaves well by undertaking to practise in a morally good way. In practice, elements in professional codes are weighted in favour of the professional rather than the client and a profession's self-interest can sometimes lead to protecting it from clients, rather than in providing a trustworthy service to them. For this reason professions are subject to external regulation. Many trades, including journalism, have aspired to professional status and have set up codes of practice.

Ethics are about the nature of good behaviour. Most societies believe that there are differences between good and bad acts and human society is better the more good behaviour there is. There are three grand theories of ethics. The oldest is deontological or rule-based ethics. Societies either agree (or have imposed upon them) rules of behaviour that distinguish between right and wrong. Good behaviour consists of accepting the rules and abiding by them. Problems arise when rules for different aspects of behaviour are contradictory, or when individual rules become irrational if applied blindly in all contexts.

The second theory is utilitarianism (also known as consequentialism). The principles involved here are summed up in such phrases as 'the greatest good to the greatest number' or 'the ends justify the means'. Here, a bad act can be justified if its consequences produce a greater overall good. While this seems intuitively sensible, problems arise in assessing the levels of disadvantage and benefit to make rational utilitarian judgements. The third system is virtue ethics. Here, the issue of moral worth is placed on individuals. How should a morally good person behave, can a life be judged from a lifetime's behaviour? The emphasis here is on individual self-reflection, it is not on adherence to arbitrary rules, nor does it depend on a calculus of cost/benefit.

News and the fourth estate

A sociological account of news describes what is written in newspapers and provides one basis for deciding what news is (as explored in Chapter 10). But the moral philosopher Matthew Kieran argues that this is an inadequate starting point. It does not take account of what the news media ought to contain. Only then can actual news be compared against a rational standard.

One high-minded description of the role of journalists is that they are a 'fourth estate'. This phrase derives from Macauley's comment in the British Parliament in the 1860s. Referring to the press box he said, 'the gallery in which the reporters sit has become the fourth estate of the realm'. In social democracies government typically resolves into three branches (or estates), the legislature (parliament), the executive (the civil service) and the judiciary (judges and the law courts). Macauley's 'fourth-estate' role for the press was to act as an independent check on the three governing estates. An alternative description is that journalists act as tribunes of the people on whose behalf government and parliament supposedly act. The press guard (or oversee) the guardians, answering the key Latin question about checking governance, *quis custodiat custodes*?

On this basis, news is any matter of public interest concerning how the state is governed. The central professional duty of the journalist is to develop the necessary expertise, knowledge and skill to describe, evaluate and investigate government on behalf of the governed. On this model, critical reporting of politics and the mechanics of government are the mainstays of good journalism. Failing to spot error, corruption, misgovernment or poor morals in the governors is the essence of bad journalism.

Kieran is well aware that media organizations are commercial operations and that they must entertain as well as report on the political sphere. Nevertheless, he takes the hardline position that journalists should be concerned primarily with what the audience ought to know, rather than with what they want to know. Journalism is bad to the extent that it merely entertains and fails to explore and expose the forces that determine the political, economic and cultural realities of our lives. Belsey and Chadwick take the same high-minded view of the moral purpose of journalists. Media interest should be focused on big human issues and they see titillating coverage of celebrity, scandal and lifestyle, not just as a cause for shame but as a moral crime.

Journalism as 'rule-based' or utilitarian practice?
For Kieran, trust in the media must derive from the rule-based behaviour of journalists and their editors. To the extent that they break moral rules and lie, cheat, steal, bribe, invade privacy or deceive, they undermine public trust and their ability to act as effective guardians. The whole mediated world of which we have no direct personal experience is represented to us by journalists. We

can only believe what we are told if we can trust journalists to tell us what they believe (in the light of their training and experience) to be the truth about the world.

Jackson takes a more utilitarian line on possible justification for lying and deceit. For her, deciding whether lying is justified depends on whether the deceit leads to a betrayal of trust, and the extent to which those lied to retain an obligation to expect trust. If trust is not betrayed, or if those lied to have effectively forfeited any right to expect trust, then lying is justified. Actual journalistic practice then revolves round deciding when lying does not betray trust in the honest, and to what extent those with something to hide have forfeited the right to expect trust.

Trust, truth, disinterest and detachment

Kieran follows his own rule-based logic and argues that truth-telling, impartiality and writing for the audience are central journalistic virtues. Writing deliberately untrue stories breaks a primary reporting code; a commitment not to fabricate data or use one's skill to tell a fictional story as if it were true, although as we have argued in the scenario the issue is not as clear-cut as it seems.

But it is hard to defend the actions of young Jason Blair on the *New York Times*. An internal investigation of Blair's 73 news articles written between October 2002 and April 2003 found evidence of plagiarism, deception and inaccuracy in 36 of them. Blair was sacked and the *NYT* ran a 14000-word commentary of apology and excuse. The paper used the 'one rotten apple' defence; Blair had problems from childhood deprivation and adult addictions to drink and drugs, the fault lay with this maverick reporter not with the newsroom or with *NYT*'s journalistic practices. That defence fell apart when senior executives were forced to resign several months later because the newsroom was revealed as a hotbed of cronyism and competitive attitudes. Blair claimed that this dysfunctional newsroom drove him, a black reporter in a white elitist Ivy League culture, to fraud and deceit in order to survive.

Journalists (like scientists) should be disinterested in what they report. For instance, they should not themselves be aspiring politicians, actively playing the stockmarket, or too closely identified with the interests of those they are reporting on. However, Williams argues that collusion inevitably occurs between the military and war reporters during conflict. Journalists may get such a thrill from being on the ground with the forces that they accept all kinds of reporting restrictions, although they know that these will lead to partial reporting.

Kieran argues that journalists have a moral duty to write stories appropriate for their audiences. Journalists must write plainly in accessible language to maximize reader understanding. All jargon and specialized language should be avoided (making science writing especially difficult). But we have already seen that this is idealistic, because to get published and acquire reputations, journalists also have to write for their editors, their peers, or to impress the community they are writing about, rather than solely for their reading audience.

The bugbear of objectivity

Objective reporting must surely be a prerequisite of truthful representation of events; it is certainly a dominant feature of journalistic professionalism. The main characteristics of such objectivity are an accumulation of the virtues we have already listed; a position of detachment and neutrality towards the matters being reported, a lack of partisanship, an attachment to accuracy and other truth criteria, and a lack of ulterior motive or service to a third party.

Where facts are reported, their presentation is supposed to conform to truth criteria; the facts must stand up to independent verification and be consistent when reported by several sources. Whatever is reported must also be relevant, defined as information that affects most people, most immediately and most strongly.

Few can doubt that news events reported in reputable media happen, but there is a choice of things to report and ways of reporting them. Journalists produce different interpretations of events because they have different life histories, experiences and bring different value judgements to bear. In practice, these differences may not be all that significant, since news coverage in multiple sources is often depressingly similar. It seems that most journalists agree about how and why things happen. A naïve empiricist might take this as evidence that journalistic interpretations are 'true'. Others would say that the common interpretation reflects a common set of news values and the unifying effects of media culture. Probably the strongest truth-telling claim that journalists can make is that a report they have produced is true according to current media conventions. It is thus relative and contingent truth. The central journalistic norm of truth-telling is not a chimera, although there is often more than one candidate for the honour of being the most truthful account.

There is no reason to rule out a journalist being partisan. O'Neil believes that if his/her 'bias' is transparent for all readers to see, the reader is not deceived, and trust is not betrayed. But, for Kieran, the proper position of a journalist must always be detachment, the reporter must always stand apart from that reported. He feels that partisanship implies commitment and believes that any such emotional involvement is always morally bad journalism.

The issue of privacy

The media have a critical role in ensuring the existence of free speech, although British law has not been much concerned with actively protecting free speech. Article 10 of the European Convention of Human Rights, however, does provide protection for the right to free expression, to holding views and opinions, and to receiving and imparting information, and the Convention was introduced into British Law in 2000. But it must be said that most of the running in the early application of the Convention in the UK has invoked Article 8, concerned with the protection of privacy (largely invoked by celebrities resisting media intrusion).

Where are the limits to public interest to be drawn? What can legitimately be regarded as private and therefore effectively secret, not for exposure to media gaze? There are no clear-cut answers to these questions, the boundaries ebb and flow with cultural change. In the UK the problem of public interest and privacy has been particularly troublesome. It became a major issue in the 1980s (and is emerging again in the twenty-first century) when tabloid newspapers pushed the boundaries, using the defence of free speech to cover unreasonable harassment of the private lives of celebrities. While they did this to provide entertainment, they hypocritically invoked the justification of defending democracy, a pretty open and shut case of morally bad journalism.

Archard thinks that there are no good ethical reasons why public figures should lose their right to a private life, although there are valid reasons why such private affairs might be of public interest. He goes so far as to claim that 'what interests the public' might be a valid reason for the exposure of private life. This is normally dismissed because it seems merely to satisfy public prurience and sell more papers, but Archard argues that it is justified by the principle that gossip is essential social glue. This is refreshing because it moves away from the po-faced focus on the quality of political information and admits the significance of other cultural functions for the media.

Declaring an interest

Journalists are increasingly subjected to the blandishments of public relations people. Entertainment, fashion and 'lifestyle' journalism only work because so much material is supplied to journalists free by companies seeking publicity. To take the most obvious examples, food, drink, restaurant and travel coverage depend on suppliers, holiday companies, bars and restaurants providing samples of their services or wares free to interested journalists. These practices are potentially corrupt, but are usually considered trivial.

However, these comfortable compromises may be breaking down. More public relations practitioners are waking up to the fact that editors are more likely to accept work from freelance journalists than from press releases or press conferences. This has led to 'selling in'. Here, a public relations person commissions a freelance journalist to attend a conference or write a report. The journalist then sells the idea or story to a periodical, as if it was an independent activity of hers, untainted by formal sponsorship. The corruption is then aggravated if the journalist is paid twice, once by the PR firm and again by the periodical. Unreasonable pressure is often applied to such journalists; sponsors often make it a condition of payment that a minimum number of pieces are published.

THE REAL WORLD?

This emphasis on the good journalist in his/her role in fourth-estate mode, criticizing and exposing the defects and malpractices of powerful individuals and institutions, is certainly idealistic. A great deal of actual journalism falls far short of these ideals in behaviour and purpose. But this does not alter what journalists ought to be doing, what is supposed to be the moral justification for their existence. Scientists fall short of their professional codes on occasion, probably not as often as journalists. Some of us persist in expecting high standards of journalism because protecting and strengthening democracy seem worthwhile objectives. These high moral standards should apply as much to media coverage of science as to that of any other powerful institution.

BIBLIOGRAPHY

Archard, D. (1998). Privacy, the public interest and a prurient public. In Kieran, M. (ed.). *Media Ethics.* Chapter 7. London: Routledge.

Belsey, A. (1992). Privacy, publicity and politics. In Belsey, A. and Chadwick, R. (eds.). *Ethical Issues in Journalism and the Media.* Chapter 6. London: Routledge.

Belsey, A. and Chadwick, R. (1992). Ethics and politics of the media: the quest for quality. In Belsey, A. and Chadwick, R. (eds.). *Ethical Issues in Journalism and the Media.* Chapter 1. London: Routledge.

Blair, J. (2004). The truth this time. *The Guardian*, Weekend Review, 6 March, 22–9.

Edemariam, A. (2004). The story teller. *The Guardian*, G2 Section, 10 May, 8–9.

Gibbons, T. (1998). *Regulating the Media*. 2nd edition. London: Sweet and Maxwell.

Hanlin, B. (1992). Owners, editors and journalists. In Belsey, A. and Chadwick, R. (eds.). *Ethical Issues in Journalism and the Media*. Chapter 3. London: Routledge.

Jackson, J. (1992). Honesty in investigative journalism. In Belsey, A. and Chadwick, R. (eds.). *Ethical Issues in Journalism and the Media*. Chapter 7. London: Routledge.

Kampfner, J. (2003). The truth about Jessica. *The Guardian*, G2 Section, 15 May, 2–3.

Kieran, M. (1997). *Media Ethics. A Philosophical Approach*. Westport CT: Praeger.

Kieran, M. (1998). Objectivity, impartiality and good journalism. In Kieran, M. (ed.). *Media Ethics*. Chapter 3. London: Routledge.

McQuail, D. (2005). *Mass Communication Theory: an Introduction*. 5th edition. London: Sage Publications.

O'Malley, T. and Soley, C. (2000). *Regulating the Press*. London: Pluto Press.

O'Neil, J. (1992). Journalism in the market place. In Belsey, A. and Chadwick, R. (eds.). *Ethical Issues in Journalism and the Media*. Chapter 2. London: Routledge.

Paton, N. (2001). When is a story not a story? *The Guardian*, G2 Section, 22 October.

Preston, P. (2003). Reporter on the spike. *The Observer*, 18 May, 12.

Sanders, K. (2003). *Ethics and Journalism*. London: Sage Publications.

Snoddy, R. (1992). *The Good, the Bad and the Unacceptable. Hard News about the British Press*. London: Faber and Faber.

Williams, K. (1992). Something more important than truth: ethical issues in war reporting. In Belsey, A. and Chadwick, R. (eds.). *Ethical Issues in Journalism and the Media*. Chapter 11. London: Routledge.

Wolff, M. (2003). Phonies and cronies. *The Guardian*, Media Section, 9 May, 4.

Wolff, M. (2003). Will the buck stop here? *The Guardian*, Media Section, 9 June, 2–3

Yonge, G. (2003). Reporter's plagiarism claims scalp of editor as *New York Times* becomes the news. *The Guardian*, 6 June.

Zellor, N. (1995). Narrative strategies for case reports. In Hatch, J. A. and Wisniewski, R. (eds.). *Life History and Narrative*. London: Falmer Press.

12 The influence of new media

In the City of London there is a statue of a city trader 1980s style, a yuppie from the early years of deregulated financial markets. What marks him out as a figure from history is the brick-sized mobile phone clasped to his ear. The early cell phone was large, expensive, ostentatious and used by loud-mouthed young men to keep 'in touch' with office or trading floor. The devices (and their owners) proved a major irritant when used on commuter trains to activate their partners to pick them up from the station.

Then the phones began to shrink and got much cheaper. While their capacity to irritate did not decrease, their value for gossip increased sharply, especially when teenagers discovered text messaging. My class of Science Communication students circa 1996/97 marked an early stage in this transition of the mobile phone from braying yuppie accessory to necessary adjunct to social life. One young woman, after agonizing for weeks, decided it was worth investing in a mobile. There may have been other early adopters in her class, but the excitement caused by her decision suggests that many still found the idea of owning a mobile phone outrageous.

By 2000 it was unusual if a student did not have a mobile phone, two or three years more and most owned camera phones. Two or three years more and most of them could send photographs to their friends and on the most expensive services could get (not-too-good) internet access. By late 2008 so-called 3G (third-generation) phones were the norm as universal communication and data-processing devices; simultaneously phones, cameras, video cameras,

MP3 audio players, text-generators, e-mail and internet accessible.

The 3G phone is the ultimate new media machine, an astounding technological achievement, which rolls together once disparate experiences drawn from newsprint, books, radio, television, film, audio recording, the telephone, and the internet. The cultural consequences are wide-reaching but it is all happening so fast that analysis can scarcely keep up. We may have to wait for new media technologies to stabilize before really understanding what they are doing to us.

THE BIRTH OF THE WORLD WIDE WEB

In 1990 CERN, the international particle physics research facility in Geneva was the biggest academic internet site in Europe. Tim Berners-Lee and Robert Cailliau suggested that, to further improve computer communication, it should set up an elaborate networked system to allow sites on the internet to interact with each other with text, sound and pictures. It required the development of new software (browsers) and modifications to existing hardware (servers). Berners-Lee invented the concepts and necessary software for Uniform Resource Locators (URLs), the Hypertext Transfer Protocol (HTTP) and standards for a programming procedure to allow non-computer programmers to set up sites (now web pages) with ease, using Hypertext Markup Language (HTML). Berners-Lee came up with the name 'World Wide Web' in the CERN cafeteria in 1990.

The prototype World Wide Web was up and running in 1991 and all the first-generation sites were particle physics laboratories. By the end of 1992 there were still only 50 Web servers world-wide, increasing to 250 by the end of 1993. The breakthrough to mass use followed the introduction of user-friendly browsing software, developed by Marc Andreesen and Eric Bina. The system was called

Mosaic and then developed into *Netscape Navigator* when Adreesen founded a new company in partnership with Jim Clark in 1994. *Netscape* used the mouse-driven, point and click, easy-to-use graphical interface characteristics already common in business and entertainment computer environments.

The wide availability of *Netscape Navigator* finally unlocked the commercial and social potentials of the internet, way beyond the academic community. Almost any Tom, Dick or Harriet could set up a homepage accessible by anybody with a browser anywhere in the world. By the end of 1995 there were over 73 000 host sites and, from that point on, the World Wide Web was essentially synonymous with the internet.

Building a website in the 1990s still required modest computer skills which discouraged ordinary people from setting up their own web pages. Personal sites remained restricted to those with some computer literacy, but institutional and commercial websites grew rapidly, serving educational and business markets for information, goods and services. At that time the majority of desktop computers had only limited speed and processing power and were without broadband facilities. User-friendly web page building software, more powerful domestic and office computers, and widely and cheaply available broadband connections were necessary before the modern era of new media could develop.

GREAT TECHNICAL NETWORK: WHAT WAS THE CONTENT TO BE?

The internet began as a private system of exchange among the scattered academic community. The private system had been taken forward by computer buffs in the 1970s and 1980s on an ideology of free exchange of material and ideas. This sat uneasily with the development of commercial services which followed in the 1990s. This expanded system needed to generate revenue. Internet Service Providers (ISPs) charge users for telephone access to servers. These service providers and the telecommunication companies who are responsible for the physical infrastructure provide visible services, which are paid for by subscription.

It is less clear how web content (the information that consumers access) can be paid for. In the late 1990s, it seemed the content would be cut-price goods and services. A huge growth was predicted in such e-commerce through these dot.com companies, symbolized by pioneers like *Last.minute.com* and *Amazon*. There was a feverish investment bubble on the expectation of vast profits. Like all such bubbles it eventually burst in summer 2000, losing a lot of people a great deal of money. All the prognoses had been too optimistic, consumer and business culture could not change fast enough and the e-businesses were bogged down in the logistics of storing, moving and dispatching real products. The largest category of dot.com survivors into the twenty-first century were mostly agencies (brokering suppliers and users of services) including *Last.minute.com* and a tumescence of dating agencies, pornography, gambling and tie-in sites to television reality shows.

Before the dot.com collapse, many companies were experimenting with high grade content made possible by broadband telephone connections, but most of them failed in the dot.com collapse. It was then an uphill battle to persuade people they should spend money on a broadband upgrade, if all it offered was speedier access to the unexciting and the seedy. Nevertheless, broadband uptake in the UK was reasonably rapid post-2000 and much of this resurgence was to gain access to goods and services from established retailers who developed internet trading arms.

Just as many idealists were vexed by the failure of old media to properly serve democratic interests, so they were initially disappointed with parallel failures in new media. Rather than a commercial system based on consumption, they favoured a model promoting cultural exchange: a high-minded combination of super-library, people's university and self-help bureau. But, making this erudite model work would have needed extensive legal and cultural reform, especially in the area of intellectual property rights. In practice, such a free-exchange system did emerge, Web 2.0 social networking, which ignores (or tries to bypass) intellectual property issues like copyright with easy-to-use file sharing software.

MAINSTREAM JOURNALISM GOES ONLINE

This new social network age began with some radical fusions of old and new media. In journalism a significant novelty was run in the UK in the late 1990s from an attic in London by an ex-Reuters man, Paul Eedle and his wife, *Out There News*. Eedle and his colleagues were journalists, but what they did with *Out There* was to collect and e-publish stories from people directly involved in news zones; eye-witness accounts from participants which did not often appear in conventional media. Eedle claimed that these accounts were nearer the 'truth', and that this bottom-up approach provided an alternative news analysis to that provided by professional journalists in conventional media channels.

A similar radical initiative was *Ohmy News*, in South Korea. This was also started by a journalist, Oh Yeon Ho, in 2000 as an online newspaper with stories written largely by ordinary people, 'citizen reporters' as Oh called them. Over 17 000 people had submitted articles to the paper by summer 2004, the reporters being largely young male students or office workers, together with a sprinkling of professional journalists. All articles carried a comment zone for reader feedback, allowing Oh Yeon Ho to use two further catch-phrases, 'news as debate' and 'participatory journalism'. In 2004 the material was edited by a staff of 35, who also contributed the 20% of content given over to complex news. The presentation was professional and modest payments were made to contributors whose pieces occupied prominent positions, but otherwise writers were not paid. Because everything was filtered through an attractively packaged, single brand site, it could be financed from advertising.

This online newspaper model worked well in South Korea where conventional media are conservative. There were doubts about whether the model would work so well elsewhere, although an ideal opportunity cropped up in America in 2002/2003 for an 'underground' press opposing the pro-government, pro-Iraq War stance of mainstream media such as *Fox News* (and many others). But, in America these events triggered an explosion in personal blogging instead, which turned out to be an even more radical form of participatory journalism.

BLOGGING

It is hard to define the term 'web log' or trace the origins of web logging or blogging. It is a form of vanity publishing, a cyber-version of the print culture of amateur fanzines and other home-produced underground magazines prepared by enthusiasts desperate to have their opinions widely circulated in a 'permanent' form, rather than simply airing them in the pub or on the sofa. Much of this pre-web material consisted of critical reaction to musical, literary and other cultural production. Since the mid 1990s it has been possible to produce such 'zines more cheaply and easily online as internet home pages, which still needed some understanding of software and principles of website design.

In the early twenty-first century, easy-to-use blogging software appeared which allowed self-publishing critics, aspiring literary figures and citizen journalists of all types onto the web. Bloggers think that others might be interested in their personal selections of cultural products and that their opinions and accounts of their daily doings (through diaries, or more salaciously webcams) would benefit from wider circulation. The blogging culture, combining web logging, 'zine writing, newsletter preparation and online journalism grew rapidly. Both professional and new amateur writers and opinion formers emerged, some with wide readerships, some earning money from voluntary subscriptions by their readers.

A famous pioneer was Salem Pax, the 'Baghdad Blogger' who used his site to provide first-hand reports of life in Baghdad as the Iraq War raged in 2003. He then went mainstream, his dispatches published in *The Guardian* newspaper. On a similar site, *Eye to Eye*, young Palestinians reported on life inside refugee camps in the violent stand-offs between Israel and Palestine. In America an early player was Matt Drudge's *Drudge Report*, famous for breaking the Monica Lewinsky scandal in the dying phase of the Clinton presidential administration in the late 1990s, and the *Huffington Post* edited by Ariana Huffington, which became a major player in political commentary surrounding the presidential race between Barack Obama and John McCain in 2008. Local, city or state-orientated blogs also made a big contribution to this election, especially in mobilizing local Democrat activism and support, using cyberspace in place of (and as well as) knocking on doors.

Commercial companies became interested in blogging because of its influence on consumer behaviour. Corporations employ blog monitoring services, which detect what is the 'word on the street' about new products. Many also use blogs for marketing, alerting enthusiasts about new products or services. The power of the blog in consumer and citizen contexts seems to lie in the degree of trust we place in sources of information. While certain professions, such as doctors, receive overwhelming trust as information sources, the next category of informant that surveys show we trust are family, friends and 'people like us'. While academics and other concerned professionals wring their hands about the problems of authenticity and trust that people place in online information sources, bloggers are seen by most net users as an extended network of family and friends, 'people like us' and thus as trusted sources, which helps explain their powerful cultural effects.

Blogging took off because new software made it simple for amateurs to produce professional-looking text and picture homepages. Since high-quality audio and video web logs can also be produced, more and more enthusiasts are making their blogs either audio or video based. Net listeners can download audio blogs onto MP3 players such as iPods, and carry these narrowcasts round with them.

Over its short lifespan, the blogosphere has stratified. Some lay reporters and commentators are having influence well beyond their immediate social groups. They are becoming 'citizen journalists' and both they and some commentators think they are pioneering a new form of 'bottom-up' journalism, which will ultimately threaten conventional mass media, although research in America suggests that their influence remains limited and that they do not often break news stories. Imitations of *Ohmy News* have appeared in America claiming to combine the editorial responsibility of mainstream media with the 'bottom-up' reporting and attempts at resetting the news agenda of blogs. Unlike blogs, they have to raise money to keep an editorial team going and this may count against their success in the longer term.

SOCIAL NETWORKING

While blogs and blogging continue to grow, technological progress has stimulated more organized and efficient systems of exchange and promulgation of matters more trivial than citizen journalism. The critical and journalistic functions of blogs have been combined with the social networking functions of group e-mail and tele-texting to generate the social networking sites of Web 2.0.

These sites allow participants to put all kinds of material up on the web with the minimum of technical effort and no expense. Social exchange and chatter about this material and their personal lives is then easy for all (potentially many million) members of the network who tend to behave in cyberspace as real friends and colleagues would at actual social gatherings. While much of the material is commentary on existing cultural output, the distinctive feature of the networked sites is that participants provide masses of cultural product themselves (as text, pictures, performances, recordings, videos and so on).

These sites have grown at astonishing speed since 2003. Most famous are *MySpace*, *Facebook*, and *YouTube*. Teenagers who have grown up with personal computers as an integral part of their lives interact a great deal on these sites. The level of conversations and quality of much of the generated materials are not high, but having this level of interaction with a potentially infinite number of contacts is popular. The free exchange culture of these sites is somewhat spoiled by their commercial value, the wealth of their founders and the fact that mainstream media organizations have paid very good money to take them over. While members go about their business for free, the sites are packed with paid-for advertising and it is open to site owners to allow commercial companies to infiltrate the sites for marketing and sales efforts.

Growth and development of Web 2.0 activities and static and mobile hardware like micro-laptops and super interactive mobile telephones happened at dizzying speed towards the end of the first decade of the new millennium. The cultural effects are probably going to be deep, although hard to predict. Web 2.0 itself is replete with learned (and not so learned) pundits on these issues, and it is too early to say who is likely to have got their predictions right.

NEW TYPES OF GATEKEEPER?

The access by ordinary citizens to web-based information, goods and services, and their ability to generate cultural product for themselves with global distribution, feels revolutionary. Certainly, such reliable and facile web access in the UK threatens the viability of retail stores and, more importantly in the context of communication, to shrink the markets of the old media of print, radio and television. The most radical advocates of change are convinced that the massive self-publishing power available to everybody via the web will produce huge changes in the production and dissemination of both news and culture as they both become 'bottom-up' activities to which anyone can contribute.

But the evidence so far of cultural shift suggests that this is unlikely to happen on quite the scale the radicals imagine. While the costs of printing, storage and distribution have been taken out of e-publishing, the editorial gatekeeping function of traditional media (seen by radicals as restrictive and elitist) may become more important as a means of navigating through the huge volume of material available (we have seen in Chapter 3 that this seems to be true for professional science communication). Few people have the time or energy to scan and evaluate the whole web for what they want and will continue to rely on gatekeepers of some type to select what is worth attending to. These new media editors will be different in background and task from their old media counterparts, but paradoxically they may eventually turn out to be even more influential in guiding culture and reportage.

BIBLIOGRAPHY

Berners-Lee, T. and Fischetti, M. (1999). *Weaving the Web.* London: Harper Collins.

Burkeman, O. (2005). The new commentariat. *The Guardian*, 17 November, 8–15.

Connon, H. (2001). Phone giants' brave new world still disconnected. *The Observer*, Business Section, 4 March 2001.

Garfield, G. (2004). New kids on the blog. *The Observer*, Review Section, 4 April, 1–2.

Garfield, G. (2006). How to make 80 million friends and influence people. *The Observer*, Review Section, 18 June, 6–8.

Gibson, O. (2002). Broad but not so deep. *The Guardian*, Media Section, 4 March, 38–9.

Gibson, O. (2005). The bloggers have all the best news. *The Guardian*, Media Section, 6 June, 12–13.

Gibson, O. (2005). The man who put teenagers' lives online. *The Guardian*, Media Section, 3 July, 5.

Gillies, J. and Cailliau, R. (2000). *How the Web was Born. The Story of the World Wide Web.* Oxford: Oxford University Press.

Hammersley, B. (2004). Audible revolution. *The Guardian*, Online Section, 12 February, 27–8.

Hafner, K. and Lyon, M. (1996). *When Wizards Stay up Late: the Origins of the Internet.* London: Simon and Schuster.

Hargrave, S. (2004). The blog busters. *The Guardian*, Media Section, 9 August.

House of Lords Select Committee on Science and Technology (2000). *Tenth report*, http://www.publications.parliament.uk/pa/cm200304/cmselect/399/39903.htm, visited 25 October 2004.

Mansell, R. (2002). Where all citizens should be free to meet. *Times Higher Education Supplement*, 22 February, 17–18.

Martinson, J. (1999). Sleeping with the enemy. *The Guardian*, Media Section, 22 November, 6–7.

Mattin, D. (2005). We are changing the nature of news. *The Guardian*, Media Section, 15 August, 10.

McClellan, J. (2003). Newbiz on the blog. *The Guardian*, Online Section, 30 January, 1–3.

McIntosh, N. (2002). The 3G roll out begins. *The Guardian*, Online Section, 10 October, 1–3.

Moody, G. (2004). Dambusters. *The Guardian*, Online Section, 11 November, 23–4.

Moody, G. (2004). Risk-free rebellion. *The Guardian*, Online Section, 11 November, 19.

Naughton, J. (1999). *A Brief History of the Future: The Origins of the Internet*. London: Weidenfeld and Nicolson.

Paton, M. (2001). The word in his attic. *The Guardian*, Media Section, 15 October.

Pearse, J. (2003). Content rules at 3GSN. *New Media Age*, 6 March, 22.

Schofield, J. (2004). Hacks of all trades. *The Guardian*, Online Section, 22 July, 23–4.

Seenan, G. (2004). Forget the bloggers, it's the vloggers showing the way on the internet. *The Guardian*, 7 August, 11.

Wadman, W. (2001). Publishers challenged over access to papers. *Nature*, **410**, 29 March, 502.

Waldman, S. (1999). Stop the presses … *The Guardian,* Media Section, 11 January, 6–7.

Waldman, S. (2004). Who knows? *The Guardian*, G2 Section, 26 October, 2–3.

13   How the media represent science

Professor Janet Docherty was smart, personable, articulate and running an important cell biology research group investigating the behaviour of cell lines taken from mouse cancers. She had no trouble getting research grants; she was a star at conferences, and eligible for election to the Royal Society. The organizations funding her and her university were keen to publicize her work and Janet herself was perfectly willing to do all that she could in talking to the media.

The press liaison offices at her university and at a leading research charity tried to build news stories round her best papers. Press releases were carefully drafted; press conferences organized at prestigious London venues, the press officers and Janet herself were careful to get to know the leading science and health correspondents personally and always to respond to requests from journalists for interview. Janet was the very model of a modern media-savvy professor and her labours and those of her press officers were rewarded, her work always attracted interest and a certain amount of low key coverage. But media attention did not reflect her professional status as a leading cancer researcher.

Then, one day in a faraway corporate laboratory in a rustbelt American city a small team announced a breakthrough in the treatment of lung cancer, a drug which might stop one of the most intractable cancers of all. It worked in rodents, but still had to go through the whole series of clinical trials in humans. Announcing it at this stage was a huge risk for the pharmaceutical company concerned but it was small, in need of more investment, and generated the publicity to attract it.

The announcement caused a huge stir, but the company was cagey about how the drug worked, but mentioned Docherty's work as the basis of its action. Janet's phone never stopped ringing, she appeared on television with pictures from a hastily assembled news conference. A long appearance on BBC *Newsnight* coinciding with a televised address at a cancer conference threatened to turn her into a media star. But she backed away. She was in the dark on the details of the drug's action and still no one was interested in her long-term goal of finding new ways to deal with cancer.

Four weeks later it had all died down and for several years the university press machine again tried to publicize Janet's work but with little success. Should she have ridden the drug story harder? Probably not, those who sup with the media need long spoons. Two years later the clinical trials on the American drug came undone, the company collapsed and all those closely associated with it found themselves hounded as charlatans. Janet emerged unscathed but resolved not to seek media attention quite so assiduously in the future.

The media are interested in science because it is a powerful social institution with potential to improve or damage the lives of ordinary people. Many British science organizations have learned the importance of having specialist press teams to help with getting messages about their work into the media, and to absorb or deflect unfavourable commentary. But the crucial factor in the success or failure of such communication effort is its relationship to the news agenda. That agenda, based on news values and media logic, makes an imperfect and flawed set of criteria but it is what the media play by. The lesson for science is that successful publicity demands playing by media rules, not by the institutional values of science.

And publicity is a multi-edged sword. The media or the public may misinterpret what is said and can make unfavourable negative associations or ludicrously positive ones. Such 'misreadings' are seldom irrational; they are entirely explicable from the conventions of media behaviour and from the sociology of media/audience interactions. These are worlds remote from science, but it is these factors that determine what science becomes news, how the audience reacts to it, and what they think about it. The alien nature of these agendas alarms some scientists who see media handling of science as inevitably devious, distorting and unfavourable. They might reflect, however, as we have seen in Part II, that science still retains enormous trust and respect with the public. The media are not out to get science but journalists have a duty to be properly critical of much of what it does.

A BRIEF HISTORY OF POST-WAR SCIENCE

Coverage in the British press

Science and technology were discussed extensively in periodicals (and to a lesser extent newspapers) in the late Victorian and Edwardian eras. The first specialist (albeit part-time) appointment in science journalism in the UK was made when J.G. Crowther joined the *Manchester Guardian* in 1928, managing to convince the editor, C.P. Scott, that he could find original science news stories and write them for lay audiences.

As Chilvers shows, Crowther held strong left-wing views and told Scott that his mission as a science journalist was to help the public realize the greatness of science and its significance for society and the human mind: he was a proponent of the 'enlightened rationalism' of science. He saw his task as educating people about science within an overtly left-wing framework based on the idea that society should be organized on scientific principles, what we would now call 'scientism'. Crowther had excellent contacts in the Cavendish Laboratory at Cambridge in the 1930s, where key progress was made in subatomic physics, and his reports on the drama of the new science made his reputation and convinced other editors that covering science was worthwhile. In 1932 the young Ritchie Calder started out as the second official member of the new British profession. So, specialized media science coverage began by celebrating the wonder and progress of science and favouring a more significant cultural role for scientists. This positive positioning has remained dominant and is favoured for obvious reasons by the scientific community, but does not perhaps fulfil the critical role that journalism at its highest level is supposed to take.

Martin Bauer and a small team produced a long-term quantitative study of science coverage in newspapers in the UK from 1946 to 1990. They found that a steady 5% to 6% of space was devoted to news with a science and/or technology content. While the level of coverage remained constant, attitudes towards science changed. At the beginning (1950–65), coverage was positive and celebratory, but then science reporting became increasingly negative and critical (1966–90). In the first period, emphasis was on the benefits of science and technology, while in the second, risks were given more prominence. The subject matter also changed over time. Physical science dominated the first phase but, after the mid 1960s, it was steadily replaced by a combination of social/human and biomedical sciences. Only about a quarter of articles were concerned with science controversy and, in most cases, this was not manipulated by the media. The controversy was within science and dutifully reflected in media coverage.

Hansen and Dickinson conducted a detailed analysis of science coverage in the British press and broadcasting in April and May 1989. The dominance of biomedical and social science coverage revealed by Bauer's team was reinforced, comprising nearly three-quarters of the total in the press and on the radio, and two-thirds of the total on television. In the quality press specialist correspondents wrote much of the material, while scientists themselves wrote the articles in 6% of cases. Refining Baur's analysis, Hansen and Dickinson showed that science coverage was not uniform in tone within a single newspaper or one television channel. Newspaper feature articles tended to be different in tone from news items. In broadcast news, science was often portrayed as certain and uncontroversial, but science documentaries actively explored opposing views and controversies. In another survey Hansen analysed newspaper coverage of biotechnology between 1990 and 1992 and found that most quality papers carried about 100 articles a year but the *Financial Times* carried more than 350 a year. This extra *FT* coverage was about the economics of companies in the biotechnology sector. All tabloid titles together carried only 96 articles in the 2-year period.

There was reasonably wide UK quality newspaper coverage of key biotechnology issues such as DNA fingerprinting, the Human Genome Project (HGP), and the biotechnology industry. However, the patterns of news coverage were very different. Genetic fingerprinting was most prominent but see-sawed wildly. Coverage of the HGP showed a steady rise but was generally low level, while biotechnology industry coverage was stable but at a higher level than HGP. A rather different pattern emerged in the coverage of the first UK BSE controversy in the later 1980s and early 1990s. News coverage of this issue showed a steady low rate most of the time but with a huge peak in the summer of 1990 and another, smaller one, in 1992.

Hansen argued that these patterns showed that coverage of science-related issues was clearly determined by factors other than those intrinsic to science. Genetic fingerprinting came up in crime and identity reporting, although there was little or no reporting of the underlying science. The same applied to BSE, there was no progress in the relevant science of dementias, scrapie or other prion diseases so little scientific advance to report. The coverage was driven by socio-political news events. The huge 1990 BSE reporting covered the high-profile attempts by the British Minister of Agriculture at the time, John Gummer, to overturn the politically and economically damaging ban on the export of British beef to Europe.

Hansen's analysis of the coverage of genetic fingerprinting demonstrates some standard features of the reporting of new and unfamiliar science. Coverage almost always stressed the certainty of the technique, little attention was paid to its complexity and consequent uncertainty; it was not completely safe and there was the chance of mistakes being made. It was reported as a breakthrough that could bring certainty where previously there had been doubt, and the media conveyed this certainty through a rhetoric of numbers; there were said to be huge odds against a genetic fingerprint being wrong. The value of the quoted numbers (which were variable) did not really matter, so long as they were sufficiently large to symbolize near certainty. The perceived power of the technique was increased with its use in analysing fossil DNA which needed only tiny amounts of material (the rhetoric of the very large therefore combined with that of the very small). These were both positive arguments in favour of the technique in a news context.

One of the most striking conclusions from Hansen's surveys was that half of all science coverage was in articles not specifically about science, the main subjects being crime, politics or moral issues. This tendency for scientific issues to be embedded in, and diverted by, the wider news agendas is emphasized by Guy Cook's team. They analysed coverage of genetic modification in British newspapers in 2003, the year in which a government sponsored 'official' debate on the issue took place. But the main news agenda was set by 'the war on terror'; specifically, the invasion of Iraq. Cook's team reported that officials, scientists, GM protagonists and protesters were all irritated by public ignorance of the government sponsored public consultation on GM. The public absorbed GM coverage as part of the 'general' news agenda and constructed connections between the GM and Iraq stories over the issue of 'trust'. How much trust the audience placed in government, industry and protest group statements in these two stories became a common denominator between them. This was not an outcome foreseen by those who initiated the 'GM debate', but their frustration reflects a failure to see the importance of news agendas and how audiences (with their different social contexts and interests) will interpret news and information in ways different from those intended by people disseminating the information. This point is reinforced in work carried out by Bates. He argues that public knowledge of genetics derives from a wide range of media sources and that people process the information they encounter in complex ways, fitting it into their particular personal, social and cultural agendas.

Despite the rhetoric that science speaks with certainty and a single voice, media coverage often reflects the reality that science speaks with multiple, sometimes contradictory, voices. For instance, events during the British Foot and Mouth outbreak in 2001 found ministers and government scientists wrong-footed by independent epidemiologists like Roy Anderson from Imperial College. His models of how Foot and Mouth spread, rather than veterinary advice from government scientists, were the basis for the unpopular government policy of extreme culling of at-risk farm animals, championed by the newly appointed Chief Scientific Advisor to the government at the time, Professor David King. Given the ground rules, the rather brutal Anderson/King advice turned out to be more effective than anything available from the Ministry of Agriculture. But there is a caveat in the phrase 'given the ground rules'. These excluded vaccination largely on political grounds to do with international meat and livestock trading. But the merits of vaccination as an alternative to culling in dealing with Foot and Mouth clearly need more careful examination, although the rules over meat and livestock trading will make scientific evaluations more complex. But, even at the purely scientific level, there is an unresolved debate over the relative benefits of culling versus vaccination in the control of Foot and Mouth disease.

ANALYSIS OF THE BRITISH MEDIA AND CLIMATE CHANGE, THE MMR VACCINE CONTROVERSY, CLONING AND GENETIC MEDICAL RESEARCH

A group led by Ian Hargreaves from Cardiff University School of Journalism undertook a comprehensive survey of media coverage of aspects of science during the 9-month period from January to September 2002. They chose to monitor three issues with a strong science component: climate change (essentially global warming), the controversy over a possible link between the MMR (measles, mumps and rubella) triple vaccine, bowel disease and autism, and cloning human stem cells as a tool for medical research. Their survey was based on two early evening television news programmes, the BBC Radio 4 *Today* programme, and several daily and Sunday newspapers including tabloids and quality titles. The three stories appeared on more than 2200 items during the survey period.

The team also investigated public knowledge about these issues, based on 1000-person questionnaire surveys at the start (April 2002) and end (October 2002) of the analysis period. They also undertook some analysis of all stories in their sample where the word 'science' or 'scientist' appeared, to provide a snapshot of the range of issues covered in the media. This latter survey only included about a third of the pieces covering the three main stories under investigation, the majority of which were run without overt reference to science. Here they found a subject breakdown of coverage very similar to those described by Bauer and Hansen for earlier periods, with medical and health stories dominating.

Focusing on the three issues investigated in greater depth shows that these science stories were not like ordinary news. Unusually, the news subjects themselves, the scientists, were the main sources of information in 44% of articles and the general public in 15%. More conventional news sources; pressure groups, politicians, government, business and so on, were only minority contributors.

The research was undertaken in traditional 'public understanding of science' mode; that lack of public knowledge of science is a political problem and media should work harder to increase scientific literacy. The two knowledge surveys were devised to discover whether the public 'learned' more about the three phenomena as a result of 7 months of media coverage. Not surprisingly, the surveys gave near identical results, longer exposure to news coverage did not increase the number of 'right' answers in the surveys of understanding of the technical issues. These results suggest that media reflect the general level of understanding of phenomena among the public, rather than leading them to greater insight. People did respond best to questions based on what was covered by the media (so there had been an element of agenda setting) but, in terms of technical detail, their answers were more often wrong than right.

In climate change news items the surveys showed that only 3% of stories tried to explain the key phenomenon of 'greenhouse effect', demonstrating the point that news culture makes explanation difficult. Although people were generally conscious of the climate change problem, they confused global warming with thinning of the ozone layer, a situation often found before among journalists and public.

In the MMR controversy, there was a high level of understanding that the connection being made and questioned was between having the triple vaccine and the risk of autism among children who had been vaccinated. There was good understanding that the fall in vaccine uptake could trigger outbreaks of childhood diseases with possibly serious consequences. Many people knew that it was Andrew Wakefield who had first raised the matter but there was little understanding that his own co-authored paper did not provide good evidence for the connection, or that the weight of evidence from other studies did not support it. The Cardiff authors claim a degree of media culpability for this situation, although even coverage that put Wakefield in the foreground usually gave the other side of the argument as well.

The biomedical community saw this as an example of grossly misleading media coverage with serious public health consequences. The journalistic concept of fair reporting of controversy through 'balance' confronted the scientific concept of 'greater weight of empirical evidence'. But it seems likely that the real focus in this controversy was autism rather than MMR, fuelled by public alarm at the apparent rise in autism in children for which the medical and scientific establishments can provide no explanation. The ghost of the BSE and other controversies hovers here. The government then said that beef was safe to eat, but it wasn't. Here, the government insists that MMR vaccine is safe and yet autism is rising. The public finds common ground in these two issues, as they did between government positions on risk in the cases of terrorism and genetic manipulation.

On the issue of cloning and medical research, public attitudes were mixed. They were prepared to accept that, if research led to better medical treatment, it was a good thing, but were confused by the detailed ethical and legal arguments about embryos and stem cells. Overall, the Cardiff Group conclude that, to an extent, the media do mislead and the public do misunderstand. They had no simple solutions to rectify the situation. They do not subscribe to any agenda for more detailed science force fed into the media to improve understanding. Without engaging public interest or concern, any diet of 'science for science's sake' will be ignored, a conclusion repeatedly found in other PUS analyses as we saw in Part II.

THE COMPLEXITY OF MEDIA REPRESENTATION OF SCIENCE

Stephen Hilgartner's thoughts on this theme have had considerable influence. He conducted a case study of the diffusion of material from a key review paper by Doll and Peto, 'The causes of cancer: quantitative estimates of avoidable risks of cancer in the United States today', published in the *Journal of the National Cancer Institute* in 1981. Doll and Peto reviewed all the literature on the subject and wrote this paper specifically for 'interested non-specialists'. They came up with a set of 'best guesses' of the environmental causes of cancer and how many cancer deaths could be attributed to each cause. They provided ranges (often wide) and surrounded their figures with caveats.

Hilgartner showed that the further away any report of this material was from the Doll and Peto source, the more certain the numbers become with their ranges and caveats dropped. The firmer figures were then widely quoted in specialist and popular magazines and newspapers as part of a debate about the relative importance of personal lifestyle as opposed to workplace practices as the main causes of cancer.

The dominant framework for analysing science popularization, in which scientists generate new knowledge, and popularizers then disseminate news about it to a wider audience, is not adequate to explain what is going on here. The key issue is how to separate 'scientific knowledge' from 'popularized' versions of that knowledge. While there is a world of difference between a scientific journal report and a news story of that report in a newspaper, there is a continuous spectrum of communication forms between one and the other. There is no logical way to decide where the boundary lies between writing for scientists and popular writing. The communication spreads along a continuum from events like technical seminars, scientific meetings and laboratory shop talk, through intermediating documents such as scientific papers, technical literature reviews, grant proposals, editorials and news items in the house literature of the scientific profession, through to policy reports, monographs, textbooks, popular books and ultimately the mass media. With its hybrid purposes, the Doll and Peto paper does not fall firmly into any science or popularization categories. The existence of the spectrum of sources probably suggests that the diffusion model itself is wrong for thinking about science popularization generally.

THE SCIENTIST AS A SOURCE OF NEWS

Dunwoody showed trends in what kinds of scientist were involved in initiating news stories in the United States in the 1980s. University and government scientists were more likely to be story sources than industrial scientists; publicity for research is part of the public ethos, while industry has a culture of secrecy for commercial protection. Nevertheless, industry would like certain aspects of its science to be covered, and conducts considerable public relations (PR) activity to

Bronsdon, S. (1998). Attitudes of academic staff to the dissemination of science in the media. Unpublished M.Sc. dissertation, Imperial College London.

Brown, B. (2003). ... the answer is five. *The Guardian*, Media Section, 19 May, 2–3.

Brown, B. (2003). Where's the next Winston? *The Guardian*, Media Section, 2 June, 2.

Chilvers, C.A.J. (2003). The dilemmas of seditious men: the Crowther-Hessen correspondence in the 1930s. *British Journal for the History of Science*, **36**, 417–35.

Cook, G., Robbins, P.T. and Pieri, E. (2006). Words of mass destruction: British newspaper coverage of the genetically modified food debate, expert and non-expert reactions. *Public Understanding of Science*, **15**, 5–29.

Coward, R. (2005). Back to nature. *The Guardian*, Media Section, 9 May, 6–7.

Cozens, C. (2003). Tomorrow's World now yesterday's news. *The Guardian*, 4 January, 7.

Dingwall, R. and Aldridge, M. (2006). Television wildlife programming as a source of popular scientific information: a case study of evolution. *Public Understanding of Science*, **15**, 131–52.

Friedman, S., Dunwoody, S. and Rogers, C.L. (eds.) (1986). *Scientists and Journalists. Reporting Science as News*. Washington: American Association for the Advancement of Science.

Hansen, A. (1994). Journalistic practices and science reporting in the British press. *Public Understanding of Science*, **3**, 111–34.

Hansen, A. and Dickinson, R. (1992). Science coverage in the British mass media: media output and source input. *Communications*, **17**, 365–77.

Hargreaves, I. (2000). Is that Frank – or Frankenstein? *The Guardian*, Education Section, 19 September, 14–15.

Hargreaves, I., Lewis, J. and Speers, T. (2003). *Towards a Better Map. Science, the Public and the Media*. London: Economic and Social Research Council.

Herman, D. (2003). Thought crime. *The Guardian*, Weekend Review, 1 November, 18–19.

Hilgartner, S. (1990). The dominant view of popularization: conceptual problems, political uses. *Social Studies of Science*, **20**, 519–39.

King, D. (2002). Inaugural Graduate School of Engineering and Physical Sciences lecture. November, Imperial College London.

Mabey, R. (2003). Nature's voyeurs. *The Guardian*, Weekend Review, 15 March, 4–6.

Monbiot, G. (2002). Planet of the fakes. *The Guardian*, 17 December, 13.

Nelkin, D. (1995). *Selling Science*. 2nd edition. San Francisco: W.H. Freeman.

Rajan, L. (1995). Research into the popularization of science by scientists and engineers at Imperial College. Unpublished M.Sc. dissertation, Imperial College London.

14 How should science journalists behave?

Gerald Wheeler was both an American university teacher and a television science presenter. His presenter experiences show clearly that successful science communication is subservient to media agendas and that popularization should not aim to be too ambitious. Almost by accident Wheeler was asked to do a series of Saturday science shows for children, which he called 'sidewalk science'. He approached these shows as an opportunity to jazz up what he was already teaching to undergraduates but that approach didn't work. Running shows round principles like 'forces' was of no interest to anyone. He had been lulled into supposing that people were interested in that kind of thing from his captive undergraduate audiences. They wanted to be physicists or engineers and had to pass the exams. Schoolchildren at leisure had no such incentives.

He also learned that classroom science demonstrations and classroom pace were not effective on television. He had to have a 'tease' at the top of the programme and everything had to be much faster and less hedged with caveats than a lecture or class. While he got better at entertaining his juvenile audience, his colleagues criticized him for the 'errors' he was introducing. At first this worried him, until he realized that such 'error' is inevitable and did not matter for the purposes of his audience.

Later he acted as an advisor on another television show for young viewers and observed how scientists and media people talked in different languages and were focused on different issues. It took a long time to work out situations that were scientifically correct but also worked as television. In the light of his experiences Wheeler argued that, while children's television science shows can act as a stimulus and raise consciousness, they cannot go much further.

The science education framework had to be carefully adjusted to conform to the norms of children's television magazine programmes. In a similar way science journalists have to negotiate between the science research agenda and the culture of the newsroom.

THE NORMS OF PROFESSIONAL SCIENCE JOURNALIST BEHAVIOUR

The differences between the ethos of science and the ethos of news

Friedman and her colleagues produced a classic book in the 1980s, reporting on research among American science journalists and other science communicators (it contained Wheeler's story). Much remains fundamental to science journalism today.

Standard media logic limitations of space and time are harder for science specialists to cope with than most, because they feel they need space to explain complex issues. The hard news agenda does no favours to science and considerable effort goes into forcing it to fit, with inevitable distortions. Thus science often comes across in the media as a series of breathless 'breakthroughs', many of which turn out to be damp squibs. Good news stories have drama and human interest, which militate against science reporting where both elements may be lacking. Applied science is easier to write about than pure science, so much science has to be dressed in a suit of application to make it newsworthy. All these factors lead some in the science community to accuse the media of unnecessary sensationalism in science coverage.

Science usually advances slowly, with evidence added incrementally. Newspaper articles often report on a single research study with no mention of how it relates to earlier work, failing to portray the cumulative and collaborative nature of science. Reports on single studies with significant results, presented enthusiastically, give the public the impression that such a study constitutes 'proof'. This impression reduces the credibility of science because subsequent studies often 'prove' the opposite. Journalism also tends to give too orderly a picture of science, allowing little room for the notion that scientific discovery involves hunch and accident. Dorothy Nelkin has commented strongly on the tendency for journalists to see science as value-free, and to view scientists as neutral arbiters of truth.

Management and loyalty

Editors have a huge influence on science reporting, as they do on all reporting. Science writers face editors who often have little feel for science and do not believe readers are interested, although audience surveys repeatedly show that people want more science, technology and medicine news. There are more specialist science journalists now, but they may face a status problem in both their professional worlds. Scientists regard them as 'mere' writers, lacking authority in their own right, while other journalists often consider them marginal in the newsroom, specialists 'on tap' rather than central contributors to the news operation.

In theory, journalists from different papers and broadcast organizations are in competition with each other to cover stories but this may be less important for science reporters and was especially so for the 'inner club' of science specialists working in the USA in the 1980s. They formed a cooperative group after their accidental assignment from the reporting pool to cover the space race in the 1960s. They formed a group for mutual support and self-help in an unfamiliar environment. They trusted each other and willingly shared expertise and information, operating together in press conferences so that they could collectively probe deeper. While such a cartel helps journalists produce stories against deadlines it may operate against the public interest. The topics covered tend to be narrow and gee-whizzy rather than broad and socio-political. There is some evidence that, in UK media, specialist journalists (on science, health, etc.) have a similar ethos of mutual respect and support.

Distortion of science

Much early American analysis showed that media 'distort' science. This approach may not be helpful, given the separate professional cultures within which journalists and scientists operate. In any case Hansen and Dickinson reported that problems with accuracy of media reporting were not a serious issue for most scientists. They know that journalists work under tight constraints and feel they do a reasonable job of reporting in the circumstances. When controversy appears in the press, there is a tendency to say that this is because journalists are distorting the story. But most publicly reported controversies are within science itself and not trumped up by journalists. Furthermore, it is not in the interests of science journalists to misrepresent their sources, since they are so dependent on them and have no desire to alienate them.

The self-image of science journalists

Hansen investigated in some detail the professional practice of British science journalists and found that they see themselves as 'journalists' first and 'science journalists' second. They selected from the potential stories flowing through the newsroom using news value criteria such as controversy, breakthrough, proximity, suddenness, unexpectedness of event, and so on. A frequently expressed criterion was the combination of 'human interest' and 'relevance to everyday life'. They understood very well that, for science to become newsworthy, it must be linked with developments in more routine news forums such as politics, crime or the economy. They reject the idea that they have a duty to educate the public or to proselytize on behalf of science; their role is to provide interesting, informative and entertaining coverage of science. On the whole, there was little enthusiasm for undertaking investigative work or for adopting any self-consciously fourth-estate mode of critique of science and its institutions.

Quality newspaper science journalists enjoy considerable autonomy. They set their own agendas and are trusted to develop what they feel are important issues, although they accept that they have to work to sell their stories to the news desk. There is sameness in science covered by all papers, partly because of common assumptions on news values and partly by the collaborative behaviour of a small group of specialized journalists. While the popular paper writers are very clear that their audience is the general public, quality paper writers feel they should write for their peers and their sources as well; they value the respect and status this gives them.

Nelkin reported that American science journalists did not see themselves as public relations people for science, but nor did they feel any call to be particularly critical of science or scientists. She believed there to be a general problem of lack of criticism in science journalism. Relations between science journalists and their sources are often too close, journalists accept the 'mind-frame' of their sources, and there is none of the critique characteristic of political or cultural media coverage. Journalists identify with their sources rather than challenging them. Nevertheless, she recognized the tensions between the two communities. She noted (as have others) that the reporting of science is often simplified and expressed in the language of certainty, and journalists often seek human interest and play up scientific controversy to create reader interest, while scientists prefer their disputes to remain internal until they are 'professionally' resolved.

Steven Rose believes that too many science journalists still take what scientists and their PR machines say too much at face value. Scientists remain too used to being treated deferentially and (unlike other public figures) are unused to their authority being challenged. Rose thinks they should get used to it and that science journalism should be a more demanding trade where practitioners have the necessary expertise to be properly critical.

As part of a more recent survey of science and the public in the UK, Hargreaves and Ferguson asked a number of science communication specialists about their work. They were drawn not only from newspapers, but also from radio, television, the internet and specialist science journals. The survey showed science specialists conforming generally to the norms of journalistic culture, but there were significant differences. The Hargreaves/Ferguson sample certainly felt closely allied with the science community and deplored the sensational way in which controversial, science-related issues can be presented in the media. Among this group, in contrast to Hansen's findings with print journalists, there was a strong urge to educate the public. Science specialists were unusual in tending to shun the obvious rewards of media work; being in the public eye and expressing their own opinions. Rather science journalists see themselves as conduits for information flow from science to the public, not as representatives of their readers or as critical experts with authority in their own right. In these senses they fail to aspire to the highest journalistic standards.

Visions of science communication drawn from British and American experience are not universal; the situation in Canada and parts of Europe is different. Members of the Canadian science writing community often reflect on their trade in their house journal *Science Link* and there have been several Canadian academic reports on these matters as well. Very few specialist science reporters in Canada have scientific qualifications and nor are they fully engaged with science, having it only as part of their job description. While they are taught to be aggressive and confrontational with authority (acting as tribunes of the people), they find this is not a good mode for science reporting or for keeping their sources happy. Very few use primary scientific literature or conferences as story sources but rely extensively on public and corporate Public Relations. Some specialist writers (on medicine particularly) have a very strong public education ethos and an obsession with accurate representation, to the extent of getting draft copy approved by the experts consulted before going to print. Many resent the news ethos under which they work; they really want to spend time on explanatory features for which their editors make little demand.

SCIENTISTS AND JOURNALISTS STILL MISUNDERSTAND EACH OTHER

While scientists and journalists now have a better understanding of each other's professional behaviour, it does not take much to awaken old fears. A *New York Times* article in May 1998, written by Gina Kolata reported Judah Folkman's work on cancer at the Children's Hospital in Boston. His team had discovered that endostatin and angiotensin had regressive effects on tumours in mice, apparently by choking the blood supply to the cancer. The headline was 'A cautious awe greets drugs that eradicate cancers in mice'. Caution was stressed repeatedly in the body of the text, and the uncertainties of the science were well explained. But the article also reflected the buzz of excitement and contained optimistic quotes from James Watson and Richard Klausner, head of the National Cancer Institute. Watson was quoted as saying 'Judah is going to cure cancer in two years', while Klausner apparently said the therapy was, 'the single most exciting thing on the horizon' and added, 'I am putting nothing on higher priority than getting this into clinical trials'.

The story conformed to the endlessly repeated 'medical cancer breakthrough' format and had commercial and medical consequences. Firstly, the market value of the biotech firm making the substances rocketed from $12 to $80. It then fell back to $52 on the Monday afterwards, falling again to $33 by the end of the week, while the shares in two other biotech companies making similar products also rose by significant amounts. Secondly, cancer physicians complained that they were inundated with calls from patients demanding the substances, while the work at that point was confined to mice. Both of these are reasonably common effects of newspaper drug breakthrough stories, although this was more dramatic than usual.

The article attracted savage calumny from the scientific, medical and investment banking communities. The bankers grew hot under their collars about the 'artificial' roller-coaster in biotech shares the report had stimulated, as if rumour-induced bumps and grinds in share values were in any way unusual. The biomedical community pointed out that the story was not 'news' in their terms, since Folkman had been talking about his results for months and his team was not alone; others had actually got similar substances in clinical trials. But these are 'news values' as seen within the scientific institution, not those of the wider media agenda.

A *Nature* editorial thundered disapproval at the behaviour of the 'media' (as if it was not itself a commercial periodical publication). But, it actually found it hard to fault Kolata's text and therefore set about blaming news editors for forcing their journalists to 'hype' science articles to get them published, and for not ensuring the appropriate balance of excitement and caution in their stories. Watson and Klausner rapidly back-pedalled on the quotes attributed to them, but the *New York Times* stood by its version of what they had said and neither speaker denied the euphoric tone of their statements. *Nature* had the brass neck to end its diatribe, 'And they [news editors and science journalists] can help avoid the bad consequences of their craft by a better understanding of the damage so often done by naïve or, worse, disingenuous reporting of distinguished scientists' unbridled expressions of anticipation'. This therefore admits that top scientists gave 'unbridled expressions of anticipation', but then blames the press for reporting them.

So, despite better mutual understanding between scientists and journalists, there is some way to go. Scientists can still be alarmed when their university press offices insist on publicizing their work, but its complexity means that general reporters reach for the simplest take-home message they can find and once again a mythical breakthrough occurs. Journalists do actively try to repair the damage, for instance, by advising scientists to befriend specialists rather than leave themselves at the mercy of general reporters. But even specialist reporters must combine publicity for research with a good story.

In any case, the more media-aware members of the scientific community already know how to play the media agenda. Hargreaves suggests they complain about misrepresentation, while at the same time manipulating the media for their own ends. For instance, the Royal Institution Science Media Centre in London was set up self-consciously as a public relations agency for science. It actively helps the scientific community to negotiate the media agenda and learn how to get their points across. The Centre is perhaps the best British example of the operation of a science information unit.

THE ROLE OF SCIENCE INFORMATION PEOPLE

Science information professionals are the external relations and public relations people acting as midwives between the worlds of science and media producers. Journalists claim they do not respond to PR, although the reality is different, their diaries are driven by 'staged' media opportunities. Scientific information people work for public and private corporations and are usually ex-journalists or ex-scientists. Some posts were created altruistically by science bodies to provide information to the media and the public, others are genuine PR, trying to place their organization and its work in the most favourable light. Generally, scientific information people act in one or more of three ways: as advisors, communicators and mediators.

As an advisor, there are two roles, working with senior officials on organizational presentation and policy, and working with scientists on how to talk, write and generally handle the media. From this activity in the UK have sprung a number of 'how-to' manuals on being interviewed, writing, speaking and so on, and to groups of media professionals giving 2 to 3-day courses for scientists in media skills. The communicator role usually involves editing in-house newsletters and magazines and providing public- and media-friendly information and education material for circulation outside the institution. As mediators (or facilitators), scientific information people liaise between scientists and the media, through briefing contacts, preparing news releases, organizing news conferences and handling press facilities at conferences. The job's outcomes are hard to quantify, yet it seems likely that this mediation has a huge effect on what science appears in the media and how it is interpreted.

Scientific information people often find themselves holding the ring between the conflicting interests of scientists, institutional management, the press and their own feelings about the place of their organization and its image in the world. The more progressive manuals of public relations argue that PR departments should genuinely mediate; conducting a dialogue with public audience and consumers and encouraging their organizations to respond to public opinion by modifying their objectives and behaviour where necessary.

HOW ARE SCIENCE JOURNALISTS DOING?

Science journalists are members of a larger set of subject specialists whose tasks are made difficult by the complexity and unfamiliarity of the activities upon which they report. There is an almost inevitable drive to a default position where their central professional role is to explain technical issues to lay audiences. Specialists are clearly much better at doing this than general reporters. However, science specialists, despite the central place of explanation in their work, generally do not see their role as openly educational; they do not see themselves as lay science teachers, presenting material to be learned.

Making the explanation of science a central professional norm opens science journalists up to the accusation of being too close to their sources, not only to their professional scientific agendas, but to their political and social mind sets as well. Journalists need to keep these sources on side and, since scientists are used to deference, journalists do this by seeking respect from their sources; representing them as they would like to be represented, generally as neutral technical experts doing good and useful work. While that perception is partly true, science journalists may fail to aspire to the highest ethical standards in journalism because they are not focused hard enough on the interests of their audience but too much on the interests of their sources. They, therefore, fail to set science in its wider social, cultural and political context and fail to act in effective fourth-estate mode by holding the scientific community to account, to critique and probe the shape and effectiveness of the social contract between science and society. To be a 'good' science journalist is not an easy task. It is perhaps a central task for the profession to develop a stronger set of ethical and behavioural norms to allow it to carry out its responsibilities to its audiences more thoroughly.

BIBLIOGRAPHY

Anon. (1998). Problems with gatekeepers. *Nature*, **393**, 14 May, 97.

Cathcart, B. (2004). Witness to the atomic age. *The Guardian*, Life Section, 26 February, 11.

Clayton, A., Hancock-Beaulieu, M. and Meadows, J. (1993). Change and continuity in the reporting of science and technology: a study of *The Times* and *The Guardian*. *Public Understanding of Science*, **2**, 225–34.

Friedman, S., Dunwoody, S. and Rogers, C.L. (eds.) (1986). *Scientists and Journalists. Reporting Science as News*. Washington: American Association for the Advancement of Science.

Hansen, A. (1994). Journalistic practices and science reporting in the British press. *Public Understanding of Science*, **3**, 111–34.

Hargreaves, I. and Ferguson, G. (2000). *Who's Misunderstanding Whom? Bridging the Gulf of Understanding Between the Public, the Media and Science*. London: Economic and Social Research Council.

Kirby, A. (2004). Learning to love the reptiles. *Biologist*, **51**, 120.

Kristiansen, C.M. (1983). Newspaper coverage of disease and actual mortality statistics. *European Journal of Social Psychology*, **13**, 193–4.

Lipsett, A. (2004). As seen on TV. *The Guardian*, Education Section, 6 July, 24.

Lougheed, T. (1998). Speak gently and carry an interesting explanation. *Science Link*, **18** (3), August.

Michaels, E. (1999). The do's and don'ts of medical reporting. *Science Link*, **19** (3), December.

Nelkin, D. (1995). *Selling Science*. 2nd edition. San Francisco: W.H. Freeman.

Rose, S. (2004). Stop pandering to the experts. *The Guardian*, Life Section, 1 April, 6.

Rose, S. (2004). Revolutionary tracts. *The Guardian*, Life Section, 23 September.

Saari, M.-A., Gibson, C. and Ostler, A. (1998). Endangered species: science writers in the Canadian daily press. *Public Understanding of Science*, **7**, 61–81.

Science Media Centre (2002). *SMC Newsletter*. London: Royal Institution, Number 1, autumn.

Smith, S. (2000). The media and science journalism in Canada. *Science Link*, **20** (1), March.

Wadman, M. (1998). Cancer 'cure' stirs up hot debate and reporter backs away from lucrative book deal. *Nature* **393**, 14 May, 104–5.

Young, L. (2004). Brum boffins in breakthrough. *The Science Reporter*, April/May, 4–5.

Part IV The origins of science in cultural context: five historic dramas

15 A terrible storm in Wittenberg: natural knowledge through sorcery and evil

The storm blew out of nowhere at about 11 o'clock, first with violent showers then towards midnight with rain, thunder and lightning, throwing an eerie light over the little university town cowering before the onslaught. In a students' antechamber the great door shook in its frame sending vibrations through the walls, while water ran under the door and soaked the floor. By midnight, it was too noisy to sleep. The students made out other sounds; louder, sharper and hideous because both human and anticipated. Tough young men clung to each other in terror.

Well before dawn the storm had passed, the students dozed fitfully and shivered. At first light, they awoke, and watched the door to the inner chamber materialize from the shadows as the room grew brighter. Rising and stretching, the students inched towards the chamber door.

"He locked it," said the first, "we won't be able to get in."
"You're right," said the second, "we had better go round the
   other way."
"Let's try it," said the third, "he may have unlocked it later."

He gingerly lifted the latch and the door eased open and swung towards them. Someone or something had indeed unlocked it. The great study beyond was in chaos, furniture broken, books torn, and blood, hair and hunks of gristle smeared over the walls. The far door was open and numb with distress they passed into the garden. Several body parts were scattered among the garden sweepings and kitchen filth of the compost heap in the corner.

There had been murder and butchery, almost beyond human comprehension. But humans had not done it. Superhuman forces had torn a body to shreds and flung the fragments among the detritus of the spoil heap. Mephistopheles had come for Faust's soul and had been none too picky about ripping the flesh apart to get at it.

PACTS WITH THE DEVIL

This Gothic comeuppance by the forces of evil on the unfortunate Dr Faustus of Wittenberg features in an English chapbook of 1590, *The Historie of the Damnable Life and Deserved Death of Dr John Faustus*, and in the so-called B-text of Christopher Marlowe's play, *The Tragicall Historie of the Life and Death of Doctor Faustus* printed in 1624. The chapbook was a translation of a German *Volksbuch* by Johann Spies of 1587, *Historia von D. Johann Fausten*. The English chapbook translation was the main source for Marlowe's play, first performed in 1594, the year after Marlowe's death in a Deptford pub brawl. Faust's gruesome postmortem details were missing from the first printed edition of the play (the A text of 1604). Marlowe evidently did not see the need to embellish his tragedy, but an anonymous hand later bulked out the original, rather spare text with additional details for the B-text.

Everyone knows the Faust story. In exchange for 24 years unlimited access to secret knowledge Faust agrees to sell his soul to the Devil and to spend eternity in hell. The story has huge staying power. It pre-dates Marlowe and has survived into the twenty-first century. Because it equates the search for knowledge with evil it questions the legitimacy of encroaching on God's creation of the human and natural worlds, or of making new artefacts and therefore encroaching on His prerogative. Scientists, engineers and artists can all be seen as morally transgressive, their activities open to censure and their persons to persecution.

Johann Georg Faust was a quasi-historical figure (or possibly two figures), probably born in Wittenberg around 1480, and put to death at Staufen in 1540. A number of stories were told about him as scholar, alchemist, magician, astrologer, and as charlatan and conjurer. In the chapbook version, Faust was born in Weimar of God-fearing parents and showed himself an able scholar from an early age, mastering the Bible, medicine, maths, astrology, sorcery, prophesy and necromancy. His wish to form a pact with the Devil arose from frustration at the limits to knowledge he could acquire. He conjured the Devil up at a cross-road in the Spesser Forest one night and negotiated a deal in which the Devil agreed to serve Faust in his lifetime, to provide him with whatever information he might ask, and never to tell Faust a lie. In return, Faust promised to surrender his body and soul to the Devil after 24 years, signed the pact with his own blood, and renounced his Christian faith.

For the agreed time, the Devil did answer all Faust's questions and he was able to travel the Earth and the known universe (and even to look into hell). He became a famous astrologer whose horoscopes all turned out to be true and gathered a coterie of dedicated students around him. But Faust also lived pretty high on the hog until towards the end of his time. He gathered all his students together on the night of his death. A huge storm broke out and they heard their mentor screaming. At dawn, they entered his room to find blood and body fragments over the walls and his dismembered corpse outside on a manure pile. They learned the lesson that Faust had failed to grasp, to keep faith with God and reject the Devil and all his works.

In the most straightforward versions of the story, the Devil collects his dues and Faust's damnation is the punishment for any Christian who embraces evil. But the case seldom is straightforward; the power of many retellings lies in subverting this expectation of eternal punishment and offering hope and redemption. Stories of pact-making with the Devil long pre-date the Faust myth and occur in many earlier European folk traditions. The protagonists sometimes enter into the pact for entirely base motives (seducing virgins or enjoying huge wealth), but often they are men frustrated in their efforts to achieve good aims who turn to the Devil for help. When they are scholars, the pact usually includes access to unattainable knowledge. Contrary to Faust's fate, the protagonists in the early stories are quite often saved and their souls go to heaven, either because of intervention on their behalf by saintly figures, or because they repent. In other cases the Devil does get the soul, because the seller sees the light too late and cannot manage enough redeeming acts before his time is up. So from their beginnings, pacts-with-the-Devil stories are ambivalent about the motivation of people who make such bargains and what will happen to them. These same ambiguities (and others) haunt the Faustian corpus.

The historical context of the Faust myth

The first version of the *Faust* story emerged in Germany in the mid sixteenth century at the same time as Martin Luther's bid to reform the Catholic Church and at the early height of the European witch craze. Faust's special sinfulness reflects the cultural context in which it was written. The Catholic Church was on the defensive and ready to use anything to sustain its long-standing spiritual and secular power. It found witchcraft a useful phenomenon to demonize and attack. Before the sixteenth century, sorcery and black magic were not taken all that seriously and magical events were often seen to be conjuring tricks. Male black magicians were wizards (or sorcerers), the females were witches although, when witchcraft became subject to widespread persecution, the term witch was used for both women and men. The witch craze in Europe lasted 200 years and between 200 000 and 500 000 witches were probably executed, 85% of them women.

The case for the persecution was set out in two texts, Jacquier's *Flagellum Haereticorum Fascinariorum* (1458) and Sprenger and Kramer's *Malleus Maleficarum* of 1487–89. These books persuaded people that witchcraft was not a harmless fantasy but a serious heresy. They claimed that witches were possessed of the Devil, that they flew to sordid Sabbath ceremonies, indulged in sexual orgies with devils, and ate unbaptized infants. The second book attempted to prove by sophistic argument that those who did not believe in witches were themselves victims of witchcraft, and provided methods for recognizing witches, and how to investigate and persecute them.

The social and economic framework of the feudal and largely agricultural medieval world had been sanctioned by the Catholic Church. By the fifteenth century, substantial urbanization had occurred and deaths from plague had greatly reduced the labour force and therefore increased the power of the smaller surviving populations. The feudal authorities and the Catholic Church saw these changes as threats and countered them by finding other enemies, the origin of the drive against witches. Women were the main targets because the labour shortages encouraged women into employment. Large numbers of unmarried women outside the traditional authority of husbands or fathers threatened men with visions of sexual availability and their wives with fear that such women would bewitch their husbands. The witch hunts finally declined from the mid seventeenth century, probably because economic stability was re-established and religious pluralism accepted in societies now based on nation and city states, rather than on feudal and Catholic religious authority.

Since Faust embraces sorcery to satisfy his lust for knowledge in the late sixteenth century, this marks him out as an extreme sinner. In Marlowe's play, Faustus is a scholar and teacher at the University in Wittenberg, but there is always more to learn and Faust is interested in the fastest way to learn it. In the first scene he tries to read a book of sorcery but the text is so arcane he needs the assistance of two black magicians who agree to initiate him into 'the art' and its 'ceremonies' to summon devils.

By Scene 3, Faust has learned the correct incantations, how to inscribe a circle appropriately with signs of the Zodiac, and successfully 'conjures up' Mephisto, one of Lucifer's fallen angels. Despite the blandishments of a good angel anxious to help him onto the straight and narrow, Faust agrees to make a pact with the Devil in which he will undermine and attack God whenever he can and give his soul to Lucifer after 24 years. In return Mephisto will be his constant servant, doing everything that he is bid. Faust briefly wonders if the pact is worth it, but the heavyweight trio of Mephisto, Beelzebub and Lucifer remind him that any appeal to God will be punished with instant death and immediate loss of his soul without even 24 years of worldly benefit, so he goes through with the bargain.

Faust is able to travel widely and learn much astronomy, astrology and other natural philosophies so that, when he returns to Wittenberg, he is acknowledged as an expert. But he does not show any high moral purpose in using these gifts. He spends a great deal of time playing magic tricks on Papists and simple people, and pandering to the vain demands of the great. He is well rewarded for these tricks and his use of devil-given powers is not so base as that of buffoons who come across black magic by accident and just want to slake their lust and enjoy a drunken good time. As the 24 years draw to a close, Faust doubts the wisdom of what he has done, but his own shallowness prevents him from repenting. Parallels are often drawn between the fictional Faust and the real Dr John Dee, Court mathematician and natural philosopher to Elizabeth the First, who fell from grace when he claimed to have conjured up angels who dictated learned books to him. Dee claimed his familiars were angels but many people suspected they were devils.

FAUST REVISED

Later reworkings of the Faust myth by Goethe and others remove much of the stigma of black magic and sin and re-express the pact-with-the-devil in virtuous terms. Goethe's *Faust* took 60 years to complete (the two parts were published in 1808 and 1831) and Faust no longer goes to hell, because seeking knowledge has now become a good thing. In Goethe's version, the Faustian pact to gain knowledge and control over nature does not lead to eternal damnation.

Faust is saved and raised to heaven. Enquiry is now seen as a good that counterbalances any evil (or selfish) desire for knowledge. In Goethe's version Faust abjures sloth, self-satisfaction, worldly pleasure, and the pride of wanting glorious moments to last forever in exchange for being allowed to strive for knowledge. Only if Faust fails in these virtuous behaviours can Mephisto call the bet in and carry his soul to hell, a significant softening of the terms of trade from Faust's point of view. He does successfully resist these sins until he dies; so his soul is saved. Goethe lets natural philosophers off the hook, they are allowed to strive for new knowledge and encroach on God's understanding provided they exhibit good moral behaviour.

In the later nineteenth and early twentieth centuries, Faust becomes an even more positive figure. Seeking new knowledge is perceived as intrinsically good and Faustian figures are increasingly artists (rather than scholars or scientists) struggling to let their creative genius out and having (now permissible) God-like powers. Overreaching pact makers became virtuous. This inversion of the Faust myth reached an extreme in the work of the German philosopher, Nietzsche, and the practical Nazi ideology of a super race for whom the quest for power and knowledge is justified at any price. Not surprisingly, liberal German intellectuals re-instated the original reading of Faust; that the Nazi era was an intrinsic evil, where a metaphorical pact with the Devil must have been made. The destruction of the German state was the inevitable price to be paid for such transgression.

Thus Thomas Mann's response, the novel *Dr Faustus* written during the Second World War in America, is essentially a straight re-telling of the original myth but about an artist, the composer Adrian Leverkuhn, whose creative gifts seem devil-given and who believes his unhappy life is the price he must pay for creative insight from a pact he believes he made with Lucifer; here a series of insane imaginings. Mann has Leverkuhn invent atonal music with its 12-note scale, in reality, a system invented by Arnold Schönberg at about the same time. Not surprisingly, this upset Schönberg and Mann was forced to include a postscript pointing out that the 12-note scale was Schönberg's invention.

There are also wholly secular Fausts, especially in America. The American *Faust* is a pure overachiever, a person of huge gifts and early achievement, who pays for this success with a later life of failure. The two classic literary American examples are Captain Ahab in Melville's *Moby Dick* and Jay Gatsby in Fitzgerald's *The Great Gatsby*. America's most famous real Faustian figure is probably Orson Welles, the wunderkind who made the most critically famous film of all time, *Citizen Kane*, by the time he was 25. But, after *Citizen Kane*, it was downhill all the way for Welles as he brooded round global film and television studios, never again able to come near his initial triumph. He described himself as a Faustian figure, his first Broadway appearance in 1937 was as Marlowe's *Faust*, and he claimed that all the roles he played were versions of Faust.

SORCERY AND MAGIC HAUNT THE ORIGINS OF 'SCIENCE'

The early curse of association with sorcery and black magic has coloured the popular reception of natural philosophy (and later science) from the beginning and, despite the more positive later revisions of the Faust myth, continues to have some influence on opinion about science to this day. Natural philosophy emerged in the sixteenth and seventeenth centuries from several overlapping, older traditions for explaining and controlling the natural world. These include sorcery, white magic, alchemy, orthodox Christianity, and several pagan theologico-philosophical heresies. The dividing lines between mature science and its occult origins are not as clear-cut as they seem, and some traces of their association remain. Other key dramas of the Jacobean and Restoration periods in the seventeenth century further explore these sources of natural philosophy.

BIBLIOGRAPHY

Ashliman, D.L. (2005). *Faust legends*. http://www.pitt.edu/~dash/faust.html, visited 11 January 2005.

Ben-Yehuda, N. (1989). Witchcraft and the occult as boundary maintenance devices. In Neusner, J. *et al.* (eds.). *Religion, Science and Magic. In Concert and in Conflict.* New York: Oxford University Press, pp. 233–45.

The Ecole Initiative. Pacts with the Devil. Faust and precursors. http://www.usao. edu/~facshaferi/FAUST.HTML, visited 11 January 2005.

Faust Timeline. *Variations of the Faust myth.* www.ucalgary.ca/~esleven/faust/fausttimeline. html, visited 7 January 2005.

Haynes, R. D. (1994). *From Faust to Strangelove. Representations of the Scientist in Western Literature.* Baltimore: Johns Hopkins University Press.

Jackson, K. (2004). American Faust. *The Independent on Sunday,* ABC Section, 26 December, 6–9.

Jolly, K. L. (1989). Magic, miracle, and popular practice in the early Medieval West: Anglo-Saxon England. In Neusner, J. *et al.* (eds.). *Religion, Science and Magic. In Concert and in Conflict.* New York: Oxford University Press, pp. 166–81.

Jolly, K. L. Magic in the Middle Ages: a preliminary discussion. *ORB: The online reference book for medieval studies,* http://orb.rhodes.edu/encyclop/culture/magwitch/orbmagic.htm, visited 2 January 2003.

Katz, D. (2007). *The Occult Tradition. From the Renaissance to the Present Day.* London: Pimlico.

Mann, T. (1968). *Doctor Faustus* (trans. Lowe-Parker, H. T.). London: Penguin (originally published Secker and Warburg, 1949).

Marlowe, C. (1989). *Dr Faustus* (ed. Roma Gill, 2nd edition). London: A. and C. Black.

16 A terrible storm in the Mediterranean: controlling nature with white magic and religion

Once upon a time a Witch of considerable power lived on a mythical island in the Southern Mediterranean. In stereotypical fashion she coupled with the Devil to produce a monstrous offspring whose hideous appearance reflected his evil personality. She also had a familiar spirit to do her bidding. Angry with this spirit she trapped him in a cleft pine tree and left him there, dying before she thought to release him.

The spirit was saved by a Wizard arriving on the island with his little daughter. Using his magical powers the Wizard freed the spirit and enslaved the Witch's misshapen offspring. The spirit undertook the Wizard's morally good bidding but the deformed child remained evil. To work his magic, the Wizard put on a magical coat, used a magic wand, stood within circles inscribed on the ground, and used incantations to summon the spirit.

The Wizard used his powers to right past injustices. He had been a Duke but, obsessed with occult study, passed the rule of his Dukedom to his brother. That brother, in cahoots with the King to which the Dukedom was vassal, usurped the Dukedom and would have killed the brother and little daughter had not a kindly counsellor intervened with the scheme for casting them adrift. Years later the exiled Wizard was able to bring his brother, the King, and their retinues into his power when they sailed close to his island. The Wizard conjured up a storm which wrecked the ship and cast the nobles ashore.

The Wizard used his magic to make the King's son fall in love with his daughter. With other good interventions and the union of the Dukedom and the Kingdom through the marriage of the Wizard's daughter with the King's son, the Wizard reclaimed his Dukedom, while his usurping brother and the conniving King saw the error of their ways. All past injustices were forgiven and the Wizard, now a restored Duke, forsook the practice of magic and freed his spirit from bondage.

BLACK AND WHITE MAGIC

In a nutshell this is the plot of Shakespeare's last play, *The Tempest*, first performed in 1612, where Prospero, the usurped Duke of Milan with his daughter Miranda are marooned on an island with the monster Caliban and the spirit Ariel. Prospero is a wizard, but he is not a sorcerer. He is a magus, a white magician, a wise man of great knowledge, wisdom and understanding, who takes care to use magic power for virtuous ends. Such moral rectitude meant that white magicians like Prospero were respectable in the eyes of the Church. Leading medieval proto-natural philosophers such as Thomas Aquinas and Roger Bacon were considered to be magi.

Faust's sorcery and Prospero's white magic seem fantastic, yet audiences watching *Faust* or *The Tempest* at the time, while aware that much magic was merely conjuring, accepted that elements of the plays might actually happen. Even the sophisticated considered both black and white magic feasible, believing it possible by diligent study to become adept and to use magic to influence the natural world, or cause harm or benefit to other people. Incantations could conjure up familiars to undertake the adept's commands. But, magic practice was not all spells and ritual; it shared rational principles with natural philosophy. Magic manipulation of nature implied the existence of forces governing the natural world.

White magicians also observed religious moral precepts. Although the creation stories of the Old Testament, like the Faust myth, set limits on the knowledge humans could legitimately acquire and the Church strongly supported these limits to retain its spiritual and secular power, white magic could escape censure if there was proper humility and religious observance. This tolerance was eventually extended to black magicians and sorcerers in the later incarnations of the Faust myth in the nineteenth century. The theoretical principles of white magic derive from non-Christian philosophies, many originating in ancient Greece and incorporated into Christian thinking in the Middle Ages. According to many of these philosophies, the 'real' world, and how it appears to us, is not a good guide to how it is controlled. The real strings and levers are hidden, but can be manipulated by various types of magic.

THE RATIONAL BASIS OF MAGIC

In magic practice, two types of force are assumed to be at work, sympathetic and contagious. In sympathetic magic the magician manipulates something resembling the phenomenon he wants to influence. A common malicious example would be making images of people to whom harm is to be done, and harming these images in the way the subject is to be harmed, while reciting a relevant spell, charm, or incantation. A benevolent application would be a farmer whose sheep had broken a leg binding up the leg of a chair and preventing anyone from sitting on or moving it. The binding of the chair leg is supposed, through sympathetic magic, to heal the animal leg.

In contagious magic two objects which have once been in contact can influence each other even after they have been separated by long times or distances. The most familiar application is that anything in contact with a person can be manipulated to produce (usually bad) effects on him. Thus hair, nails, teeth, blood or other body fluids, afterbirths, or (less powerfully) clothes or possessions, or weapons used to harm a person, should be destroyed or kept safe in case they fall into the hands of a magician who might use them to

texts from randomly associated words. All the projectors are poverty struck and filthy, their obsessions preventing them from managing their ordinary lives.

Ludicrous though the natural philosophy rehearsed by Shadwell and Swift seems, they drew most of their examples from the pages of the *Philosophical Transactions of the Royal Society*; things at first sight ridiculous were actually taking place. The satires demonstrate that natural philosophy was publicly recognized as a discrete activity by the second half of the seventeenth century and that observation and experiment were clearly the starting points from which explanatory theories could be devised. The new knowledge about nature was supposed to lead to improved technology. The satirists, however, thought observation and experiment largely trivial and natural philosophy satisfied only the curiosity of the philosophers, with no practical benefits for anyone else. But, there were more sympathetic commentators who pointed out that, while natural philosophy seemed bizarre, the explanations of the natural world did have intellectual, social, and practical value.

But, the satirists had one valid point. Natural philosophers (and later pure scientists) were centrally concerned with persuading each other of the truth of their theoretical explanations rather than applying knowledge to useful ends. It is also true, despite the claims of natural philosophy (and later science) to the contrary, that technical development depends on more factors than new natural knowledge. On other matters, though, satirical scorn was clearly misplaced. A fresh approach to explaining nature was emerging, although magic, alchemy, theology and older philosophies were not really abandoned. The key elements of natural philosophy's new methods were articulated clearly by Sir Francis Bacon in the early seventeenth century.

BACONIAN PHILOSOPHY

Bacon's views on natural philosophy were rooted in several of the ancient traditions we have already considered and with Aristotle's thought, although Bacon believed he was mounting an attack on the Aristotelian school of philosophy. He made a number of criticisms of Aristotelian methodology as practised in his day. For instance, that data collection was too much governed by the preconceptions of investigators, who in turn were too much influenced by the teachings of Aristotle himself. But, Bacon followed Aristotle in accepting that the laws governing nature could be deduced from observation of actual phenomena, although these laws were disguised by the complexity of phenomena and had to be teased out by careful observation and analysis. The observer should empty his head of all pre-suppositions and gather data comprehensively, becoming 'a child before nature'. Bacon also strongly advocated the use of experiment. The ancient philosophers generally believed nature's behaviour would then be unnatural and provide false information.

Bacon distrusted intuitive leaps of imagination in devising explanations and understood the limitations of the inductive method, the method of reasoning which dominated natural philosophy (and later science). If a phenomenon is observed a number of times and it looks the same each time, inductive logic assumes that the limited observations are representative of the phenomenon as a whole. If the phenomenon is always observed behaving in the same way, it is assumed to be a fact of nature. This assumption is logically weak because a long series of confirming observations can be demolished by a single counter-example. The classic case is the general observation that 'all swans are white'. Someone with limited observations of swans might be tempted to believe that this is universally true, but a single observation of a black swan contradicts any number of sightings of white ones. Natural philosophy (and science) faces the logical problem that any interpretation based on empirical observation may be proved wrong by later counter-observations.

Bacon therefore tried to shore up the logical strength of the inductive method by a rhetoric of numbers, accumulating huge numbers of observations (preparing a massive database in modern parlance) about nature from which laws of behaviour could be abstracted. From these huge repositories of pure facts, careful analysis would draw out low-order associations and small-scale patterns. From these low-level associations, more all-embracing principles would be induced and so on up a scale of abstract explanatory power to Bacon's ultimate explanatory principles, which he called *forms*. Bacon hoped that, by making each step small, certainty could be guaranteed, while accidental or false relationships could be excluded. The 'method of exclusion' to achieve this was to involve the cross-referencing of huge tables of presence/absence/degree among phenomena with the rejection of any correlation where an inconsistency could be found. While scientific method has moved on a long way since Bacon and the early virtuosi of the Royal Society, the primacy of observation and experiment in the presentation of science persists.

For Bacon, the whole point of understanding nature was to gain control over it. Bacon argued that technology could be improved by better understanding natural phenomena. He advocated that governments should finance natural philosophy, the cost justified by the benefit of the technological improvements that would arise. Bacon supported 'experiments of fruit', as did the Royal Society in its earliest days, although the Society's fellows soon preferred 'experiments of light', work in pure science (in modern parlance). This was partly because they found such experiments more interesting and partly because the gentry who undertook natural philosophy had little respect for the practical, and found it difficult to liaise with socially inferior technical workers.

Bacon was also much influenced by visions of a group known as the Rosicrucians. While the practical aspects of alchemy transformed into chemistry, its philosophy persisted in the utopian visions of Rosicrucians. Their *Rosicrucian Manifestos* called for the spiritual regeneration of society through social, economic, political and religious reform. This Rosicrucian movement proved popular and was a major stimulus to Bacon's own manifesto on a great revival of learning, the first step in allowing man to take effective control over nature. Bacon's vision of natural philosophy was not all that far removed from alchemy. It differed in calling for an open and communal way of working (in opposition to the secrecy of alchemical work) and reform of the language of communication to emphasize transparency. Much of the Royal Society's early emphasis on issues of technical improvement to trade came in part from the Rosicrucian Manifestos.

Bacon's reform of language was not simply a matter of stylistic change from elaborate rhetoric to plain expression; he also abandoned the view that the language of important documents contained secret meanings. This conviction that somewhere hidden in the language of texts was great truth explains the minute attention given to the exegesis of ancient and biblical texts by all medieval and early modern scholars (including those later identified as proto-scientists). Even the greatest hero of the rationalist 'scientific revolution', Isaac Newton, was an active exponent of Neo-Platonism and alchemy and a studious searcher after hidden messages in the text of the Bible.

WAS THERE A SCIENTIFIC REVOLUTION IN THE SEVENTEENTH CENTURY?

The existence of these beliefs of Newton's is strong evidence that the textbook notion of a seventeenth-century 'Scientific Revolution' may be misleading. We have been careful to use the term 'natural philosophy' to describe the work of the virtuosi at the early Royal Society and their continental peers. Their greatest achievements (the heliocentric view of the planetary system and Newton's universal theory of gravitation) are always popularly described as a scientific revolution. But, the hesitant emergence of natural philosophy from a richer stew of religion, pagan philosophy, magic and alchemy suggests the word 'scientific' here is misplaced. Historians such as Cunningham and Perry Williams argue that modern science is better considered a product of the nineteenth century.

The seventeenth-century scientific revolution was described in the 1940s and 1950s by a pioneering generation of historians of science working in America and Great Britain; those in Britain including Herbert Butterfield and his student (and my doctoral supervisor) Rupert Hall. Their view of the emergence of modern science as a reaction against magic, sorcery, alchemy and religion still dominates the textbooks. There was a 'mechanisation of the world picture'; animistic, organic or other 'primitive' interpretations of nature were displaced by mechanistic explanations of natural phenomena.

These historians interpreted events in the light of assumptions about science derived from its practice in the mid twentieth century. But, modern scientists were different beasts from their seventeenth-century natural philosophical ancestors. Butterfield, Hall and others worked with four assumptions about science, none of which is acceptable today.

The first was that science has a particular method of enquiry producing causal laws expressed in mathematical form. But seventeenth-century natural philosophers still used spirits and powers as explanatory principles and thought within an overtly theological framework. Secondly, science was seen as an essentially moral pursuit, embodying values of freedom, rationality, truth and goodness; it was an engine of social progress. Scientific knowledge and attitudes were viewed as guarantors of justice and democracy and the source of technology that could banish want and suffering. This vision reflects closely the attitudes of democracies threatened by Fascism in the twentieth century rather than the situation in the seventeenth century.

Thirdly, science was seen as a universal phenomenon, the expression of an innate human curiosity to understand the world. The historians saw the scientific revolution as the emergence of free thought, with contemporary politics, religion and philosophy holding up its progress. But, in reality, these contextual factors facilitated rather than impeded 'scientific' thought. Finally, the ancient Greeks, the seventeenth-century revolutionaries, and modern scientists were all seen as engaged in solving essentially the same problems. But, it seems naïve to read a common set of objectives into their work; their mental frameworks and philosophical objectives were actually quite different.

None of this is to deny that dramatic events took place in the seventeenth century or that the pioneer figures of the 'scientific revolution' were not undertaking extraordinary work. But, many historians think it makes sense to locate the emergence of modern science in the nexus of socio-political and cultural changes that created the modern world. The scientific way of thought is not a natural feature, common to humans at all times, but an invention made at a particular time and place. The 'revolution' to modern scientific attitudes should perhaps better be located at the same time as the series of parallel revolutions in politics, philosophy and economics, between about 1760 and 1848.

SIR ISAAC NEWTON LEADS THE REVOLUTION FROM THE BACK

Recent investigations reveal the persistence of magical, alchemical, religious and philosophical ideas in the thinking of even the greatest figures of the 'scientific revolution'. We know that Newton was an alchemist and student of Bible exegesis, as well as a leading natural philosopher. Alchemically, Newton believed in a hidden 'vegetative principle', which animated the entire natural world, which he thought analogous to light, and that God used this vegetative principle to animate the universe. He assumed that all true knowledge must be knowledge of God, that reason based on observation and experiment and revelation were supplementary to God's truth, a truth that appeared both in revealed scriptures and in nature. He believed that God still acted on the world and that He used the hidden alchemical spirit for this task.

Newton's religious faith was also heretical. On the surface he seemed to be a conforming Anglican, but he dissented from the Trinitarian orthodoxy of the Church of England, and his beliefs were much closer to those of the arcane Socinian sect (also known as the Polish Brethren). This sect argued rigorously against the Trinity and

believed that there was only one God. The source of this faith is a
literal reading of the Bible, where only the father is designated as
God. While Newton was never a Socinian as such, he rejected the
idea of the soul's immortality and the existence of evil spirits; there
was no Devil or associated demons.

While Newton never revealed his heretical beliefs in public,
rumours about them abounded. He may well have moved to London
from Cambridge in the 1690s because career progress was more
dependent on Anglican orthodoxy in Cambridge than in London.
Newton worked hard on interpreting biblical prophecies. Once these
were decoded, he (like so many others) believed they would unlock
hidden secrets. This was a long, powerful obsession of Newton's, and
he thought he had decoded several leading prophesies, especially in
the books of *Daniel* and *The Apocalypse of St John*, although his
interpretations were not published until after his death. Recently
examined Newton manuscripts show that he believed the Pope to
be the Antichrist on Earth, a view too extreme for most Anglicans
at the time.

Cambridge was dominated in Newton's time by Neo-Platonism.
The Neo-Platonists were 'modern' in opposing scholasticism in theology and natural philosophy, but 'ancient' in their search for wisdom
in old texts. Natural magicians of various kinds were increasingly
using careful observation and experiment, already subscribing to a
major element of what would become 'scientific method'. Although
Bacon censured alchemists and natural magicians, he shared many
of their suppositions and attitudes. The historian Charles Webster
was one of the first to see a smooth transition, rather than a revolutionary break, from magic and alchemy to experimental natural philosophy. He saw no clear discontinuity between natural philosophy
and black magic, sorcery and witchcraft. Given the amount of self-
serving propaganda that the early Royal Society issued about itself, it
is surprising that it missed the opportunity to attack witchcraft.

This seems to have been deliberate, arising from fear of too
much enthusiasm for materialism, which excluded God from nature

and was therefore potentially blasphemous. To dismiss the idea that witchcraft was the work of the Devil might imply disbelief in the Devil, and therefore disbelief in God (although in Newton's case, it was perfectly possible to believe in God while dismissing the existence of the Devil). But evidence suggests that many Fellows of the Royal Society accepted the danger of witchcraft on standard theological grounds and (like the Neo-Platonists and Hermeticists before them) had to work hard to prevent their own practices being seen as witchcraft. The decline in the persecution of witches during the latter half of the seventeenth century did not happen because the new natural philosophers had rationally explained it away.

BIBLIOGRAPHY

Brumfiel, G. (2004). Newton's religious screeds get online airing. *Nature*, **430**, 19 August, 819.

Cunningham, A. and Williams, P. (1993). De-centring the 'big picture'. The origins of modern science and the modern origins of science. *British Journal for the History of Science*, **26**, 407–32.

Dobbs, B. J. T. (1991). *The Janus Face of Genius. The Role of Alchemy in Newton's Thought*. Cambridge: Cambridge University Press.

Haynes, R. D. (1994). *From Faust to Strangelove. Representations of the Scientist in Western Literature*. Baltimore: Johns Hopkins University Press.

Hookyas, R. (1972). *Religion and the Rise of Modern Science*. Edinburgh: Scottish Academic Press.

Shadwell, T. (1966). *The Virtuoso*. Nicolson, M. H. and Rodes, D. S. (eds.). Lincoln: University of Nebraska Press.

Snobelen, S. D. (1999). Isaac Newton, heretic: the strategies of a Nicodemite. *British Journal for the History of Science*, **32**, 381–419.

Swift, J. (1985). *Gulliver's Travels*. Dixon, P. and Chalker, J. (eds.). London: Penguin.

Turner, W. *History of Philosophy*, Chapter 20, Neo-Pythagoreanism and neo-Platonism, Jacques Maritain Center, http://www.nd.edu/Departments/Maritain/etext/hop20.htm, visited 2 January 2003.

Webster, C. (1982). *From Paracelsus to Newton. Magic and the Making of Modern Science*. Cambridge: Cambridge University Press.

19 Is scientific knowledge 'true' or should it just be 'truthfully' deployed?

The true tale of Galileo and the Roman Catholic Church is as well known as the fictional Faust story. The great Italian astronomer used the newly invented telescope to reveal secrets of the Sun, planets, moon and stars, and to confirm the truth of Copernicus's earlier idea that the movements of bodies in the night sky are better explained by assuming that all the planets revolved round the Sun, rather than round the Earth. These ideas were opposed by the Catholic Church as heretical errors contradicting the Bible. As the most prominent exponent of the heliocentric view Galileo came up against the Papal Inquisition and was forced to recant his views on pain of torture and possibly death.

History has proved Galileo right and the Catholic Church wrong, making him a hero in the supposed struggle between reason and science, on the one hand, and religious superstition, on the other. But just as the Faust myth can be re-interpreted, so can Galileo's. He was indeed right, no one seriously denies that the Earth and other planets revolve round the Sun, but it is not that truth alone which determined his success. The role of cheer leader for the heliocentric universe fell to Galileo because of his skill with the politics of patronage and his clever use of presentational rhetoric.

While Galileo was scientifically right, the consequences of his discoveries were not value-free. At other times, when the consequences of science turn out to be morally undesirable, Galileo can be seen as a failure; someone who refused to take moral responsibility for the uses to which his knowledge was put. Galileo can be accused of concern only with the philosophical truth of his position and not with the implications of its use if control passed to others. The most famous modern retelling of the story, Brecht's *Life of Galileo*, makes just this point. At the time when Brecht was writing in the 1940s and 1950s, nuclear weapons were proliferating and Brecht took the view that atomic scientists had too easily given up their role as uniquely informed public intellectuals who could have guided us to world peace. Instead, they allowed ideological politicians and the military to use atomic physics to develop weapons of mass destruction. Brecht's Galileo is a scientist whose lack of courage allowed the authorities to deny his insights. As with Faust, a figure's moral status can vary with the cultural framework in which his actions are interpreted.

THE ROLE OF PUBLICATION AND POLITICS IN GALILEO'S 'SUCCESS'

Galileo had to use considerable publishing skill to establish himself as a natural philosopher and persuade people of the truth of the Sun-centred Copernican planetary system. Most natural philosophers of the seventeenth and eighteenth centuries were financially secure gentlemen, but Galileo was no gentleman and therefore had to make extensive use of his powers of persuasion to acquire the financial resources to undertake research and the social and political authority to have his ideas accepted. This meant gaining the patronage of a powerful social leader, to become a high-grade servant or low-grade courtier.

The historian Adrian Johns has shown that Galileo's fame was not solely the result of the novelty of his work and the ultimate 'correctness' of the Copernican world-view. It was also the result of astute manipulation of patronage. Galileo's first successful book, *Sidereus Nuncius*, published in 1610 contained evidence from telescopic observations about the surface of the moon, that the Milky Way was a collection of discrete stars, and the discovery of four previously unknown moons orbiting Jupiter. Galileo paid for the printing and distribution of an entire edition of several hundred copies of the book himself. He looked upon the publication as a speculative investment. His aim was to use it as his passport to join the court of the Florentine prince, the Grand Duke Cosimo II de Medici.

Once in Florence he would become a paid retainer to provide high-brow entertainment through public debate with other philosophers of Cosimo's entourage and those of other princes. The point of leverage in his book was that the planet Jupiter formed part of the coat of arms and insignia of the Medici family, so an account of these moons formed the centrepiece of his book. He originally called them 'Cosmian' satellites but he was informed that the Grand Duke did not approve and therefore changed them to 'Medicean'. Unfortunately, this essential piece of information did not reach Galileo until half the books had been printed. He had to glue the new name over the old in the copies that had already been run off.

He took a copy of the book personally to Cosimo, together with a telescope to allow him a private view of the new phenomena. Only after he had obtained Cosimo's approval did he send copies (through Cosimo's diplomatic service) to other princes and cardinals in Europe with an enclosed spyglass so that they themselves could see the evidence for his claims. Galileo's political and financial initiative paid off; he became a court philosopher in Florence and, as a consequence, found his ideas circulated and discussed across Europe. Galileo the mathematical philosopher cannot be separated from Galileo the political operator. The authority and acceptance of his discoveries was only possible once he had persuaded a patron to accept them.

Not only did Galileo carry no innate authority as a natural philosopher, at that time he could not copyright his book. In the edition for which he was responsible, he had supervised production;

especially of the illustrations. But, before the year was out, a pirated edition of the book appeared, followed by many others none of which took proper care over the illustrations. In these pirated editions the illustrations of his observations were unconvincing. If these distorted illustrations had been the only ones available and he had had no princely patronage, it is unlikely his ideas would have been accepted as readily as they were.

Galileo's ultimate ambition was to persuade the Catholic authorities to accept the Copernican heliocentric model as the true representation of the universe. To achieve that, Galileo knew that he must persuade the Pope himself and therefore set about moving his power base from Florence to the papal court in Rome. His first moves were extremely successful. A supporter of his, Maffeo Barberini, was elected Pope as Urban VIII in 1623. Galileo immediately redirected the dedication of his next book *Il Saggiatore* to Urban rather than Cosimo and wrote and published a book on the tides that explained them using an overtly Copernican framework. He received news that these works were well received.

Galileo therefore set about writing his exposition of the Copernican position in the famous *Dialogo* (the dialogue about the two world systems), confident that he had the support of the Pope. Although originally intended to come out in 1630, the book was not actually published until 1632. It was not obviously scandalous and had passed through the Papal licensing hoops necessary to permit publication. But the 2-year delay in printing proved nearly fatal. The book was sunk by political events that had nothing to do with natural philosophy. Galileo's contact and advocate at the papal court was one Ciampoli, but he had the ill fortune to fall from grace just as the book was published. At the same time Spanish interests complained that the papacy was lacking in zeal in the pursuit of both heresy and the Thirty Years' War. Urban was therefore primed to be tough on heresy and the causes of heresy, and associated the new book with the unpleasant events surrounding Ciampoli's disgrace.

Thus what Urban in 1630 might have read as witty intellectual dialogue that could be accepted as truth, in 1632 he read as attacks on himself and his court. Politically wrong-footed, the ambitious Galileo had to face the Inquisition in Rome, recant his support for the Copernican world-view, and endure house arrest for much of the rest of his life. On the more extreme reading of power politics, Galileo's rise and fall had as much to do with his political timing as the truth of his natural philosophical credentials.

BRECHT'S GALILEO

Galileo might have been less famous if his political luck had held and the Catholic Church had accepted the heliocentric view. The trial, the rebuff and the house arrest have lent drama to the story of rational natural philosophy overturning a view of the Earth and its place in the universe, apparently based on religious myth. In 1939 when Brecht wrote the first version of *Life of Galileo* he followed the conventional line on Galileo as a rational progressive fighting against the mental shackles of authoritarian repression. Science is good because it leads to truth, while repressive government and religion are bad because they support error. But as Brouwer and Schroeer have separately shown, in subsequent revisions of the play, the power of nuclear weapons and growing realization of what the Marxist regime in East Germany (to which Brecht returned after the War) was doing, shifted Brecht's interpretation of Galileo's historical role.

Brecht wrote the first version in Denmark in 1939, where Galileo is such a determined scientist that his concession to the Church is a compromise that allows science to advance. The second version (written in the USA between 1945 and 1947) and the third German version (developed in Berlin from 1954 to 1956), both revise the emphasis. By the third version, Galileo condemns himself as a traitor to science for relinquishing control to the authorities when he should have used it for social benefit (seeing clearly that knowledge is not simply good of itself). Brecht's contemporary parallel was atomic scientists ceding control of knowledge to governments, which led to an expensive arms race rather than an out-and-out effort on atoms for peace.

Brecht wanted a Hippocratic Oath for scientists to prevent them allowing their work to be prostituted for military excess. His third Galileo is deeply concerned about the possible misuse of science, it is a tragedy that the triumph of human reason can so easily be misused. But the negative Church reaction shows a proper concern for social stability. The Church wants to keep the scientific revolution divorced from any social revolution, to use the new natural philosophy to aid navigation, but to keep the implications of loss of philosophical authority from the people. But, ultimately Galileo sees the resistance by authority to change (then as now) as wrong because it is motivated by the desire to preserve the status quo. In the third version of the play Galileo's own faith in the power of reason is shaken by his denial of truth under threat of torture.

But, while there may have been a major shift in Brecht's intentions by the time he wrote the third version, his audiences did not necessarily follow him. An analysis of the contemporary critical reactions to productions of the play in Berlin in 1957 and Milan in 1963 shows that in neither case were scientists' responsibilities for the wider consequences of their work seen as the central issue. Science-as-power, science as destroyer, Galileo as anti-hero, intellectual courage, and science and faith were all more important for one or both of these audiences. Galileo Mark One persisted, his iconography too powerful to allow immediate Brechtian revision. The strength of Brecht's re-interpretation of Galileo's position took time to sink in.

BIBLIOGRAPHY

Brecht, B. (trans. Willett, J., commentary Rorrison, H.) (1986). *Life of Galileo*. London: Methuen (original text 1955).

Brouwer, W. (1988). The image of the physicist in modern drama. *American Journal of Physics*, **56**, 611–16.

Cuomo, F. (2006). Berliner ensemble 1957 – Piccolo Teatro 1963. Science in the reception of Brecht's Galileo as from the press reviews of both stagings. *SISSA Journal of Communication*, **5**, http://jcom.sissa.it/.

Findlen, P. (1993). Science as a career in enlightenment Italy. *Isis*, **84**, 441–69.

Hye, A.E. (1996). *The Moral Dilemma of the Scientist in Modern Drama*. New York: The Edwin Mellen Press.

Johns, A. (1999). *The Nature of the Book*. Chicago: University of Chicago Press.

Schroeer, D. (1980). Brecht's Galileo: a revisionist view. *American Journal of Physics*, **48**, 125–30.

Part V Science in literature

20 Science and the Gothic: the three big nineteenth-century monster stories

We have seen in Part IV that some seventeenth- and eighteenth-century authors treated the precursors to science (magic, alchemy and natural philosophy) with considerable cynicism. Science did not get off to a good literary start and Haynes has shown that Western literary culture continued to view science in a poor light. This literary image of science was further blackened by its role in three of the best-known and long-surviving nineteenth-century horror stories, which are constantly retold in new stage and screen adaptations.

These are Mary Shelley's *Frankenstein or the Modern Prometheus* (1818 and revised in 1831), Robert Louis Stevenson's *Strange Case of Dr Jekyll and Mr Hyde* (1886), and Bram Stoker's *Dracula* (1897). The overall conclusion from these stories is that science can lead to horrible consequences, exemplified by acronyms like 'Frankenfoods' to describe foodstuffs prepared from genetically modified crops. But the associations in these stories were initially more subtle, the science often being a force for good, rather than a cause of evil. The ambivalent position of science in these stories mirrors the ambivalent relationship between reason, progress and good government in so-called Enlightenment thought in the eighteenth and nineteenth centuries, and its antithesis in traditional, aristocratic and reactionary government epitomized by feudalism. The literary expression of the tensions between progress and reaction is the Gothic; in which horror is often associated with science.

In popular interpretation, science in *Frankenstein* is bad because Dr Frankenstein cannot control the artificial being he has created by the appliance of science; science over-reaches itself and produces uncontrollable and horrible consequences. In *Jekyll and Hyde* the science of chemistry has the power to reverse human evolution and bring out the animal, the uncontrolled, and the evil which in the nineteenth century were thought to lie concealed beneath the veneer of civilization separating the human from the animal. Here, a scientist uses his scientific knowledge to liberate the degraded beast within. In *Dracula* the great cultural triumphs made possible by science, industrialization and urbanization, are prey to evil and destructive forces, often metaphorically represented as syphilis or vampires. Optimistically, these can be overcome by the forces of science if anyone applies them. In *Frankenstein* progressive science produces a degenerate monster, in *Jekyll and Hyde* science is used to re-activate a primitive individual, in *Dracula* progressive and scientific forces overcome this tendency to revert to the primitive in communities as a whole.

THE GOTHIC TRADITION

In so far as these three stories can be pigeon-holed into a literary genre, they are often included in the Gothic tradition, characterized by Botting as stories of fear, transgression and excess, suffused with gloom, which contemplate the awesomeness of the 'sublime'. The rational philosophers of the eighteenth- and early nineteenth-century Enlightenment saw the earlier medieval and feudal arrangements of society as horrible, to be overturned by rational, progressive systems of government such as democracy. For progressive philosophers and politicians, the medieval world stood for ignorance, degradation and despotism; physically manifested by gloomy and decaying Gothic architecture.

But the despised medieval Gothic became a rallying point for those opposed to the Enlightenment project. Another symbol of this reversion was the replacement of distaste for wilderness (because it was uncivilized) by pleasure derived from contemplating the wild and untamed; the 'sublime'. Emotional response to wild natural beauty was preferred to admiration of harmonious agricultural landscapes. The Gothic and the sublime were often combined in their literary expression.

In the eighteenth century, Gothic tales were usually set in crumbling castles, in the nineteenth century they moved to isolated country houses, and in the twentieth century they were increasingly set in alienating cities. In early Gothic, terror is exerted by outside agents such as ghosts, vampires or evil aristocrats, but in later Gothic these external forces are replaced by the stresses of inner psychological disintegration. In the eighteenth century, anxiety was induced by supernatural forces but in the more rational nineteenth century, these were partly replaced by the alienating forces of science and technology. The laboratory full of electrical apparatus and writhing glassware provided a satisfying alternative Gothic setting to the gloomy castle or the lonely country house.

The original type specimen of the Gothic romance is usually taken to be Horace Walpole's *The Castle of Otranto* (1764). Walpole was himself an aristocrat with an obsession with the medieval, building his country house as a mock Gothic castle at Strawberry Hill in Twickenham. The story was a fantastic romance revolving round the disputed ownership of a castle between two families and the dastardly behaviour of both, laced with many supernatural and ghostly goings on. Initially, Walpole was little imitated, but in 1777 Clara Reeve's *The Champion of Virtue* introduced another stock element of the genre, the virtuous heroine resisting assault and seduction. Two more Gothic tales appeared in the mid 1780s, Sophia Lee's *The Recess* (1783–5) and William Beckford's *Vathek* (1782 in French, in English in 1786). Beckford was another wealthy medievalist who built Fonthill Abbey in the Gothic style and introduced another source of sensation and fear; Arab Orientalism.

In all these Gothic tales, social order is either unreliable (genuinely medieval) or modern civilization breaks down and primitive anarchy and chaos re-emerge. In the late 1780s the social breakdown in France following the French Revolution saw life imitate art, triggering the publication of hundreds of Gothic romances in the UK in the later 1780s and 1790s. Conservative writers such as Edmund Burke (*Reflections on the Revolution in France*, 1790) saw virtues in medieval Gothic institutions like the monarchy, the aristocracy, landed property, and the Church as bulwarks against the revolutionary anarchy unleashed in France. But radical authors like Tom Paine (*The Rights of Man*, 1792) Mary Wollstonecraft (*A Vindication of the Rights of Women*, 1790), and William Godwin continued to believe that society would be better if it was rationally organized, based on enlightened politics with individual responsibility and rights, more democratic government and fairer distribution of wealth. They did not let the degeneration of the French Revolution discourage them.

William Godwin used Gothic fiction as a device to spread his radical ideas, notably in the novel *Caleb Williams* (1794). The humble but politically progressive Caleb attacks persistent medieval, feudal power and wealth, but models himself on his apparently noble employer, Falkland. But, he finds that despite his nobility, Falkland is deeply flawed. Falkland's guilt, despair and remorse spread to Caleb as well and neither can escape a lethal fate. Godwin and Wollstonecraft were Mary Shelley's parents, and she was as politically progressive as they were. Yet she was also the creator of the iconic Gothic (and by association, reactionary) tale of Dr Frankenstein's monster created by re-animating a collection of dead organs. Frankenstein and Caleb are both rational and enlightened people, whose faith in the virtues of enlightened thinking are shaken by encounter with their opposites, Falkland and the monster. But these sources of evil are not innate. Poor social circumstances lie behind their bad behaviour. In a more progressive society they would turn out better.

The later nineteenth-century Gothic story turned in upon itself. Horror was aroused by single characters who possessed opposing personality traits (fragmented psyches), or individuals with one set of features having doubles or doppelgangers behaving in the opposite way. These vampires and doppelgangers re-appear in English literature with a dying flourish at the end of the nineteenth century in Stevenson's *Jekyll and Hyde* and in Stoker's *Dracula*. The sources of fear are science, industrialization, and urbanization, the latter especially seen as the source of social breakdown through increased crime and unleashed female sexuality.

The image of science in this Gothic material was multivalent. It could be seen as the root of modernity, and was cursed excessively by those who saw modernity as bad, and unreasonably praised by those who saw it as good. Science was blamed for the horrors of industrialization; poverty, degeneration, industrial pollution and misery among the labouring classes, but on the other hand, mechanization and industrialization were viewed as positive changes associated with increased wealth and greater political freedom. Some saw science's detached rationalism, and its neutral and amoral stance, as models for a positive, rationalist view of society. But others saw such neutrality as dehumanizing and destructive of community and social coherence. Science and its applications were sometimes deemed to lead to better societies because they were rationally and scientifically designed, but at other times the consequences of science were seen as out of control, leading instead to destruction and disintegration.

Gothic remains very much alive in the twentieth and twenty-first centuries. Those who want to accentuate the continuity of Gothic subsume science fiction within it, suggesting the only difference is that cultural anxiety has been shifted from the past to the future. Twentieth-century Gothic fears lie in the dehumanizing influence of mass markets, mass media, automation and computerization and excessive regulation through onerous and punitive bureaucracies. High literary expressions of twentieth-century Gothic include Conrad's *Heart of Darkness* (1902) and *The Secret Agent* (1907) and perhaps most powerfully Kafka's short story 'Metamorphosis' (where a man transforms into an insect) and his grim satires on extreme bureaucracy, *The Trial* (1925) and *The Castle* (1926). The core tales in the Gothic tradition have proved fruitful and lastingly popular. The cultural explanation of this popularity is complex. But to the extent that science has been associated in this Gothic material with the reactionary, the backward, and the horrible in these stories its image has been traduced. By contrast, actual science and its factual popularization were perceived as overwhelmingly positive during the same late eighteenth- and nineteenth-century period.

FRANKENSTEIN, HOW SHOULD WE CLASSIFY VICTOR AND HIS MONSTER?

The Gothic Frankenstein

Literary critics have crawled over this text and generated a cornucopia of interpretations. Here there is only space to focus on a few issues. For Rosemary Jackson *Frankenstein* is a pioneer text in a specific sub-genre of Gothic stories, those about psychological fragmentation. A central leitmotif of these stories is the division of good and evil between two opposites, often two characters who are 'really' aspects of the same person. Another is the internalization of good and evil (previously symbolized by God and the Devil) into aspects of the psychological make-up of a single character. Good and evil explained in a 'modern' way do not need the super-agents of religious belief to explain why humans behave well or badly.

Jackson thinks it significant that Mary Shelley was William Godwin's daughter. Her father was certain that evil was the result of repressive laws and their manipulation by the ruling classes; it was not innate in the characters of the criminal or the poor. Jackson argues that, just as Caleb Williams and Falkland are aspects of the same character in Godwin's *Caleb Williams*, so Mary Shelley's monster is a grotesque reflection of Victor Frankenstein. The monster is literally made up of fragments of other disintegrated selves, re-assembled body parts fused into life by an electric storm.

Frankenstein *as science fiction before its time*

For Brian Stableford, *Frankenstein* does not fit the Gothic tradition. It shares conventions of horror but he thinks the story lacks other typical features such as ancient edifices, evil conspiracies, hideous apparitions, the threat of sexual violence or intimations of incest. He prefers to read it as proto-science fiction, although to make this acceptable he has to accentuate the strand in science fiction of nightmare vision (essentially the British Science Romance movement) and rather ignore its positive incarnation of science as social salvation and progress.

The book's subtitle is *The Modern Prometheus*. For Mary's husband, the poet Percy Bysshe Shelley, the ancient Greek Titan Prometheus was a hero, and so he probably was for Mary. Prometheus symbolized technological progress and Percy Shelley believed the actions of the Gods in chaining him to a rock as punishment for stealing fire represented unreasonable tyranny. If Prometheus is a technological hero, and his torment by the gods unjustified, this suggests that Mary's Victor Frankenstein (the New Prometheus) is neither a failure nor someone who must be punished for going too far in acquiring knowledge. Like Prometheus, Frankenstein's punishment (his creation turning against him and destroying him) is unreasonable, he has not committed a sin which demands this degree of punishment. St Clair argues that Mary Shelley was trying to express a politically progressive message, entirely consistent with her father's radical thinking; that treating a person (or a monster) badly leads to malevolence and selfishness. How has the story come to be read as an awful warning to science not to over-reach itself?

Stableford argues that it derives from the constraints under which the story was written. It had to be a horror story, because that was what Percy Shelley, Lord Byron, Mary Shelley and others agreed to produce to fill in time on a Continental holiday ruined by bad weather. This constraint forces Victor to be involved with something horrible. Apparently, the central scene in the book, of Frankenstein's first encounter with his escaped creation, occurred to

Mary as a dream. The image was so powerful that she wrote the rest of the story round it; the first part had to lead up to it, the latter to outline the consequences. The nightmare scene had to be 'explained' through the plot. For Mary Shelley, the supernatural conventions of the Gothic novel were unacceptable, to achieve the effects needed a human who could undertake such tasks for himself, hence Victor Frankenstein was a scientist. The point of the story, Stableford argues, was not to reflect on the nature of scientific knowledge, the application of science was simply a plot device to get to the central confrontation.

Frankenstein *as a popular myth*

Jon Turney provides a comprehensive discussion of the cultural significance of *Frankenstein* and argues that one element of the story has been extracted to become a powerful modern myth. The basic script of this myth is that a scientist creates a living being, which grows monstrous and turns on its creator. While Shelley's book is more nuanced than this, it is this simple script that has emerged to resonate with older myths of man acquiring knowledge beyond his right to know and being punished for his presumption. Powerful taboos surround human access to the secrets of life and in so far as activities have been dedicated to finding these secrets, such as alchemy or witchcraft, they have been universally condemned. Turney argues that the *Frankenstein* myth translates these ancient stories into a modern version. The *Frankenstein* story differs from earlier myths in having man himself able to create life, without recourse to divine, magical, or other supernatural forces.

The *Frankenstein* myth is a modern version of the fear of creating life. Victor Frankenstein starts out positively, wanting to undertake science for social and medical benefit. He is no evil genius creating life for selfish reasons. But the full text is not itself the myth. The myth is the bald script; a scientist creates a living being which grows monstrous and turns on its creator. How did this pared down version emerge from the more complex text? It arose partly from accidents of publishing history and partly from the successful reworking of the story for the stage (and ultimately for the screen). St Clair shows that Mary Shelley had difficulty finding a publisher; the book was too sensational and anti-religious for most circulating libraries and their conservative readers. The book was originally anonymous, but references to Godwin in the preface warned the staid readership that it was probably an unsavoury work by some snarling progressive from Godwin's group. The only publisher prepared to take it in 1818 was Leckington who ran off an edition of 500, which turned a quick profit because he sold the whole edition in one go. But Leckington was the publisher of desperation. Dealing with him played against Mary Shelley's serious intentions because he published books on magic, pseudoscience, horror and the supernatural. Readers expected the horror story, but were unprepared for any serious message it might contain.

The potential for a stage version was spotted early and the first theatre version was performed in 1823 and aroused enough interest to produce a second edition of the book. This sold better than the first but not well because it was still aimed at the middle-class market. Shelley sold the copyright of a revised version of the book outright to Bentley in 1831 but he too failed to exploit the schlock value with cheap editions. Sales limped on and the book was essentially out-of-print from the 1850s to the 1870s. When the copyright expired in the 1880s, the story was well known from the stage, and only then did cheap editions of the book for the artisan market pour off the presses to big sales. Only by simplifying the plot and ignoring Mary Shelley's progressive messages did the book become a bestseller.

Turney discusses the theatrical life of the story. Staging the drama forced writers to abandon the multi-layered narratives of the book, to focus on the Gothic background, demonize the monster, and play up the alchemical overtones of the laboratory. Mary Shelley's complex and plausible Victor Frankenstein was simplified to a figure challenging the gods over the creation of life and receiving appropriate punishment for such hubris. In the cinema, *Frankenstein* appeared on screen relatively early in an Edison silent version in 1910 but the key film text is James Whale's Universal sound picture in 1931. Whale's film was based on an American stage production, so all the simplifications of stage versions were carried over to film. Universal had already made a version of *Dracula* in 1930, which had been so successful that they cast about for another story in the same vein. If *Dracula* and vampires have proved long-running staples of film horror, *Frankenstein* and his clones have been even more successful. Peter Cushing, who played Victor Frankenstein opposite Boris Karloff's Monster in Whale's version, said that he based his interpretation of Victor on the notorious body snatching Victorian surgeon, Robert Knox, a deliberately negative representation.

Dr Jekyll and Mr Hyde; *the dark side of evolution theory*

The form of Gothic in which a single character has within him a fragmented dualism of evil and good is obvious in Stevenson's *The Strange Case of Dr Jekyll and Mr Hyde*. The urbane and educated Jekyll liberates his suppressed 'animal' self through chemical manipulation to turn himself into the deformed Hyde, a fearsome breaker of all the taboos of late Victorian London. The power of science is used to release backward, ancient tendencies, a form of regression to the bestial, a relapse into depravity as the animal displaces the rational and moral human.

This release of the underlying animal was a common fictional motif after the publication of Darwin's *On the Origin of Species* in 1859. Biological work on the human brain revealed that its intellectual capacity might be separate from the emotional. Did the recently evolved human intellect perhaps barely suppress the emotional, interpreted as primitive and bestial by later Victorians? Man had developed from the animals and presumably this 'progressive' forward process could be reversed and he might revert to the bestial, the motif also famously explored ten years later by H.G. Wells in *The Island of Dr Moreau* (1896), although this is generally included by convention in science fiction because Wells is considered the founding father of that genre.

Stevenson's protagonist is genuinely two people (Jekyll and Hyde) in the same body. McNully and Floresco describe how the tale derives from the real biography of William Deacon Brodie (1741–88), an Edinburgh citizen who led a double life, a story known to Stevenson from childhood as one of the many tales told him by his nanny. Brodie was a respectable businessman by day and a criminal mover in the city's darker regions by night, keeping two mistresses and five children. He was eventually caught, tried and hanged. The fictional Jekyll and Hyde conversion between personalities is more extreme, and happens in London rather than Edinburgh.

Stevenson saw his native Edinburgh as a divided city, where as a youth he led a double 'Brodie' life in the taverns and among the prostitutes of the old town at night, while respectable in the new town by day. The Jekyll and Hyde story started from a dream in September 1885 which Stevenson eventually converted into a 25000-word novella. After a poor start, favourable reviews began to appear early in 1886 and it became an international bestseller, initially selling 40000 copies in the UK and two million in the US.

Like *Frankenstein*, the long-term survival of *Jekyll and Hyde* has depended on its re-incarnations on stage and screen. As with *Frankenstein*, film and theatre simplified the plot, Jekyll becomes all good, Hyde pure evil. Jekyll is transmuted into a noble victim, not someone whose irresponsible behaviour meant he deserved his fate. Freudian interpretations have science reviled as the cause of psychological problems (it dehumanizes and destroys personal life). The long theatrical/cinema tradition is again based on early stage versions; the book itself is seldom an immediate source.

DRACULA; LATE REVIVAL OF THE VAMPIRE

In *Dracula* Bram Stoker revisited the ancient Gothic fantasy of the vampire, the night-dwelling undead who preys on the living by sucking blood and converting them also into the limbo of vampirehood, neither properly human nor capable of liberation through death to the afterlife. Stoker adapted the story of a semi-historical Transylvanian tyrant, Vlad Dracul (Vlad the Devil), who becomes a vampire and lives on as Dracula (son of the Devil). Vampires and witches share a world of hidden sexual fantasy. The vampire and his victims are the suppressed, sub-human mirror of respectable Victorian propriety. As with the fragmentation of *Frankenstein* and *Jekyll and Hyde*, the hero of *Dracula*, Jonathan Harker, sees himself mirrored in Dracula the vampire, and as Frankenstein's monster threatens Victor's love, Elizabeth, so Dracula threatens Harker's girlfriend, Mina.

Stoker made his living as the actor-manager, Henry Irving's, business manager at the Lyceum Theatre. He was interested in applied science and, in many of his stories, the technically competent survive because problems are solved and tight scrapes avoided by appropriate technical solutions. Stoker generally took a positive view of science and technology as aids to progress. In *Dracula* the forces of reason and science, the Crew of Light, oppose the forces of unreason and darkness (and evil) in the form of Dracula and his female vampires, and vanquish them. The action cuts between remote, backward, medieval Transylvania, and late Victorian England where Dracula is intent on buying an estate to undermine the modern city of London by spreading his exotic, antiquated evil.

Jonathan Harker is a thoroughly modern man, using shorthand for his journal, memorizing train timetables to enable him to travel efficiently, and taking pictures of Dracula's castle with his little Kodak camera. He and his wife Mina are central to the Crew of Light, together with Dr Seward, Arthur Holmwood, Quincey Morris and Dr Van Helsing. Renfield the madman and Lucy, Mina's friend, are, at different times, part of the crew or associated with Dracula. The Dracula crew are nocturnal undead who consume human blood. They are disorder and fear, which may overthrow rational, modern society.

Mina is also a very modern young woman, classifying and organizing the mass of evidence the Crew of Light accumulates. She can take shorthand and use a typewriter. Her friend Lucy is far more passive, sleepwalking and dreaming a great deal; an ideal subject to fall in with Gothic and evil. Dr Seward runs an asylum and is thoroughly committed to modern science as a way of understanding the brain and also obsessively collects data, from the analysis of which he hopes to tame the world. The asylum inmate, Renfield, is well educated and a believer in science, even though his own descent to madness shows that science has limitations. Van Helsing is a universal scholar of medicine, the humanities and law, and the medicine is modern although centred round the poorly understood practices of transfusion and immunology (the science of blood, parallel to Gothic vampire concern with the same substance). But Van Helsing tends to be impulsive rather than systematic, an unscientific trait and does not believe that science can solve everything. This perhaps enables him to understand and meet the forces of magic and folklore.

Dracula is entirely Gothic, medieval in mind set and environment, supernatural, aristocratic, a sexually depraved villain who threatens young women. The book is a mainstream Gothic text in its tone and content but the evil, supernatural and dark forces are defeated not just by moral correctness and heroic behaviour, but by science and technology, which are used to analyse and then attack the weak points in Dracula's strategy. Some reviewers found the mixture of medieval and modern disturbing and most film versions have played up the Gothic, thriller and heroic elements at the expense of the scientific.

THE LEGACY OF THE MONSTERS

The original literary texts, from which the long-lasting theatrical and cinematic myths of Victor Frankenstein, Dr Jekyll, and Dracula originated, contained reasonably subtle treatments of the risks and benefits of science. These texts are therefore closer to contemporary Victorian feelings about science, which were essentially positive. There was fascination with the theories derived by science and people were impressed with advances in technology for which science claimed the credit. The theatrical and cinematic myths all accentuated the Gothic and either ignored the science or turned scientists into over-achievers, whose hubris was inevitably met with the nemesis of their downfall. But the literary versions live on in parallel with the dramatic and cinema versions. The books are never out of print and new plays and films keep exploiting fresh variations of the three monster themes. It is difficult to understand the cultural contradictions and connections between the literary texts and their dramatic offspring, or between the positive portrayals of real science in factual media and the less positive ones found in fiction, including these Gothic stories.

The cultural asymmetry, which allows survival of canonical popular and literary fictional texts, while factual material and short pieces of fiction published in periodicals and magazines disappear, is unfortunate. Material in the periodicals is ephemeral; it is archived but seldom re-published or re-read by later generations. But the full-length fictional stories and their dramatic and cinematic offspring often survive indefinitely, in the case of science carrying forward negative feelings and fears while the more positive factual and periodical material is lost. The central place of literature in education and culture ensures that the novels survive and are subjected to continuous commentary and analysis. Such recycling does not help non-fiction books to survive; they date rapidly and become historical period pieces, their positive interpretations of science lost as well. The same asymmetry follows the survival of science fiction and literary fiction, as we shall see in the next two chapters.

We can notice a couple more parallels and paradoxes in the monster stories. There are strong parallels between the themes of *Jekyll and Hyde* and *Dracula*. In both, the veneer of civilization is thin, in the individual's case in *Jekyll*, in society in *Dracula*. In so far as science is responsible for nineteenth-century civilization, it does not seem to have done the job thoroughly enough. Technical advances are not accompanied by equivalent moral advances, so that society finds it difficult to deal with the consequences of science and technology.

In the dramatic and cinematic *Frankensteins* we have modern versions of the old taboo that there are matters that humans are not supposed to understand because they are properly the province of Divine beings. Victor's science is seen as a new way of exploring areas previously exclusive to the supernatural, in earlier times this had been done with magic or alchemy. To the extent that magic, alchemy and science break spiritual taboos they are all evil activities. There is also the continuity we suggested in Part IV. Science is not a modern reaction against ancient magic or alchemy; it grows as much out of them as against them.

BIBLIOGRAPHY

Botting, F. (1996). *Gothic*. London: Routledge.

Garrett, P. K. (2003). *Gothic Reflections. Narrative Force in Fiction*. Ithaca: Cornell University Press.

Haynes, R. D. (1994). *From Faust to Strangelove. Representations of the Scientist in Western Literature*. Baltimore and London: Johns Hopkins University Press.

Jackson, R. (1981). *Fantasy. The Literature of Subversion*. London: Routledge.

McNally, R. and Florescu, R. (2001). *In Search of Dr Jekyll and Mr Hyde. The True Life Story behind the Ultimate Tale of Horror*. London: Robson Books.

St Clair, W. (2000). The impact of Frankenstein. In Bennett, B. T. and Curran, S. (eds.). *Mary Shelley and her Times*. Chapter 3. Baltimore: Johns Hopkins University Press.

Senf, C. A. (2002). *Science and Social Science in Bram Stoker's Fiction*. Westport: Greenwood Press.

Stapleford, B. (1995). Frankenstein and the origin of science fiction. In Seed, D. (ed.). *Anticipations. Essays on Early Science Fiction and its Precursors*. Liverpool: Liverpool University Press, pp. 46–57.

Turney, J. (1998). *Frankenstein's Footsteps. Science, Genetics and Popular Culture*. New Haven: Yale University Press.

21 Science fiction: serious literature or low grade entertainment?

"Joanna how can you read that stuff? Garish covers, cheap production values, it's all so repetitive. Science fiction looks clever to an adolescent, especially when you start to learn science. I used to read it myself, but when you grow up, it all seems pretty immature!"

"David, you've used the right word; garish. The covers are brazen and they're saying 'pick me up! Read me! Don't be afraid! Here are adventures!'"

"Exactly, they're just thrillers set in deep space or time. There are no real characters; they don't face any moral challenges."

"That's so patronizing." Joanna chucked her rather dog-eared paperback at him but missed. "Conventional literary stuff is not the point. Science fiction is about ideas, what will happen if certain technological breakthroughs occur, if different political or philosophical ideas are played out? All these future scenarios warn us about what might happen."

"Oh yeah, well most of them seem to rely on scientists being put in charge and monkeying about with what it means to be human to make us susceptible to control. I don't much like solutions to our troubles that depend on having Strangeloves in charge with robots and ray guns. Proper literature teaches us about the human condition, solving human problems needs humanity not science."

"OK." Joanna suddenly grinned. "Is Doris Lessing a proper literary figure?"

"Silly question." From David, "of course she is, she won the Nobel Prize for Literature."

"Then pass me down that copy of Stapleton's *Last and First Men*".

David reached for it and handed it over with some disgust. "Olaf Stapleton, unreadable, fake histories of the future, mad propositions! You made me read his *Starmaker* last year, said it would be a revelation in scope and ideas. But what was it? A mish-mash of imaginary worlds with weird results from evolution, a hymn to fantasy mental collectivism, and the physical universe having a mind of its own. Cod philosophy, cod physics, cod biology. If you want to understand some philosophy, or science, or theology, then read good philosophers, scientists or theologians, not disguised lectures by a half-baked fantasist."

"You may be right," said Joanna but she had opened the copy of *Last and First Men* near the back and, grinning, shoved it in front of David, "but look who wrote an afterword saying what a wonderful book this is and how much it had influenced her as a star-gazing girl in Africa – Doris Lessing!"

"Huh," from David glancing at the by-line, "you've always been an incorrigible smartarse."

"You said it," from Joanna laughing, "science fiction is for intelligent people."

THE STRANGE GENRE OF SCIENCE FICTION

Joanna makes the case for taking science fiction seriously. It is a genre widely read by scientists and aspiring scientists and a format in which a number of scientists themselves are tempted to write, often showing high levels of creativity and style. But, despite (or because of) its popularity, science fiction has been widely ignored in the literary mainstream.

Damien Broderick argues that science fiction has failed to attract serious attention because it is seen as bad art and false science. It also tends to focus on the natural world and on intellectual disciplines like philosophy, although it tries to do this by using stories about people and their relationships. In most literature the emphasis is reversed, human subjects and their behaviour are in the foreground, the world in which they live and their intellectual mind sets the framework. But science fiction shares with science a primary concern with the nature of the external world.

Broderick notes that science fiction is not much concerned with actual science. It either deals with the consequences that science and technology have on society, or can be read as allegory (defined as a parable or fable, a tale illustrating certain moral principles), which has a surface plot with local meanings but which can also be interpreted at deeper levels. Science fiction stories are about intellectual, philosophical, theological, moral or political arguments with the surface plot serving as a metaphor, cover, disguise or irony. Broderick claims that science fiction deserves to be taken more seriously because it deals with important issues which no other literature does and he rejects the conventional literary view that it is little more than low-grade entertainment.

Most histories of science fiction argue that the form we recognize today emerged in the 1940s and 1950s. It melded together two separate traditions of scientific speculative fiction, which developed independently from the 1890s until the Second World War. The British tradition is Scientific Romance, in contrast to the American genre of Science Fiction. The most important trigger for both was the publication in 1895 of *The Time Machine* by the young schoolmaster H.G. Wells. What Wells wrote was not itself revolutionary, and nor did his scientific romances (all published between 1895 and 1905) lead directly to modern science fiction. But Wells's output was a significant point in the evolution of the genre.

The man who did more than most to pin down the science fiction movement was Hugo Gernsback, founding editor in 1926 of the American pulp fiction magazine, *Amazing Wonder Stories*. This magazine focused on a niche market in adventure fiction initially called by Gernsback, 'scientifiction'. His editorials in the early 1930s defined what this American genre was. Science fiction stories were clearly romances (narratives dealing with events and characters remote from everyday life). Gernsback thought they should be stories like those of Jules Verne, H. G. Wells, or Edgar Allen Poe, romances intermingled with scientific fact and prophetic vision. They should be educational, specifically concerned with introducing the discoveries of modern science to scientifically illiterate audiences. And they should be prophetic, generating ideas about the future that would be largely determined by technological inventions and scientific advance.

Gernsback hoped that actual science and technology would be influenced by these futuristic visions and evolve along the pathways suggested by the fictional stories. Such a proposal is not as far-fetched as it might sound provided the science involved is accurate and plausible. In Gernsbeck's vision, science would become a cultural force of wide application, replacing the humanities as the best way to understand and organize human society. In other words he advocated scientism, the view that society would benefit greatly if governed by scientists on scientific principles. Gernsback was very sure that this future would be better than the present. He refused to accept stories in Gothic vein about dysfunctional societies. *Amazing Wonder Stories* would not publish dystopian propaganda intended to inflame the public against science, machines or inventions in general. It was this optimistic American vision of science fiction that dominated its post-Second World War global development.

The student of the British tradition, Brian Stableford used the term 'scientific romance' to describe the scientific speculative fiction produced in the UK between 1890 and 1950. He argued that there was a close association between British scientific romance and the non-fictional speculative essay. British scientific romance in this period focused on the consequences of evolution and philosophical materialism in biology, rather less on the paradoxes of post-Einstein physics.

Stableford suggested that the speculation at the heart of scientific romance did not have to be scientifically accurate, but plausible enough to separate scientific romance from the supernatural or fantasy. Most subsequent definitions of science fiction also insist that the genuine article has to be scientifically plausible. Pre-war British scientific romance ranged from high seriousness to broad farce and tended to be iconoclastic, putting forward a rhetoric of science as the 'best' way to both natural and cultural truth, batting away the 'idols' of what their authors saw as false beliefs and popular follies that passed for truth. British scientific romances had a tendency to be dystopian and critical, if you like, to wear Gothic clothes. Quite a lot of attention was paid to how to harmonize science with spirituality and religious belief.

THE ORIGINS OF SCIENCE FICTION

H.G. Wells's *Time Machine* (1895) fitted into the framework of an emerging movement, for he was not alone in writing stories about the future. Many stories in British Victorian periodicals were proto-science fiction and introduced new scientific concepts and possibilities to the public; including evolution, entropy, time travel, the fourth dimension, and scientific speculation about nearby planets. These romances had earlier roots, which Edward James distinguishes into discrete categories, although many stories were an amalgam of two or more of these types.

The imaginary journey

These stories abound in folklore and include voyages to the moon, the planets and beyond. What singles out the scientific romance from the imaginary journey is scientific plausibility. Jules Verne was the nineteenth-century master of such voyages, and had a huge influence on British scientific romance, although he was poorly served by his translators. About one-third of his adventure stories fit reasonably in the modern category of science fiction. His heroes were virtuous and their scientific and technical adventures based closely on actual science. This was done as a contribution to educating his (predominantly young) readers about science and technology. In the late nineteenth century, as the globe became thoroughly explored, fantasy journeys shrank to isolated valleys or lost mountain ranges, creating a new sub-genre of 'lost race stories'.

Tales of science

These stories tell of marvellous inventions and were relatively common before Wells and often involved mad or dangerous scientists bent on destruction and mayhem. Most modern versions of this genre concentrate on the creations and inventions themselves and pay less attention to the process of producing them. Wells himself was atypical with his focus on the scientist and his moral dilemmas.

Interest in the consequences of science and technology at the end of the nineteenth century is not surprising; the products of 'science' were transforming people's lives (steam trains, factories, gas, electricity, machines and gadgets of all types). The leading American exponent of the scientific tale was Luis Philip Senarens and his protagonist, Frank Reade Jr, with tales of electric robots, submarines, tanks and powered and unpowered flight in the 1890s. Such tales became staples of the American 'dime' novel. The name 'Edisonades' was given to stories where clean-cut American hero inventors use their ingenuity to save themselves, their friends and the nation from foreign oppressors.

Utopian and dystopian fantasies

Stories of hypothetical ideal societies are almost as old as imaginary voyages. Most have satirical elements as authors clearly felt that humans were not well adapted to lives in heaven. While authors were speedy to adopt new technology to travel to their utopias, they took longer to see that technology could be problematic for society. Dystopias dominated the British scientific romance movement, leading to the most influential dystopian fantasies of all, Huxley's *Brave New World* in the 1930s and Orwell's *Nineteen Eighty-Four* in the

1940s. H. G. Wells to an extent bucked the trend; remaining generally a builder of utopias. The early American science fiction tradition was different. Science and technology were always progressive forces.

Future wars

This genre was begun by Lieutenant-Colonel Sir George Tomkyns Chesney with *The Battle of Dorking: Reminiscences of a Volunteer* (1871), a fantasy which questioned British military ability in the Imperial era. It was pessimistic and expected the destruction of civilization by barbaric forces. Many of these fantasies stuck close to existing military technology until George Griffith produced *The Angel of Revolution* in 1892, which explored future warfare with airships, submarines and powerful explosives. Once again, there is a sharp contrast between the UK and the US. The Americans had no tradition of future war story, but in Britain concern about the Empire and its future was an everyday feature of cultural life.

Evolutionary fantasies

A wide range of reactions to evolution theory were common after Darwin published *On the Origin of Species* in 1859. Evolutionary implications permeated quality literature, but evolution did not trigger speculative fiction for some time, apart from Samuel Butler's *Erewhon* in 1872 (where machines evolve to be fitter than men). The absence of such tales is surprising. It was left to H. G. Wells to explore most of the speculative consequences of evolution theory in his romances at the turn of the twentieth century.

Eschatological fantasies

These are fantasies set deep in metaphysical time and space, visions of heaven, hell and so on, found in Jewish and Christian religious texts. Mary Shelley's *The Last Man* (1826) is in this tradition, and fantasizing about the death of civilization was picked up by Richard Jefferies in *After London* (1885) and an entire sub-genre of later science fiction is concerned with it. Many versions of these fantasies in the scientific romance defend religious metaphysics against the onslaught of atheist science.

Scientific romance and metaphysical fantasy

Scientific romance went out of its way to separate itself from superstitious fantasy. Paradoxically such fantasy was common, despite the waning of supernatural belief in the face of scientific determinism. The paradox was resolved by reconciliatory stories that fused elements of the old religious world-view with the modern scientific one. The logic of atheism met the continuing emotional need for spirituality. These tensions between old and new were obvious in 'new age' philosophies like Theosophy, Christian Science, the activities of the Society for Psychical Research (which looked for scientific evidence of occult phenomena) and Spiritualism.

Persistence of the 'occult'

In most of this precursor material and in science fiction itself, issues of spirituality, religion, and the occult are powerful and sometimes dominant elements. As we shall see in the next chapter, these things are also important for more serious literary authors. It seems that, while science itself (especially biology) strives hard to cut itself off from wider culture, including its occult origins, much science fiction and fantasy celebrates the possibility of reuniting the scientifically rational with the mystical and spiritual. Indeed, strange nineteenth-century movements such as spiritualism, Christian Science, Theosophy and psychical research were patronized and supported by many leading late nineteenth- and early twentieth-century scientific figures. Rational neutrality and cultural isolation seem to be philosophical stances that some elements within science find it hard to maintain.

THE DIVERGENT TRADITIONS IN BRITAIN AND AMERICA

The publication of scientific romance increased in the UK in the 1890s, partly because of social change following industrial growth, partly *fin de siècle* feelings about a new century, but mainly because of changes to the British magazine and book markets. The British book market in the nineteenth century had been divided between two extremes, expensive, three-decker, high-brow novels of literary worth and low-brow fiction churned out as cheaper penny or two-penny dreadfuls. There was no middle market of single-volume books, or middle-brow, middle-class magazines, both of which existed in America and Continental Europe. Serious short fiction did not exist in the UK because there was no publishing niche for it. Anyone with literary pretensions had to write at least three volumes. The single-volume form that suits speculative science fiction (lacking intricate character development or extensive descriptive background) was not available.

British publishers only began to cater for the middle market in the 1890s. Cheap single volumes began to appear and middle-brow weekly and monthly magazines (such as the *Strand* and *Pearson's Weekly*) appeared in large numbers, mixing fiction with non-fiction. These outlets were suitable for scientific romance and tyro writers of speculations (scientific and otherwise) could now make a living. Other romantic story categories flourished as well, for instance, detective fiction by Conan Doyle, occult romances by Marie Corelli and African adventures by Rider Haggard.

While scientific romances were perfectly placed to occupy new British middle-brow magazines, the market for them fell sharply in the early twentieth century before an aggressively expanding daily popular national press. Surviving magazines strove for respectability and abandoned scientific romance as too sensational. By the First World War, periodical outlets for British scientific romance had almost disappeared. Instead, it had to be published in single-volume book form and the scientific romance in Britain hovered for a while on the edge of literary respectability.

In America at this time there were very cheap dime novels and a new breed of periodical, unique to the USA, pulp magazines, crudely produced from thick wood pulp paper with hideously garish covers. Middle-class magazines printed on expensive paper were 'the slicks'. Most American science fiction in the first half of the twentieth century turned up as short stories on the pages of the pulps, while a small amount of British scientific romance appeared in America in full-length novel form.

There were other cultural contrasts. American and British experiences of the First World War were very different and American science fiction was gung-ho and optimistic compared with the dystopian character of British and other European science romance. 'Futurology' became a respectable intellectual pursuit in the UK in the 1930s which kept science fiction just this side of respectable. Leading examples of non-fictional futurology were J. B. S. Haldane's *Daedalus; or, Science and Future* of 1924 and J. D. Bernal's *The World, the Flesh and the Devil* of 1929. These reinforced an ongoing agenda for the scientific community to claim for science a special cultural role in the future.

By contrast, American pulp science fiction was teaching people to wonder and be amazed, not to think or criticize. In America the 'doc' Smith tradition produced the superhero and the space opera. Big-scale action and size of spectacle became ends in themselves. The American superhero was incredibly popular but criticized by intellectuals for his rabid anti-democratic attitudes. But embedded in the all-action American approach was some more thoughtful material about ideas, moods and characters and from this eventually emerged the 'modern' post-war American science fiction of Asimov, Heinlein and others.

THE AMERICAN AND BRITISH APPROACHES COMBINE

Middle-brow literary tradition kept scientific romance out of the paperback book trade in the UK as it emerged in the 1930s. This was dominated by Allen Lane with Penguin Books, which aped the serious tradition of good literature and searched through the back catalogue to republish good literary material on this new 'platform'. But in America, paperbacks replaced cheap pulps and published a wide range of popular literature. After the war, in the UK, new paperback publishers (Corgi and Pan for instance) adopted the American low-brow model, specializing in gangster novels and salacious sex. They cast about for new genres and came across American pulp-based science fiction and began to publish it over here (before the Americans put it into paperback themselves). But, by this stage, under pressure from the better magazine publishers, American science fiction writers were beginning to go upmarket, meeting the new British taste for trashier science fiction on the way down. From this fusion, on both sides of the Atlantic, post-war science fiction authors began to combine the philosophical and critical elements of old British science romance with the sense of wild adventure from America.

In Britain in the 1950s, two leading pioneers of the new science fiction (or of fully mature science romance) were John Wyndham with *The Day of the Triffids* (1951), and John Christopher with *The Death of Grass* (1956). Both these authors found readers outside the group of hard-core science fiction/scientific romance fans. To an extent they broke into the conventional literary market, and were immediately followed by three British authors who became the respectable arm of science fiction, Arthur C. Clarke, Brian W. Aldiss and J. G. Ballard. By the 1960s and 1970s, even 'literary' authors were prepared to write books in the science fiction genre.

In America, in 1938, John W. Campbell Jr became editor of the second science fiction pulp magazine, *Astounding Stories of Superscience*. In the 1940s he nurtured four of the leading writers who set the benchmarks for American science fiction in the classic period, Robert A. Heinlein, Isaac Asimov, A.E. Van Voght and L. Ron Hubbard. Campbell encouraged more mature writing and physically altered the look and feel of the magazine from pulp to slick. Campbell, like Gernsback, thought that science fiction should be serious, instructive and above all prophesy. The science in science fiction was to be accurate, the predictions serious and plausible. Robert Heinlein developed five basic precepts for science fiction, of which the fifth was that everything that occurs in science fiction must obey the laws of science or what can reasonably be extrapolated from them. If unexplained or implausible science is used, then the tale is fantasy, not science fiction, which means that much recent work in the science fiction tradition is excluded by hard-core fans. Science fiction must start with the science and social organization of the present day and project future events that could plausibly develop.

Campbell insisted on scientific accuracy because he knew that many of his readers (and writers) were scientists and engineers (there was a big readership in Los Alamos in the 1940s and at NASA in the 1960s) and, like Gernsback, he hoped they would respond to the prophetic element in science fiction by turning the predictions into reality. He, too, played to the culture of scientism, that science would not only explain the universe, but determine the future and produce a better society. Campbell was clear that science fiction must deliberately have a different form from conventional literature, so that it could have greater freedom to express ideas in a more powerful way. He saw that science fiction must embrace sociology, psychology, parapsychology and history but his vision was soon undermined because his writers did not want to produce the didactic polemics he envisaged, but rather to entertain and play intellectual games.

While there were liberal American science fiction writers in this period, the Campbell years of science fiction in *Astounding* were dominated by right-wing, hard-line attitudes. History was seen as endlessly cyclic, civilization was always followed by degeneration and this would continue into the future. Maintaining civilization was a series of long struggles against degeneration demanding tyranny because the human race was too stupid to take political decisions for itself. It does not take much imagination to see what sort of people *Astounding* writers thought such tyrants should be; a strong scientific elite who could guide society in the 'right' direction. To the *Astounding* fraternity any long-term hope of restoring democracy depended on 'improving' humanity to enable the public to understand the importance of scientific rationality and to overcome what science fiction writers saw as unacceptable levels of irrationality, ignorance and emotionalism. Parapsychology and brain-washing techniques featured strongly in classic science fiction as potential methods for human psychological growth.

In a more sinister turn of events L. Ron Hubbard took his ideas out of the realms of fiction and developed the pseudo-religious cult of scientology. To join this self-defining elite, supplicants had to undergo a form of brain-washing known as dianetics, auditing their past traumas and becoming 'clears' who could participate fully in scientological practice. The full panoply of scientological beliefs is bizarre; for instance, its creation myth involves invasion and destruction of galactic beings on Earth 75 million years ago, whose radioactive souls waft through the atmosphere to this day, implanting 'false' religious ideas from which only high-level scientologists are immune. The Church of Scientology claims ten million members in 159 countries and is thought to be worth billions of dollars.

THE MEANING OF SCIENCE FICTION

The strong argument for science fiction is that it allows philosophical, social and political ideas and tensions to be worked out. These stories are said to be 'moral' tales from which we learn the future consequences of present behaviour. Defenders argue that science fiction is the only literary genre to address big problems (like overpopulation, unemployment, poverty, warfare, sexism, environmental pollution, global warming and so on) and ask how to solve them. But science fiction has never become respectable; many mainstream readers still consider it adolescent and imitative.

Just as with Gothic, the largest platform for science fiction turned out to be film and television. As with Gothic, the lowest common denominator ruled, cinematic science fiction never aspired to the serious level of literary science fiction, drawing mainly on the pulps and comic strips for inspiration to generate space operas and superhero movies, in which evil from outer space is seen off by clean-cut officer types. Most 1950s science fiction in film and television was not 'hard science fiction' but closer to fantasy, with participants using scientific 'patter' to sketch in imaginary science, much of it pseudoscience, crank theories and ideas such as ufology, astrology and 'psychic' thinking. While America was optimistic that science would win the post-war peace, it also felt increasingly threatened by science in potential nuclear holocaust as the Cold War deepened.

Another figure feeding into American 1950s science fiction was the comic book superhero, his position compromised as he had to defend a good country (America) with bad weapons (atomic bombs). Bartter argues that this made him complicated, although overall he still possessed the benevolent masculine values of a cowboy frontiersman. Locke's work on superheroes in comic books shows that both positive and negative images of science and scientists co-existed, science displacing the magical, while also taking on magically transcendent properties, with scientists perceived as wizards or priests. In the UK in the 1950s a very high-minded strip was devised for the comic *Eagle* by the Reverend Marcus Morris to counteract the degrading effects of imported American comics and pulp fiction. This was the astronaut *Dan Dare* whose adventures in space resembled those of a conscientious early twentieth-century Imperial Officer in the far reaches of British Empire.

By the end of the 1950s, most of the classic themes of science fiction had been explored by the leading writers; space exploration and colonization, encounters with alien races, and the constant struggle to keep civilized galactic empires together against the forces of degeneration. Science fiction seemed to help many people come to terms with nuclear fear. Real governments behaved like their science fictional galactic counterparts in trying to defuse this unease. They accentuated the benefits of nuclear power and justified the continuation into peacetime of state power, scientific exploitation, and secrecy as key features that had won the war and could therefore bring prosperity in peacetime. Supposedly democratic Western governments got away with this in the immediate post-war period but, as the 1950s wore on, popular culture (in Heinlein and Dick's post-nuclear holocaust scenarios and especially in the cinema) revealed the strength of underlying fear. Nuclear fear scenarios reached a crescendo with Nevil Shute's book *On the Beach* in 1959 and Stanley Kubrick's film *Dr Strangelove* in 1963.

But, it is hard to generalize about cultural stereotypes and they never stand still. Comparisons of American science fiction stories published in the 1950s with those from the 1990s provide hints of change. Snyder found in a sample of 1950s stories that one-third had scientists as main protagonists and just under half showed scientists in a negative light (confirming earlier work on the content of science fiction in this period). However, in the 1990s, scientist protagonists occur in nearly half the stories and are nearly always positively portrayed.

THE SCIENCE FICTION COMMUNITY

Science fiction has an intense audience and modern science fiction conventions attract thousands of attendees. In the classic period fans had an almost religious fervour, worshipping the benign future apparently available in deep space from the appliance of science (almost oblivious of the fact that it was fiction). Fandom creates a sense of community among those who 'know the truth' and fans can feel they are missionaries bent on enlightening 'ordinary people'.

Thomas Disch believed science fiction had wide influence in American culture because it was popular, commercial, low-brow, not educational or elitist, and he traced these characteristics in American science fiction to the lurid tales of Edgar Allen Poe in the 1830s–1840s. Poe was pure entertainer, generator of schlock horror stories unredeemed by moral precept and an early user of scientific scenarios to set up gore and mystery. While Disch conceded the influence of British science fiction writers on the American genre, he thought the classic tradition derived more from Poe.

Disch also suggested Poe was the starting point for spiritualism and, later, for similar cults. A year after Poe's death in 1849, stimulated by his stories of resurrection from the dead, the Fox sisters of upstate New York claimed they could contact the dead who tapped out messages to them (faked by the sisters cracking their toe joints against the floor). They became the first mediums and the spiritualist craze spread like wildfire. Disch saw this as a direct forerunner of various cults springing from over-enthusiastic science fiction fans, such as UFO spotting and stories of encounters with aliens. From spiritualism arose 'Madame' Blavatsky's Theosophical Society, founded in 1875 as a form of 'religion' in which some humans were evolved to higher states than ordinary people, a set of spiritual guides known as the Great White Brotherhood of Masters. The parallels with L. Ron Hubbard and scientology are obvious. Disch also believed Poe was a strong influence on Mary Baker Eddy, whose cult of Christian Science is a belief in the reality of the spiritual and in the illusion of reality.

Science fiction spawned cults and sects, several of which have turned out to be dangerous. L. Ron Hubbard was not the only science fiction author who realized the power of his writing. Others deliberately set out to create sects, believing themselves divinely inspired. On the whole, they have only managed to assemble a few cranks, although entirely blameless writers have found their works used by deranged fantasists. Robert Heinlein's texts were central to Charles Manson's 1970s cult of violence and Asimov's *Foundation* to Arum Shivikyo, leader of the Shoko Asahara cult responsible for the sarin gas attack on the Tokyo underground in the 1990s. Members of these cults are convinced that their vision and prophesies are right and that everyone else is wrong. That conviction of the special status of their beliefs entitles them (in their minds) to treat unbelievers in any way they wish because such people are essentially worthless.

On a lighter note, perhaps the most obsessive and benign fan groups have gathered round the television series *Star Trek* and *Dr Who*. There have been several series of *Star Trek* and a large community of *Trekkies* exhibit obsessively detailed interest in the soap opera lives of the crew of the *Enterprise*. The original series in the 1960s resonated with the liberal civil rights and anti-Vietnam war community, since the crew was multiracial and plot lines were pointedly liberal. Spock's relationships with the rest of the crew started the female fan base. Disch argued that the *Enterprise* was also symbolic of corporate America, the crew behaving like a project team in a good management consultancy. But other critics attack *Star Trek*'s claims to have been strongly anti-racist and anti-sexist. Having females and mixed race aliens on the bridge of *Enterprise* was not enough. Deconstruction of the plot lines and characters shows that racism and sexism were alive and well throughout all three *Star Trek* series.

But science fiction on television has not received the critical attention it deserves apart from discussion of *Star Trek*. Some critics argue that the success of television science fiction reflects its quality as art, while others, Bould for instance, argue that science fiction is not a sophisticated art. What makes science fiction successful is its soap banality. It does what television does best; develop exploitable fictional packages for popular consumption.

SCIENCE FICTION AFTER THE CLASSIC PERIOD

Science fiction took off in fresh directions in the 1960s, once the classic writers had worked out most future possibilities. In England the new wave was centred round *New Worlds* edited by Michael Moorcock and written by leading lights including Brian Aldiss and J. G. Ballard. Moorcock called for more characterization, more depth, and more emotional commitment and thought that surrealism and the fantastic should feature heavily to force readers to consider humanity afresh and from different angles. Following Moorcock's clarion call, writers went overboard on experiment, which did not always prove popular with readers. The American version of the new wave started a little later and aimed to improve the existing traditions, rather than move to other ground altogether.

From the 1970s the genre has become increasingly fragmented. Space opera continued among core fans as 'hard science fiction' but science fiction also explored the cultural themes of the period; sex, drugs and both extreme liberal and extreme right political positions and their implications. All this annoyed the hard science fiction community. Feminist and fantasy science fiction became increasingly common, the fantasists treating science and technology as forms of magic which authors had no obligation to get 'right' or even plausible. In the 1970s the first fantasy role-play games emerged, such as *Dungeons and Dragons* and the first computer game, *Adventure*. Whereas many adolescents up to that point read science fiction, they turned to computer games. Feminist science fiction moved human relationships back to the centre of the genre, which had otherwise been dominated by space hardware and the broad sweep of history and psychology. British writers remained relatively marginal figures apart from Arthur C. Clarke whose reputation became international.

A new sub-genre was born in the 1980s with cyberpunk, a vision of emerging domestic technologies centred round home computerization and the elision of man and machine through implants, prosthetics, neurochemistry and artificial intelligence to improve the mental equipment of dim human populations. While these worlds were hi-tech, in some senses they were also sordid and run-down because the corporations running this version of the future cannot maintain infrastructure. Leading lights are Bruce Sterling and William Gibson, whose *Neuromancer* of 1984 is often taken as the ur-text, where drug fuelled hackers live most of their lives in virtual reality cyberspace. Cyberpunk represents a victory for dystopian science fiction (with a very Gothic feel) over the progressive, largely utopian visions of classic space opera.

SCIENCE FICTION AS 'SERIOUS' SCIENCE COMMUNICATION

Writing books of popular science and of science fiction is sometimes a way for scientists to promulgate heterodox ideas which are not acceptable to fellow scientists. Jane Gregory argues that Fred Hoyle, serious scientist and popular radio presenter on astronomy in the

1950s, exploited his media profile to branch out into science fiction, in which he first articulated elements of his life-from-space thesis, only later presented as formal scientific papers and factual books. For Hoyle, science fiction came first because his novels were widely read by other scientists who were not prepared to consider the idea as a 'serious' proposition in the professional press. These novels could therefore be considered part of the mainstream communication of science.

In its mature form Hoyle's theory was bold, proposing that cosmic dust was coated with organic molecules, that life fell to Earth from such dust brought by comets, that the influx of organic matter from space still drives terrestrial evolution, and that a Superior Intelligence guides the universe. While the first hint of the idea appeared in the popular factual book *Frontiers of Astronomy* in 1955, the thesis is much better worked out in dramatic form in the novel *The Black Cloud* (1957) and in *A for Andromeda* (1961), a BBC television drama. Hoyle's main papers on the theme in the professional science press only appeared in the 1970s (mainly in *Nature*) and the first factual popular book version, *Life Cloud*, not until 1978. By this stage he was attracting obloquy from the establishment in biology, who thought his concepts were nonsense, their view reinforced when he spoke, in court, on behalf of creationists in Arkansas in the 1980s. In the end Hoyle's life-from-space thesis moved from respectable heterodoxy to crackpot vision in the eyes of the scientific establishment.

The example of Fred Hoyle's work shows there can be serious educational and cultural motivations behind writing science fiction. Yet, despite evidence of sound moral and philosophical purpose, science fiction remains a genre not taken seriously by the literary establishment. Is it, as Broderick argues, because future predictions about science are inevitably false science, and too many science fiction authors are simply bad writers, not able to bring off satisfying treatments of human motivations, behaviour, moral choice, or relationships? Perhaps science fiction simply cannot illuminate the human condition, however well it can describe theories of nature or deal with intellectual dilemmas around science, spirituality, politics and philosophy?

Or perhaps the difficulty lies with the exposition versus narrative problem, discussed in other literary contexts in the following chapters. Are discussions of abstract intellectual ideas or scientific theories simply incompatible with the development of stories about the moral dilemmas of human characters? The answer is clearly 'no' because ethics and morality are explored in all forms of literature at a variety of levels. This is because these philosophical principles can be analysed and worked out in the context of human behaviours and relationships. But when it comes to philosophical and scientific ideas about nature, it is extraordinarily difficult to develop these through conventional stories focused on the behaviour of human characters. In English and American literature, attempts to do this in 'novels of ideas' are seldom critically successful. To render science fiction respectable, it seems to need some high-order re-engineering and re-invention to allow abstract ideas and human stories not just to co-exist, but to enter mutually satisfying relationships with each other.

BIBLIOGRAPHY

Bartter, M.A. (1988). *The Way of Ground Zero. The Atomic Bomb in American Science Fiction*. New York: Greenwood Press.

Bould, M. (1999). Wither our understanding of sf. *Public Understanding of Science*, **8**, 57–63.

Broderick, D. (1995). *Reading by Starlight. Postmodern Science Fiction*. London: Routledge.

Disch, T.M. (1998). *The Dreams our Stuff is Made of. How Science Fiction conquered the World*. New York: The Free Press.

Fayter, P. (1997). Strange new worlds of space and time: late Victorian science and science fiction. In Lightman, B. (ed.). *Victorian Science in Context*. Chapter 12. Chicago: University of Chicago Press.

Gregory, J. (2003). The popularization and excommunication of Fred Hoyle's 'life from space' theory. *Public Understanding of Science*, **12**, 25–46.

James, E. (1994). *Science Fiction in the Twentieth Century*. Oxford: Oxford University Press.

Hammerton, M. (1995). Verne's amazing journeys. In Seed, D. (ed.). *Anticipations. Essays on Early Science Fiction and its Precursors*. Liverpool: Liverpool University Press, pp. 98–109.

Lambourne, R., Shallis, M. and Shortland, M. (1990). *Close Encounters? Science and Science Fiction*. Bristol: Adam Hilger.

Lewenstein, B. W. (1995). From fax to facts: communication in the Cold Fusion saga. *Social Studies of Science*, **25**, 408–24.

Locke, S. (2005). Fantastically reasonable: ambivalence in the representation of science and technology in super-hero comics. *Public Understanding of Science*, **14**, 25–46.

Reitman, J. (2006). Inside scientology. *The Observer*, Review Section, 9 April, 7–10.

Snyder, L. H. (2004). The portrayal of scientists in science fiction. *Strange Horizons*, 24 May, http://www.strangehorizons.com/2004/20040524/portrayal.shtml.

Stableford, B. (1985). *Scientific Romance in Britain, 1890–1950*. London: Fourth Estate.

Westfahl, G. (2002). Of plagues, predictions and physicians. Introduction to Westfahl, G. and Slusser, G. (eds.). *No Cure for the Future. Disease and Medicine in Science Fiction and Fantasy*. Westport CT: Greenwood Press.

22 Science in British literary fiction

Self-consciously modernist writers of the early twentieth century such as Henry James, Joseph Conrad or Virginia Woolf held that a novel should be a work of art and an end in itself. They argued against those like H.G. Wells and Aldous Huxley who believed that novels should be means to ends, commenting and critiquing the human condition with a view to changing or improving it. We know from the subsequent reputations of these writers which position most literary commentators have taken. To use a cricketing analogy, James and Conrad are opening batsmen for genius, while Huxley and Wells are sloggers well down the order in the second 11. Subsequent modernists have followed James, such that literary art was set up in opposition to science, an argument rehearsed in two famous historical spats; T.H. Huxley's duel with Matthew Arnold in the nineteenth century, and the infamous F.R. Leavis/C.P. Snow 'two cultures' row in the mid twentieth century.

The great polymath immunologist, Sir Peter Medawar, questioned the validity of the myth underlying the whole dispute, that imagination and reason are antithetical, or independent ways of understanding the world. He argued that they are complementary and, in science at least, both are essential. The idea of their mutual hostility arose from serious mistakes made by thinkers on both sides. Those who favoured the rapid insights of creative imagination overdid their propaganda that truth derived through reason was slow and trivial. Reductionist philosophers of science compounded the false dichotomy by claiming that rational analysis was the only tool used in science.

For Medawar the latter was nonsense; scientists used imagination and told stories when devising their hypotheses, in much the same way as literary authors. Science then proceeds to evaluate and modify these hypotheses to see if they correspond with reality. Medawar's gripe with literary writers was their reluctance to use either reason or correspondence to reality to evaluate their stories, assuming that imaginative literary truth went beyond simple correspondence with reality. Medawar conceded that fictional authors tried to make their theories internally consistent and satisfying but for him this was not enough. He would not tolerate the claim that literary truth is somehow better than the scientific one. Such a claim he called poetism, dismissing it as the equivalent of scientism, the equally misconceived belief that the world would be a better place if it was run by scientists.

SCIENCE IN LITERARY CULTURE

We live in a society where science and technology are integral to our economy, industry and business, where scientific thinking and attitudes reach deep into many aspects of our lives, and yet they are poorly represented in our elite cultural products such as literary fiction. In so far as scientists are represented, Haines shows that, in canonical Western literature, they are seen in a negative light. This elite literary distaste might arise because scientific ideas and explanations are difficult and counter-intuitive, or because the forces central to scientific explanation are invisible.

But there may be a more pernicious reason for the lack of coverage of science as such in serious literature; elite literary practitioners and critics identified themselves as bastions of resistance to what they believed were the undesirable consequences of science; technological change leading to industrialization and urbanization. They saw themselves as champions of more humane attitudes supposedly swept away in modern industrial societies. Despite industry and the machine being iconic symbols of modernity in art and architecture, modern literature has generally chosen not to celebrate them but to attack their supposedly undesirable consequences. This oppositional stance may explain why there is so little overt science and scientists in literary fiction.

But, if science is not solely the cause of technological change and industrialization, it cannot be blamed for their evil consequences (and, symmetrically, nor can it take all credit for their success). We could therefore dismiss the whole contentious war between reason and imagination (and between science and art) as vacuous. But, in the real world, the academic critic F. R. Leavis and his predecessors, undertaking the 'new literary criticism' of the first half of the twentieth century, did read strong anti-science and anti-industry messages when interpreting the works of those writers deemed to be the leading figures of modernist English literature, especially Thomas Hardy, Virginia Woolf and D. H. Lawrence.

Since the Leavis/Snow debate in the second half of the twentieth century, academic literary critics have somewhat back-pedalled from this position. They discovered that, while science and scientists were seldom represented in nineteenth-century literature, scientific thinking (especially positivist philosophy and Darwinian evolutionary thought) pervaded much canonical literary work. Many scholars have unearthed this influence in plots, character development, and above all in metaphors and other literary tropes based on scientific ideas. Such connections between science and literature are now expressed in a variety of ways, including the literary analysis of popular and professional factual science writing. There is a paradox that English literature made the case that literature and science were two separate world-views and dismissed science as inferior, but to do this it used methods borrowed wholesale from the very sciences it sought to undermine. Turner argues that the paradox is even deeper because the scientific tools they borrowed are out of date and do not represent the modern nature of science at all.

Revisionists such as Ingersoll question whether modernist writers did actually take the strong anti-science positions ascribed to them. Most writers certainly opposed industrial urbanization, which critics have perceived as based on science. It seems much less certain whether the authors themselves felt the blame should rest with science. D.H. Lawrence is the key witness for the literary prosecution although careful cross-examination reveals that he may not be all that reliable. In Lawrence's world, manual labour on the land is liberating, factory work is slavery and, by implication, Lawrence is categorized as anti-science. But mining and civil engineering are the professions of many of his characters and he himself was an enthusiastic botanist (the acceptable science for a ruralist). Authorial attack on his engineer characters is based on their anti-ruralism, rather than being anti-technology or anti-science per se. And, among later twentieth-century writers, Alan Sillitoe's working class Arthur Seaton in *Saturday Night and Sunday Morning* is a capstan lathe operator and therefore an industrial slave with bad consequences for him and his social group. But he enjoys the actual work he does, and treats his machine as a sort of friend.

Academic analysts and literary critics have focused on the use of scientific metaphor (and other linguistic tropes using science) in literature and on interpreting the apparently anti-science attitudes of canonical literary authors. Much less common has been analysis of science and scientists as narrative actors in novels, although a certain amount has been done and what follows are brief reports on research in this area.

PHYSICS FICTION IN AMERICAN LITERATURE

The rarity of science and scientists as fictional subjects is confirmed by Friedman's analysis of 'physics fiction' in the work of six American post-Second World War authors. Physics is certainly present, but its treatment is largely indirect. There is some material on the impact of scientific change on culture and society (the standard subject matters of science fiction extended into literary fiction), frequent use of scientific metaphors and other tropes to discuss the human condition, but science as an explicit subject of the novel occurs on only a few occasions. In his analysis of tropes Friedman believes ideas from modern physics (relativity and quantum theory for instance) leak across into general culture in three metaphorical contexts; order and disorder, cause and effect, and unity between the human and physical universes.

Friedman finds order/disorder treated metaphorically in Thomas Pynchon's *Entropy*, *The Crying of Lot 49* (1966) and *Gravity's Rainbow* (1973) and in William Gaddis's *JR* (1975). The underlying science metaphor is the second law of thermodynamics in its crude meaning of increasing chaos and entropy. In the cause and effect category, the uncertainty principle appears metaphorically in Robert Coover's *Universal Baseball Association Inc. J. Henry Waugh Prop* (1968) and Joseph McElroy's *Look out Cartridge* (1974). Both of these also have overtones of engineering communication problems: signals and messages are hard to receive because of noise interference.

Unity between the arts and sciences is the theme in Don DeLillo's *Ratner's Star* (1976), Robert Pirsig's *Zen and the Art of Motorcycle Maintenance* (1974) and Joseph McElroy's *Plus* (1977). DeLillo's and McElroy's books are quasi-science fiction but also deal to an extent with the nature and process of science, as does Pirsig, more directly. In *Ratner's Star*, a 14-year-old mathematician thinks maths has no contact with the real world but finds, on the contrary, that abstract ideas touch physical and human universes with consequent suffering. In *Plus*, following fatal radiation exposure, a scientist allows his brain to be used for an experiment and the brain tries to reconstruct a previous life, developing a strange new personality, part human–part machine, creating a sympathetic alien being.

In Pirsig's *Zen* the narrator had previously gone mad trying to re-unite the separated classical and romantic aspects of reality and has a new personality created by electric shock treatment. He goes in search of his past self providing a series of lectures on the relations between science, technology, and the humanities where he seeks the underlying unity which he perceived in his previous incarnation. The book contains a lot of material drawn from Zen Buddhism and science but Pirsig disclaims accuracy, the material is not 'right' or true in a real science sense. Friedman concludes that, with the exception of *Ratner's Star,* the views of science expressed here are not stereotypically negative or confrontational and that the most satisfactory use of physics in fiction arises when it provides metaphor. In none of these books does the practice or theory of physics form the actual subject of the story.

SCIENCE AND SCIENTISTS IN NINETEENTH- AND TWENTIETH-CENTURY ENGLISH NOVELS

I have reviewed the rather rare appearances of scientific characters and their science in nineteenth- and early twentieth-century English canonical novels. During the nineteenth century, both writing and science were career options opening up to a wider range of participants than had been possible before. Scientific research and literary writing were just two of a range of new professions emerging to organize an increasingly complex industrial society.

The patterns of authorship and portrayal of science characters in nineteenth-century fiction reflect the social changes that allowed this wider access to the professions. The early authors of mid century (George Eliot and Elizabeth Gaskell) came from gentry or emerging professional backgrounds and their scientific characters, in books set in the 1820s and 1830s, belong to the pre-professional cadre of well-off hobbyists who did not need to make a living from their work, or who were members of other professions (notably medicine) undertaking scientific research in their spare time. By this stage science researchers needed specialized education and technical competence to guarantee the quality of science, although paid careers in science were still almost impossible. By the later nineteenth century, the demand for specialists increased and more widely available education allowed members of the artisan and lower middle classes to take up both paid writing and scientific careers.

Thomas Hardy sits at the transition between the old and new patterns and was himself a pioneering member of two emerging professions (architecture and literature). The scientist characters in his novels are still located in older, unpaid contexts, but career possibilities were opening up, at least for members of the gentry. With George Gissing and H.G. Wells at the end of the nineteenth century and into the twentieth, both authors came from artisan backgrounds and were holders of university degrees. Some of their scientific characters shared that background and succeeded in making science a paid career. But the characters, like their creators, were often frustrated that the full benefits of such a life were not open to them. Very few scientists could earn a living in research; that was only possible for a small number of university teachers. The new entrants were concentrated in scientific services, the majority working as analysts for the chemical industry or in school teaching. The lives of science figures in literary novels reflected these changing professional patterns in the real world and provide additional insight into the lives of those who experienced these changes, insights not easily available from other sources.

I have also looked at popular novels written between the 1930s and 1960s by English writers who also trained as scientists, most of them 'new men' following in the tracks of Wells and Gissing emerging into the twin professions of science and authorship from humble backgrounds. They were active during a particular period in British cultural history from 1930 to 1970, when economic and political collectivism dominated British society after the economic collapse of free market capitalism in the early 1930s. This collectivism persisted through the Second World War and continued into the three decades of the long economic boom which followed it. This was a time when the vaunted promise of science seemed to come true; scientific research led to technological innovation which then led to economic growth, all within an economy dominated by state-run industries with central planning orchestrated by the government. There was a general cultural approval and support for science in the UK, which continued well into the 1960s. The British economy was effectively operated as a military/industrial complex with huge official support for science and engineering education and training. The five writers all benefited educationally from this surge of interest in science and technology and were able to use their professional lives in science as source materials for fiction, which proved sufficiently popular for large sales.

The 15 or so books by these five authors dealt with the process, sociology and, to an extent, philosophy of science, and these topics were sufficiently interesting for readers to buy the books. The five authors have received variable treatment since their heyday. C. P. Snow had literary pretensions as a writer, and five of his novels dealt with the mechanics of science and its role in the wider contemporary, political environment. He remains well known but scarcely read, his style now unfashionable. Three novels by the very popular writer of medical novels, A. J. Cronin, explicitly dealt with the difficulties and benefits of a career in biomedical research. Cronin was seldom troubled by attention from the literary establishment; he was an unashamedly popular writer but first-class story teller. He is remembered now through repeats and DVDs of television adaptations of his books (famously *Dr Finlay's Casebook*) and the flow of lurid paperback versions of his books reprinted well into the 1980s.

The other three have faded from view, although Nigel Balchin and William Cooper have always had critical adherents and their reputations may rise again. E. C. Large has pretty well disappeared, probably because he only wrote full-time for about 4 years, sandwiched between an earlier career as a chemical engineer and a later one as a plant pathologist. This generated two satirical novels about industrial science and a much longer lasting book of factual popular science still on university library shelves, *The Rise of the Fungi*.

H. G. WELLS AND ALDOUS HUXLEY, SCIENCE IN THE SECOND ELEVEN

Roslynn Haynes reviews the fictional scientists portrayed by Wells in his romances, short stories and socially realistic novels, and concludes that, in the early novels, Wells took a negative view, his scientist characters showing a range of unfavourable attributes and often behaving in a Faustian way. In the more mature books his view is more positive and realistic. Wells seldom gave any details of research, either because explaining science was difficult or because he was more concerned with the intellectual, philosophical, or human consequences of science, than in the practice of science itself.

Wells is best known for the early scientific romances, which were firmly rooted in contemporary science and technology and proved popular. When he does have to explain science, Wells uses techniques like wrapping the unfamiliar up within the familiar, and a great vagueness in technical matters combined with great precision on irrelevant detail (used to great effect in *The Time Machine* where the machine itself is vaguely sketched in, while the library and dining room in the traveller's house are set out in great detail). When it was necessary to explain scientific principle, Wells was very good at embedding it in the story. There are seldom any freestanding 'science bits'. His technique boiled down to providing a strong narrative line (often constructed within a familiar genre such as mystery or detective) combined with a focus on the technological, philosophical or other implications of the science, rather than on science itself. Where explanation was necessary, he integrated it into the story through devices like an assistant recording and commenting on technical events, or a non-scientific character asking perceptive questions. If a didactic passage could not be avoided, he used humour. He also made a great deal of incorporating news of current science and technology into his stories.

June Deery dissects Aldous Huxley's relationship with science, which was tied closely to his interest in religion. He was a founding figure in the New Age Movement, which can perhaps be described as mystical science, an under-researched area of science in popular culture. Huxley thought literary people ought to be interested in the cultural and philosophical consequences of science and he himself engaged with these issues at some level in most of his books. Being part of a great biological dynasty helped, but he also had an extensive circle of scientific friends and drew on contemporary science popularizers such as Eddington and Jeans. He even read a number of primary science journals regularly.

Huxley felt that literature should draw attention to the evil ends to which 'morally neutral' science could be put. He wanted literature to retain a public intellectual role, not become the kind of specialization that modernists insisted literature, art and music should be. Huxley dropped in scientific and technical facts liberally, with the weird, the odd and the surprising rather predominating. Science was much less often a substantial plot presence. Fantasy was the only genre where he allowed science a central role, in *Brave New World*, *Ape and Essence*, and *Island*. The fantasies allowed him to cover his literary weaknesses, especially the failure to create three-dimensional characters. But he had the privilege of writing one of only two modern fantasies with a major influence on both elite and popular culture (his being *Brave New World*, the other Orwell's *1984*). Only in these fantasies could he clearly articulate relationships between science and society.

In Huxley's literary novels there are relatively few scientist characters. They only occur extensively in *Genius and Goddess* (1955), a form of scientific biography used as a vehicle for debating scientific issues. Otherwise, scientists have only minor roles; the novels are stereotypically about private, not about professional life. Where they do occur, his scientists are generally child-like, cold and dysfunctional. These portraits seem rather at odds with his more positive general view about science and scientists. The chief scientific portraits are Lord Edward Tantamount (*Point Counterpoint*), Illedge (*PCP*), Maartens (*Genius and Goddess*) and Shearwater (*Antic Hay*). All have elements of the absent-minded professor, although none are dark obsessives in the Faust, Frankenstein, Jekyll and Hyde mould.

Too often, and in contrast to Wells, Huxley failed to integrate the emotional with the intellectual in his novels. The ideas sit awkwardly as lectures rather than as integrated dramas. He was a much better essayist than novelist. The essay puts expository skills before those of narrative and the essay is a better format for developing ideas. His expository tendencies mean that Huxley's novels can become tracts, tediously didactic 'novels of ideas'. Huxley's fictional scenes are often contrived and superficial; they don't arise organically from the plot, the characters, their behaviour and emotions. Only in short stories could Huxley handle plot and character properly.

Philosophically, Deery defines Huxley as a badly shaken realist who understood that reason did not lead to a 'true' interpretation of reality, but nevertheless clung to a rational, positivist agenda, although appalled at the reductionist turn of modern science. He saw that science's dependence on language entailed subjectivity, that scientific language was to an extent rhetorical and emotive, and he also saw that experiment was not the ultimate arbiter of reality because of the problems of perception and the aesthetic properties of theories, which protect them from refutation by empirical evidence. But he had little understanding of how personality and politics impinge on the practice of science.

Huxley was much attracted by Oriental mysticism, and used psychedelic drugs. While his book, *The Doors of Perception* helped popularize drug culture of the 1960s, Huxley wanted drug use restricted to elite intellectuals, not to be widely disseminated. Mysticism was a route to enlightenment, which allowed him to resolve tensions between science and literature. He seems to have followed modern physics pioneers in admitting that science had limitations, so that even scientists could accept religion, closing the schism between science and religion that had opened up after Darwin's theory of evolution in the nineteenth century. Huxley's legacy is visible in the founding text for the New Age 'misty-science'; Frifjof Capra's *The Tao of Physics* (1975). Capra and others also tried to marry Western physics with Eastern mystic thought, interpreting science as a soft and spiritual pursuit. In the New Age view, physical science especially has opened fresh ways to spirituality and religious belief, a position pioneered by Huxley in his romances.

The critical neglect of Wells and Huxley stems partly from their espousal of unfashionable literary attitudes, but there is also no doubt that they are flawed novelists. While philosophically convinced of the importance of science in culture, Huxley lacked the literary skills to express this belief in narrative fiction, although Wells was more successful in writing novels with science. Both found it easier to discuss science in essays and articles. In fictional mode, they were forced to use fantasy as the narrative genre to explain science and its consequences, facing the problem of being taken seriously in a trivial genre. Despite speaking out about the importance of science in culture, neither of them had a straightforwardly positive attitude towards science. They were ambivalent and their most significant works are science dystopias, although their general position seemed to be that science itself was neutral, good or evil consequences arising from how it was used. Unlike Brecht, they did not seem convinced that the main responsibility for how science is used lies with scientists themselves.

MEDICAL RESEARCH NOVELS

Phillip Scott investigated English and German medical novels in the first half of the twentieth century, where a medical doctor also undertakes research, and identified a number of themes from a corpus of 18 novels.

Attitudes towards medicine and science

Fictional protagonists with the twin tracks of medicine and research always find the demands of clinical medicine and scientific research conflict. Scott uses Sinclair Lewis's 1926 novel *Arrowsmith* as the exemplar for the exploration of these issues. The novel follows the career of Martin Arrowsmith from medical student, to rural general practitioner, to scientist at a Public Health Institute, who finally winds up as a researcher living and working in isolation in the woods.

Lewis's message is that science demands enormous sacrificial effort, the direct application of science to medicine leads to corruption, and doing medical science seems incompatible with clinical work.

Other novels echo these professional conflicts between medical compassion and scientific objectivity. The duel career always generates problems of time commitment, objectivity and of detachment versus involvement. Scientists must be fanatical in the pursuit of research if they are to succeed and protagonists have their commitment to research tested severely. Mentally, they behave like artists; they are creative, skilled craftsmen and imaginative dreamers.

Self-image and attitudes towards life and success

The chief exemplar here is Angela Koldewey in Ewwebeck's novel of the same name published in 1939, the story of a woman in medicine and research driven by a need to achieve immortality from her work. Dedication to medicine and science leads her to abandon her fiancé and work on a difficult disease for her doctorate, malignant granuloma. This gives her a creative focus to life; she will find a cure. But she goes down with the disease herself and realizes she won't live long enough to achieve it. She re-orientates her goals towards husband and family as the only genuine fulfilment, but then returns to research (with her husband's help) as she weakens. She achieves her goal, they find the cure and it is announced at a major conference after which she dies, apparently ecstatically happy.

Few protagonists enjoy cultural or other leisure pursuits because nothing is so fascinating as research. Many characters knowingly risk their lives in research and the link between sickness, madness and creative zeal is frequently made. Many protagonists do not eat or sleep properly because their work dominates their lives and some experience alcohol or other substance abuse.

Close relationships with other people

Scientist characters trained to suppress emotions in their professional lives may do this in their personal lives as well and have few intimate relationships. Only one hero is a good parent. Work colleagues are often friends; sources of personal or emotional support. Of 16 marriages, 4 end in divorce and 1 in murder, largely because the protagonists have such commitment to work. The protagonists do not have much connection with their parents, even if their domestic circumstances in childhood had quite a lot to do with their becoming doctors or researchers in the first place.

Attitudes toward social issues, culture and recreation

Authors have to make their characters interesting, so they sometimes have 'outside' interests to provide breadth, but face the eternal problem of finding time for them. Josef Zeppichmann in *The Fire and the Wood* is a young doctor/researcher developing a polyvalent tuberculin which he must test during the novel's story time. He comes from a poor Jewish background and is obsessed with research success as a means of personal fulfilment. He remains focused on this project 20 hours a day despite working in 1930s Germany. Politics finally impinge on him when he is arrested and sent to the labour camps, but he is still sustained only by love of his patient Minna and his laboratory notebooks. Eventually, he does realize the horror of the situation and, as an exile, becomes more humane; still focused on Minna and research to the exclusion of all else, but now with a view to the benefits of his work for mankind. But despite their levels of intellectual and emotional commitment to science, most protagonists do not put all their faith in science, they often believe in a force operating in nature and human affairs, whether God or fate. Almost every novel addresses the possibility of reconciling scientific principles with these supernatural beliefs.

Despite German and English national and ethnic differences, these fictional researchers share many features of outlook and personality. The mythology of the scientific life is uniform; the medical scientist must find social and intellectual isolation in order to serve humanity best in the long run. After 1950, the medical research novel changed and came closer to science fiction or medical detective work. Authors seek wider cultural resonances (individual or human) from these fictions rather than dwelling on the research process for its own sake. Scott mentions four major successes, Michael Crichton's *The Andromeda Strain* (1969), Robin Cook's *Coma* (1977) and *Outbreak* (1987), and Paddy Chayevski's *Altered States* (1978). These can be classified as techno-thrillers, and may form an analytical category in their own right.

ARE SOME TECHNO-THRILLERS IN A SEPARATE CATEGORY OF LITERATURE?

Soren Brier makes a case for the existence of a genre of techno-thriller, which he calls Ficta, fictions in which real scientific implications are addressed as central themes; problems with serious current consequences for culture and civilization. He argues that such a popular genre can treat serious issues. His type specimen is Michael Crichton and his books *Jurassic Park* (1990) and *The Lost Worlds* (1995). Explorations of dramatically opposing scientific ideas are central in these books. But, while Crichton and other authors deliberately set these ideas in the centre of their works, readers often fail to realize, 'getting' only the surface thriller message, while in the film versions the ideas are entirely left out, producing pure techno-thrillers. Brier believes books like Crichton's should be considered as works of science popularization, not just novels, and is on a mission to force readers to take the science seriously and learn from it ('Ficta' as a form of textbook through entertainment).

He sets out a list of popular science genres of varying literary complexity leading towards his category of 'Ficta', defined as a radically entertaining genre where the author intends to impart some science or culture of science, in a fictional genre such as horror, thriller or detective. Along with Crichton he includes books like Greg Egan's *Distress* and Douglas Adams' *Hitchhiker's Guide to the Galaxy*. He also puts *Star Trek* here rather than in science fiction. As precursors to Ficta, he includes the Mr Tompkins books, where George Gamow explained the curiosity of the quantum world by showing what the real world would be like if quantum principles applied there; an extended metaphor.

Michael Crichton is his star exhibit, a trained scientist, all of whose techno-thrillers have explorations of scientific issues at their core. Brier thinks his presentation echoes new journalism where the writer is embedded and experiencing the world he is investigating, in anthropologist–ethnographer mode. The simile resonates with him because Crichton (like the new journalists) makes a fetish of getting the science right. Brier views *Jurassic Park* as a form of dramatized dialogue about classical versus indeterminist chaos science. The classical determinists believe they can plan and build a safe park, while the indeterminists say that it is bound to fail, as indeed it does.

But without guidance the average reader may miss the science in the action and librarians find it hard to classify or advise on these works. Are they novels or are they popular science? The genre situation will determine how they are read and Brier worries that the 'serious' is missed in the thriller (but if it was reclassified as serious, readership would plummet). Brier really believes this material has a mission to explain science before its obligation to entertain, although it is not clear what Crichton felt about that. All this is an echo of the problem faced by Penguin Books when republishing Olaf Stapleton's novels in the 1940s (disparagingly described by David in the scenario in Chapter 21). In the end they badged them as factual non-fiction rather than as works of science fiction.

SEARCHING FOR MORE FICTIONAL SCIENCE

Science fiction is not a respectable genre, while literary fiction does not carry much science. But this absence may be more apparent than real. It ignores the large amount of scholarship dedicated to scientific metaphors and culturally embedded expressions of scientific ideas in literature. The more straightforward (and in literary terms less interesting) analysis of scientists and their science in literature (and other texts) may simply be suffering from neglect. If scholars and critics looked harder, they might find more.

For instance, the major American literary figure, John Steinbeck, had as his most intimate friend the ecologist Edward Ricketts, and their joint scientific and philosophical discussions underlay many of the themes in Steinbeck's novels, while in two of them, *Cannery Row* (1945) and *Sweet Thursday* (1954), there were elaborate pen portraits of a character based closely on Ricketts (known as 'Doc'), and aspects of his biological work. There has been a certain amount of scholarly interest in this relationship, but there is more to explore. Steinbeck has suffered critical neglect compared with other leading American writers for the same reasons that Huxley and Wells have been neglected in the UK; his use of fiction as a mechanism for critique of society rather than as a self-conscious work of art. It is more than possible that less fashionable modernist (or parallel non-modernist) and post-modernist authors may provide a rich hunting ground for anyone searching for more literal connections between science and literature.

BIBLIOGRAPHY

Beer, G. (2000). *Darwin's Plots*. 2nd edition. Cambridge: Cambridge University Press.

Brier, S. (2006). Ficta: remixed generalised symbolic media in the new scientific novel. *Public Understanding of Science*, **15**, 153–74.

Broks, P. (1996). *Media Science before the Great War*. London: Macmillan.

Cantor, G., Dawson, G., Gooday, G., Noakes, R., Shuttleworth, S. and J.R. Topham (eds.) (2004). *Science in the Nineteenth Century Periodical. Reading the Magazine of Nature*. Cambridge: Cambridge University Press.

Dale, P.A. (1989). *In Pursuit of Scientific Culture. Science, Art and Society in the Victorian Age*. Wisconsin: University of Wisconsin Press.

Deery, J. (1996). *Aldous Huxley and the Mysticism of Science*. Basingstoke: Macmillan.

Forgan, S. and Gooday, G. (1996). Constructing South Kensington: the buildings and politics of T.H. Huxley's working environments. *British Journal for the History of Science*, **29**, 435–68.

Friedman, A.J. (1979). Contemporary American physics fiction. *American Journal of Physics*, **47** (May), 392–5.

Haynes, R.D. (1980). *H.G. Wells Discoverer of the Future. The Influence of Science on his Thought*. London: Macmillan.

Haynes, R.D. (1994). *From Faust to Strangelove. Representations of the Scientist in Western Literature*. Baltimore and London: Johns Hopkins University Press.

Henson, L., Cantor, C., Dawson, G., Noakes, R., Shuttleworth, S. and J.R. Topham (eds.) (2004). *Culture and Science in the Nineteenth Century Media*. Aldershot: Ashgate.

Huxley, A. (1963). *Literature and Science*. London: Chatto and Windus.

Jordanova, L.J. (1986). *Languages of Nature. Critical Essays in Science and Literature*. London: Free Association Books.

Ingersoll, E.G. (1992). *Representations of Science and Technology in British Literature since 1880*. New York: Peter Lang Publishers.

Levine, G. (1988). *Darwin and the Novelists. Patterns of Science in Victorian Fiction*. Cambridge MA: Harvard University Press.

Medawar, P.B. (1972). *The Hope of Progress*. London: Methuen.

Myers, G. (1989). Science for women and children: the dialogue of popular science in the nineteenth century. In Christie, J. and Shuttleworth, S. (eds.). *Nature Transfigured: Science and Literature 1700–1900*. Chapter 8. Manchester: Manchester University Press.

Postlethwaite, D. (2001). George Eliot and science. In Levine, G. (ed.). *The Cambridge Companion to George Eliot*. Chapter 6. Cambridge: Cambridge University Press.

Russell, N.C. (2007). Science and scientists in Victorian and Edwardian literary novels: insights into the emergence of a new profession. *Public Understanding of Science*, **16**, 205–22.

Russell, N.C. (forthcoming). The new men. Scientists at work in popular British fiction between the early 1930s and the late 1960s. *Science Communication*.

Scott, P.A. (1992). *The Medical Research Novel in English and German 1900–1950*. Bowling Green OH: Bowling Green State University Press.

Shuttleworth, S. (1986). *George Eliot and Nineteenth Century Science. The Make Believe of a Beginning*. Cambridge: Cambridge University Press.

Smith, J. (1994). *Fact and Feeling. Baconian Science and the Nineteenth Century Literary Imagination*. Madison: University of Wisconsin Press.

Turner, M.A. (1993). *Mechanism and the Novel. Science in the Narrative Process*. Cambridge: Cambridge University Press.

23 Science on stage: the politics and ethics of science in cultural and educational contexts

Henrik Ibsen's play, *An Enemy of the People*, was published in 1882. The hero (or anti-hero according to taste) is the physician Dr Tomas Stockmann who cannot understand why his scientific demonstration that a local pulp mill is poisoning the water supply is not accepted by any segment of local society; industry, politicians, the media or ordinary people. But acknowledging and dealing with the problem is not in any of their short-term interests. It will cost the mill owners money, politicians and the media do not want to ruin the tourist trade, and local labour leaders do not want workers to lose their jobs, so at a public meeting Stockmann is branded an enemy of the people. Scientists might like to read this play as an attack on the small-mindedness and stupidity of non-scientists in the face of heroic efforts by a scientist to improve their lot. But the opposite reading is equally valid; the scientist is naïve if he supposes that scientific analysis alone can solve the problem, if the practical consequences so clearly go against the political realities of the lives of those affected.

Something similar happens in William Golding's play *The Brass Butterfly* (1958) where an inventor is banished from ancient Rome for railing against people and politicians who will not use his machines for human benefit rather than to gain political power and destroy their enemies. The politicians banish him because such a dangerous idealist is better out of the way.

BACON RE-EXPRESSED. THE PURPOSE OF SCIENCE SHOULD BE FOR HUMAN BENEFIT

Brouwer notes the common dramatic dilemma of scientists whose new knowledge has undesirable implications. The scientists may be essentially good, well-intentioned people who do not seek to do harm or acquire power for selfish ends. For Brouwer, as for many others, in Brecht's *Life of Galileo* the great natural philosopher is accused of betraying science because its primary purpose should be to improve the lot of mankind by easing the hardship of existence. Such ideals are corrupted once scientists allow themselves either to undertake science at the whim of their masters or (just as bad in Brecht's eyes) do science only to find new knowledge, passing responsibility for its use to others. In either of these situations, or the Ibsen and Golding scenarios of scientists whose work affects their community, Brouwer argues that scientists in drama are politically naïve if they believe that rational scientific arguments alone based on established facts, must inevitably provide the best solutions to the problems besetting society, or that science will only be used for human benefit.

There have been many plays about science in the twentieth century and, as we might expect, it is the social and political consequences of scientific advance and the moral dilemmas of scientists' responsibilities for these consequences that most interest dramatists. The moral character of the scientist is central. His professional or personal involvement with science, or the science itself seem less interesting to dramatists and their audiences.

It was not only Brecht who focused on physics as the key scientific discipline; it has been dominant in the majority of science drama since 1945. Orthofer recently reviewed the 'big three' physics dramas from Brecht's *Galileo* (final version 1956), through Friedrich Durrenmatt's *The Physicists* (1962), to Michael Frayn's *Copenhagen* (1998). The first two show scientists as supermen whose discoveries can destroy the world. The playwrights ask what scientists ought to do with their knowledge; to whom should they owe allegiance, how can they best try to mitigate or control 'evil' consequences that may result from their discoveries?

Orthofer believes Tom Stoppard's plays *Hapgood* (1988) and *Arcadia* (1993) show a more subtle treatment of science. These are farces and explore scientific ideas which Stoppard finds interesting in their own right. His characters act out metaphorical versions of their scientific ideas, while exploring their moral implications in more refined ways than just demonstrating the over-reaching individualism which dominated the earlier period, when Brecht's influence was paramount. Frayn's *Copenhagen* continues Stoppard's more subtle approach, not as farce but as something more serious.

Biographical and historical themes are common in late twentieth-century science dramas and they often use time shift between past and present, for instance, Stoppard's *Arcadia* or Shelagh Stephenson's *An Experiment with an Air Pump* (1998). The audience follow the implications of a well-known piece of science, which example is then used to help describe less-familiar science which triggers similar dilemmas. Science itself is seldom the point; the moral implications provide the drama, although they are no longer necessarily produced by the god-like figures of physicists making awful discoveries. Big physics with big moral dilemmas are no longer the only dramatic games in town.

THE CONTEXT OF THE MAIN PHYSICS PLAYS IN MORE DETAIL: BRECHT, KIPPHARDT, DURRENMATT AND FRAYN

Hye has looked at many of these twentieth-century physics plays, which began with Brecht most famously in *Life of Galileo*. Since this was discussed in Part IV, it will not be revisited here. All Brecht's Marxist drama is didactic; the audience is supposed to follow an argument, remain detached and critical, understand why things are happening and thus go out and correct the social wrongs demonstrated in the play. He deliberately abandoned the conventional theatre of emotional involvement with character, believing such engagement prevented people from following arguments. He aimed to suppress the audience's expectation of such engagement by using 'alienation effects' such as scene titles giving away the plot, actors coming out of character to address the audience, and so on. For him, this was theatre for the 'scientific age'. Kipphardt and Durrenmatt who followed took a similar didactic approach.

Brecht was fascinated by the emergence of the new physics of relativity and quantum mechanics and used indeterminacy and statistical causality to explain the complex relationships between individuals and society. Most Marxists retained old Newtonian certainties when applying science to society; if there was enough data about social cause and effect, then social action is explained and political intervention can be rationally designed to change it. Any model of society based on the new indeterminate physics made that impossible, yet Brecht embraced the new ideas. Only masses (sociologically) were subject to statistical measurement and characterization, individuals behaved more like subatomic particles whose behaviour could never be wholly determined.

The Ocean Flight and *The Badener Didactic Play of Agreement* were the first pair of plays Brecht wrote after his 'conversion' to Marxism and premiered in 1929. They are concerned with science in terms of its application in technology. They both addressed the question of man's striving nature and technological prowess. *The Ocean Flight* was a short radio play based on Lindbergh's trans-Atlantic flight of 1927 and presents a struggle between the aviator and the elements, personified voices of fog, snowstorm and water, which resent his presence and try to bring him down. Fatigue also tries to lull him to sleep, but human ingenuity and technology keep the plane flying despite its weakness amongst the larger forces of nature. The flier then adds his indomitable spirit to ensure success. In the eighth scene the flier reflects that the human race no longer needs religion; science can explain everything that was once the realm of religion and new knowledge will allow man to overcome the exploitation of capitalism.

The *Badener Didactic Play* has a pilot and his three mechanics crash a plane and seek help from the locals among whom they have landed, represented by a learned chorus (mouthing the attitudes of the Communist Party). Essentially, the plane crashes because the team were only interested in technological glory and individual achievement. Their flight did nothing to help society. The correct attitude should be humility and the plane is rebuilt to carry out sociologically useful transport, not simple glory. To a modern audience the heavy-handed Marxism feels peculiar, perhaps the view that science has displaced religion less so, though we should note that spiritual feelings among scientists seem strongest in fundamental physics and cosmology.

Heinar Kipphardt's (1922–82) *In the Matter of J. Robert Oppenheimer*, is a dramatization of the 1954 American Atomic Energy Commission enquiry to determine the security clearance of Robert Oppenheimer, the scientist who had been in charge of the American laboratories in the Manhattan Project to build the first atomic bomb during the Second World War. The 3000-page transcript is distilled into 120 pages of dramatic text, 40 witnesses are reduced to 6, some witnesses are combinations of two or more actual voices, and new speeches are interpolated as expressions of the views Kipphardt believes can be attributed to the leading actors.

The key question is whether Oppenheimer in the early 1950s hindered his colleagues in the development of the hydrogen bomb; and hence could be seen as a traitor to America during the Cold War. At the hearings, Oppenheimer focused on the professional duty of physicists, but his interrogators concentrated on politics and military matters. If physicists are forced to conform to onerous social norms, this will undermine their value in producing creative advances in physics. But these advances can (and have) led to 'bad' social consequences; weapons of mass destruction and the arms race. Some physicists, their position represented by Oppenheimer in the play, felt they had been 'blackmailed' into developing the atomic bomb by fear that Hitler was doing the same thing in the 1940s and into developing the hydrogen bomb by the Soviet threat to Western democracy in the 1950s.

In the play Edward Teller does not share Oppenheimer's doubts and puts his knowledge loyally at the service of the state to defend democracy. Such a duty justifies the development of more and better weapons of mass destruction. In the end the Atomic Energy Commission does not restore Oppenheimer's security clearance and in a final speech he says he will never work again on war projects. He sees scientists as professionally and morally flawed in handing over research to the military without considering the consequences. Brecht was preparing the third version of *Galileo* as this hearing was taking place, and his third *Galileo* echoes Oppenheimer's position closely. Later, the Berliner Ensemble produced *Oppenheimer* using the sets from *Galileo* to emphasize the parallels between the historical and contemporary ethical dilemmas over the use of scientific knowledge. Both Oppenheimer and Galileo were victims of power politics; their moral authority attacked to lend credibility to the charges against them. Both accepted that they were guilty of turning their knowledge over to these authorities and were therefore traitors, not to Church or state, but to science itself.

The Swiss playwright Friedrich Durrenmatt's (1921–90) *The Physicists* premiered in 1962. Durrenmatt was much influenced by Brecht and the post-war Theatre of the Absurd, where the chaos and tragedy of the late twentieth century could only be addressed as surrealist comedy. Written at the height of the Cold War, the play considered (once again) the key issue of human passion for knowledge and its dangerous consequences.

The plot is bizarre. In a sanatorium a nurse is killed. The murderer must be one of three patients, one of whom claims to be Sir Isaac Newton, the second (who conducted a previous murder) claims to be Albert Einstein, and the third patient claims to be Johann Mobius, and is haunted by visions of King Solomon and of the murdered Nurse Stettler. She had believed that Mobius would marry her and had obtained permission for him to leave the sanatorium. But he killed her because he wanted to stay inside to prevent the misuse of his ideas. The other two 'physicists' turn out to be foreign agents trying to get Mobius to work for their governments, but he convinces them to remain cut off in the sanatorium as well. But it is no good; the psychiatrist in charge has been copying Mobius's notes and exploiting them for her international cartel. The only counter-measure would have been for the physicists to keep all their knowledge to themselves, but that is simply not a viable option either.

Michael Frayn's *Copenhagen* (1998) is set in a post-mortal limbo where the great physicists Niels Bohr and Werner Heisenberg, together with Bohr's wife Margrethe, meet to dissect a strange and significant event in their lives, the visit by Heisenberg from Germany to Bohr in German-occupied Denmark in 1941. It remains unclear to this day exactly why Heisenberg came, what conversations took place and with what outcomes. Frayn explores the possibilities in the context of the time (Heisenberg a scientist who has agreed to serve the Nazi regime, Bohr half-Jewish in an occupied state), in the personal and professional relationship between Bohr and Heisenberg who had been teacher and student and generated several key concepts of quantum mechanics in the 1920s, and in the military consequences implicit in quantum mechanics; the development of nuclear weapons. Frayn explains the quantum mechanical concepts of the uncertainty principle and complementarity which are then used as metaphors for human and political relationships. The physicists here are no longer God-like generators of powerful knowledge. Instead, they and their science are beset by uncertainties parallel to the uncertainties of quantum physics.

While the play is not a comedy, there is a great deal of wit and insight, and one might speculate that what drew Frayn to write a play about this incident was an interest in farce (which he shares with Stoppard). The play's structure of interlocking and unravelling story lines is farce-like and was an unexpected hit with both critics and public. It was also performed when there was intense interest in the Copenhagen meeting among professional historians. Frayn courted their attention by writing an extensive postscript to the play discussing the historical background and including a bibliography. He has since been engaged in wearisome discourse with the historians about what may actually have happened and what responsibility he might carry for 'misrepresenting' the events if, in any dominant reading, he got it 'wrong'. These academic history issues have rather hijacked discussion of the play, epitomized by a 2-day international historical conference held in Copenhagen in September 2001. Cathryn Carson in her concluding remarks about this meeting takes the historians to task for their po-faced critiques of Frayn's interpretations in the play, pointing out that some of their own analyses are more imaginative than Frayn's.

Some commentators do not like this academic, historical focus on Frayn's play. They want to consider it as drama, to ask why this play was a success. Johnston points out that the play is in the form of an old-fashioned whodunit, reconstructing an event from the limited evidence available and participant memories. Frayn does not provide a single, linear answer to the question (which is what historians want him to do), but shows that we cannot know that any answer is correct, another expression of the metaphor of uncertainty derived from quantum mechanics. There may be no satisfactory single account of any event, the stories we tell depend on how we want the narrative logic to proceed.

Frayn's other great strength is that the core of the play is the complex clash of personalities and relationships between the main characters. These characters are sufficiently three-dimensional for the audience to engage with them. Those relationships are, to a large extent, delineated by the characters' scientific and political concerns, so the relationships, central to emotion and drama, arise naturally from their science and politics. They are not, as is so often the case in plays of 'ideas', merely one-dimensional spokespersons for particular intellectual positions. A piece of drama has first and foremost to work as a piece of drama. Even Brecht, despite his avowed rejection of emotional engagement in favour of didactic instruction, anchored his most famous play in a compelling dramatization of Galileo's character, despite the alienation effects he may have inserted to try to stop such engagement from occurring.

DIDACTIC DRAMA

Physical theatre

Modern plays about science considered so far are all by literary artists who sometimes take science and its implications as dramatic themes. Many scientists are rightly impressed by the way they expound scientific principles. Stimulated by these successes, some scientists have decided to have a go at drama writing themselves. Ball is a dramatist from the science camp who argues that, since science is inherently theatrical (a point shared with literary academic analysis by Shepherd-Barr and others), science theatre should take advantage of its physical and visual potential (science as spectacle) rather than emphasizing knowledge and theory articulated through dialogue. Dramatists should show as well as tell. He concedes that word-based playwrights are good at using science as metaphor but are often hamstrung by the audience's lack of familiarity with science; so that much of the dialogue must be devoted to disguised tutorials. Like most critics he much prefers it if science in theatre is neither metaphor nor lesson, but arises naturally within the narrative. Brecht's *Life of Galileo* falls into this category and it is also relatively easy for the audience because the story of Galileo and the Inquisition is mythic folktale. The context (at least in its stereotypical form) is familiar to most of the audience.

Ball himself is an enthusiast for visual and physical theatre, where all forms of performance are combined, many not dependent on words; including circus, mime, dance, clown, puppetry, maskwork, and so on. When physical theatre puts on shows around science, he believes they work if they generate engagement rather than aiming to teach. Ball is also keen to harness the benefits of the Victorian lecture demonstration, where visual and physical experiments were incorporated into the discourse. In the end his plea is that science theatre must entertain before teaching, a fundamentally sound principle.

Demonstrating the physics of Copenhagen

Ball's principles were put into practice by some of the Faculty in the Physics Department of Stockholm University who used *Copenhagen* as a trigger for a public lecture-demonstration on quantum mechanics. They leafleted audiences at the play during its Stockholm run, advertising a 2-hour demonstration, from which they filled a lecture hall for a 1-night physics show.

They built a set of demonstration activities round the problem of the wave-particle duality of light, resolving the paradox through the quantum mechanics of subatomic particle behaviour. The theoretical background was provided as a lecture, then paradoxes discussed with the audience and simple experiments demonstrated to resolve them, which generated more interpretation and further resolution through guided audience discussion. The success of this lecture led to an installation version of the event and experiments in the Stockholm Science Laboratory, an interactive centre designed primarily for school children but with access also for the general public. Here visitors could undertake many of the demonstration experiments for themselves (though whether they 'mean' what the audience guided in the carefully choreographed lecture understood seems doubtful). But the organizers believe that the link with the play through the installation title, 'The physics of *Copenhagen*' encourages audiences to explore the physics issues seriously.

Nobel injustices

Another academic, this time a Norwegian historian of science, Robert Friedman, was also stimulated by *Copenhagen*, in his case to see if other critical episodes in the history of physics might be dramatized. He sees clearly that drama must make its ethical, polemical or historical points arise from emotional character inter-action; having characters just as mouthpieces will not work. He was also much attracted by Frayn's device of having characters in limbo revisiting key events in their past in an effort to understand what really happened. He also sees that accurate historical analysis probably cannot be portrayed dramatically. In order to present the essential matters in a way to which an audience can relate, historical accuracy has to be abandoned. The process of dramatization has to distort the 'reality' of history, just as it distorts the 'reality' of sci-ence. Dramatic and fictional truths demand some sacrifice of both historical and scientific truth.

Friedman chose to try to correct a commonly accepted his-torical wrong by showing how chicanery among her colleagues prevented Lisa Meitner from receiving a Nobel Prize for her work on the discovery of nuclear fission. The timing of this discovery in Berlin just before the Second World War, with some of the scientists involved having to flee from Nazi persecution, set up endless misun-derstandings. Meitner left Berlin for Sweden in 1938 but her critical contributions to the Berlin work of Hahn and Strassman (the Nobel Prize winners for fission) after she had left were ignored, while her reception in Siegbahn's laboratory in Sweden as a refugee created another series of misunderstandings. Friedman wrote a one-act play around this story for an International Science Festival in Gothenburg in Sweden. Two hundred people watched the performance and took part in the lively panel discussion afterwards. He and others judged it so successful that he worked on a full-length play to bring out the whole story more clearly.

Carl Djerassi: Revealing the behaviour of the scientific tribe in fiction and drama

Carl Djerassi is famous for pioneering work in the 1950s on the syn-thesis of progesterone which formed the basis of the contraceptive pill. He became a Professor of Chemistry at Stanford, generating over 1200 scientific articles and 100 patents. He embarked on a late literary career in 1983, when he was already 60.

He started by writing 'science-in-fiction' with the object of describing the tribal culture of contemporary science, and his first book, *Cantor's Dilemma*, deals with a piece of Nobel Prize-winning work, which may or may not be replicable, an example of ethical and practical problems arising from the innate competitiveness of science. The book was well received, has appeared in seven languages and been used in a range of American science, technology and society courses on the ethics of research, science in literature, sociology of science, and so on. The novel's success and its use in academia encouraged Djerassi to pursue fiction writing for didactic reasons, to instruct while entertaining.

He called this project 'science-in-fiction' to distinguish it from 'science fiction', because he believed that, to be taken seriously, his fictional science and scientists must be realistic in plausible contemporary settings. He talks of smuggling science facts into a scientifically illiterate public, but these novels are more about the behaviour of the scientific tribe and expose how the scientific institution works rather than telling the public facts and theories. The success of *Cantor* led him to write three further novels with interlocking characters.

Djerassi is also an enthusiastic theatre-goer. He decided to try writing plays himself after watching Stephen Poliakoff's *Blinded by the Sun* in 1996. Although written by a non-scientist, Djerassi felt this play came close to being 'science-in-theatre' because the plot sprang from the behaviour of the characters in their professional capacity as members of the scientific tribe, and there were scientific facts and theories incorporated as well. Djerassi has written four plays and in the second, *Oxygen*, he put his own subject, chemistry, on stage co-writing with the Nobel Prize-winning chemist and poet Roald Hoffman. *Oxygen* explains what an act of scientific discovery is and why being first matters so much in science, and succeeds in explaining these in an entertaining framework. For his third play, *Calculus*, he focused on the priority disputes that often follow scientific discoveries when different protagonists claim to have discovered the same thing. He explores the early eighteenth-century Newton–Leibniz altercation over who first discovered the calculus.

TEACHING OR ENTERTAINING?

What links many of these theatrical explorations of science and its wider implications is a covert (and sometimes overt) attempt to teach. Perhaps this is inevitable; the general public does not have extensive science education, so any play dealing with scientific issues is forced to find ways to generate enough understanding of the science (or its context) to allow the audience to follow the moral or other dramatic points. The more recent plays present scientists as open to doubt and interpretation; they are no longer Brechtian figures with omniscience drawn from the power of science. The nuclear consequences of fundamental physics (for good or ill) were ubiquitous in the politics, economics and culture of nations in the post-war period with demonstrable applied consequences of the correctness and certainty of scientific knowledge. It is not surprising that Brecht and others had little to say about the science itself; the drama was all in the applications. But, in more recent plays like *Copenhagen*, the same events are explored more thoroughly through the complex interplay between scientific truth, scientific uncertainty and technological application. The messages in the recent dramas are subtle and sophisticated; better representations of the science they explore.

The overt 'mission to instruct' re-introduces starkly a problem already discussed, the tension between exposition (describing or arguing the principles of some abstract discipline) and storytelling (emotional engagement with characters in response to plot). The problem is common in documentary film as well as in fiction, drama and fictional film. There are a variety of ways to resolve it. Classically, texts try to force the audience to follow an exposition by making abstract matters sufficiently engaging that the audience will attend (and even learn). In drama this happens with Brecht at his most didactic (preaching as his critics claim), in documentary it is the voice-over exposition accompanied by illustrative pictures, in Ficta (to use Brier's category) it is the 'science bits' interpolated into the narratives of *Jurassic Park* and other techno-thrillers. At the other end of the scale, the exposition is worked seamlessly into the emotional drama of character interaction, usually by going back to real or imaginary scientists and allowing the science and its controversies to emerge naturally from the professional and personal lives of the protagonists. Brecht could bring this off on occasion (*Life of Galileo*), while Frayn's *Copenhagen* is the apogee of such treatment. Intellectual ideas (including science) can also be valuable material in farce and physical drama. Stoppard's *Arcadia* is the star witness here. Perhaps the centrality of plot and the satirical treatment of characters who 'stand for' professions, ideas or attitudes, can work in farce in a way that would grate in more realistic drama.

But on balance, whether we consider fiction or drama, bringing science and its implications to life remains a challenge. Few great literateurs are close enough to science, and few scientists possess the necessary literary skills (though many are good at exposition, particularly in the popular essay format). The usual solution on stage or in film is to collaborate; to bring scientists, writers and performers together. Such collaborations are necessary for the drama-doc format (for instance, the classic BBC production of *Life Story*), or in physical theatre companies, such as The Complicite Company's recent production *A Disappearing Number*, where theatrical business of a very sophisticated kind keeps the audience engaged round an abstract theme, in this case around the significance of prime numbers in mathematics.

BIBLIOGRAPHY

Badash, L. (2003). From security blanket to security risk, scientists in the decade after Hiroshima. *History and Technology*, **19**, 2441–56.

Ball, P. (2002). Beyond words: science in visual theatre. *Interdisciplinary Science Reviews*, **27**, 169–72.

Ball, P. (2004). Playing dirty. *Nature*, **430**, 729.

Bergstrom, L., Johansson, K.E. and Nilsson, C. (2001). The physics of Copenhagen for students and the general public. *Physics Education*, **36**, 388–93.

Brecht, B. (translated by Willett, J. commentary by Rorrison, H.) (1986). *Life of Galileo*. London: Methuen (original text 1955).

Brouwer, W. (1988). The image of the physicist in modern drama. *American Journal of Physics*, **56**, 611–16.

Carson, C. Placing Frayn's play in the historical tradition. Conference on *Copenhagen and beyond*, http://www.nbi.dk/NBA/files/sem/symp/carson/html, visited 9 February 2005.

Complicite (2007). *A Disappearing Number*. London: Oberon Books.

Djerassi, C. (2001). *This Man's Pill. Reflections on the 50th Birthday of the Pill*. Oxford: Oxford University Press.

Djerassi, C. (2002). Contemporary 'science-in-theatre': a rare genre. *Interdisciplinary Science Reviews*, **27**, 193–201.

Djerassi, C. and Hoffman, R. (2001). *Oxygen*. Chichester: Wiley.

Durrenmatt, F. (trans. Kirkup, J.) (1962). *The Physicists*. London: Samuel French.

Frayn, M. (1998). *Copenhagen*. London: Methuen.

Friedman, R.M. (2002). Remembering Miss Meitner: an attempt to forge history into drama. *Interdisciplinary Science Reviews*, **27**, 202–10.

Hye, A.E. (1996). *The Moral Dilemma of the Scientist in Modern Drama*. New York: The Edwin Mellen Press.

Ibsen, H. (trans. Watts, P.) (1964). *A Public Enemy*. In *Ghosts and Other Plays*. London: Penguin, pp. 103–219 (original text 1882).

Johnston, I. (March 2001). Lecture on Frayn's *Copenhagen*. http://www.mala.bc.ca/~johnstoi/introser/frayn.htm, visited 9 February 2005.

Kipphardt, H. (trans. Spiers, R.) (1967). *In the Matter of J. Robert Oppenheimer*. London: Methuen.

Orthofer, M.A. (2002). The scientist on the stage: a survey. *Interdisciplinary Science Reviews*, **27**, 173–82.

Poliakoff, P. (2001). *Blinded by the Sun*. London: Samuel French.

Russell, N.C. (2006). The Play's the thing … *The Scientist, Thursday online*, 21 July, http:// www.the-scientist.com/news/display/24008/#24029.

Shepherd-Barr, K. (2006). *Science on Stage. From Dr Faustus to Copenhagen*. Princeton NJ: Princeton University Press.

Stephenson, S. (1998). *An Experiment with an Air Pump*. London: Methuen.

Stoppard, T. (1998). *Arcadia*. London: Faber and Faber.

Index